Essentials of
American Government

Essentials of Political Science

James A. Thurber, American University, Editor

The Essentials of Political Science series will present faculty and students with concise texts designed as primers for a given college course. Many will be 200 pages or shorter. Each will cover core concepts central to mastering the topic under study. Drawing on their teaching as well as research experiences, the authors present narrative and analytical treatments designed to fit well within the confines of a crowded course syllabus.

Essentials of American Government, David McKay

TITLES FORTHCOMING FOR 2000

Essentials of Political Research, Alan D. Monroe

Essentials of
AMERICAN
GOVERNMENT

David McKay
University of Essex

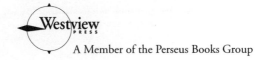

Westview
PRESS

A Member of the Perseus Books Group

Essentials of Political Science

Copyright © 2000 by Westview Press, A Member of the Perseus Books Goup

Published in 2000 in the United States of America by Westview Press, 5500 Central Avenue, Boulder, Colorado 80301-2877, and in the United Kingdom by Westview Press, 12 Hid's Copse Road, Cumnor Hill, Oxford OX2 9JJ

Visit us on the World Wide Web at www.westviewpress.com

Library of Congress Cataloging-in-Publication Data
McKay, David H.
    Essentials of American government / David McKay.
        p.   cm.—(Essentials of political science)
    Includes bibliographical references and index.
    ISBN 0-8133-6755-7 (pbk.)
    1. United States—Politics and government.   I. Title.   II. Series.
JK274.M5143   1999
320.473—dc21   99-048143
                                                                         CIP

The paper used in this publication meets the requirements of the American National Standard for Permanence of Paper for Printed Library Materials Z39.48-1984.

10   9   8   7   6   5   4   3   2   1

Contents

Illustrations

Preface

Perhaps the most distinctive feature of American government over the past thirty years has been the juxtaposition of quite dramatic changes in political institutions with an essentially unchanging political culture. Few question the transformation in the presidency since Vietnam and Watergate. In contrast to the midcentury incumbents, few recent presidents have been free to set the domestic policy agenda, and none has emerged from the experience unscathed by scandal or failure, or both. Congress, too, is a very different institution from that body thirty years ago. Congress used to be collegial, procedurally conservative, and deferential both to its own leaders and to presidents. Today it is combative, ideological, and rarely accommodating to the appeals of leaders. Ideologically, the Supreme Court has made the transition from liberal activism to an uncertain and often passive conservatism. Finally, the role of the states has been transformed. Once regarded as unprofessional, regressive, and often corrupt in relation to the federal government, they are today at the forefront of policy initiation and experimentation. In total, these changes have increased the institutional fragmentation that has always been a feature of the American system. They have also made the United States a harder place to govern.

Yet in spite of these institutional changes, no equivalent shift has occurred in the fundamentals of how Americans view politics. True, distrust of political authority and especially the federal government has increased appreciably. But the conviction that limited government is good government has always been a defining theme of American political culture. At the same time, at least since the New Deal Americans have had high expectations of the federal government, whether measured in terms either of the moral authority of individual politicians or of the specific benefits the government can provide.

High public expectations in the context of a culture of limited government and institutional fragmentation is the theme of this book. Almost every text on American government stresses the institutionally fragmented nature of the political system. This was, of course, part of the founders' original design, with federalism and the separation of powers being the most distinctive features of the new republic. The stock argument is that these features not only have persisted through time but also have become more pronounced, so that today fragmentation makes the business of building winning coalitions at the federal level extremely difficult. Hyperpluralism, gridlock, and ungovernability are some of the more vivid descriptions applied to this phenomenon.

In one important sense, however, these analyses are now out-of-date. The gridlock literature was fueled by perceptions that the U.S. economy was performing poorly compared with other countries, that the budget deficit was out of control, that nothing could be done to reduce welfare dependency, and that domestic pressures would make it impossible to define the U.S. world role. In 1999 the performance of American government in relation to all these problems was looking remarkably good, and especially so in comparative perspective.

Notwithstanding the view that recent improvements may be temporary—or even illusory—today it is clearly inappropriate to identify failure as the defining feature of American government. Instead, the mark of its uniqueness is the combination of high public expectations with a philosophy of limited government. Both a Republican Congress and Democratic president extol the virtues of less government but continue to grapple with demands for improved education, health care, transportation, and so on. All praise the virtues of lower taxes and at the same time promise improvements in the quality of public services. The same tension applies in the courts, in state politics, and indeed throughout the system. Foreign and defense policies are also affected by it: Support for a major U.S. world role remains high, but serious tensions exist over the costs implicit in an active world role, whether measured in terms of money or the lives of American service personnel. Recent successes such as a balanced budget have been achieved in part because the limited-government philosophy has been on the ascendant and has won support from all shades of political opinion. At the same time, conflict over the distributional questions of who gets what has hardly subsided.

This theme works well when comparing the United States with other nations for two reasons. First, in few countries is the philosophy of limited government as well established as in the United States. Lower taxes are not a dominant value in Germany, France, Italy, or the UK, for example. Second, in few countries is democracy so well developed and access to the institutions of government so easy as in the United States. The U.S. political system is highly accessible to public demands, yet satisfying those demands is difficult to reconcile with limited government. *Essentials* therefore strives to make students aware of this unique combination through selected comparative references.

David McKay
Santa Barbara, California

Acknowledgments

I owe a debt of thanks to a number of individuals and institutions. The Department of Political Science, University of California, Santa Barbara, provided an amenable environment for much of the writing of the book. Thanks to Stephen Weatherford and Lorraine McDonnell for their hospitality and support. I must also thank my home institution, the Department of Government, University of Essex, for continuing to provide a stimulating and always challenging intellectual environment in which to work. Leo Wiegman of Westview Press was always encouraging and supportive, as was the series editor, James Thurber, and a number of the publisher's readers and referees. Finally, thanks to Sherri Singleton for her forbearance and encouragement amid much transatlantic comings and goings.

D. M.

1

Limited Government in the Age of High Expectations

Americans expect a lot from their government. They expect government officials to be honest. They expect them to represent their interests faithfully. They also expect the products of government—public policies—to be provided on an adequate and fair basis. Social security should be properly funded; HMOs should be sufficiently regulated to provide quality health care; educational standards should be maintained at a high level; the environment should be protected; and a strong national defense should always be available to protect the nation from outside aggression. At the same time, Americans have always been deeply ambivalent about government. Unlike the citizens of most Western European states—and indeed of America's immediate neighbors, Mexico and Canada—Americans have historically mistrusted big government. Low taxes and limited public spending have been populist rallying cries since the beginning of the republic. Ambivalence about the role of government in society—in particular, the tension between a *general* philosophy of limited government and *particular* public demands for more and better government programs and services—forms the theme of this book.

At the inception of the republic, no question aroused as much passion as did the proper scope of the federal government. The founding fathers decided on an institutional structure that required the assent of several diverse constituencies (those electing the House, Senate, and president) before a bill was passed. The veto power provided an additional check on government, as did the institution of federalism, which served further to fragment government in the new

republic. These institutional features were a product of, and were reinforced by, a public philosophy of limited government. From the
very beginning, Americans accepted that government was a necessary evil and that essential services such as law and order, sanitation,
and education should be provided by state and local governments
rather than the federal government. The first ten amendments to the
Constitution (the Bill of Rights) provided citizens with legal protection from a potentially intrusive central government. In particular,
the First Amendment rights of freedom of speech, assembly, and religion were, and remain, bulwarks against the power of the state.
Americans also mistrusted standing armies. Instead they placed their
faith in a people's militia or, later, in armies and navies that would be
largely disbanded once a national emergency had passed.

The remarkable feature of the ensuing 150 years of American history is how powerful an influence this public philosophy was. Not
until the 1930s and 1940s did the federal government assume a permanent and extensive role in social policy and defense. But many
Americans remain deeply ambivalent about these new functions.
Support for the particular benefits provided by a range of social programs such as Medicare and Social Security is high, but antipathy remains to the general notion of the federal government supporting
those in need. Politicians from all sides preach the virtues of less government and lower taxes while promising to defend existing programs. A similar tension exists in a range of conscience issues. Those
who want to protect "family values" are usually opponents of big
government, yet the advance of their agenda would require strong
government action in such areas as abortion, school prayer, and the
rights of sexual minorities. Politicians known to be tough on crime
support an extension of the powers of government, including those
of federal agencies such as the FBI. But these very same politicians
often preach the virtues of limited government.

Foreign and defense policies are also affected by the tension between limited government and calls for strong federal action. Public support for a major world role remains high—but only if associated costs in terms of taxation and the lives of American service
personnel are kept low. In fact, this tension has almost become the
defining feature of American foreign policy since the end of the
Cold War, as attested by the Gulf War and U.S. involvement in Somalia, Bosnia, and Kosovo.

Of course, the balance between limited government and an expanded federal role ebbs and flows as historical events such as re-

cessions and wars change values and interests. But the tension is always there and has increased since the 1980s. Surveys have shown increasing support for limiting the scope of government and a deepening disillusionment with the institutions of the federal government. At the same time, there is little evidence that, on the whole, the role of the federal government has been reduced. As later chapters will show, the percentage of GDP (gross domestic product) accounted for by federal spending has declined only slightly since 1980. Defense spending has fallen, but the decrease has been offset by increased expenditures on Medicare, Social Security, and other programs. And the effective elimination of the budget deficit has been achieved not by radical reductions in spending or by tax hikes but by containing spending increases in the context of the enhanced tax revenues that flow from a period of sustained economic growth. Similarly, there is little evidence that those areas of federal government activity not easily measured in economic terms, such as regulation and law and order, have been reduced in size and scope, in spite of the prevailing philosophy of limited government.

For an introductory textbook, the theme of limited government in the context of high public expectations has a number of advantages over more historically specific themes. It facilitates international comparison. In few countries is the philosophy of the limited state as well established as in the United States. Lower taxes are not a dominant value in Germany, France, Italy, or the UK, for example. As will be shown in Chapter 2, citizens in these countries will often support parties that openly propose higher taxes to fund social programs. Moreover, they often see it as a *duty* of the government to provide for the disadvantaged and needy. Such sentiments have been the exception rather than the rule in American history. *Essentials of American Government* will constantly make comparisons of this sort as a means of highlighting the importance of a set of uniquely American beliefs and values.

These values are, of course, articulated in the context of the institutional structure of American politics. Still, this structure has been the subject of much criticism in recent years. Critiques have been based in part on specific institutional arrangements—in particular, the separation of powers. With one party controlling the presidency and another the Congress, governing has, so the argument runs, become more difficult than in the past. Underpinning this critique is the simple fact that American citizens have an un-

usually high degree of access to their political institutions—
whether at the local, state, or national levels. Access is facilitated
not only by the sheer number and variety of democratically accountable political institutions, from local school boards through
to the U.S. Congress, but also by Americans' strong belief in their
First Amendment right to express their views. Thus the many
points of access for the expression of the democratic will is combined with a high expectation on the part of citizens that their demands will be translated into policy. In this sense, the American
system is much more democratic than comparable systems that
often place great actual or potential power in governments and political leaders.

The great paradox of America's institutional arrangements is, of
course, that open and free access to decisionmakers does not always
translate into the satisfaction of public demands. Often the very complexity of the system cancels out competing demands and leads to incremental rather than radical change. This dynamic explains many of
the policy failures of recent years, such as the Clinton health care reforms and attempts to reform the campaign finance laws. Institutional arrangements thus fit nicely with the theme of the book. They
facilitate the airing of sometimes strident public demands while often
limiting what governments can tangibly do.

A final and related advantage of this volume's theme is that it
helps to make sense of the growing social and economic inequality
that characterizes American life. In democratic political systems, reductions in inequality occur when, in response to public demands,
governments act decisively to transfer resources from advantaged to
disadvantaged citizens. At least twice in recent U.S. history—during
the New Deal in the 1930s and the Great Society in the 1960s—just
such redistributions occurred. In recent years, however, the fragmentation of public demands into myriad competing claims operating in
a complex institutional environment has made it especially hard to
build winning coalitions for redistributions. This is especially so
given that the philosophy of limited government has also been on the
ascendant. Hence there persist inequalities in such areas as health
care and education. In both cases, reducing inequalities would require a substantial increase in public spending. Many—perhaps
most—citizens agree that worsening inequality needs to be addressed, but building a coalition in the presidency, in both houses of
Congress, and in the states in support of the required tax increases
has proved difficult if not impossible.

*　　*　　*

This book follows a conventional format. Discussion focuses on the main institutions of American federal government while at all times incorporating the designated theme as a device to add interest and perspective to the subject. Chapter 2 is devoted to analysis of the role of beliefs and values in American politics and how these link in to the broader society and economy. As such, it places a special emphasis on the remarkable way in which the tension in American political thought between the philosophy of limited government and high public expectations of the democratic process has been accommodated within a uniquely *American* ideology. Chapters 3 through 12 cover the main institutions and processes of American government, with each chapter designed to provide basic information and to discuss the relevance of historical trends as well as the relevance of recent research findings in political science. Special attention is paid to the relationship between, on the one hand, the institutional structure of government and, on the other, the public's expectations of the performance of politicians and political processes. Chapters 13 through 16 are designed to add substance and perspective to previous chapters by examining the policy process in four currently crucial areas: social policy, economic policy, the regulation of public morality in such areas as civil rights, and foreign policy. Chapter 17 returns to the main theme of the book and attempts to assess the performance of American government at century's end. Through the use of comparisons with other countries, the chapter offers an audit of the political system and encourages readers to evaluate their government critically in terms of democratic responsiveness and public accountability.

The general orientation of these chapters reflects my conviction that the study of political institutions can be productive only when placed in the broader comparative and historical perspective. The alternative is to condemn the reader to an uninspired descriptive account, which is a disservice to anyone studying what should be one of the most interesting subjects in social science.

2

Beliefs, Values, and American Society

It has been our fate as a nation not to have ideologies but to be one.

—Richard Hofstadter

So powerful is the dominant ideology in this country that existing economic and political arrangements frequently appear not merely as the best possible arrangements but as the only possible ones.

—Ira Katznelson and Mark Kesselman

The Nature of American Beliefs and Values

One of the most enduring debates in social science concerns the relationship between the mass public's beliefs and values and political authority. Liberal scholars label these beliefs "political culture," or "a historical system of widespread, fundamental, behavioral, political values actually held by system members (the public)."[1] Political culture therefore embraces the dominant pattern of beliefs and values that are acquired and that modify and change as a result of a complex process of socialization and feedback from the political system. In other words, individual citizens acquire attitudes toward politics through learning from parents and their environments (socialization), and these attitudes adapt and change as political authorities produce particular responses or policies over time (feedback). Political culture is the sum of individual beliefs and values, and, crucially, it is essentially *independent* of political authority. In some systems it may be incompatible with prevailing political institutions—as in Spain during the 1970s when an authoritarian regime was replaced

6

by democracy, or in Weimar Germany before the rise of Hitler—in which case, regime change occurs. In other systems, ethnic, religious, racial, cultural, or linguistic divisions may be so great that no single political culture and institutional structure can accommodate these differences. In such cases civil war may ensue or the country may disintegrate. The breakup of the former Soviet Union, Yugoslavia, and Czechoslovakia can be explained in this way, as can the American Civil War in the mid-nineteenth century. In other cases, the political culture supports and succors the political system. Liberal scholars invariably label the modern American system in such terms. U.S. politics and political culture may change, but they tend to be mutually supportive. Regime change is extremely unlikely in such a situation.

Radical critics of the political-culture perspective argue that public beliefs and values are imposed from above by those in positions of power. Beliefs constitute an *ideology*, therefore, whose function is to legitimate the prevailing system of political authority and economic organization. This radical perspective identifies the United States as a country where a dominant ideology imposed by powerful elites is particularly influential:

> The dominant ideology is more powerful in the United States than in any other capitalist democracy. Most political debates in the United States take place within the framework of this ideology. . . . So powerful is the dominant ideology in this country that existing economic and political arrangements frequently appear not merely as the best possible arrangements but as the only possible ones.[2]

These two apparently incompatible positions are not as far apart as they may seem, for when American beliefs are examined, both liberals and radicals accept the importance of similar public attitudes and values. Samuel Huntington has summed these up as "liberty, equality, individualism, democracy and the rule of law under a constitution."[3] As the following summary shows, within this system of beliefs and values, the tension between the need to limit government and simultaneously to ensure good government has always been present.

Liberty

Survey research from the 1950s and early 1960s found a high level of support among Americans in favor of *general* statements of free speech and opinion (for example, "people who hate our way of life should still have a chance to talk and be heard"), but much lower support for *specific* statements (for example, "a book that contains wrong political views cannot be a good book and does not deserve to be published").[4] Moreover, the level of support for specific freedoms was much higher among elites (politically influential people) than among the mass public. This disjunction between general and specific support is not exclusively American; citizens of many countries would answer positively to general statements advocating freedom. Clearly, freedom of expression is not an absolute value, and there have been times in American history when public tolerance of "un-American" values has been very low. The red-baiting periods following World Wars I and II demonstrated just how limited freedom could be in the United States.[5] And until the mid-1960s the attitude of white Americans in the South toward the African American population was the very opposite of libertarian, based as it was on systematic racial segregation and discrimination.

Since the 1960s, however, there has been evidence of some important changes. Racial tolerance has generally improved, and attitudes toward "un-American" beliefs (communism, atheism) have become more liberal (Table 2.1). In spite of these changes, antipathy to "non-American" values clearly remains, so it would be misleading to characterize the United States as a country where "freedom of expression" or "liberty" is assigned an inviolate status.

Three final qualifications need to be added to this conclusion, which should serve as a warning against simple overgeneralizations in this area. First, as later chapters will show, there have been quite dramatic advances in the legal protection of all individual rights, and especially freedom of expression since the 1960s. Not all these advances have been simply procedural; objectively, American citizens, newspapers, and other media enjoy much more freedom than they used to. As this development can often cause governments and officials serious difficulty and embarrassment, it seems to contradict claims that Americans are being manipulated by dominant elites.

Second, the American political system is uncommonly fragmented and devolved. Some of the worst examples of the infringement of individual freedom have occurred within *state* and *local* jurisdictions with the open acquiescence of local populations. This applies particularly to racial questions and criminal procedural rights. As society has become nationalized, so such activity has been exposed and has led to the spread of uniform, federally imposed standards. The na-

TABLE 2.1   Public Opinion on Civil Liberties, 1940–1996 (percent)

Issue/Year	Allow[a]	Don't Forbid[b]
Public speeches against democracy		
1940	25	46
1974	56	72
1976a	55	80
1976b	52	79

Issue/Year	Allow to Speak	Allow to Teach College	Keep Book in Library
Atheist[c]			
1954	37	12	35
1964[d]	–	–	61
1972	65	40	61
1973a	65	41	61
1973b	62	39	57
1974	62	42	60
1976	64	41	60
1977	62	39	59
1978	63	–	60
1980	66	45	62
1982	64	46	61
1984	68	46	64
1985	65	45	61
1987	69	47	66
1988	70	45	64
1989	72	51	67
1990	73	50	67
1991	72	52	69
1993	71	52	67
1994	73	52	70
1996	73	55	68
Admitted Communist[c]			
1954	27	6	27
1972	52	32	53
1973a	60	39	58
1973b	53	30	54
1974	58	42	59

(continues)

TABLE 2.1 *(continued)*

Issue/Year	Allow to Speak	Allow to Teach College	Keep Book in Library
1976	55	41	56
1977	55	39	55
1978	60	–	61
1980	55	41	57
1982	56	43	57
1984	59	46	60
1985	57	44	57
1987	60	46	61
1988	60	48	59
1989	64	50	62
1990	64	52	64
1991	67	54	67
1993	69	56	67
1994	67	55	66
1996	64	57	65
Racist[c]			
1943[e]	17	–	–
1976	61	41	60
1977	59	41	61
1978	62	–	65
1980	62	43	64
1982	59	43	60
1984	57	41	63
1985	55	42	60
1987	61	44	64
1988	61	42	62
1989	62	46	65
1990	63	45	64
1991	62	42	66
1993	61	43	64
1994	61	42	66
1996	61	46	64
Admitted homosexual[c]			
1973	61	47	53
1974	62	50	55
1976	62	52	55

(continues)

TABLE 2.1 *(continued)*

Issue/Year	Allow to Speak	Allow to Teach College	Keep Book in Library
1977	62	49	55
1980	66	55	58
1982	65	55	56
1984	68	59	59
1985	67	58	55
1987	67	56	57
1988	70	56	60
1989	76	63	64
1990	74	63	64
1991	76	63	68
1993	78	69	67
1994	79	71	69
1996	81	75	69

NOTE: – indicates not available

[a] Question: "Do you think the United States should allow public speeches against democracy?"

[b] Question: "Do you think the United States should forbid public speeches against democracy?"

[c] Question: "There are always some people whose ideas are considered bad or dangerous by other people. For instance, somebody who (is against all churches and religion/admits he is a communist/believes that blacks are genetically inferior). If such a person wanted to make a speech in your (city/town/community), should he be allowed to speak or not? Should such a person be allowed to teach in a college or university, or not? If some people in your community suggested that a book he wrote (against churches and religion/promoting communism/which said blacks are inferior) should be taken out of your public library, would you favor removing this book or not?" (Slight variations in wording across groups.)

[d] In 1964 the question was as follows: "Suppose a man admitted in public that he did not believe in God. Do you think a book he wrote should be removed from a public library?"

[e] In 1943 the question was as follows: "In peacetime, do you think anyone in the United States should be allowed to make speeches against certain races in this country?"

SOURCE: Harold Stanley and Richard G. Niemi, *Vital Statistics on American Politics 1997–98* (Washington, DC: Congressional Quarterly Press, 1998), table 3.14.

tionalization of standards has, of course, involved a more intrusive federal government. Many on the right argue that this expanded federal role represents an extension of governmental power beyond its proper limits. A very small minority on the extreme right go further and refuse to recognize the authority of the federal government. As discussed in later chapters, attempts to reduce the power of the federal government by returning power to states and localities may indeed limit the scope of government, but it can also result in fewer freedoms for some.

Third, if the definition of liberty or freedom is expanded to include economic individualism or the freedom to accumulate wealth and pass that wealth on to the next generation, then there is no doubting that the United States is a free country.

Equality

Early foreign observers of the American scene, from Alexis de Tocqueville to Charles Dickens and James Bryce, noted the remarkable absence of deference to position or status in the United States. "Equality of estimation" is what Bryce called it, or the tendency of Americans to treat each other as equals, whatever their education, occupation, or social class. This notion remains broadly true—although, of course, other countries have been moving in the same direction. "Equality" was one of the earliest rallying cries of Revolutionary America, but from the very beginning it implied an equality of opportunity rather than equality of condition. The argument ran something like this: Provide equal status for all citizens (except slaves, of course) under the law, and every individual would be capable of achieving self-fulfillment. As the country developed, people came to accept that the precondition for equality of opportunity was a certain standard of education. Consequently, education achieved—and retains—a very special status in American social policy. Almost alone among major social programs, education generates broad consensus that it should be provided out of public rather than private funds.

Critics argue that the constant stress on equality of opportunity helps legitimize what is a very unequal society. Originally the emphasis was on the frontier and unlimited land. More recently the appeal has shifted to education and all the benefits this can bring. By constantly being reassured that everyone can succeed given personal effort and a good educational base, citizens are, so the argument runs, being duped into accepting what are considerable material inequalities in the society. No doubt there is something to this—certainly Americans have traditionally believed that their economic position (or the position of their children) would improve[6]—but such a perspective fails to distinguish between equality before the law and the material or economic benefits that equality of opportunity can bring. The former, which is close to equality of dignity or esteem, is highly developed in the United States and recognized as an important element in citizenship. Legislation designed to prevent unfair or unequal treatment by private individuals and public authorities is far-reaching and, compared with similar laws in other countries, is quite rigidly enforced. In recent years discrimination against women and racial minorities has been the main focus of these laws, but the idea that all citizens, irrespective of background, should be treated equally is deeply entrenched.

Clearly such laws can be implemented in such a way that they conflict with those notions of individualism that underpin the philosophy of limited government. As the next section will highlight, by placing the interests of the group above those of the individual's worth, affirmative action can cause serious tensions between equality of individualism.

Individualism

Nothing more accurately seems to represent Americanism than a stress on individual rather than collective action. Trade union membership in the United States is low, collectivist political parties of the left (and also of the right) have failed to win mass support, and the society is infused with a degree of self-reliance rarely found in other countries. This spirit of self-reliance has its roots in the Puritanism that flourished in both colonial and postcolonial America, and it remains a potent force, as shown in public antipathy to welfare dependency and, in comparison with most European countries, a surprisingly wide acceptance of job insecurity. Some general indicators of American self-reliance in comparative context are detailed in Table 2.2.

As far as the distribution of resources is concerned, Americans prefer private to public institutions. Indeed, the "state" as such is held in quite low esteem compared with its status in other countries. But we should be wary of inferring that Americans are always antipathetic to state-provided goods and services. The evidence

TABLE 2.2   Comparison of Attitudes Toward Various Government
Activities (percent)

Agree government should . . .	*United States*	*West Germany*	*Britain*	*Austria*	*Italy*
Control wages by legislation	23	28	32	58	72
Reduce working week to create more jobs	27	51	49	36	68
Control prices	19	20	48	–	67
Provide health care	40	57	85	–	67
Finance job-creation projects	70	73	83	–	84
Spend more on old-age pensions	47	53	81	–	80
Reduce differences in income between those with high and low income	38	66	65	70	80
Agree/strongly agree that . . .					
Wearing seat belts should be required by law	49	82	80	81	81
Smoking in public places should be prohibited by law	46	49	51	58	89

SOURCE: Various, summarized by Seymour Martin Lipset, *American Exceptionalism: A Double Edged Sword* (New York: Norton, 1996), table 2.3.

suggests that when questions on government benefits are couched in general terms, Americans show antipathy to government provision, but when asked about specific programs such as Social Security, health care, or education, they show a high level of support.[7] As was suggested in Chapter 1, this tension between an ideology of limited government and demands for more government activity has mounted as increasing numbers of citizens have come to expect government regulation and support from federal programs.

America's tradition of antipathy to government has a number of roots. One of particular significance is that this tradition has at least in part depended on the continuing success of capitalism. From the country's inception, self-reliance and economic individualism were the very essence of the new society, and capitalism flourished as in no other country; not until the 1930s did it need sustained support from government. The Industrialization, infrastructure development, and urbanization were provided by the private market rather, as in most European countries, by the central government. Government played a role, but mainly at the state level and in response to the needs of capitalism, not as a leader and director of investment and resources.

Thus, when government today intrudes into almost every aspect of society, it continues to be treated with suspicion by many Americans, an attitude deeply embedded in the American political culture. In comparable countries, including America's main economic competitors in Europe and Asia, and where governments have been dominant in economic development or in dictating the central—often elitist—values of the society, citizens are generally more accepting of a prominent central state.

Two further points on individualism should be noted: First, observers make the mistake of inferring a general *cultural* individualism when noting the undoubted prevalence of *economic* individualism in the United States. Yet as the discussion of freedom and references to religion suggests, Americans are often influenced by collectivist thinking. Whether it be McCarthyism, fundamentalist Christianity, or a sometimes violent rejection of outsiders from carefully protected local communities, there is no shortage of examples of Americans moving, sometimes blindly, in masses. By this measure, many local communities have shown less respect for cultural variety than applies in more centralized "cosmopolitan" countries such as Britain and France.

Second and related is the fact that laws designed to provide equality of opportunity often conflict with notions of individualism. Positive discrimination in favor of ethnic minorities, women, or the disabled can mean the application of rules and standards intended to benefit whole social *groups*. In such instances, the merits of *individuals* are sometimes subordinated to those of the group. Hence racial or gender quotas applied to employment or admission to college give preference to particular groups at the expense of "advantaged" individuals who are not members of these groups (usually white or Asian males). This tension between equality and individualism has become an important issue in American politics. Although it is difficult to generalize in this area, many on the right and in the Republican Party favor laws that respect individual merit, whereas many on the left and in the Democratic Party favor laws that respect the collective interests of disadvantaged groups. In 1997 voters in California passed a law rejecting affirmative action, but the courts have yet to endorse a total ban on all positive discrimination programs.

Noteworthy about this issue is the intensity of feelings it arouses, for although affirmative action is an issue in many countries, only in the United States does it provoke such passionate debate. This is, perhaps, because equality and individualism are so central to the American creed, and conflicts between them have been recurring themes in American history. At the same time, the issue brings into sharp focus the conflict between the philosophy of limited government and the need for strong government action to redress what is seen as the long-term effects of inequality and discrimination.[8]

Democracy and the Rule of Law

If "democracy" is defined in terms of a simple devotion to *majoritarianism,* then there is no doubting that Americans believe in it. Majority opinion carries a weight and independent value in the United States that is unusual elsewhere. This attitude not only translates into a broad acceptance of the legitimacy of elections and, at the state and local levels, of initiatives and referendums, but it also means that on occasion ill-judged policies and programs have been adopted following a surge of (often populist) moral fervor. Such was the case with prohibition and, arguably, some of the tax-cutting measures of the 1978–1981 period when citizens in a number of states voted to reduce property taxes to levels insufficient to provide for local services. More recently, politicians have scrambled to be among the first supporting "quick fix" solutions to America's crime problems. Hence in the 1990s many states passed laws designed to ensure that repeat violent offenders were sent to prison for good. These "three strikes and you're out" laws led to all sorts of anomalies, including the imposition of life sentences for minor offenses and the release of long-term violent offenders to make room for repeat offenders.

As far as general political arrangements are concerned, American attitudes present something of a paradox, for they combine strong *general* support for the Constitution and the system as such with considerable disillusionment with *particular* processes and institutions. One of the first and most impressive of the political-culture studies discovered that Americans were overwhelmingly supportive of the political system and Constitution compared with other countries. True, this survey dates from the early 1960s when people were generally more optimistic about society, but there is still evidence that Americans believe their system to be basically sound (few want to emigrate, and most greatly admire the constitutional framework).[9] However, since the mid-1960s, increasing numbers of people have become disillusioned with the party system, the presidency, Congress, and the federal bureaucracy.

Confidence in government reached a low by 1980 following the events of Vietnam, Watergate, and the Iranian hostage crisis. With the Reagan presidency, some confidence returned—but not to the levels of the 1960s. During the 1990s, confidence levels resumed their downward trend, only to recover somewhat during the prolonged economic boom years of the second Clinton administration (Figure 2.1).

But too much can be read into these shifting sentiments. Citizens may be disillusioned with particular institutions, governments, or politicians, but they are not *alienated* from the system in a way that threatens the regime.[10] The institutions and processes that succor American democracy and the rule of law are highly respected. If anything, recent evidence of declining trust in government reflects an increasing sophistication among voters, who are now making more conscious connections between what parties and politicians promise and how they perform. This tension is, of course, the theme of the book and is explored further in later chapters.

Claims that the system is essentially stable appear to be supported by the relative absence of regime-challenging parties and protest movements in American history. The Civil War apart, most protest activity has been inspired by single issues (civil rights, the Vietnam War) or has been accommodated within existing parties and institutions. Radical critics are quick to point out that this stability is because truly revolutionary movements have been nipped in the bud by an unholy alliance of corporations and government. But much more repressive tactics have been employed in other countries to no avail. Why should much less extensive measures have been so successful in America?

More convincing perhaps is the claim that, unable to mobilize politically against the prevailing ideology, increasing numbers of Americans have turned to nonpolitical violence and antisocial behavior. There can be no doubting that America is a violent society (more than 19,000 people were murdered in 1997 alone), but it is extraor-

FIGURE 2.1   Individual Confidence in Government, 1952–1996

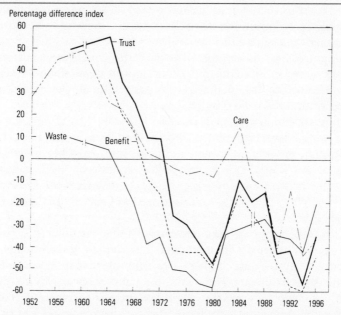

NOTE: Broken line indicates question not asked that year in the biennial National Election Study Questions: (Care) "I don't think public officials care much about what people like me think" (Trust) "How much of the time do you think you can trust the government in Washington to do what is right—just about always, most of the time, or only some of the time?" (Benefit) "Would you say the government is pretty much run by a few big interests looking out for themselves or that it is run for the benefit of all people? (Waste) "Do you think that people in the government waste a lot of money we pay in taxes, waste some of it, or don't waste very much of it?" The percentage difference index is calculated by subtracting the percentage giving a cynical response from the percentage giving a trusting response.
SOURCE: Harold W. Stanley and Richard G. Niemi, *Vital Statistics on American Politics 1997–98* (Washington, DC: Congressional Quarterly Press, 1998), figure 3.7.

dinarily difficult to make clear causal connections between this sort of pathology and political values and institutions. Violence and crime have always been a part of what was for many generations a frontier society. Until the 1960s (and possibly beyond), violence and intimidation in the South were part of a Southern social structure built on racism and exploitation. Obviously this was as much a political as a social or economic phenomenon. As significant is the continuing high (but falling) levels of random violence and serious crime among the racial and ethnic minorities of America's inner cities. There seems little doubt that these citizens are often politically excluded, isolated, and socially alienated. For them, the optimism, materialism, and egalitarianism that continue to dominate political discourse and that are encouraged by the highly commercial media either must seem an irrelevance or must serve as a diversion from their everyday lives.

In sum, undoubtedly the most important feature of the American political culture is its ability to accommodate apparently deep divisions over the role of government in society without challenging the constitutional order or what many have defined as "Americanism." Such is the devotion to Americanism that it has been uniquely effective in overpowering other systems of beliefs and values. Samuel Huntington has made this point well:

> It is possible to speak of a body of political ideas that constitutes "Americanism" in a sense which one can never speak of "Britishism," "Frenchism," "Germanism" or "Japaneseism." Americanism in this sense is comparable to other ideologies or religions. "Americanism is to the American," Leon Samson has said, "not a tradition or a territory, not what France is to a Frenchman or England to an Englishman, but a doctrine—what socialism is to a socialist." To reject the central ideas of that doctrine is to be un-American. There is no British Creed or French Creed; the Académie Française worries about the purity of the French language, not about the purity of French political ideas. What indeed would be an "un-French" political idea? But preoccupation with "un-American" political ideas and behavior has been a recurring theme in American life. "It has been our fate as a nation," Richard Hofstadter succinctly observed, "not to have ideologies but to be one."[11]

This ideological consensus is supported by virtually all social and political groups—however antagonistic toward one another they may appear. As Michael Foley has noted, "Americans fight each other in their efforts to expand the American creed."[12] Even citizens from as close a country (geographically and culturally) as Canada find this phenomenon startling, as exemplified in this description of a Canadian's first encounter with the United States in the 1960s:

My first encounter with American consensus was in the late sixties, when I crossed the border into the United States and found myself inside the myth of America. Not of North America, for the myth stopped short of the Canadian and Mexican borders, but of a country that despite its arbitrary frontiers, despite its bewildering mix of race and creed, could believe in something called the True America, and could invest that patent fiction with all the moral and emotional appeal of a religious symbol. . . . Here was the Jewish anarchist Paul Goodman berating the Midwest for abandoning the promise; here the descendant of American slaves, Martin Luther King, denouncing injustice as a violation of the American way; here an endless debate about national destiny . . . conservatives scavenging for un-Americans, New Left historians recalling the country to its sacred mission.

Nothing in my Canadian background had prepared me for this spectacle . . . it gave me something of an anthropologist's sense of wonder at the symbol of the tribe. . . . to a Canadian skeptic, a gentile in God's country [here was] a pluralistic, pragmatic people bound together by an ideological consensus. Let me repeat that mundane phrase: *ideological consensus.* For it wasn't the idea of exceptionalism that I discovered in '68 . . . it was a hundred sects and factions, each apparently different from the others, yet all celebrating the same mission.[13]

In this discussion of the deep ambivalence many Americans show toward the role of the federal government in society and economy, it should always be remembered that no matter how fierce the ensuing ideological battles, almost all of the protagonists believe their positions are true to essentially *American* political values. This orientation explains why what seem to be deep and bitter political divisions in America almost never become the basis of challenges to the constitutional order. The rest of this chapter examines how these values interact with the growth and present-day functioning of the American society and economy.

Values and American Society

Immigration and Demographic Change

Until the mid-nineteenth century, the United States was an "imperialist" continental power, constantly expanding its territory by treaty, annexation, and conquest. It was expansionist both in the sense that it dominated the other continental powers—Mexico,

Britain, France, and Spain—and in the sense that numerous Native American tribes were overwhelmed by a technologically more advanced and populous society. Above all, it was America's economic might that enabled the new nation to swallow up huge tracts of territory during this period (see Map 2.1). Population increases were also considerable and did not fall below 20 percent per decade until 1920 (Table 2.3). Ever since then, the population has continued to grow rapidly and remains at around a 10 percent increase a decade—a remarkably high figure for an advanced industrial country with a small agrarian population. Both high natural increases and immigration account for this population growth, although since 1971 there has been a small natural *decrease* for the white population.[14]

The United States was virtually built on an ideology of immigration, with successive generations of Americans promoting the country as a land of freedom and opportunity. The appeal was simple. Free from the corruption and oppression of Europe and rich in land and natural resources, the United States could and did absorb vast numbers of immigrants, first mainly from Britain, then from Germany, Ireland, southern and eastern Europe, and most recently from Asia, Mexico, Cuba, Canada, the Caribbean, and South American countries. As Table 2.4 shows, a high level of immigration continues even today, with more than 7 million new immigrants arriving in the 1990–1996 period.

In comparative context this is a high figure, for no other industrial country allows such an influx. During periods of labor shortage or political emergency, many European countries have encouraged some—often temporary—immigration, but none permits a continuing high level of immigration that persists even during periods of high unemployment and low rates of economic growth. However, mass immigration has not gone unopposed in the United States. During and following the truly massive waves of immigration from southern and eastern Europe in the 1880–1910 period, opposition to what for many Americans represented an "invasion" by alien cultures was fierce and finally culminated in the 1924 Immigration Act. This law limited immigration to 150,000 and established preference quotas for the immediate family members of U.S. citizens. The effect was to favor immigration from Canada and northern and western Europe. Immigration fell dramatically during the 1930s and 1940s as depression and war took their toll both on economic opportunity and on freedom of movement.

MAP 2.1   U.S. Territorial Expansion
NOTE: Dates under state names denote year of statehood.
SOURCE: *Statistical Abstract of the USA 1981*, figure 7.2, p. 208.

With immigration increasing once more after 1950, criticism of
the patent biases in immigration law intensified, and in 1965 a new
law was adopted with fairer, more balanced quotas. Nonetheless,
and following further amendments to the law in 1980, 1986, and
1996, immigration continued at between 2 percent and 3 percent
of the total population per decade; during the 1980s, some 7.3 million immigrants arrived in the United States.[15]

Since about 1970 the immigration controversy has been fueled
anew by substantial illegal immigration, mainly from Mexico, and
by the social tensions that large numbers of Cuban, Haitian, and
Central American newcomers have brought, particularly to California and Florida. Illegal immigration has accelerated as poorer Mexi-

TABLE 2.3 Population and Area, 1790–1997

	Resident Population		Increase over Preceding Census		Area (square miles)		
Census Date	Number	Per Square Mile of Land Area	Number	Percent	Gross	Land	Water
Conterminous US[a]							
1790 (2 August)	3,929,214	4,5	n.a.	n.a.	888,811	864,746	24,065
1800 (4 August)	5,308,483	6.1	1,379,269	35.1	888,822	864,746	24,065
1810 (6 August)	7,239,881	4.3	1,931,398	36.4	1,716,003	1,681,828	34,175
1820 (7 August)	9,638,453	5.5	2,398,572	33.1	1,788,006	1,749,462	38,544
1830 (1 June)	12,866,020	7.4	3,227,567	32.5	1,788,006	1,749,642	38,544
1840 (1 June)	17,069,453	9.8	4,203,433	32.7	1,788,006	1,749,462	38,544
1850 (1 June)	23,191,876	7.9	6,122,423	35.9	2,992,747	2,940,042	52,705
1860 (1 June)	31,443,321	10.6	8,251,445	35.6	3,022,387	2,969,640	52,747
1870 (1 June)	39,818,449	13.4	8,375,128	26.6	3,022,387	2,969,640	52,747
1880 (1 June)	50,155,783	16.9	10,337,334	26.0	3,022,387	2,969,640	52,747
1890 (1 June)	62,947,714	21.2	12,791,931	25.5	3,022,387	2,969,640	52,747
1900 (1 June)	75,994,575	25.6	13,046,861	20.7	3,022,387	2,969,834	52,533
1910 (15 April)	91,972,266	31.0	15,977,691	21.0	3,022,387	2,969,565	52,822
1920 (1 January)	105,710,620	35.6	13,738,354	14.9	3,022,387	2,969,451	52,936
1930 (1 April)	122,755,046	41.2	17,064,426	16.1	3,022,387	2,977,128	45,259
1940 (1 April)	131,669,275	44.2	8,894,229	7.2	3,022,387	2,977,128	45,259
1950 (1 April)	150,697,361	50.7	19,028,066	14.5	3,022,387	2,974,726	47,661
1960 (1 April)	178,464,236	60.1	27,766,875	18.4	3,022,387	2,966,054	54,207
United States							
1950 (1 April)	151,325,796	42.6	19,161,299	14.5	3,615,211	3,552,206	63,005
1960 (1 April)	179,323,175	50.6	27,997,377	18.5	3,615,123	3,540,911	74,212
1970 (1 April)	203,211,926	57.4	23,888,751	13.3	3,618,467	3,540,023	78,444
1980 (1 April)	226,545,805	64.0	23,243,774	11.4	3,618,770	3,539,289	79,481
1990 (1 April)	248,709,873	70.3	22,164,068	9.8	3,787,425	3,536,342	251,083
1997 (1 April)	267,901,000	n.a.	n.a.	n.a.	n.a.	n.a.	n.a.

[a] excludes Alaska and Hawaii.

SOURCE: *Statistical Abstract of the USA*, 1996, tables 1 and 2, updated from 1998 ed., table 2.

TABLE 2.4   Immigration, 1820–1996

Year	No. (1,000s)	Rate[a]	Year	No. (1,000s)	Rate[a]
1820–1989	55,458	3.4	1970	373	1.8
1820–1830[b]	152	1.2	1971	370	1.8
1831–1840[c]	599	3.9	1972	385	1.8
1841–1850[d]	1,713	8.4	1973	400	1.9
1851–1860[d]	2,596	9.3	1974	395	1.9
1861–1870[e]	2,315	6.4	1975	386	1.8
1871–1880	2,812	6.2	1976	399	1.9
1881–1890	5,247	9.2	1977	462	2.1
1891–1900	3,688	5.3	1978	601	2.8
1901–1910	8,795	10.4	1979	460	2.1
1911–1920	5,736	5.7	1980	531	2.3
1921–1930	4,107	3.5	1986	602	2.5
1931–1940	1,528	0.4	1987	602	2.5
1941–1950	1,035	0.7	1988	643	2.6
1951–1960	2,515	1.5	1989	1091	4.4[g]
1961–1970	3,322	1.7	1990	1536	6.1
1971–1980[f]	4,493	2.1	1991	1827	7.2
1981–1986	3,466	2.4	1992	974	3.8
1965	297	1.5	1993	904	3.5
1966	323	1.6	1994	804	3.1
1967	362	1.8	1995	720	2.7
1968	454	2.3	1996	916	3.5
1969	359	1.8			

[a] Annual rate per 1,000 U.S. population. Rate computed by dividing sum of annual immigration totals by sum of annual U.S. population totals for same number of years.

[b] Oct. 1, 1819–Sept. 30, 1830.

[c] Oct. 1, 1830–Dec. 1, 1840.

[d] Calendar years.

[e] Jan. 1, 1861–June 30, 1870.

[f] Includes transition quarter, July 1 to Sept. 30, 1976.

[g] Includes persons granted residence under the "amnesty" program of the 1986 Immigration Reform and Control Act.

SOURCE: *Statistical Abstract of the USA*, 1996, table 5, updated from 1998 ed., table 5.

cans have sought employment across a long and poorly policed border. Estimates of the numbers involved vary widely but are at least in the low millions. In 1994 voters in California approved an initiative (Proposition 187) that denied welfare and other state benefits to illegal immigrants. In general, Republican politicians take a hard line on illegal immigration; Democrats, although they condemn it, are more prepared to accept that the government has some responsibility toward supporting the families of illegal immigrants. In spite of these differences, very few politicians are openly anti-immigrant, and America's comparatively liberal attitude to immigration continues to echo the long-standing conviction that once in America, people of all backgrounds will be provided with an equal opportunity to succeed.

As the country and economy have grown, so both the composition and spatial distribution of the population have changed. The mass immigration of the nineteenth and early twentieth centuries made the country more ethnically diverse, and although these earlier immigrants are now generally assimilated into American society, many retain some national, ethnic, or religious identity that has European origins. More recently, immigration and high relative birthrates have led to substantial increases in the African American and Hispanic populations. By 1995 some 26.8 millions (10.2 percent) of Americans were Hispanic (mainly Mexican, Puerto Rican, and Cuban), and 33.1 million (12.6 percent) were African American. In the case of the Hispanic population, a linguistic as well as ethnic dimension is involved, for Spanish is the mother tongue for many, and in some areas, notably California and the Southwest, demands have been made for an official bilingualism. However, no state has such a policy, and in recent years state initiatives have been introduced to limit bilingualism in elementary and secondary education. These measures reflect the continuing conviction that in spite of its great ethnic and religious diversity, the United States should share one essentially *American* system of beliefs and values underpinned by freedom and equality of opportunity.

America today is a highly urban society, with more than 75 percent of the population living in cities with populations over 2,500 in 1995. A more meaningful measure of urbanism is, perhaps, the number of people living in metropolitan areas, which in 1992 held no less than 79.7 percent of the population. One interesting post-1970 trend has been an increase in the nonfarming rural population. In the last census period (1980 to 1990), nonmetropolitan areas grew by 18.2 percent, while metropolitan areas grew by just

11 percent. These new rural dwellers are not, in the main, farmers, but people seeking a new lifestyle away from the crowded cities and suburbs. Indeed, the growth of smaller towns and rural areas is a general phenomenon in advanced industrial societies.

Nonetheless, urban areas are still growing, although not in a uniform or even manner. The inner or central areas of the older industrial cities continue to decline, although during the 1980s and 1990s a number of these cities experienced a revival of their downtown areas. In addition, there have been some quite dramatic changes in the distribution of population among the largest metropolitan areas. Two broad trends can be discerned. The first is the rapid growth of southern and western cities and the relative decline of northern cities. This trend, of course, is part of the "Sunbelt-Snowbelt" divide much talked of in the 1970s. Second, since 1990 there have been clear signs of revival among some of the older metropolitan areas, with the Chicago, Detroit, and Cleveland areas showing renewed growth. At the same time, some of the Sunbelt cities' growth rates began to slow—although admittedly from a very high level. These figures should, however, be treated with some caution. The metropolitan census areas cover large urban agglomerations, which contain within them many variations. Within the Detroit region, for example, the central part of the city of Detroit continues to decline, whereas many of the surrounding suburbs, towns, and cities are growing quite rapidly.

An interesting feature of American urbanization is that for the most part it has not resulted in what in some countries is identified as a dominant metropolitan culture centered on one or a few dominant cities. Unlike Britain, France, Russia, or Mexico, no American urban area has a monopoly on economic, social, and political power. In addition, Americans have always mistrusted urban sophistication. They have instead idealized rural and small-town America, which many continue to see as the representation of traditional American values such as democracy and community.

Economic Change

From very humble beginnings, the American economy had grown to the world's largest by the end of the nineteenth century, and by 1945 the United States had established an effective global hegemony in economic affairs. America's per capita income was easily the highest in the world for a large country, and the economy had achieved a remarkable degree of self-sufficiency. By 1998 the economy had grown to a staggering $8 trillion and per capita income exceeded $26,000. As the economy has grown, there has been a shift in sectors, first out of agricultural employment to manufacturing and, most recently, out of manufacturing into service industries. By 1996 less than 3 percent of the labor force was employed in agriculture—even though the United States is the world's largest food producer. Of the nonagricultural labor force, those employed in goods-related jobs (mining, construction, and manufacturing) fell from 37.7 percent in 1960 to 23 percent in 1994, while service-sector jobs increased to over 70 percent of the total. With most Americans working in the service sector, talk of a postindustrial society is not entirely misplaced—although it is only through great productivity advances in agriculture and manufacturing that the economy is able to sustain such a diversity of service-sector jobs.

In spite of these advances, the American economy began to experience difficulties in the early 1970s, which led many to challenge the long-held notion that the United States was the land of economic opportunity and upward mobility. Some of these difficulties derived from world economic problems, but others were a result of peculiarly American circumstances. In general, U.S. productivity increases did not keep pace with those of major competing countries. Concern at the apparent U.S. "deindustrialization" increased perceptibly during the early 1980s as unemployment rose and industrial output fell. However, between 1982 and 1989 the economy recovered well, with both unemployment and inflation falling rapidly (Table 2.5) and U.S. productivity rates improving in relation to other countries, with the notable exception of Japan. But much of this new growth was in the service sector, which generated mainly low-paid unskilled jobs.

By the early 1990s the economy had slowed once again, with unemployment rising to 7.4 percent (Table 2.5). There was general acceptance that the recession of the early 1990s resulted in part from excessive borrowing (by the government and individuals) during the 1980s. Indeed, by 1992 there was an emerging consensus that the boom of the 1980s had been built on very shaky foundations. U.S. investment levels had remained relatively low, and few American families had seen their real incomes rise during the decade. Indeed, the poorest 20 percent of families saw their incomes decline (Figure 2.2). This fact, above all, led to a major reappraisal of the role of government in the economy during the 1990s. A new con-

TABLE 2.5   U.S. Unemployment and Inflation, 1960–1999

	Annual Percentage Change in the Consumer Price Index	Unemployment (percentage of total civilian workforce)
1960	1.6	5.5
1965	1.7	4.5
1970	5.9	5.0
1975	9.1	8.3
1980	13.5	7.2
1982	6.1	9.7
1984	4.3	7.5
1986	2.0	7.0
1988	4.4	5.5
1989	4.6	5.3
1990	6.1	5.5
1991	3.1	6.7
1992	2.9	7.4
1993	3.0	6.8
1994	2.7	6.1
1995	2.7	5.8
1996	1.9	5.3
1997	1.9	4.8
1998	1.0	4.6
1999 (est)	1.2	5.0

SOURCE: *Economic Report of the President, 1998,* updated from Organization for Economic Cooperation and Development (OECD), *Economic Outlook* (Paris: OECD, December 1998), p. 38.

sensus emerged on the need for a balanced budget—an imperative that happily coincided with a long and steady economic recovery between 1993 and 1999. Unemployment fell (Table 2.5), and the long-term decline in real wages was arrested, if not reversed. The economic traumas of the 1970s and 1980s led many observers to claim that the American dream was over—that the ever improving well-being of the country that was the very foundation of equal opportunity and democracy had come to an end. By the late 1990s, however, the good times had returned with record low inflation and unemployment, although the booming economy did not result in economic well-being for all Americans.

A relatively new aspect of the American economy is that government is now inextricably involved in managing economic change. By 1998 some 35 percent of the gross national product (GNP) was accounted for by government spending. This figure is not high in comparative perspective (see Table 15.1 in Chapter 15), but it is dramatically higher than before the Great Depression, the 1930s, and World War II transformed the ways in which the federal government intervenes in society. As already established, Americans remain deeply ambivalent about this role. On the one hand, they *expect* the federal government to provide a wide range of social benefits, to regulate the market, and to ensure that growth and employment are kept on an ever upward curve. On the other hand, the public bemoans higher taxes, and the media are constantly reminding the citizenry of waste and inefficiency in government programs. This ambivalence extends to what has become the very complex ways in which the American economy interacts with the rest of the global economy. As will be stressed in Chapter 15, the U.S. economy is now undoubtedly more interdependent with the economies of other countries. As a result, further limits exist on the ability of politicians to deliver what they promise in economic policy.

Social Structure

A fundamental issue in social science is the relationship between social structure and political activity. In most countries, social class, race, gender, religion, language, and region are important determinants of how people think and behave in relation to political authority. The purpose of this section is to provide some background on American society as a prelude to later analysis of political attitudes and behavior.

Income and Wealth. The preeminence of equality of opportunity as an underlying value in American society has undoubtedly limited the growth of an explicitly class-based politics in the United States. Americans are supposed to be essentially middle class, eschewing both the working-class and aristocratic values associated with many European countries. By many objective indicators, the United States should indeed have a predominantly middle-class culture. In 1996 more than 45 percent of all workers were in professional, technical, managerial, or administrative jobs. Only 30 percent of all workers were in blue-collar jobs, with a further 22 percent in service jobs and 3 percent in farm employment.* Americans are also highly educated and enjoy a high level of home ownership, two indicators commonly

---

*This is a narrower category than implied by service *sector* and includes workers in catering and domestic service.

FIGURE 2.2   Rate of Real Annual Family Income Growth by Quintile

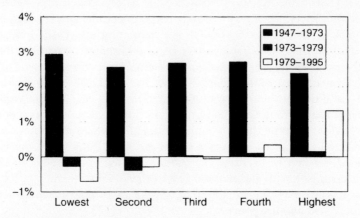

SOURCE: Data from the Bureau of the Census, 1997, Internet site
http://www.census.gov/hhes/income

employed to measure social class. In 1996, 80 percent of all eighteen-
year-olds had achieved a high school certificate, and of these approximately 30 percent went on to complete a four-year undergrad-
uate degree, a high percentage in cross-national context. As notable
are the housing figures, with more than 60 percent of all housing
units being owner-occupied. Another measure of the middle-class nature of American society is the high level of stock (share) ownership
in corporations. More than 60 percent of American families own
stock or hold stock in a variety of pension funds, dramatically more
than in most developed countries, although most stockholders have
less than $30,000 of equity.

Some sociologists have questioned these "objective" indicators,
arguing that the relationship between employed and employer is
little different for white- and blue-collar workers. Moreover, these
figures reveal nothing about the distribution of wealth and income
or about the continuing existence of many truly poor Americans. In
fact, most measures rank the United States at or near the bottom
when comparisons of income and wealth inequalities are made
across countries. There has also been a trend toward increasing inequality of U.S. incomes since the late 1970s. As illustrated in Figure 2.2, the poorest 20 percent of the population suffered falls in
income in the period 1979–1995, while the richest 20 percent experienced increased income.

These figures do not always translate into increased levels of poverty. In fact, measuring the number of poor people in the United States is difficult. Poverty is a relative concept and is extraordinarily hard to measure accurately. There is in fact an *official* poverty measure, and there is a broad acceptance that families living below 125 percent of this level are effectively living in poverty. This translated into an income of around $18,000 for a family of four in 1996. As can be seen from Table 2.6, the incidence of poverty has remained roughly at around 14 to 16 percent of the population since 1980. The biggest single drop in recent years occurred between 1960 and 1966 when many of today's social programs were first enacted.

Regardless of how poverty is measured, one certainty is that America does have a large population of poor people. They are not perhaps poor in the sense of living below subsistence level, but they are certainly poor in the sense of having little hope of full-time, secure employment and access to good housing and an acceptable living environment.

Of course, poverty is not randomly scattered throughout the country. Its incidence is highest in the southern states and in rural and inner-city areas. Blacks and one-parent families headed by women are also greatly overrepresented among the poor (Table 2.7).

In spite of these inequalities, most of which have been characteristics of American society for many generations, class has not emerged as a major social cleavage in American politics. True, there have been occasions when at least the embryo of a national working-class or populist movement could be identified. And in particular geographical areas, class-based political parties have achieved some considerable success. But their impact has been slight compared with the effects of radical movements on the national politics of other countries. Scholars have pondered long and hard as to why this should be so. As later chapters will show, institutional arrangements—in particular, federalism and the electoral system—militate against minority and radical political parties. Probably more important is the absence of a feudal and aristocratic past, with all the deeply rooted social cleavages such arrangements imply. Related is what has been called a dominant ideology of equality and liberty, with its promise of unlimited opportunity and social mobility. Certainly the United States has in the main been a remarkably successful country economically. Even by the mid-nineteenth century, the American standard of living exceeded that of

TABLE 2.6 Families Below Poverty Level and Below 125 Percent of Poverty Level, 1960–1996

	Number Below Poverty Level (1,000)				Percent Below Poverty Level				Below 125 Percent of Poverty Level	
	All Races[a]	White	Black	Hispanic[b]	All Races[a]	White	Black	Hispanic[b]	Number (1,000)	Percent
1960	8,243	6,115	n.a.	n.a.	18.1	14.9	n.a.	n.a.	11,525	25.4
1970	5,260	3,708	1,481	n.a.	10.1	8.0	29.5	n.a.	7,516	14.4
1974	4,922	3,352	1,479	526	8.8	6.8	26.9	21.2	7,195	12.9
1975	5,450	3,838	1,513	627	9.7	7.7	27.1	25.1	7,974	14.2
1976	5,311	3,560	1,617	598	9.4	7.1	27.9	23.1	7,647	13.5
1977	5,311	3,540	1,637	591	9.3	7.0	28.2	21.4	7,713	13.5
1978	5,280	3,523	1,622	559	9.1	6.9	27.5	20.4	7,417	12.8
1979	5,461	3,581	1,722	614	9.2	6.9	27.8	20.3	7,784	13.1
1980	6,217	4,195	1,826	751	10.3	8.0	28.9	23.2	8,764	14.5
1981	6,851	4,670	1,972	792	11.2	8.8	30.8	24.0	9,568	15.7
1982	7,512	5,118	2,458	916	12.2	9.6	33.0	27.2	10,279	16.7
1983	7,647	5,220	2,161	981	12.3	9.7	32.3	25.9	10,358	16.7
1984	7,277	4,925	2,094	991	11.6	9.1	30.9	25.2	9,901	15.8
1985	7,223	4,983	1,983	1,074	11.4	9.1	28.7	25.5	9,753	15.3
1986	7,023	4,811	1,987	1,085	10.9	8.6	28.0	24.7	9,476	14.7
1987	7,005	4,567	2,117	1,168	10.7	8.1	29.4	25.5	9,338	14.3

1988	6,874	4,471	2,089	1,141	10.4	7.9	28.2	23.7	9,284	14.1
1989	6,784	4,409	2,077	1,133	10.3	7.8	27.8	23.4	9,267	14.0
1990	7,098	4,622	2,193	1,244	10.7	8.1	29.3	25.0	9,564	14.4
1991	7,712	5,022	2,343	1,372	11.5	8.8	30.4	26.5	10,244	15.3
1992	8,144	5,255	2,484	1,529	11.9	9.1	31.1	26.7	10,859	16.1
1993	8,393	5,452	2,499	1,625	12.3	9.4	31.1	27.3	11,203	16.4
1994	8,053	5,312	2,212	1,724	11.6	9.9	27.3	27.8	10,721	15.5
1995	7,532	4,994	2,127	1,695	10.8	8.5	26.4	27.0	10,223	14.7
1996	7,708	5,059	2,206	1,748	11.0	8.6	26.1	26.4	10,476	14.9

n.a. Not available.

a Includes other races not shown separately.

b Persons of Hispanic origin may be of any race.

SOURCE: *Statistical Abstract of the United States, 1998*, Washington, DC, 1998, table 764.

34

TABLE 2.7   Persons Below the Poverty Line, 1995

Group	Percentage of Group That Is Poor	Group as a Percentage of All Poor People
Race/ethnicity		
White	11.2	67.1
White (not of Hispanic origin)	8.5	44.7
Black	29.3	27.1
Hispanic origin[a]	30.3	23.5
Family status		
Female householder, no husband present		
White	29.7	19.3
Black	48.2	18.0
Hispanic[a]	52.8	8.4
All other families		
White	6.6	29.0
Black	10.8	4.5
Hispanic[a]	22.1	11.8
Age		
Under 18	20.8	40.3
65 and over	10.5	9.1
Dwelling		
Metropolitan residents	13.4	77.8
Nonmetropolitan residents	15.6	22.2
Region		
Northeast	12.5	17.7
Midwest	11.0	18.6
South	15.7	39.7
West	14.9	24.0
All persons	13.8	100.0

[a] Persons of Hispanic origin may be of any race.

SOURCE: Harold W. Stanley and Richard G. Niemi, *Vital Statistics on American Politics, 1997–98* (Washington, DC: Congressional Quarterly Press, 1998), table 10.5.

Britain, then one of the most affluent of the old European powers. Combined with bountiful and cheap land, this factor must constitute at least part of the explanation for the failure of socialism.

Nonetheless, rapid urbanization and industrialization had their social costs, just as they did in other countries, and the U.S. economy has by no means always performed well. During the Great Depression, for example, social distress was high among both working- and middle-class people. Given this, many historians and social scientists are obliged to fall back on the explanations based on beliefs, values, and ideology when accounting for the absence of a powerful socialist party.

Some scholars have argued that a repressive state (mainly at the state and local levels), in cooperation with repressive private (corporate) power, prevented the emergence of a radical trade union and socialist movement during the late nineteenth and early twentieth centuries. But comparisons with equivalent events in Europe appear seriously to weaken this argument. There certainly was repression in the United States, but its character was essentially fragmented, erratic, and uncoordinated, compared with the often quite draconian and highly centralized measures employed by some European governments.

Race and Ethnicity.   As noted, the United States is highly diverse in its ethnic and racial makeup. Within the white population, it is increasingly difficult to find distinctive characteristics based on ethnicity. To be sure, many Americans still describe themselves as Italian Americans or Irish Americans, but these labels have less meaning than they used to as groups are assimilated into the broader American culture. Not surprisingly, this integration is less true of more recently arrived immigrant groups, most of whom are Hispanic or Asian. "Hispanic American" is a broad category and embraces people of Mexican origin who have been in the United States for many generations (some in the southwestern states since before the founding of the republic) as well as immigrants from Mexico, Central and South America, and some parts of the Caribbean. Chinese, Vietnamese, and Japanese make up the majority of the Asian population, although there are increasing numbers of arrivals from other parts of Asia, including the Indian subcontinent. Finally, there are around 1.8 million Native Americans living (often in abject poverty) mainly in the West and Southwest.

As can be seen from Table 2.8, the numbers of Hispanic and Asian Americans have been increasing particularly rapidly in recent years, reflecting both high birthrates and immigration. With the partial exception of some Asian groups, these minorities are generally poorer and less well educated than the white population. Although some improvement in the status of African Americans and Hispanics has occurred since the 1970s, by many measures the position of blacks in particular has deteriorated. There are sound historical reasons for the disadvantaged status of African Americans. Until the 1960s they suffered from what was effectively an apartheid system in the southern states. Further, the continuing collapse of the black family unit since the 1980s has been cited by many commentators as a major cause of the cycle of poverty and disadvantage that affects so many African Americans, especially those living in inner-city areas.

One particular problem for African Americans is that because they are greatly overrepresented among blue-collar and low-paid jobs, they are more vulnerable to fluctuations in the economy than are other social groups. This problem has become particularly serious as the labor market has become more flexible and unions have weakened. An official acknowledgment of this situation was made in the 1995 *Economic Report of the President,* which pointed to the deterioration in the earnings of many black workers during the 1990s.[16] Better-educated and professional African Americans, by contrast, have continued to improve their position in society.

Although the political behavior of the black population is distinctive (discussed in Chapter 6), black separatist or nationalist movements have never achieved any significant success. Along with other ethnic minorities, African Americans have tended to mobilize politically within the context of established institutions and political parties. This is not to deny the importance of an ethnic dimension to politics; within the Democratic Party, for example, and at the level of local politics, ethnicity has been and continues to be a significant voting and organizational cue. But the United States has never nurtured an ethnic politics based on separatism or a complete rejection of the dominant "American" values and political institutions. In marked contrast to such countries as Canada, Belgium, Ireland, and Spain, ethnic divisions have not manifested themselves in ways that challenge the constitutional order.

In one key area, blacks and other minorities have made considerable advances: They now hold more important political offices than at any time in their history. However, an inverse relationship exists

TABLE 2.8   Resident Population by Ethnic-Origin Status, 1980–1995; and
Projections, 1996–2050 (in thousands, except as indicated)

	Total	Hispanic Origin[a]	White	Black	American Indian, Eskimo Aleut	Asian, Pacific Islander
1980 (April)	226,546	14,609	180,906	26,142	1,326	3,563
1981	229,466	15,560	181,974	26,532	1,377	4,022
1982	231,664	16,240	182,782	26,856	1,420	4,367
1983	233,792	16,935	183,561	27,159	1,466	4,671
1984	235,825	17,640	184,243	27,44	1,512	4,986
1985	237,924	18,368	184,945	27,738	1,558	5,315
1986	240,133	19,154	185,678	28,040	1,606	5,655
1987	242,289	19,946	186,353	28,351	1,654	5,985
1988	244,499	20,786	187,012	28,669	1,703	6,329
1989	246,819	21,648	187,713	29,005	1,755	6,698
1990 (April)	248,718	22,354	188,306	29,275	1,796	6,988
1991	252,138	23,381	189,692	29,825	1,829	7,411
1992	255,039	24,272	190,832	30,310	1,856	7,768
1993	257,800	25,198	191,852	30,757	1,882	8,112
1994	260,350	26,099	192,735	31,187	1,907	8,421
1995	262,755	26,994	193,523	31,591	1,931	8,715

Projections
Middle series:

	Total	Hispanic Origin[a]	White	Black	American Indian, Eskimo Aleut	Asian, Pacific Islander
1996	265,253	27,804	194,353	31,999	1,956	9,141
1997	267,645	28,680	195,091	32,396	1,980	9,497
1998	270,002	29,566	195,786	32,789	2,005	9,856
1999	272,330	30,461	196,441	33,180	2,029	10,219
2000	274,634	31,366	197,061	33,568	2,054	10,584
2005	285,981	36,057	199,802	35,485	2,183	12,454
2010	297,716	41,139	202,390	37,466	2,320	14,402
2020	322,742	52,652	207,393	41,538	2,601	18,557
2030	346,899	65,570	209,998	45,448	2,891	22,993
2040	369,980	80,164	209,621	49,379	3,203	27,614
2050	393,931	96,508	207,901	53,555	3,534	32,432

Percent Distribution
Middle series:

	Total	Hispanic Origin[a]	White	Black	American Indian, Eskimo Aleut	Asian, Pacific Islander
2000	100.0	11.4	71.8	12.2	0.7	3.9
2010	100.0	13.8	68.0	12.6	0.8	4.8

(continues)

TABLE 2.8   *(continued)*

2020	100.0	16.3	64.3	12.9	0.8	5.7
2030	100.0	18.9	60.5	13.1	0.8	6.6
2040	100.0	21.7	56.7	13.3	0.9	7.5
2050	100.0	24.5	52.8	13.6	0.9	8.2

Percent Change
Middle series:

2000–2010	8.4	31.2	2.7	11.6	12.9	36.1
2010–2020	8.4	28.0	2.5	10.9	12.1	28.9
2020–2030	7.5	24.5	1.3	9.4	11.1	23.9
2030–2040	6.7	22.3	−0.2	8.6	10.8	20.1
2040–2050	6.5	20.4	−0.8	8.5	10.3	17.4

ᵃ Persons of Hispanic origin may be of any race.

SOURCE: *Statistical Abstract of the United States, 1996,* Washington, DC, 1996, table 19.

between the status of the office and the number of African Americans represented. By 1997, 8.5 percent of members of the House of Representatives were black (compared with 12 percent represented in the population as a whole). Only one incumbent in the more prestigious U.S. Senate was black, however. At the state and local levels, the advance of blacks is equally patchy: In 1992 twenty-five of the nation's largest cities had black mayors, including Detroit, Atlanta, Chicago, New York, and Los Angeles; in the same year only 1.5 percent of all elected U.S. officials were African American.

Gender.   A major development in American society since the 1970s has been the changing attitude toward the status of women. Until the late 1960s, although women enjoyed full legal and voting rights with men, few women held important positions of political and economic power. By the late 1990s, however, most objective indicators were pointing to some improvement in the position of women. This said, women continue to earn less than men do (Table 2.9), although the relative improvement in the twelve years to 1997 was considerable. Younger women, however, made little relative progress in this period. Few women occupy the very top positions in society, whether in the professions, government, or industry and commerce. In one crucial area, childcare, the United States lags behind comparable countries. There are few government-provided or -subsidized preschool facilities, and childcare became an important

TABLE 2.9   Median Weekly Earnings by Gender, 1985 and 1997 ($)

	1985 Earnings	Percent of All Males	1997 Earnings	Percent of All Males
Males	406		579	
Age 16–24	240	59	317	55
Age 25 and older	442	109	615	106
Females	277	68	431	74
Age 16–24	219	52	292	50
Age 25 and older	296	73	462	80

SOURCE: *Statistical Abstract of the United States, 1998,* Washington, DC, 1998, computed from table 696.

political issue during the 1990s. In 1993 a family-leave bill sponsored by the Clinton administration was passed by Congress that gave workers in all larger companies the right to take time off work for pregnancy and family emergencies.

One reason the status of women has changed relates to the flat or declining real hourly earnings of American workers. As earnings have declined, more women have entered the labor force in order to maintain the real value of family incomes. They have often found lower-paid jobs in the service sector, while the number of higher-paid traditionally "male" jobs in the manufacturing sector has declined. Indeed, by the late 1990s the unemployment rate for men was higher than for women—although women's rate of participation in the labor force was lower—and this is a trend likely to accelerate in the future.

Given these developments, it is not surprising that women have mobilized politically to elevate a range of issues from childcare to abortion and family leave to the top of the political agenda. Women have also become more active in politics generally and are increasingly regarded as politicians in their own right irrespective of their positions on "women's issues." As can be seen from Table 2.10, however, they still have a long way to go.

Religion.   Americans are a highly religious people—more so indeed than the populations of most comparable countries. There is also a multiplicity of religions, sects, and denominations, and some commentators have argued that religion has been a prime source of the "creedal passion" associated with various reform movements in American history.[17] Yet in spite of this and the clear links between re-

TABLE 2.10   Women in Elective Office, Selected Years, 1975–1997 (in percent)

Elected Officeholders	1975	1981	1987	1991	1997
Members of Congress[a]	4	4	5	6	11
Statewide elected officials[b]	10	11	15	18	n.a.
State legislators	8	12	16	18	21

[a] Includes the U.S. House of Representatives and the U.S. Senate. Includes one nonvoting delegate to the House from the District of Columbia elected in 1990.

[b] Does not include officials in appointed state cabinet-level positions, officials elected to executive posts by state legislatures, members of judicial branch, or elected members of university boards of trustees or boards of education.

SOURCE: Official stastics reproduced from Paula Ries and Anne J. Stone, *The American Woman, 1992–93 Status Report* (New York: Norton, 1992), updated from Harold W. Stanley and Richard G. Niemi, *Vital Statistics on American Politics, 1997–98* (Washington, DC: Congressional Quarterly Press, 1998), various tables.

ligion and politics, religion has not constituted a major social division in American society equivalent to the role played by denomination in Ireland, the Netherlands, Belgium, or even Germany. Like ethnicity, religious differences are important in the United States, but they have usually been subsumed under a dominant set of peculiarly *American* beliefs, values, and institutions.

Nevertheless, in recent decades, the Christian right has asserted itself in national politics as the Supreme Court and Congress have increasingly set national (and often liberal) standards on such issues as abortion, religious prayers in schools, gay rights, and women's rights in employment. It would be wrong, however, to argue that Americans are becoming more religious. As Andrew Greeley has shown, in terms of the most commonly used indicators—belief in God and the afterlife, and church attendance—religious attitudes have remained remarkably constant in recent decades.[18] And although the preferred party political candidates of the religious right have been on the ascendant during this period, their electoral success has been mixed. In Congress, most Republicans are now associated with the agenda of the religious right (a point that will be developed in later chapters).

In presidential politics, however, candidates supported by the religious right have had very limited success. Indeed, the evidence indicates that the support may as often hurt rather than help presidential candidates, as the examples of George Bush in 1992 and Bob Dole in 1996 demonstrate.

Region. Region has played a somewhat different role in American history. From the very beginning, the South was culturally and economically separate from the rest of the United States, and although a rising sense of national identity strengthened North-South linkages during the 1820–1850 period, this was shattered by the Civil War and its aftermath. Only very slowly between 1865 and 1970 was the South reincorporated into the mainstream of American society. The South's distinctiveness was, of course, based on its slave and later segregationist economy, which produced a system of social stratification with no parallel in the rest of the country. It was also a one-party region dominated by racist and often corrupt local and state Democratic parties. But the South was different in other ways. Until the post-1945 period it was predominantly rural and poor. Immigrants avoided the region; industrial and infrastructure investment was sparse; change came only slowly. Not until what had effectively become an economic and social backwater was jolted by the rapid economic growth of the 1950s and 1960s, and by an increasingly strident civil rights movement, did southern society begin to change. Since 1960, in fact, many southern states have been transformed by migration, urbanization, and economic growth. To the casual visitor, many parts of the South are today indistinguishable from the rest of the country. Democratic Party hegemony has broken down, although, the black population apart, the region remains essentially conservative. But old-style southern society has by no means disappeared, especially in the poorer, less developed states (notably Arkansas, Mississippi, and Alabama). Racism still exists, as does a peculiarly "un-American" resistance to change. But the South can no longer lay claim to the very special and separate status that for so long distinguished it from the rest of the country.

No other region has the distinctiveness of the South, but each is no less complex and diverse for that. Perhaps the most remarkable feature of these other states and regions is that they have not been the springboard for successful separatist or even third-party movements—a fact that speaks volumes for the strength of universally held *American* values and beliefs.

Communications

Compared with comparable European countries and Japan, the United States is geographically vast. It has about four times the population of the United Kingdom, yet the U.S. population per square mile in 1994 was 74 compared with 623 for the UK. From the very beginning of the republic, communications have assumed a central place in American life. Today modern air transport has shrunk the size of the country considerably, but intra–U.S. business still must be conducted in four time zones (six including Alaska and Hawaii).

Until the advent of radio in the 1920s and 1930s, almost all news in America was locally generated. Even today virtually every one of the over 1,500 newspapers in the United States has a local base (the major exceptions being *USA Today* and *The Christian Science Monitor*)—although some like the *New York Times* do now publish national editions. The vast majority of the more than three thousand television and radio stations are also locally based.

It would be misleading to claim that most *news* is local, however, or that Americans do not have a consciousness of national affairs and events. On the contrary, most Americans are reading, listening to, or viewing the same national news most of the time, for several reasons. First, most newspapers carry syndicated national columns put out by news services or the more prominent regional papers such as the *New York Times* and *Washington Post*. Second, and more important, most local stations subscribe to one of the three major national networks: CBS (Central Broadcasting System), ABC (American Broadcasting Corporation), and NBC (National Broadcasting Corporation). Each puts out a nightly national newscast, and all have high viewership. In addition, CNN (Cable News Network) broadcasts national and international news around the clock.

The three national networks are available to all television viewers, but more than 60 percent of citizens subscribe to cable television that provides access to dozens of additional channels. Most radio stations broadcast music. "Talk radio," as Americans call it, is limited mainly to news and religious programs, many of them broadcast nationally. For all these reasons, information dissemination in the United States has a strong national dimension—stronger, for example, than in Canada. This is not to say that local news is unimportant or disregarded but rather that Americans have a strong sense of both national and local events. International

FIGURE 2.3   Media Usage by Consumers, 1989–1999

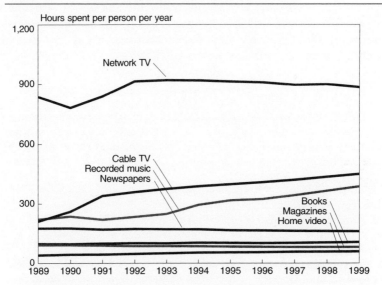

NOTE: Data for 1995 to 1999 are projected.
SOURCE: Chart prepared by U.S. Bureau of the Census.

events tend to come a distant third in terms of people's consciousness. Only international events with a clear American dimension—for example, the Gulf War or fighting drug barons in Columbia—receive extensive attention from the media.

As Figure 2.3 shows, the viewing of network television declined slightly during the 1990s, whereas cable TV viewing increased. Note the flat or declining usage of other media outlets over this period. Figure 2.3 does not include Internet usage, on which there is little systematic information. However, there were more than 35 million Internet subscribers in the United States as of 1997—more than in the rest of the world combined. The dissemination of information via the Internet is much faster than by any other medium. This was amply shown in 1998 when Independent Counsel Kenneth Starr's report on President Clinton's affair with Monica Lewinsky was available instantly on the Internet but was only published in hard copy several days later. It seems inevitable that the importance of the Internet will grow rapidly in the years to come.

All of the recent technological changes in communications have had or will have an important impact on American politics. Above all, they have served to increase the quantity and quality of citizens' access to politicians and political institutions. Thus citizens are now able to make their views heard in a variety of novel and often immediate ways. How effective these communications are is, of course, another matter, which later chapters will address.

Notes

1. Donald J. Devine, *The Political Culture of the United States* (Boston: Little, Brown, 1972), p. 17. "Liberal" is used here to describe those who see society as made up of free, self-motivated individuals rather than as a description of where individuals stand on a liberal-conservative continuum.

2. Ira Katznelson and Mark Kesselman, *The Politics of Power*, 4th ed. (New York: Harcourt, Brace, Jovanovich, 1987), p. 29.

3. Samuel P. Huntington, *American Politics: The Promise of Disharmony* (Cambridge, MA: Harvard University Press, 1981), p. 14.

4. More than 80 percent of respondents to a 1962 survey agreed with the first question, and just 50 percent with the second. Herbert McCloskey, "Consensus and Ideology in American Politics," *American Political Science Review*, 8, 1964, tables 2 and 3.

5. See Seymour Martin Lipset and Earl Raab, *The Politics of Unreason: Right-Wing Extremism in America, 1790–1970* (Chicago: University of Chicago Press, 1978).

6. During the early and mid-1990s, however, falling or flat real family incomes led many Americans to doubt that their living standards would continue to rise. This fact helped secure Democrat Bill Clinton's victory in 1992.

7. This is a consistent survey finding; see the *General Social Surveys, 1972–90*, Cumulative Codebook, National Research Center, University of Chicago, 1990.

8. For a discussion, see Aaron Wildavsky, "Resolved, That Individualism and Egalitarianism Be Made Compatible in America: Political-Cultural Roots of Exceptionalism," in Byron E. Shafer (ed.), *Is America Different: A New Look at American Exceptional Exceptionalism* (Oxford and New York: Oxford University Press, 1991), pp. 116–137.

9. In the survey, 82 percent of respondents said they were proud of their constitution and governmental system compared with 46 percent of the British, 7 percent of the West Germans, and 3 percent of the Italians. Gabriel A. Almond and Sidney Verba, *The Civic Culture: Political Attitudes and Democracy in Five Nations* (Boston: Little, Brown, 1965), table 1.

10. See Jack Citrin, "The Political Relevance of Trust in Government," *American Political Science Review*, 8, 1974, for a discussion of this point.

11. Huntington, *American Politics*, p. 25.

12. Michael Foley, *American Political Ideas: Traditions and Usages* (Manchester: University of Manchester Press, 1991), p. 44.

13. Quoted in Foley, *American Political Ideas*, p. 44.

14. Deaths and abortions have exceeded live births.

15. For a comprehensive discussion, see Louis DeSipio and Rodolfo O. de la Garza, *Making Americans, Remaking America: Immigration and Immigrant Policy* (Boulder, CO: Westview, 1998).

16. *Economic Report of the President, 1995* (Washington, DC: U.S. Government Printing Office, 1995), p. 179.

17. See Huntington, *American Politics*, chaps. 1, 2, 5, and 6.

18. Andrew M. Greeley, "The Religious Phenomenon," in Shafer (ed.), *Is America Different?* pp. 94–115.

Further Reading

The classic statement on American individualism is Louis Hartz, *The Liberal Tradition in America* (New York: Harcourt Brace, 1955). On exceptionalism, see Byron Shafer (ed.), *Is America Different?* (Oxford and New York: Oxford University Press, 1991). For an overview of American political ideas, see Michael Foley, *American Political Ideas: Traditions and Usages* (Manchester: Manchester University Press, 1991). See also, Everett Carll Ladd, *The American Ideology: An Exploration of the Origins, Meaning, and Role of American Political Ideas* (Storrs, CT: Roper Center for Public Opinion Research, 1994). For an up-to-date account of exceptionalism, see Seymour Martin Lipset, *American Exceptionalism: A Double-Edged Sword* (New York: Norton, 1996). For comprehensive data on American society and economy, see the annual *Statistical Abstract of the United States* (Washington, DC: U.S. Government Printing Office).

3

Constitutional
Government

*The American Constitution is the most wonderful work ever struck
off at a given time by the brain and purpose of man.*

—W. E. Gladstone

*Good government should be sufficiently neutral between the different
interests and factions to control one part of the society from invading
the rights of another, and at the same time sufficiently controlled itself, from setting up an interest adverse to that of the whole society.*

—James Madison

Almost all governments pay formal allegiance to a written or (more
rarely) unwritten constitution, but in few countries is the constitution
a real and continuing constraint on the exercise of power. Even more
rarely do constitutions survive political and social changes, invasions,
and wars. The American Constitution is unusual, both because it has
remained almost unaltered since its ratification in 1789, and because
it continues as a major source of authority in the political system. Indeed, even the most cursory examination of America's basic political
institutions—Congress, the presidency, federalism, the electoral system—instantly shows the influence of the Constitution. To most observers, the apparent resilience of the Constitution and constitutionalism is one of the most remarkable features of American politics,
and one that requires some explanation. Several important questions
are raised by this phenomenon: Why has the Constitution been
amended so little through history? What real influence does it have

today? In particular, by limiting the power of central government, has it served to aggravate the tension between the public's expectations of government and the ability of political institutions to satisfy those expectations? Prerequisite to answering these questions is the crucial issue of why the Constitution took the shape it did.

Origins

Most dramatic regime changes following a revolution or war are quite easy to explain. France in 1789 was seething with discontent at a corrupt and insensitive monarchy. Russia in 1917 was long overdue for a revolution to sweep away an archaic, feudal order. And the numerous colonial wars of independence in the post-1945 period were predictable, given the rapid political and economic changes brought by World War II and its aftermath.

The American Revolution fails to fit any of these neat stereotypes, however. In fact, by some definitions, it was not a revolution at all. Many of the citizens of the thirteen colonies considered themselves "true born Englishmen" who, being increasingly denied the rights they thought all free citizens deserved to enjoy, were entitled to challenge the "illegitimate" exercise of power by George III. They saw their task, therefore, as one of asserting independence from a regime that had betrayed its principles. Moreover, unlike most revolutionary wars, the War of Independence and the eventual emergence of a new constitutional system had few immediate consequences for the distribution of wealth, power, and status. If anything, it reinforced trends already under way. It was essentially a conservative revolution that, in marked contrast to parallel events in France, did not lead to new class divisions in society. This is not to say that radical or revolutionary elements were absent. They were very much present, but the real power remained in the hands of a solid middle-class and professional property-owning elite.

The unusual nature of these events stems from the unique characteristics of American colonial society. From the very beginning, the British Americans had displayed a marked degree of independence and self-sufficiency. In the thirteen colonies, and especially in New England, the local community became virtually the only meaningful level of government—and even then the label "government" is far too strong and modern to attach to what were remarkably successful self-governing entities. Sam Bass Warner has captured the spirit of these seventeenth-century communities very well:

For a generation or two, medieval English village traditions fused with a religious ideology to create a consensus concerning the religious, social, economic and political framework for a good life. Each of several hundred villages repeated a basic pattern. No Royal statute, no master plan, no strong legislative controls, no central administrative officers, no sheriffs or justices of the peace, no synods or prelates, none of the apparatus typical of government then or now.[1]

Although such communities were partly transformed by economic development and population increases during the eighteenth century, the essential independence of the colonies continued to be expressed through local governments and, later, colonial assemblies whose activities were largely tolerated by Crown-appointed governors. Admittedly, considerable variation existed between different colonies—and particularly between the plantation and slave economy of the South and the more diverse agrarian and mercantilist economy of the North—but each colony respected the independence of the other.

This description implies a colonial rule that was essentially distant and benign, and such indeed was the case until the 1760s when the English, acting under a monarch determined to assert his power over increasingly corrupt and strident Whig interests at home, decided to exercise greater control over the colonists. All goods imported to the colonies had to pass through British ports, a tax (stamp duty) was imposed on all legal documents and newspapers, a revenue tax was levied, and colonial assemblies were prohibited from issuing their own paper currency.

These economic restrictions were viewed by the colonial elites as an outrageous infringement of basic rights. During the eighteenth century, the idea that men possessed certain inalienable rights spread rapidly under the influence of the social-contract theorists (John Locke, Jean-Jacques Rousseau) and pamphleteers (Thomas Paine) and became particularly popular in a colonial America infused with a spirit of liberty and independence. Life, liberty, and property were rights that governments were obliged to protect through the representation of the people in parliaments and assemblies. And should those assemblies fail to fulfill their contractual obligations to the people, then elections would ensure the substitution of new representatives charged with carrying out the people's wishes. A monarch exercising executive power outside any representative mechanism was clearly not legitimate.

Although this rather sophisticated view of governance was probably held only by educated elites, the smallholders and artisans who made up the bulk of the population did have some notion of individual rights and were, by any European standard, highly independent and assertive. Indeed, for more than 100 years up to the Revolution, acts of political (usually mob) violence were quite common, as they were in England. Most people with some stake in society—a farm or other property, or a valuable manual or intellectual skill—were quite used to resorting to extralegal methods should their grievances be ignored by established political channels. Given this tradition, with the colonists' growing sense of independence fueled by economic growth and better communications and with the sudden change in English policy, outbreaks of armed resistance were almost to be expected. In 1774 the colonial assemblies sent delegates to a national Continental Congress—the first real assertion of national independence by the colonists. By 1775 fighting had broken out in Massachusetts, and in 1776 the Continental Congress adopted the Declaration of Independence that, with stirring rhetoric, marked the true beginnings of the United States:

> We hold these truths to be self-evident, that all men are created equal, that they are endowed by their Creator with certain unalienable rights, that among these are life, liberty, and the pursuit of happiness; that to secure these rights, governments are instituted among men, deriving their just powers from the consent of the governed; that whenever any form of government becomes destructive of these ends, it is the right of the people to alter or to abolish it, and to institute new government, laying its foundation on such principles, and organizing its powers in such form, as to them shall seem most likely to effect their safety and happiness.

For the next five years, the colonists successfully fought their revolutionary war against the British and, in 1781, established a new system of government under the Articles of Confederation. In effect, this document—the first American Constitution—was little more than a formal recognition of the Continental Congress. A congress was created, but no executive or judiciary. The new government was very much a confederation: Individual states retained considerable autonomy, giving to the Congress only limited powers—namely, to declare wars, establish treaties, regulate weights and measures, oversee Indian affairs, run a post office, and establish an army and navy.

Crucially, no mandatory power to raise taxes was established. Instead, Congress had to rely on voluntary contributions from the state legislatures. Also, each state could issue its own paper money and generally regulate commerce within its boundaries.

Such a weak, leaderless system of government could not long endure, especially in the face of a number of very urgent problems confronting the new nation. Revenue needed to be raised nationally to provide a common defense. Some central control of the currency and the enforcement of contracts needed to be created, and a common external tariff was needed to protect American goods from cheap British imports. Moreover, the war had widened the gulf between better-off individuals, who had lent money to finance the fighting, and a growing class of debtors, who had mortgaged small farms and houses to raise incomes in the face of economic dislocation. In 1786 a small rebellion had broken out in Massachusetts, a state where the law on debtors was particularly harsh, when Daniel Shays led more than 1,000 men to block the proceedings of the state's high court.

Although quickly put down, Shays's Rebellion served to remind richer citizens that the new Congress was ill-equipped to provide some degree of national economic security and uniformity. Prior to the rebellion, a number of attempts had been made to strengthen Congress, and a convention to discuss trade problems had met at Annapolis, Maryland, in 1786. Although only five states attended, a resolution to meet in Philadelphia with the more ambitious aim of constitutional revision had been agreed on at the convention. Shays's protest made such a meeting that much more imperative, and during the summer of 1787, fifty-five delegates assembled in Philadelphia charged with the momentous task of producing new constitutional arrangements for the United States.

The American Constitution

Although the fifty-five delegates—often called the "founding fathers"—were not operating in the absence of political and economic constraints, they were able genuinely to combine normative judgments on what best would make for a good system, with provisions imposed on them by political necessity. They were not, in other words, engaged in the exercise of naked political power. Nor were they obsessed with retributive measures against past masters.

And, unlike many twentieth-century harbingers of regime change, their actions were not informed by a single, closed ideology. Instead, they could afford to compromise, to show pragmatism, and to draw on a number of political theories and constitutional arrangements at that time commonly discussed by the educated and liberal-minded.

The founding fathers were certainly educated; about one-half had college degrees, a high proportion for that time. They were also established (and comparatively young) men of property and status—merchants, lawyers, planters, doctors, intellectuals. George Washington presided over the meetings, although he played virtually no role in the proceedings. Inviting Washington—who came only reluctantly—was a clever ploy, as he was the one figure almost universally respected in the new nation. The real driving forces behind the convention and its proceedings were James Madison of Virginia, a brilliant young politician who had helped to write Virginia's constitution, and Alexander Hamilton from New York, onetime aide to Washington during the war, who had helped set up the Annapolis convention.

As delegates from the state legislatures, the founding fathers were not directly elected by the people—indeed one state, Rhode Island, was not even represented, dominated as it was by a disgruntled debtor class. In one curious respect, this lack of a universal popular mandate gave the delegates some extra freedom, for, meeting in secret, they could eventually produce a document as a fait accompli and then lobby hard for its acceptance by the states. In short, that is precisely what they did.

Among the main influences on the framers, four stand out: social-contract theory, representation, the separation of powers, and federalism. The idea of the social contract is its provision of obligation on both those governed and those governing. Although central to the thinking of Thomas Hobbes and Rousseau, it was Locke's vision of the social contract that most influenced the founders. To Hobbes, the contract was a one-sided affair in which the people traded their freedom for the security that a strong state would bring. Rousseau's contract was far more idealized, involving as it did the identification and implementation of the general will of the people. Locke, in contrast, made *representation* the central canon of his ideal society. Citizens, or those with a stake in society, men of property, were entitled to a government that would champion their natural rights. Through representative institutions—free elections and assemblies—the people could hold the rulers accountable for their actions. Obedience to the law (the people's side of the contract) was, therefore, conditional on the government's fulfilling its side of the contract—the protection of life, liberty, and property.

Representative government carries with it other notions, notably majority rule and the implication that there are clear limits to democracy. Both principles were accepted by the founding fathers, and their limits on democracy were, by modern standards, quite severe. Only the lower house of the legislature, the House of Representatives, was to be elected directly by the people (Article 1, Section 2).[2] Senators were to be nominated by the state legislatures (Article 1, Section 3), and the president was to be elected by an Electoral College, the members of which were to be appointed by the state legislatures (Article 2, Section 1). The framers' very limited acceptance of democracy reflected their fear of unbridled majority rule. If the people could vote for all the main officers directly, it raised the specter of an insensitive—and possibly tyrannical—permanent majority capable of riding roughshod over the minority. As Thomas Jefferson had noted some years before the convention, "an elective despotism was not the government we fought for." Further, the electoral qualifications of those who could vote for the House of Representatives were to be determined by the state legislatures (Article 1, Section 2). In most cases this meant a very limited suffrage consisting of white property-owning males. None of this was incompatible with popular sovereignty or a republican form of government. Sovereignty resided in the people (albeit a minority of them), not in a monarch or emperor. And this premise, together with the majoritarian provisions in the Constitution, guaranteed a republican system.

The framers were worried not only about the possibility of tyranny by the majority but also about the dangers of concentrating too much power in any one institution. A powerful executive suggested monarchical or despotic leadership. A powerful legislature carried with it the possibility of rule by an insensitive majority. A device existed to overcome these dangers—the separation of powers. Borrowing in part from the ideas of the French philosopher Baron de Montesquieu, who greatly admired what he thought was a division of powers in the English system, the framers created a deliberate separation of authority among legislature, executive, and judiciary. Congress was accordingly given a separate power base (or constituency) from the presidency, and although the judiciary was not given the formidable power of judicial review it was later to assume, Supreme Court and other federal judges were to be appointed by the president. The precise jurisdiction of the courts, however, as well as the final say on the appointment of judges, were powers accorded to Congress (Article 3).

To ensure that no one branch could dominate the federal government, a system of *checks and balances* was introduced. Thus, both houses of the legislature had to approve a bill, but the president could exercise a veto over it. The Senate and House of Representatives could, in turn, override a veto if two-thirds of the members present in both houses voted for it (Article 1, Section 7). Congress was also given some control over executive appointments, which had to be filled with the "advice and consent" of the Senate (Article 2, Section 2). These checks and balances should not imply an *equality* of power and authority between the institutions. There is no doubt that the framers intended the Congress, and in particular the House of Representatives, to be the key *source* of policy. This is clear from Article 1, Section 8, which enumerates the powers of Congress. Because these provisions included fiscal, monetary, and regulatory powers as well as the authority to raise armies and declare war, they were, in contemporary terms, quite comprehensive. Significantly, the directly elected chamber, the House of Representatives, was given special responsibility for revenue bills (Article 1, Section 7), thus reflecting the popular demand ("no taxation without representation") that the "people's branch" should be directly accountable to the voters on taxation matters. (The basic constitutional arrangements are shown in Figure 3.1.)

Executive and judicial branches were, in contrast, given few specific powers, although the dictum that the "executive power shall be vested in a president" (Article 2, Section 1) leaves open the question of where executive power begins and ends. Congress was, then, expected to be the source of most legislation, but its power would be checked both internally (both houses have to approve a bill before it becomes law) and by the president. These checks are essentially negative in nature, suggesting that the framers had a greater fear of the abuse of power than of an inability to exercise it. They therefore produced a document that specifically attempted to limit governmental power. In addition to the fear of majority rule and a despotic executive, some of the framers were deeply sus-

FIGURE 3.1   The Separation of Powers and the Lawmaking Process

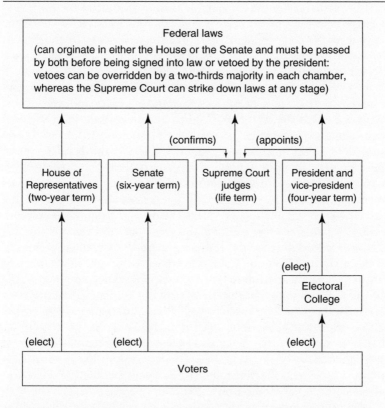

picious of the machinations of groups, parties, or "factions." James Madison, in particular, feared that government might become the creature of some class or special interest. He eloquently outlined his position in *The Federalist:*[3]

Among the numerous advantages promised by a well constructed Union, none deserves to be more accurately developed than its tendency to break and control the violence of faction. . . . By a faction, I understand a number of citizens, whether amounting to a majority or minority of the whole, who are united and actuated by some common impulse of passion, or of interest, adverse to the rights of other citizens, or to the permanent and aggregate interests of the community. There are two methods of curing the mischief of faction: the one, by removing its causes; the other by controlling its effects. There are again two methods of removing the causes of faction: the one, by destroying the liberty which is essential to its existence; the other by giving to every citizen the same opinions, the same passions and the same interests.[4]

Madison's writings leave no doubt that the only solution is to control the effects of faction. Liberty is essential, and where it exists, factions will exist. Giving an equal voice to every citizen can be achieved only in a pure democracy; pure democracy is impractical and dangerous except in very small communities. This leaves the control of faction to a republican form of government or the sort of representative system eventually adopted that had limited suffrage, some indirect elections, a separation of powers, and the operation of checks and balances.

The convention was by no means united on basic constitutional arrangements. Alexander Hamilton feared that without a strong executive, few of the nation's pressing problems would be solved. Madison, in contrast, feared both a strong executive and an overbearing legislature. More serious was the division between the larger and the smaller states over the fundamentals of the representative system to be adopted. The smaller states favored the ascendancy of state over federal power and a unicameral (one house) legislature based on equal votes for each state. They also supported the idea of a multiperson executive that could be removed by a majority of the states. Proposed by William Paterson of New Jersey, these arrangements came to be known as the *New Jersey Plan*.

In contrast, Governor John Randolph of Virginia proposed a bicameral legislature in which both houses were elected on a population basis. However, the lower house would be directly elected, while the upper house would be elected by the lower house from nominees provided by the state legislatures. The executive would be elected by Congress for a minimum of one term (this was known as the *Virginia Plan*).

After much debate, the convention eventually voted narrowly (five to four with one state delegation tied) for a compromise that contained elements of both plans. Called the *Connecticut Compromise* after being proposed by Robert Sherman of Connecticut, this established the House of Representatives on the basis of population and the Senate on the basis of equal representation of the states. In fact, debates on federalism and the delineation of powers between center and periphery were among the most acrimonious at the con-

vention, for in addition to the small-large state dichotomy, there
was the thorny problem of the very different interests represented
by the Southern and Northern states.

The distinctive economy and culture of the South posed a potentially even greater problem and was eventually resolved only by the
unsavory expedient of counting slaves as three-fifths of a free person
for the purposes of representation in the House and of distributing
federal taxes. Of course, this did not mean that slaves could vote or
play any part in the political process. They could not. Many Northern delegates disliked this compromise, but accepted it knowing that
the South would not tolerate any serious incursion into its slave-
based economy. The South was also an exporter of cotton and other
agricultural produce and had much less interest in the protectionist
(barriers against free international trade) policies that Northern
politicians favored. To safeguard their position, Southerners demanded that a two-thirds majority be required to ratify treaties in
the Senate. In this way, it was hoped that trade agreements favoring
the North would be avoided.

These controversies over the status of the South and large versus
small states should not obscure the fact that the framers were
obliged to create some sort of federal system. After all, the convention was composed of representatives of the states, and the war had
been waged against a strong central government. A centralized unitary system in the style of England was completely unacceptable to
most delegates. What eventually transpired was a highly flexible
federalism. Indeed, from the Constitution's wording, it is not at all
clear where federal power begins and ends, which gives at least
great potential power to the center.

The genius of the Constitution was that although it was the first
written constitution ever to be adopted by a country, and although
it propounded the virtues of a republican form of government—a
radical idea, indeed, in the late eighteenth century—it remained in-
trinsically *conservative* in content and implication. The founders,
and particularly the most influential and able of them, Madison
and Hamilton, were hardly social visionaries. Instead their hopes
for the new country were tinged with caution and not a little pes-
simism about human greed and selfishness. As Madison put it: "As
there is a degree of depravity in mankind which requires a certain
degree of circumspection and distrust, so there are other qualities
in human nature which justify a certain portion of esteem and confidence."[5]

As with most educated eighteenth-century men, the essentially inegalitarian view prevailed that there are worthy and unworthy, talented and talentless, wise and stupid men in the populace. The president was to be elected by an Electoral College made up, it was hoped, of wise, educated, and established citizens, free from the rabble-rousing and instant judgments that democratic processes inspired. Senators, too, were expected to be elder statesmen elected by their peers for a leisurely six years and able, therefore, to hold in line a potentially capricious and unruly lower house. What the framers hoped for, therefore, was firm, cautious, and responsible government. The Constitution was designed to provide the basic framework for such a system of stable and, above all, *limited* political power. This applied both to the legislature and the executive. Indeed, the legislature could remove the president (and any other civil officer of the United States) only for "treason, bribery or other high crimes and misdemeanors." Even then the House of Representatives was charged with impeaching (formally accusing) the president, and the Senate was given the job of trying the president, conviction requiring a two-thirds majority. These complex impeachment arrangements were designed to prevent rash and politically motivated attempts to remove presidents and other officers. By and large, they have worked. It is generally accepted that the two occasions on which presidents have been impeached—Andrew Johnson in 1866 and Bill Clinton in 1999—occurred when a politically motivated House of Representatives was intent on removal. In neither case, however, was conviction secured. By way of contrast, Richard Nixon resigned in 1974 knowing that the constitutional case against him was sufficient to secure not only probable impeachment but also conviction. (For a fuller discussion, see Chapter 9.)

The Constitution was also intended to stand the test of time—an objective greatly aided by a cumbersome amendment process. Amendments have to be proposed by a two-thirds vote in both houses of Congress and then ratified by three-quarters of the state legislatures or by a ratifying convention in two-thirds of the states. Alternatively, a national convention at the behest of two-thirds of the state legislatures can propose an amendment that in turn can be ratified by Congress or by a ratifying convention (Article 5). The first method (Congress proposing, the state legislatures ratifying) has become the normal amending mechanism, and it is testimony both to the flexibility of the Constitution and to the difficulties inherent in the amending process that, between 1791 and 1992, there have been only seventeen amendments.

Some commentators, reflecting on the personal interest the framers had in a successful economy and on the pressing economic problems the Articles of Confederation had patently failed to solve, have claimed that the exercise in Philadelphia was motivated by economic interest rather than by the higher ideals of liberty, republicanism, and civic virtue.[6] Although there is certainly an element of truth in this view, it seems odd that the fundamental disagreements that did occur on major questions involved delegates with an equal stake in economic success. Virtually all the delegates were men of property, so the more simplistic of the economic theories of the Constitution should predict no real disagreement on basic principles. Yet those who voted against the Constitution had just as much of a stake in prosperity and stability as those who voted for it. A more persuasive way to characterize the framers' motivations is to accept that they were indeed troubled by economic dislocation and the ever present threat of uncontrolled democracy but differed markedly on which system would best overcome these problems. Crucially, not only were these differences instrumental and pragmatic, but delegates also differed intellectually and represented more than one political philosophy and conception of human nature. What they all undoubtedly did agree on was the need for a stronger central government to ensure that the fragile new republic at least had a reasonable chance of survival.

Ratification

Fearful of failure, the framers wrote into the Constitution the requirement that ratification could be achieved by only nine of the thirteen states—and then by special state conventions rather than by state legislatures, some of which were dominated by politicians who believed that direct democratic control by the people was the best form of political organization. The framers also labeled themselves "Federalists," thus imposing on opposition groups the unattractive sobriquet "Anti-Federalist." Opposition was, in fact, fragmented, coming as it did mainly from the more remote rural areas. There was a geographical split but not a North-South one. Instead, ratification supporters were the commercial interests of the coastal areas, the larger towns and cities, and the big landowners of the South. The Anti-Federalists were concentrated in "the part most remote from commercial centers, with interests predominantly agricultural. It included the fractious Rhode Island, the Shays region of Massachusetts and the center of a similar movement in New Hampshire."[7] (See Map 3.1.)

Federalist lobbying in favor of the Constitution was intense and inspired the first truly national political debate in the United States. Very generally, the Anti-Federalists complained that the Constitution was insufficiently democratic and that it implied a strong and domineering central government. Complaints that individual rights were not specifically guaranteed by the Constitution were also common, and to ensure ratification in some states, the Federalists accepted that a Bill of Rights would be added as soon as the first federal government was established. Between 1787 and 1789, state conventions, one after the other, voted for ratification. Success was assured when the New York convention eventually ratified by a margin of three votes. The Federalists won because they were better organized and had all the leading politicians and statesmen behind them, and because the Anti-Federalists were obliged to fight a negative campaign, the Articles of Confederation being their only immediate alternative to the Constitution. To appease the remaining Anti-Federalists, the first Congress quickly voted for ten amendments, which, once ratified by the states in 1791, became the Bill of Rights. Interestingly, a number of additional amendments failed in Congress or during ratification, almost all of which would have made the system more democratic. One proposed that the electorate should issue binding instructions to their members of Congress, thus turning them into delegates. Another suggested that there should never be less than one member of Congress for every 50,000 inhabitants. U.S. political developments would have been strikingly different if either or both of these proposals had been adopted.

The Adaptive Constitution

Change by Amendment

No constitution can elaborate the precise relationship between institutions and political forces. Attempts to do so risk being ignored. Successful constitutions must, therefore, be flexible and open to varying interpretations. In some ways, the shorter and vaguer the document, the better. Completely unambiguous statements lead to rigidity and can render a constitution unworkable. The U.S. Con-

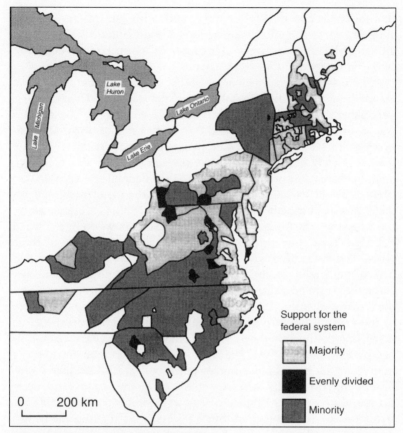

MAP 3.1   The Geography of Ratification
   SOURCE: O. G. Libby, as reproduced in J.C. Clark Archer and Peter J. Taylor, *Section and Party* (New York: John Wiley, 1981), p. 50. Reprinted by permission of John Wiley & Sons Ltd.

stitution is free of all these faults. It does, of course, lay down certain guidelines and rules, but it says remarkably little about the precise powers of the main institutions or about how authority should be shared between federal and state governments. When a comparison is made between the United States of 1789 (3.5 million people, agrarian, confined to the East Coast) and the United States of the late 1990s (263 million people, highly industrial, a continental and world power), the true success of the Constitution can be appreciated, for virtually the same document applies today as applied more than 220 years ago. Moreover, the significance of the seventeen amendments (in addition to the first ten amendments, The Bill of Rights) accepted in this period is almost certainly not as great as the changes in interpretation to which the Constitution has been subjected.

Of the seventeen amendments, some are relatively trivial, two were devoted to the adoption and subsequent rejection of prohibition, and the remainder address either electoral questions or limiting and expanding the role of the federal government.

Amendments Affecting Elections and Officeholders.   The first important amendment affecting elections was the twelfth, adopted in 1804 to simplify the election of the Electoral College, which in turn elects the president. As mentioned earlier, the founding fathers hoped that a group of elder statesmen (the Electoral College) would choose the president, but with the emergence of competing political parties, it soon became obvious that the College had become highly partisan. In 1800 the vote in the College was a tie between Thomas Jefferson and Aaron Burr. When the vote was referred to the House of Representatives, it took numerous ballots to decide the eventual winner (Jefferson). The Twelfth Amendment ensured that any election in which a candidate received less than a majority of the Electoral College would then be decided in a runoff election in the House of Representatives. Votes for president and vice-president were combined. Previously, the College had elected the two officers separately. Between 1800 and 1832, the state legislatures gradually voted to provide for the direct popular election of members of the Electoral College. Surprisingly, this system persists. Americans still do not vote directly for a presidential candidate but for members of the College. Moreover, it is a *winner-take-all* mechanism, so that the candidate who gets a majority of votes in a particular state wins *all* that state's Electoral College votes.

The number of Electoral College votes in a state is determined as follows: Each state has one vote for each representative and senator, which means that the votes are distributed roughly in proportion to population (the number of representatives in any state changes regularly in accordance with population shifts (see Chapter 6), and because there are only two senators per state, this introduces a very small bias in favor of low-population states. The major criticism of this system is that it is possible for a candidate to win the Electoral College vote but receive fewer popular votes than

TABLE 3.1   Amendments Affecting Elections and Officeholders

Amendment	Purpose	Proposed	Adopted
12	Reform of Electoral College	1803	1804
15	Voting rights extended to all races	1869	1870
17	Direct election of senators	1912	1913
19	Voting rights extended to women	1919	1920
20	"Lame duck" session of Congress abolished[a]	1932	1933
22	Presidents limited to two terms	1947	1951
23	Voting rights extended to residents of District of Columbia	1960	1961
24	Voting rights democratized— abolition of poll tax	1962	1964
25	Reform of president succession in case of disability	1965	1967
26	Voting age lowered to 18	1971	1971
27	Prohibition on members of Congress to raise their salaries before the next election	1990	1992

[a] This changed the date of new congressional sessions from March to January to shorten the period during which the old Congress could act.

another candidate. Just this happened in 1824, 1876, and 1888, although it has not occurred since. Another criticism focuses on the danger of Electoral College members failing to vote for the candidate mandated by the electorate. Again, this has happened on rare occasions, but it has never been critical.

Clearly, the Electoral College system favors the larger states. If a candidate wins just seven states—New York, California, Texas, Pennsylvania, Illinois, Florida, and Ohio—he or she amasses 210 votes even if the win is by only a narrow margin in each of these states. And only 270 Electoral College votes are needed for victory. Talk of reforming the system is never far from the surface in the United States, and the mechanism probably persists because there are only two main parties.[8] Furthermore, some bias in favor of large population centers does compensate for other biases in the system in favor of smaller states and rural areas.

Almost all the other amendments affecting elections have been designed to expand the electorate or to hold elected officials more accountable or responsive to the public (Table 3.1). These changes, together with the abolition of property qualifications for voting at

TABLE 3.2 Amendments Affecting Powers of the Federal
Government

Amendment	Purpose	Proposed	Adopted
11	Limited federal courts' jurisdiction over suits involving the states	1794	1798
13	Abolished slavery	1865	1865
14	Extended due process of Bill of Rights to the states	1866	1868
16	Established power to introduce a national income tax	1909	1913

the state level during the first part of the nineteenth century, have, in total, greatly increased the democratic element in the Constitution. None is controversial except the twenty-second, which limits presidential terms to no more than two.

Amendments Affecting Powers of the Federal Government. In one sense, changes in electoral qualifications were to be expected as the democratizing trends of the nineteenth and twentieth centuries took hold. Thus, it would not be surprising if the Constitution had been frequently amended to expand the powers of the federal government. Yet as Table 3.2 shows, only three amendments have had this purpose, the thirteenth to assert federal power over those states practicing slavery, the fourteenth imposing the Bill of Rights on the states, and the sixteenth establishing the power to introduce a national income tax. Of these three, the Fourteenth Amendment was not, in fact, applied to the states until the twentieth century.

Evidence of just how difficult it is to ratify an amendment is provided by the experience of the Equal Rights Amendment (ERA). This amendment, which reads "Equality of rights under the law shall not be denied or abridged by the United States or any state on account of sex," has, in fact, been before Congress since 1923. In 1972 Congress voted for the amendment by large majorities, and within a year twenty-five states had voted for it. It then ran into trouble, however, as some state legislators began to fear that in its implementation, women might, for example, be required to take up combat positions in battle. Eventually, the amendment died three states short of formal ratification.

The other major attempt to amend the Constitution in recent years also failed. By the late 1980s, thirty-three states had passed the Balanced Budget Amendment requiring the federal government to balance its annual budget. By the early 1990s, most commentators doubted that the amendment would win the approval of any more state legislatures. With the election of a Republican Congress in 1994, however, and again in 1996, and given Republican advances in state politics, the Balanced Budget Amendment was set for a return to the center of the political stage. The political impetus behind the balanced budget movement has been weakened only by the achievement in reality of a balanced budget for fiscal year 1997–1998.

Change by Interpretation

Much more important than amendments have been changes in constitutional interpretation that owe more to the development of American society and economy than to the wording of the Constitution as such. Four such changes can be identified:

1. Assertion of federal over state power;
2. Assertion of executive over legislative power;
3. Emergence of the Supreme Court as the final arbiter of the Constitution;
4. Growing protection of individual rights under the Constitution.

Each of these four will be dealt with in detail in later chapters. For now it is enough to point out that the first two were certainly not intended or envisaged by the framers, the third probably was, and the fourth has developed in a way that could not possibly have been predicted in 1787.

Although the Constitution is ambiguous on the question of federal-state relations, there can be no doubt that the relationship that had developed by the late 1990s was light-years away from anything the framers could have intended. Today the federal government intrudes into almost every facet of economic and social life, leaving to the states little that *constitutionally* they can call their own except perhaps their territorial integrity and equal representation in the Senate. In 1791 it was broadly expected that the Tenth Amendment's dictum, "The powers not delegated to the United States by the Constitution, nor prohibited by it to the States, are reserved to the States respectively, or to the people," would leave the states unequivocally in charge of a number of governmental functions. As the next chapter will demonstrate, this was not to be.

Similarly, Congress was expected to be the major source of legislative initiative, while the president implemented laws with prudence and efficiency. The late-twentieth-century reality is very different. Congress does play a greater role in policy initiation than almost any other national legislatures and is indisputably a powerful and independent institution, but it has largely forfeited the lion's share of the legislative function to the president and to a vast and complex executive branch.

The reasons government has become larger, more centralized, and concentrated in executive rather than legislature will be addressed in detail in later chapters. But these trends have occurred in almost all countries experiencing rapid economic and social development, the mobilization of populations by parties and groups, and the corresponding increase in demands placed on all governments, in particular central governments, which have the greatest potential for resource distribution and regulation.

In 1803 the Supreme Court asserted the power of judicial review, or the right to declare any act of Congress or action by the executive branch as incompatible with the Constitution and therefore illegal. Actions by states can also be struck down by the Supreme Court. Although used sparingly at first, this power has been utilized with increasing frequency, which has had profound consequences for the workings of the political system (as discussed in Chapter 13). Although some of the founders may have envisaged the Court playing the role of final arbiter of the Constitution, none could have foreseen the intimate involvement of the nation's highest court in such questions as abortion, electronic bugging, and political party campaign finance.

Finally, citizens' rights to free speech, assembly, religion, and privacy and to "due process" and the equal protection of the laws have slowly been extended to apply to the states. This expansion is crucial, for slavery was an institution protected by state governments and constitutions. Following the Civil War, the Thirteenth and Fourteenth Amendments swept away slavery and, in theory, discrimination. The Supreme Court failed to enforce the Fourteenth Amendment in the South until after World War II, however, thus enabling the perpetuation of segregation and the worst sort of racial discrimination.

Deference to states' rights extended to other areas such as standards of occupational safety, employment conditions, and criminal justice. For many Americans, civil rights and liberties were anything but "God-given rights." Only under federal legislation did they exist, and until the twentieth century, the federal government played only a small role in the lives of individual citizens. Beginning in the 1930s and accelerating between 1945 and 1970, this anomalous situation was slowly corrected, with the Supreme Court insisting in case after case that the Bill of Rights and the Fourteenth Amendment applied to all American governments, whatever their status. In cases involving national security, privacy, discrimination (racial, religious, and gender), and the administration of justice, the Supreme Court has mandated that all authorities have an obligation to heed constitutionally defined rights.

Of course, this extension of rights does not mean that the Court has always favored a liberal position, or that it has come down on the side of individuals rather than governments—although in recent years more often than not it has. Changes in official attitudes to civil rights and liberties parallel the growth of government noted earlier. As governments at all levels have increasingly intruded into the lives of individuals, so the need for protection from arbitrary governmental authority has grown. As will be discussed in Chapter 12, governments—and especially federal governments—have also been active in controlling the abuse of individual rights by *private* bodies, in particular by corporations. It seems highly unlikely that the framers could have foreseen that the question of individual rights would have become part of a complex web of interaction between myriad private and public institutions and individuals.

Assessing the Constitution

Some of the most dramatic changes in American government and society over the past 200 years have involved institutions and political processes not even referred to in the Constitution. Parties emerged during the early years of the nineteenth century as the major agents of political mobilization. Interest groups have grown in number and influence until today some commentators seriously argue that they are the true sources of political power and influence. Similarly, the nationally organized media, equipped with formidable electronic resources, can play a crucial role in swaying political opinion. Does this mean that the Constitution is of relatively little importance? Not at all, for all these changes have had to be accommodated within certain institutional limits that the Constitution imposes. Political and economic changes have indisputably altered the relationships between institutions and the broader society, but these relationships have not been transformed in such a way that the document has ceased to have meaning. Congress remains separated from the presidency. Interest groups, presidents, individual citizens, the media— even foreign governments—have to accept that the independent power of Congress can and frequently does thwart presidents. The courts are also independent and have shown, especially since the 1950s, that presidents and Congress must sometimes tread carefully when exercising their powers. States, too, remain important political units—although their relationship with the federal government is now one more of interdependence than of autonomy. Taken together, the two central pillars of the Constitution—the separation of powers and federalism—have undoubtedly served to limit the exercise of centralized political power.

Modern criticisms of the Constitution usually concentrate either on the continuing political hiatus between executive and legislative or on the progressive weakening of the states in relation to the federal government. Both relate to the central theme of this book. American presidents are, in comparison with chief executives in most industrial countries, uncommonly constrained by the essentially negative power of Congress. But American government is not only constrained by the separation of powers. Getting policy efficiently formulated and implemented is also affected by the complexity of the executive branch and, simply, by the many competing interests in American society that have created and nurtured so many access points to those with political power. Again, the separation of powers has served to increase the number of access points and thus has made it easier for determined minorities to block central control and regulation. Put another way, the Constitution has helped prevent the exercise of centralized power while at the same time providing citizens a multiplicity of access points for the voicing of grievances.

Federalism has had similar effects. By definition, the institution of federalism limits and fragments central political power. Arguments suggesting that the decline of the states' legal autonomy is in part attributable to the Constitution's failure to define precisely where state sovereignty begins and ends are less persuasive. Such a strict delineation of powers would have been inflexible and ultimately unworkable, and in any case the states were admirably independent until the twentieth century. The gradual erosion of their legal powers was not, therefore, a matter so much of constitutional failure as it was a consequence of the states' inability to deal with the pressing social and economic problems that industrialization and other changes brought. As the next chapter will show, however, federalism is far from dead. Indeed, in recent years the states have, in some areas, regained power. And often they have done so following popular opposition to the imposition of national standards in such areas as capital punishment and abortion.

Any assessment of the Constitution has to recognize that, as with any constitution, its continuing influence is ultimately dependent on those in positions of political power accepting its legitimacy. Had its provisions proved a major threat to power holders, it would have been ignored or radically amended. No doubt the founding fathers recognized this and, anticipating problems, deliberately opted for a short and rather vague document that would stand the test of time. But this would hardly have been enough had America been torn by fundamental divisions based on class, ethnicity, language, or religion. The framers knew that good government was all about the business of reconciling differences between competing groups and interests in society, and no doubt they were aware that the United States would experience social and political conflict of varying intensity. But the conflict between North and South apart—and this very nearly destroyed the republic—the United States has been remarkably unaffected by fundamental political divisions. Free from a feudal past and lacking deeply rooted religious, ethnic, linguistic, and, at least in recent decades, regional divides, the country was able to accommodate quite extraordinary economic and demographic changes within a single, almost unchanging, constitutional structure. Although it is impossible to measure the contribution of the Constitution to this relative consensus on political fundamentals amid rapid change—no doubt the causal lines run in many directions—it seems reasonable to conclude that by limiting the exercise of central power, the Constitution has made some important contributions in this area.

This does not mean the Constitution will continue forever, of course. And there are more than enough critics who claim that the basic division of power between legislative and executive is inappropriate for the sort of efficient policymaking needed to run an economically powerful world power at the millennium's end.

Whether this is true, later chapters will reveal. But whatever the charges, the Constitution is under no imminent threat either from domestic political conflict or from radical amendment. According to the simple measure of its ability to survive, therefore, it must be deemed a success.

Notes

1. Sam Bass Warner, *The Urban Wilderness: A History of the American City* (New York: Harper and Row, 1972), p. 8.

2. The full text of the Constitution is given in the Appendix.

3. The *Federalist Papers,* written mainly by Madison and Hamilton, were published after the convention to persuade some of the states to accept the Constitution. They comprise a remarkable collection of essays that reflect some of the most crucial debates of the convention.

4. *The Federalist,* no. 10, in *The Federalist Papers* (New York: Mentor Books, 1961), pp. 77–78.

5. *The Federalist,* no. 55, p. 346.

6. The classic statement of this view is Charles Beard's *Economic Interpretation of the Constitution of the United States* (New York: Macmillan, 1913).

7. O. J. Libby, quoted in J. C. Clark Archer and Peter J. Taylor, *Section and Party* (New York: Wiley, 1981), p. 49.

8. Should no candidate receive a majority in the College—a likelihood if the United States had a multiparty system—then the House of Representatives chooses the president on the basis of one vote per state delegation. This massive bias in favor of the smaller states would not be tolerated for long were the system put to the test—although it did occur twice in the nineteenth century. In recent years the United States has only rarely produced serious third-party candidates, and few have accumulated Electoral College votes.

Further Reading

On the revolutionary period, see Don Cook, *The Long Fuse: How England Lost the American Colonies* (Boston, MA: Atlantic Monthly Press, 1996). Also see Bernard Bailyn, *The Ideological Origins of the American Revolution* (Cambridge: Harvard University Press, 1992). Two classic accounts of the making of the Constitution and the early years of the republic are Samuel H. Beer, *To Make a Nation: The Rediscovery of American Federalism* (Cambridge: Harvard University Press, 1994), and Stanley Elkins and Eric McKitrick, *The Age of Federalism: The Early American Republic, 1788–1800* (Oxford and New York: Oxford University Press, 1994).

4

Federalism and Intergovernmental Relations

The problem which all federalized nations have to solve is how to se-cure an efficient central government and preserve national unity, while allowing free scope for the diversities, and free play to the members of the federation. It is ... to keep the centrifugal and centripetal forces in equilibrium, so that neither the planet States shall fly off into space nor the sun of the Central government draw them into its consuming fires.

—Lord James Bryce

This Nation has never fully debated the fact that over the past 40 years, federalism—one of the most essential and underlying principles of our Constitution—has nearly disappeared as a guiding force in American politics and government.

—Ronald Reagan

To many foreign observers, the practice of American federalism presents itself as something of a conundrum. On the one hand is the extraordinary variety of contrasting public policies displayed by the states. Most states levy an income tax, but ten do not; most have capital punishment, but twelve do not. State-mandated land-use planning is light-years away from the policy agenda in Texas—a state that prides itself on its free market in land—but in Hawaii state planning is a fact of life. In Louisiana laws governing the sale of in-toxicating liquors are lax, whereas Utah is close to being a "dry" state with alcohol available only on a very limited basis and mainly in private clubs. On the other hand, American observers repeatedly conclude that federalism is dying—or is even dead; that the federal government has effectively usurped the powers of the states and now plays the dominant role in American government. Federalism, so goes the message, has been transformed from a system of shared sovereignty with each level of government supreme in its own sphere and converted into a complex web of intergovernmental relations where political and economic forces, not constitutional imperatives, are the key variables.

A major purpose of this chapter is to explain the apparent paradox of continuing state variety and increasing federal power. To achieve this, attention will be paid to what has been called "fiscal federalism," or the financial relations between different levels of government, and to recent attempts to revive the institution of federalism. Finally, the discussion addresses how federalism as practiced in the United States today fits into the theme of the book, and how federal arrangements might affect the gap between the public's expectations of government and the ability of political institutions to meet these expectations.

Federalism in Theory and Practice

There are three basic forms of government operating in the modern world (see Figure 4.1). Under unitary government, sovereignty is vested in the central authorities, which can in turn decide the shape of regional and local governments. Unitary governments exist in such countries as Britain, France, and Japan. Under confederal arrangements, sovereignty is vested in the state or regional governments, whose agreement is required in order to sanction action by the central government. The U.S. Articles of Confederation and the Confederacy during the Civil War operated roughly in this way, and such organizations as the United Nations and NATO approximate confederal systems.

The defining feature of federalism is that of *dual sovereignty,* or a *sharing* of powers between state and central governments. Under federalism, each level of government is assumed to be supreme in at least one policy area. Typically the federal government would have responsibility for defense and foreign affairs, while the states would control such matters as education and law and order. The three models represented in Figure 4.1 are, of course, idealized types. In reality, most political systems, although labeled unitary or federal, share features of both.

American federal arrangements are among the world's oldest, and the U.S. example is often held up as a model of what federalism

FIGURE 4.1   Constitutional Relations in the Three Basic Forms of Government

Confederal Government

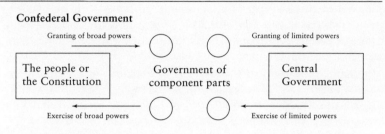

Federal Government

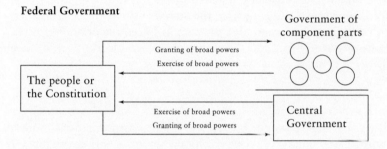

Unitary Government

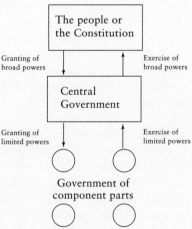

should look like. At the same time, it was not so long ago that many Europeans viewed U.S. federalism with a combination of distanced interest and condescension. A constitutional division of powers between center and periphery might, so the argument ran, suit such large and diverse countries as the United States, but they were clearly inappropriate for homogeneous countries like Britain and France, with their centralized metropolitan political cultures based on dominant capital cities. For social reformers, federalism was viewed with particular skepticism. How, after all, could resources be distributed from rich to poor areas and from the haves to have-nots of society in the absence of a powerful central government operating unhindered by "regressive" state governments? Critics pointed to the stark inequalities of American society, which seemed so often to correlate with state boundaries—abject poverty in Mississippi and Alabama, an easy affluence in Connecticut and Minnesota.

In recent years, however, the institution of federalism has experienced something of a revival. Centralized governments have been criticized as spendthrift and insensitive, and federalism has been cited as a compromise solution to the claims by increasing numbers of regions and ethnic minorities in a variety of countries for more autonomy. To the critic of the overcentralized state, federalism's advantages seem obvious. Local and regional cultural, political, and economic characteristics can be preserved; government can be brought "closer to the people"; and central power can be limited by ensuring that the administration of a whole range of domestic policies is conducted at the state and local level. Federalism is, of course, much more than the mere devolution of powers that, to a greater or lesser extent, exists in all states, unitary and federal. As indicated, *dual sovereignty* is the central theoretical condition for federalism. This involves not only the sharing of policy responsibilities between different levels of government but also the *guarantee* of constitutional integrity to state governments. No federal government can abolish its constituent states as a British government can, theoretically at least, abolish all its local governments. Naturally, the crucial question is this: Which powers should reside in the state governments and which in the federal government? Historically under "classic" or "dual" federalism,[1] defense and foreign affairs together with some aspects of financial or macroeconomic management have been considered federal government responsibilities, while most domestic policies—education, roads, welfare, the administration of justice—have been allocated to state and local governments.

Few constitutions, however, specify precisely which policy areas should be the responsibility of different levels of government. Article 1, Section 8, of the U.S. Constitution, for example, does enumerate the powers of Congress, but it does not do so in a way that unambiguously defines the federal role. Congress is given the power to regulate interstate commerce, but what does this mean? The regulation of interstate transport? Of the movement of manufactured goods across state boundaries? Of banking across state lines? Of those aspects of *intrastate* commerce that are affected by *interstate* transactions? What Congress does in this realm and what remains a *state* responsibility are matters left undefined by the Constitution.

In reality, the delineation of the federal and state roles has been left to judicial interpretation and to the ways in which the courts have reacted to shifting political and economic environments. As was pointed out in Chapter 3, workable constitutions have to be flexible and open to new interpretation, and any attempt to lay down in a permanent fashion the limits to federal or state powers would be doomed to failure. For federalism, the cost of flexibility has been the gradual and steady erosion of the states' powers by the federal government.

In strict constitutional terms, the states have but four guarantees: equal representation in the Senate (Article 1, Section 3); the right to jurisdictional integrity (Article 4, Section 3); the right to a republican form of government (Article 4, Section 4); and protection against invasion and domestic violence (Article 4, Section 4). What in reality they have retained in addition to these rights has varied with the historical period and a range of economic, social, and political forces. The states remain an important level of government, not just for constitutional reasons but also because they are a convenient jurisdictional base for a host of powerful actors and interests in contemporary America. Political parties, for example, are organized on a state rather than a national basis—a structure that gives the states a key role in nominating presidents and in electing members of Congress and senators. In short, local as well as state governments are important power bases in the American system. Localism is as strong in the United States as in any country, despite the weak constitutional position of local governments (in theory, they are constitutionally subordinate to state governments, although some state constitutions guarantee them some autonomy or "home rule"). The power of local governments is reflected in their resilience. In spite of the many pressures to consolidate into larger

TABLE 4.1   Types of Government in the United States, 1967, 1977, 1992

Type of Government	1992	1977	1967
Total	85,006	79,913	81,299
U.S. government	1	1	1
State governments	50	50	50
Local governments	84,955	79,862	81,248
County	3,043	3,042	3,049
Municipal	19,279	18,862	18,048
Township	16,656	16,822	17,105
School district	14,422	15,174	21,782
Special district	31,55	25,962	21,264

SOURCE: *Statistical Abstract of the United States, 1997*, table 470.

units—pressures that exist in all industrialized countries—the number of local units in the United States remains high (Table 4.1).

Differences in state law account for the variety of local units. Twenty states, for example, have townships, which generally have the powers of municipalities but, unlike municipalities, cover areas irrespective of population concentrations. Special districts, which continue to increase in number, have been created to perform a specific local function such as fire protection, soil conservation, water supply or sewerage. They are legally separate from, although almost always linked politically to, municipal and county governments.

In recognition of the weakness of classic or dual federalism, and of the strength of local governments, some commentators have argued that, rather than become involved in arcane discussions on the constitutional status of federalism, it is now more appropriate to talk of *intergovernmental relations* (IGR).[2] Such a focus—largely adopted in this chapter—requires examination of the political and economic relationships between different levels of government. To understand why federalism, as a constitutional concept, has changed so much over time, it is necessary to analyze the historical evolution of IGR in the United States.

The Evolution of American Federalism

That the founders opted for a federal rather than a unitary or confederal system of government in 1787 was understandable. Government under the Articles of Confederation had been minimal. A weak Congress (there was no executive branch) was obliged to rely on the cooperation of thirteen nearly independent states. In economic affairs this proved almost impossible, and internal tariff barriers, together with the absence of a common currency, rendered the new republic almost impotent against the economic might of Britain. If a confederal system that relied on the cooperation of constituent states was unworkable, the other most tried alternative, unitary government, was inappropriate for historical and political reasons. It was, after all, the centralized and highly insensitive power of England that had prompted the revolt of the colonies. Each colony had in addition its own traditions and history, which might have been threatened by a centralized system. Finally, unitary government was associated with a strong executive—not a feature likely to endear the system either to the artisans and smallholders who made up the bulk of the American population or to those sections of the elite who supported Madison's notion of limited government.

A federal system involving the sharing of authority between central authority and constituent states was a natural compromise. Hence the constitution gave to the federal government authority to raise armies, to tax, and to regulate interstate commerce—powers notably absent under the Articles of Confederation—while the individual traditions of the states were protected both by the checks and balances imposed on the central institutions of Congress and presidency and by the Tenth Amendment. ("The powers not delegated to the United States by the Constitution, nor prohibited by it to the States, are reserved to the States respectively, or to the people.") The fundamental problem that federalism attempts to solve—the tension between central authority and local autonomy—is still very much extant today. In the late eighteenth century, however, this tension took on a very different form from that presently at work in the United States. Then, a strong federal government was needed for two purposes: to defend the young republic against a hostile outside world and to provide an open and orderly market for the free exchange of goods and services within the borders of the new nation-state. At all levels, government's role was limited, and although some conflict between state and federal governments existed, it rarely reached the point where it intruded greatly into citizens' lives. In an agrarian and small town society characterized by poor communications and a strong tradition of localism, the federal government was a remote and, in terms of people's everyday dealings, a relatively minor authority.

Today, in contrast, federal, state, and local governments intervene in almost all areas of social life through a bewildering array of policies and programs. It is not surprising, therefore, that federal-state-local relations today are very different from those of late-eighteenth-century America. Initially, debate was concentrated on the *regulatory* powers of the federal government—and especially the extent to which federal law was *supreme* in the regulation and promotion of commerce. By the mid-nineteenth century, with the emergence of slavery as a national issue, the role of the federal government in protecting the rights of citizens was added to the policy agenda. These issues remain an important part of current debate on federalism, but they have been transformed by the vastly enhanced spending power of the federal government.

An examination of the more celebrated Supreme Court cases on federal-state relations confirms these shifts in emphasis. Prior to the Civil War, the most significant cases concerned such issues as the right of the federal government to establish a national bank free from state taxation *(McCulloch v. Maryland,* 1819) and to regulate interstate commerce—in this case the operation of ferries between New York and New Jersey *(Gibbons v. Ogden,* 1824). Later the Court, led by Chief Justice Roger Taney, resolutely defended the right of the Southern states to permit slavery—a right promptly removed by the Civil War and the subsequent Thirteenth and Fourteenth Amendments. Between 1870 and 1938, the Court resisted attempts by the federal government to regulate industrial and commercial life—although antimonopoly laws were upheld, and a graduated federal income tax (taxes increase as earnings increase) was eventually approved through constitutional amendment (Sixteenth Amendment, 1913). With the exception of the income tax question, which did inspire a vociferous debate on the role of the federal government, the period up to 1933 was characterized by a general agreement that the states were the proper level of government for most domestic policy formulation and implementation. Federal government power was on the increase, but presidents and congressional members generally accepted that *direct* intervention by the government in the economic and social life of the nation was undesirable.

All changed with the depression of the 1930s and the advent of the New Deal. From 1933 the federal government began to legislate in a variety of new areas, from Social Security to public works. In reaction to what it saw as an unlawful interpretation of the Commerce Clause and the Necessary and Proper Clause,[3] the Court struck down much of this new legislation in the name of states' rights. Had these decisions prevailed, Roosevelt's New Deal would have been in serious trouble, and only a last-minute change in Court opinion prevented a constitutional crisis (see Chapter 12).

Since this famous turnabout in constitutional interpretation, the executive and judicial branches have been in approximate agreement over the *economic* role of the federal government in American society, although this role once again became a matter of controversy during the 1990s. Conflict did not disappear from debate on federalism, however. The civil rights issue, in particular, inspired intense dispute between the states and all branches of the federal government during the 1950s and the 1960s. State (and more recently local) resistance to federal civil rights laws and judicial decisions should not be underestimated, but scholars have probably been right in emphasizing that conflict as such is not now the main characteristic of American federalism. Morton Grodzins was the first to recognize the cooperative nature of federalism in the 1940s and 1950s.

Using the metaphors of layer cake and marble cake to characterize conflictual and cooperative federalism, Grodzins identified the crucial transition of federalism from the intergovernmental antagonisms of the nineteenth century to the mutual interest and collaboration typical of the late 1930s to the late 1950s period.[4] Economic distress and external threat combined to transform the role of the federal government during this period. Lower-level governments responded to national emergency not with antagonism but in a spirit of cooperation and consensus. Since the 1960s, however, federalism has developed further, and cooperation is certainly not the main characteristic of intergovernmental relations today. Now, with the proliferation of programs and policies at all levels of government, a much more confused and fragmented situation exists.

There are two main aspects to the complex picture of federalism today: fiscal federalism and the continuing debate over whether national standards in public policy should prevail as opposed to standards set by state governments. These two policy areas have been the source of intense passions in modern America.

Fiscal Federalism:
The Rise and Fall of the Federal Role

Transformation of the Federal Role, 1930–1970

The federal role increased over time for complex reasons. Most relate to the close connection between administrative and political centralization and what might be called the nationalization of economic and social life. It is easy to be overdeterministic in this area—certainly the causal lines run in many directions. The evolution of mass-based political parties nominating presidents with national appeals was no doubt both an effect and a cause of the increasingly nationalized nature of economic life during the late nineteenth and early twentieth centuries. As corporations began to organize on national lines, so the need for national standards and regulations grew. Demands for minimum standards of, for example, food processing or for fair competition required the sort of political mobilization that could come only from mass-based political parties. As these strengthened, the need emerged for better and more centralized organization on the part of commerce and industry to combat (or cooperate with) the federal government. The growth of news dissemination inevitably aided this process, especially after the introduction of radio and television.

Although all these forces were important, the main impetus to the growth of federal power came from two rather different sources—economic depression and war. As previously noted, the programs of the New Deal and the massive military spending on World War II transformed the federal role. Public spending as a percentage of GNP increased from just 10 percent in 1929 to 23 percent in 1949, and the federal share of this expenditure increased from 2.6 percent to 16 percent—much of it after 1939 as a result of increased defense spending.

A major spur both to increased federal spending and to qualitative changes in intergovernmental relations was the growth of federal grants-in-aid to state and local governments. Two distinctions within any intergovernmental transfer system must be drawn if the system is to be understood. First, it is necessary to distinguish between grants and payments made directly to the population by the federal government and those paid to lower-level governments. The former—in the United States, such benefits as Social Security, Medicare, and agricultural subsidies—constitute a major part of federal spending. Grants to states and localities include both aid that goes directly to individuals through state and local governments—welfare once was the most important item of this type— and aid for programs such as highways and law enforcement, in which case the state or local government constitutes the final stage in the transfer transaction.

Table 4.2 indicates some of these distinctions through a breakdown of federal budget outlays for the 1970–1999 period. Note the rapid rise in grants to state and local governments between 1970 and 1980 and their post-1980 decline. The "payments for individuals" category includes Social Security, Medicare, and some welfare payments; however, the leveling off in this category between 1980 and 1985 resulted mainly from cuts in welfare (which is channeled through the states) rather than cuts in Social Security and other benefits, which go directly to individuals. Finally, note that government expenditure has continued to rise because of sizable increases first in defense expenditure and more recently in payments to individuals (almost entirely Social Security, Medicare, and Medicaid). Also, the burden of interest payments has increased since 1980.

A clue to the rapid rise in grants-in-aid to lower-level governments during the 1970–1980 period is the increase in general-purpose block grants after 1972. Indeed, the second crucial distinction in IGR is between *block* grants, which are general appropriations given to states and localities, and *categorical* grants, which are given for specific programs and policies and often have strings attached. For example, the urban-renewal program introduced in 1949 was categorical: It allocated funds to local governments specifically for the financing of downtown renewal. From 1954 until 1974, this money was available only if recipient governments abided by a "workable program" or general plan of how new development would fit in with existing housing and other facilities. In 1974, however, urban renewal, along with a number of related programs, was replaced by community-development block grants that carried considerably fewer restrictive regulations. This program was just one of a series of block grants introduced by the Nixon and Ford administrations between 1970 and 1976. President Nixon was the architect of the main block grant scheme, general revenue sharing, introduced in 1972 and eventually abolished during the 1980s.

The 1960s as well as the 1970s brought rapidly rising federal expenditure. Many of the programs through which this money was spent were associated with Lyndon Johnson's Great Society: model

TABLE 4.2 Percentage Distribution of Federal Budget Outlays, 1970–1999

	Amount in 1982 Dollars (billions)	Total %	Defense	Payments to Individuals	Net Interest	Aid to State and Local Governments	Other
1970	509.4	100	44.3	29.9	6.8	12.0	7.0
1975	586.0	100	27.3	45.4	6.9	14.8	6.6
1980	699.1	100	23.5	46.4	8.9	15.1	7.1
1985	849.6	100	27.1	44.7	13.7	11.1	3.1
1990	912.2	100	26.4	46.8	14.6	10.7	1.5
1996	1,612.0	100	16.3	55.1	15.9	10.8	1.8
1999a	1,733.0	100	15.0	56.5	14.0	11.5	3.0

a Estimated.

SOURCE: *Statistical Abstract of the United States, 1996*, table 5.14, updated from *Economic Report of the President 1999*.

cities (1966) to reinvigorate inner-city areas; mass transit (1966) to provide cities with more efficient public transport; subsidized housing (1968) for "moderate" and lower income families; Medicare and Medicaid (1965) and a host of smaller social welfare and other policies. In addition, Great Society policies expanded existing programs—urban renewal, public housing, welfare, Social Security.

Many of these programs—and especially the newer ones—had two features that, although not new, became more pronounced during the 1960s. First, the programs were structured generally to bypass the states and transfer funds directly to local governments. The states had long been identified as "regressive" or "backward" participants in the social reform process. Dominated by rural conservatives, state legislatures tended not to favor social reform measures. Given this, the Great Society's focus on aid to local governments was understandable. Second, local, not state, governments were the jurisdictions of the social problems that inspired increased federal aid. Urban problems—racial conflict, inner-city decay, crime, poor housing, poverty—began to dominate the policy agenda during these years.

By the mid-1970s, therefore, through a broad range of categorical and block grant programs, the federal government was providing help for most local governments as well as increasing numbers of individuals. A more analytical description is that the federal government was increasingly perceived as a provider for both *redistributive* and *developmental* policies. The former redistributes income, usually through individuals, from better-off to poorer citizens. Developmental policies are those designed to improve the infrastructure—water and utility supplies, roads, mass transit, education, and law enforcement. Redistributive policy had, since its inception in the 1930s, always been viewed as a federal responsibility, although welfare benefits were channeled through the states. Developmental policy had traditionally been considered a state and local government function.[5]

It was small wonder that these new emphases, together with burgeoning civil rights legislation, troubled both fiscal conservatives and defenders of classic federalism. Bypassing the states was bad enough, but when this was combined with huge increases in government expenditure in areas where the federal government had traditionally played little or no role, it appeared to many that not only federalism but also America's free-enterprise tradition was withering away.

The 1970s: High-Water Mark of Federal Aid

Both Nixon and Ford faced a solidly Democratic House of Representatives throughout their tenure in office, and federal aid to state and local governments increased rapidly during these years. As can be seen from Table 4.3, by 1977 no less than $125 billion, or 3.1 percent of America's GNP, was devoted to this purpose, and both developmental and redistributive benefits were growing fast. During Nixon's second term, efforts were made to cut many of these programs, but they came to little. Not only was Congress deeply hostile to this project, but the administration was itself weakened by the unfolding drama of the Watergate scandal as well. President Ford was even more constrained than was his predecessor, for in 1974 the Democrats won a landslide victory in the midterm elections. The so-called Watergate Congress was intent on a further expansion of the federal role, and federal aid to state and local governments increased more rapidly during the mid-1970s than at any time since World War II.

The election of Jimmy Carter led many commentators to conclude that the federal role would receive a further impetus. Carter was, of course, a Democrat, and at that time the influence of the "urban lobby"—supporters of grants, affirmative action, housing subsidies, and welfare—in the Democratic Party remained strong. Paradoxically, however, federal aid to state and local governments peaked during the Carter years. Carter believed in fiscal rectitude, or the idea that the first responsibility of the national government was to balance the budget. In practice, this meant holding back that part of federal spending considered "controllable," and the result was attempts to limit aid to state and local governments.

Other items on the budget were much less easy to cut. Defense spending had been reduced during the 1970s, but the latter half of the decade brought increased East-West tensions, which required greater defense expenditures. The other major budget item—Social Security—involved the distribution of automatic payments to old-age pensioners, widows, and the disabled, so could not be touched. Carter did attempt to reform the federal welfare role and even tried to forge a "national urban policy," but his plans lacked clear commitment to specific reforms in these areas and came to nothing.

A further reason for the decline in support for federal aid in the late 1970s was an increasing awareness that many of the new programs of the Johnson-Nixon era were inefficient, corrupt, or both.

TABLE 4.3 Developmental and Redistributive Federal Grants to State and Local Governments, Selected Years, 1957–1990

Function and Category	Percentage of GNP							Amount (billions of 1990 dollars)						
	1957	1962	1967	1972	1977	1982	1990	1957	1962	1967	1972	1977	1982	1990
Developmental														
Transport	0.2	0.5	0.5	0.4	0.3	0.3	0.3	4.3	11.6	15.4	14.7	12.7	11.6	15.5
Natural Resources	0.0	0.0	0.0	0.1	0.0	0.0	0.0	0.6	0.6	0.9	1.8	1.9	1.3	2.2
Safety	0.0	0.0	0.0	0.0	0.2	0.2	0.1	0.2	0.3	0.6	1.7	1.9	1.7	2.8
Education	0.1	0.3	0.5	0.6	0.6	0.5	0.4	2.7	4.9	14.6	20.7	22.1	19.6	23.2
Utilities	0.0	0.0	0.0	0.0	0.0	0.0	0.0	0.0	0.0	0.0	0.0	0.0	0.0	0.0
Miscellaneous	0.1	0.1	0.2	0.1	0.7	0.5	0.3	1.6	3.0	6.0	4.7	36.8	25.2	16.4
Total[a]	0.4	0.9	1.2	1.2	1.8	1.5	1.1	9.4	20.4	37.5	43.6	74.5	59.4	60.1
Redistributive														
Pensions/medical insurance	0.0	0.1	0.0	0.1	0.1	0.1	0.1	0.0	1.9	0.0	2.2	3.0	2.8	2.8
Welfare	0.4	0.4	0.5	1.1	0.9	1.0	1.1	7.0	10.2	15.8	37.9	37.0	41.8	60.0
Health and hospitals	0.0	0.0	0.0	0.1	0.1	0.1	0.1	0.5	0.7	1.5	3.8	3.5	3.8	5.9
Housing	0.0	0.1	0.1	0.1	0.2	0.2	0.2	0.5	1.5	2.5	4.4	7.1	9.8	10.8
Total[a]	0.4	0.6	0.7	1.3	1.3	1.4	1.4	8.0	14.3	19.8	48.3	50.6	58.2	79.5
Total domestic expenditure[a]	0.8	1.4	1.9	2.7	3.1	2.8	2.5	17.4	34.7	57.3	91.9	125.1	117.6	139.6

[a] Totals may not add because of rounding.

SOURCE: Paul E. Peterson, *The Price of Federalism* (Washington, DC: Brookings Institution, 1995), table 3.5.

In many instances, state and local governments, strapped for cash, simply diverted money from programs designed for particular purposes into general funds used to pay salaries and the like. This tactic was an especially serious problem when federal money went directly to local governments or to the private sector. Housing and urban-development programs were particularly prone to this sort of abuse. Intellectual and political opinion was turning against the view that big government was the answer to all of society's problems, for despite all the new programs and policies, generally there occurred no discernible improvement in crime, education, and urban conditions. At the same time, the economic dislocations of the 1970s led many to believe that excessive government spending was a cause of inflation and recession. An obvious step toward correcting these problems would be a reduction in federal government aid to state and local governments. It was left to the Reagan administration to implement these changes.

The Reagan Administration: Federalism Revived?

In his campaign speeches and his 1981 inaugural address, Ronald Reagan made the revival of federalism a central part of his program to rekindle traditional American values. The federal government had become inefficient, insensitive, and cumbersome and, so the argument ran, should be reduced radically in size. One way to achieve this was to revive Richard Nixon's original idea and consolidate myriad categorical grants-in-aid programs into a number of block grants. In this way, the states would be returned to their "rightful" position as the main source of domestic policies and programs. Accordingly, during 1981 the administration proposed consolidating eighty-three categorical programs into six human services block grants (health services, preventive health services, social services, energy and emergency assistance, local education services, and state education services). The total amount of federal money involved was $11 billion. At the same time, the 1981 Budget Reconciliation Act reduced federal spending in a wide range of programs. Some intergovernmental programs were eliminated altogether, while others were subject to substantial cuts.

Later, in 1982, the administration presented an even more radical plan for a "New Federalism" involving a "swap" of the three main welfare programs funded by the states and federal government on a matching basis. Welfare and food stamps would be taken over by the states, and the federal government would assume responsibility for Medicaid (medical care for the poor). This plan was combined with a massive "turnback" to the states of most other grants-in-aid programs that, initially at least, would be funded by a special trust fund. In just five years, however, the fund would be terminated, leaving the states in glorious isolation. In the meantime, an immediate 25 percent cut in funding would be imposed.

The plan was greeted with almost unanimous opposition from the states, from Congress, and even from within the Office of Management and Budget—Medicaid was the most rapidly growing item in the federal budget. Within months the swap plan was dropped, as was the grandiose scheme for a nearly complete devolution of programs to the states. In any event, Congress accepted some of the consolidations into block grants and some of the cuts. During the rest of the Reagan years, this became the general pattern. Generally, transportation, education, and capital spending programs suffered most and had been reduced considerably by 1990 (Table 4.3).

Although the grand strategy of the New Federalism had to be abandoned, Ronald Reagan succeeded in reversing the historical trend toward ever increasing federal aid for developmental purposes. This change in the policy agenda continued during the Bush and Clinton years.

Bush and Clinton: Permanent Change in the Federal Role?

In his 1989 inaugural address, not once did George Bush mention federalism and the states. Although he later pledged that he would continue the Reagan agenda of devolving power to the states, he lacked the political and emotional commitment to the idea.

During the Bush years, a Democratic Congress found itself under increasing pressure to resume higher levels of intergovernmental aid. By 1989–1990, a number of states and cities were beginning to experience fiscal stress as economic recession eroded tax bases, but politicians were unwilling or unable to increase taxes. Federal programs were, once again, viewed by states and localities as possible saviors. In 1992, first the Los Angeles riots and then the Miami hurricane demonstrated that, like it or not, the federal government was expected to provide major aid programs following local or regional disasters. In both cases the Bush administration produced emergency aid packages. In spite of these events, the Bush years brought no major reversal of the trends established during the Reagan years.

During his first campaign for president, Bill Clinton gave the strong impression that he would resume the old-style fiscal federalism of the 1960s and 1970s. He proposed an immediate $19.5 billion economic development package to stimulate the economy. He was politically close to a group of economists who believed that the federal government should play an enhanced role in the provision of infrastructure—in particular, transportation and communications—in order to facilitate faster economic growth. In practice, this notion would entail greatly increased developmental aid to state and local governments. Once elected, Clinton appointed one of these economists, Robert Reich, to his cabinet, and during the first two months of his administration, a revival of fiscal federalism looked imminent.

By the end of Clinton's first term, however, the political agenda had changed to such an extent that the administration's position on federalism resembled President Reagan's view more closely than President Johnson's. This transformation had several causes. First, Clinton's ambitious economic stimulus program immediately encountered opposition in Congress. Republican senators managed to block the legislation, and by summer 1993 many Democrats had become skeptical of the need for such a far-reaching program. Furthermore, the economy was recovering quickly, and any new federal expenditure seemed incompatible with the need to reduce the budget deficit. Within the administration, the influence of the fiscal conservatives increased while that of the proponents of an enhanced federal role declined. In short, the only important measure passed that enhanced the federal role was a crime bill providing new federal resources for local police enforcement.

The agenda changed again after the election of the Republican 104th Congress in 1994. Thereafter, proposed changes involved a reduction rather than an increase in federal aid to state and local governments. In particular, the new Congress wanted to change the redistributive as well as the developmental role of the federal government. Federal welfare programs, in particular, were seen to encourage dependency and discourage work. "Workfare" rather than welfare became the slogan of the 1990s, and the states were to be allocated a major role in a reformed welfare system. In 1996 Congress enacted welfare reform that effectively delegated the responsibility for welfare provision to the states (discussed in more detail in Chapter 14).

Although the federal government's role in developmental policy (education, housing, transportation, law enforcement) has been reduced since the 1970s, Congress continues, under pressure from its constituents, to pass old-fashioned pork-barrel bills in such areas as transportation and public safety. The federal role may have been reduced, but it has not been transformed. Most experts agree that the federal government should play the major part in redistributive policy—mainly because many of the poorer states do not have the tax capacity to provide adequate social security and welfare programs for the needy.[6] This is broadly the position adopted by the Clinton administration, although the president did sign a 1996 welfare reform act that returned much of the responsibility for welfare to the states.

Even liberal Democrats are now sensitive to the fact that the public's regard for the federal government has declined while its faith in state government has increased. This represents a sea change from the 1930s and 1940s when public opinion took precisely the opposite direction (Figure 4.2). The clear implication is that experience has taught increasing numbers of citizens that Washington cannot deliver on its promises. Instead, new federal programs often mean higher taxes with few associated benefits. State programs, by contrast, tend to be less grandiose and expensive. States have also been obliged to limit spending by constitutional constraints and direct voter pressure. Put another way, the conflict in modern American politics between a philosophy of limited government and high public expectations of federal institutions has fed directly into debates on federalism. The result has been a resurgence in the role and importance of state government.

A Changing Court Role?

As earlier indicated, in the economic and social dimension of federalism, the Supreme Court deferred to the other branches from the late 1930s onward. In other words, the issue of where the federal government's powers over the economic and social affairs of the states began and ended would be decided by the president and Congress rather than by judicial interpretation of the Constitution. Indeed, in 1985, in what seemed to be a landmark decision (*Garcia v. San Antonio Metropolitan Transit Authority*), the Court argued that the federal government could regulate the wages of San Antonio bus workers because the limits to federal power "inhered principally in the workings of the national government itself." Most commentators took this wording to mean a complete abdication of the role of the Supreme Court in arbitrating between state and federal law.

FIGURE 4.2   Public Regard for Federal and State Governments, 1936 and 1995

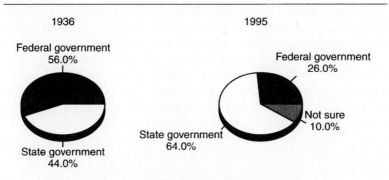

Question asked: 'Which do you favor – concentration of power in the
federal government or in state government?'

SOURCE: Gallup (1936) and Hart and Teeter Research Companies (1995)
as presented by Richard P. Nathan in "Overview Essay on Federalism and Social Policy," unpublished, University of Princeton, 1996.

However, just seven years later, the Supreme Court appeared to reverse itself with two dramatic decisions that seemed to put strict constitutional limits on what the federal government could do. In the
first, *New York v. United States*, the Court struck down a 1985 law
requiring states to dispose of radioactive waste. In the majority decision, Justice Sandra Day O'Connor invoked the Tenth Amendment
and reasoned that "The Constitution . . . [does not] authorize Congress simply to direct the States to provide for the disposal of radioactive waste generated within their borders." In 1994, the Court
appeared to go further by striking down a federal law that would
have established gun-free zones within 1,000 yards of schools. In
passing this law, Congress had invoked the Commerce Clause by arguing that high crime around schools could increase the cost of insurance and travel and thus could affect interstate commerce. The
Court held that there were limits to the interpretation of the Commerce Clause. As Chief Justice Rehnquist put it: "[This law] neither
regulates a commercial activity nor contains a requirement that the
possession [of a gun] be connected in any way to interstate commerce." In future, therefore, Congress would have to establish a
clear link between laws regulating state activity and the provisions of
the Commerce Clause.

These decisions were followed by others in a similar vein, including a 1997 case (*Printz v. United States*) that invalidated parts of the 1997 Brady gun-control bill requiring background checks on would-be gun purchasers. (For further details, see Chapter 12.) These decisions are of obvious importance, but they do not necessarily represent unambiguous limits on the ways in which the federal government can control the powers of the states. Much depends on the circumstances of individual laws and individual cases. Clearly, however, for the first time since the 1930s, the Supreme Court has recognized limits to what can be legislated in the name of the Commerce Clause. In so doing, the Court has suggested that the Tenth Amendment does have some validity and application.

The Pressure for National Standards

In some areas federal power has been in retreat, but in others it has taken on new forms. This is especially true with regard to the setting of national standards in many areas of social and economic life. Gradually since the 1970s, Congress, often acting on presidential initiative, has legislated to establish such national standards. The most important of these are federal (or congressional) *preemption sanctions* and *cross-over sanctions*.

Federal preemption, which can be statutory or attached to a condition of grant aid, is a legal requirement that states or local governments meet minimum standards or provide particular services. States cannot now, for example, establish a minimum retirement age or regulate airline, bus, or truck companies. In areas such as environmental protection, states must conform to national mandates or standards and pay to do so. Some preemption statutes provide some compensation toward the cost of implementation, but the amount rarely covers the full cost.

Cross-over sanctions require states to comply with a law or lose funds authorized earlier under other federal laws. In health care and transportation, threats of such sanctions are increasingly common. Perhaps the most famous was the Reagan administration's insistence that all states increase their minimum drinking age to twenty-one or lose federal highway funds. By 1987 all had complied. Cross-over sanctions can involve the states and localities in expensive new policies.

Federal insistence on minimum or national standards introduces a further element of conflict in U.S. intergovernmental relations.

Many of the Reagan-Bush measures were aimed at freeing the market from what were considered restrictive state laws or involved the application of minimum penalties for such matters as driving offenses. Clinton was more inclined to support minimum standards in environmental protection, civil rights, consumer protection, and occupational safety and health. These are more expensive to implement and thus are potentially more conflictual. It remains to be seen what the role of the courts will be in this area, but in light of the cases discussed earlier, it is certainly possible that a conservative Court could invalidate some of the more intrusive attempts by the federal government to use preemption and cross-over sanctions as tools to control the states.

American Federalism and Public Expectations

Most observers would agree that classical federalism, with state and federal governments each sovereign and separate in their designated area, is effectively dead—indeed, there is serious doubt that it ever applied in the United States. Cooperative federalism, which dominated intergovernmental relations from the 1930s to the 1970s, is also inappropriate as a description of the 1990s. "Competitive interdependence" is a more accurate label; but it describes federal, state, and local relations, not merely federal-state interactions. If this is now the status, what is left of federalism? Much more remains than would have been expected in the late 1980s, for not only has there been a top-down attempt to devolve power by Congress, but also the Supreme Court has made serious attempts to revive federalism by strengthening the Tenth Amendment and by reinterpreting the Commerce Clause. This shift is not the equivalent of a return to the pre-1937 era, but it does show the general trend toward the devolution of power in the United States.

Of course, the states remain important administrative and political units. As was noted at the beginning of the chapter, the states preserve variety—each continues to have its own separate legal and political system, and anyone traveling from state to state is aware of distinctive political cultures. Certainly, the states preserve a degree of local or regional political autonomy that is quite unfamiliar in more centralized political systems. The states are now also much more efficient and professional as policymakers than ever before. As state government has increased in size and status, it has attracted more capable personnel. Governors are of higher quality, and corruption, although still a part of some states' political culture, is less prevalent than it used to be. Finally, states now do a great deal more than they used to, not only in administering federal programs but also in running their own.

This resilience and growth, however, derive not so much from constitutional imperatives as from tradition and custom and from the fact that the states remain politically convenient jurisdictions for the representation of a variety of interests. State law remains preeminent in many areas of economic and social life, including industrial relations, insurance, and almost all aspects of family law. At the same time, state and local taxes are the main source of revenue for a range of distinctive state and locally provided services, including transportation, education, and law enforcement. As noted, the role of the states has increased as the federal government has required them to participate in the implementation of federally funded programs. In addition, by the late 1990s, there was an emerging consensus that the states should take on some of the tasks hitherto performed by the federal government. American society may be becoming more nationalized as federal standards increasingly apply in certain areas. The constitutional position of the states may also be weak, but in many respects they remain politically independent.

In other words, many voters expect state rather than federal authorities to be responsible for a wide range of public policies. Indeed, the states are at the very heart of some of most important issues in American politics. Federal law, for example, mandates the right to abortion. Antiabortion or pro-choice activists want to return decisions on the subject to state legislatures, many of which would abolish the right to abortion. Under pressure from voters, whether directly via initiatives or through state legislatures, the states have been assertive in a range of other areas, including affirmative action, penal policy, and education. And in contrast to the 1960s and 1970s, Congress and the federal courts have been reluctant to challenge these decisions and reassert federal power. This disinclination in turn reflects a shifting public mood in favor of a more limited form of government. As has been the case since the 1930s, however, when state authorities prove unable to cope with a particular problem—whether it be a natural catastrophe, an economic crisis such as the savings and loan collapse of the early 1990s (see Chapter 15), or acts of terrorism—these very same voters will be quick to call for federal action. Thus, as with many other facets of U.S. politics, the great paradox of American federalism at century's end is the public's deep ambiguity about the nature of federal power.

Notes

1. The classic statement on the nature of dual federalism is by Morton Grodzins, *The American System* (Chicago: Rand McNally, 1966).
2. This abbreviation is taken from Deil S. Wright, *Understanding Intergovernmental Relations* (North Scituate, MA: Duxbury, 1978).
3. Section 8, Clause 18, empowers Congress to make laws that are necessary and proper to implement its enumerated powers, including the regulation of interstate commerce.
4. Grodzins, *The American System*.
5. These distinctions are taken from Paul E. Peterson, *The Price of Federalism* (Washington, DC: Brookings Institution, 1995).
6. See Peterson, *The Price of Federalism*, chap. 8.

Further Reading

The best general account of changes in American fiscal federalism during the 1980s and 1990s is Paul E. Peterson, *The Price of Federalism* (Washington, DC: Brookings Institution, 1995). For the traditional view of the transition from conflictual to cooperative federalism, see Morton Grodzins, *The American System* (Chicago: Rand McNally, 1966). A sympathetic account of the resurgence of the states is John A. Ferejohn and Barry R. Weingast (eds.), with Thomas Nechyba, *The New Federalism: Can the States Be Trusted?* (Stanford, CA: Hoover Institution Press, 1997). A critical view of the resurgence of state power is John D. Donahue, *Disunited States: What's at Stake as Washington Fades and the States Take the Lead* (New York: Basic Books, 1997).

5

American Political Parties
in Transition

A democratic society has to provide a mode of consistent representation of relatively stable alignments or modes of compromise in its polity. The mechanism of the American polity has been the two-party system. If the party system, with its enforced mode of compromise, gives way, and "issue politics" begin to polarize groups, then we have the classic recipe for what political scientists call "a crisis of the regime," if not a crisis of disintegration and revolution.

—*Daniel Bell*

The American political party system is not an insoluble puzzle. But it does have more than its share of mysteries. The main one, arguably, is how it has survived for so long, or perhaps, how it survived at all, in a difficult and complicated environment.

—*William J. Keefe*

To the outside observer, the American party system conjures almost a caricature of American politics. Parties appear to be coalitions of many interests. They are organizationally weak and in a constant state of crisis. In contrast, most European political parties have quite vivid public images based on class, regional, religious, linguistic, ethnic, or ideological divisions.

Although this is an oversimplified characterization of the two types of party system, it remains broadly true that American parties cover a narrower band of the ideological spectrum than do their European counterparts. They are also much less *programmatic,* offering their supporters very general and diffuse policy options rather than the more structured and specific policy programs associated with European parties. What is true of almost all party systems is that they are constantly developing and adapting to rapid social and economic changes—a fact that leads many commentators to attach the label "crisis" to the most recent development or electoral event. The remarkable feature of the American system is that it has always had only two major parties—although not always the same two parties—competing for major offices at any one time. Moreover, these parties have been largely nonideological in style and policy substance, and this in a country constantly buffeted by the major social changes brought by immigration, industrialization, and urbanization.

The diffuse nature of the parties fits well into the theme of this book, for a defining characteristic of both the Democrats and the Republicans is that they have constantly sought to appeal to as wide a spectrum of voters as possible. As such, they have been obliged to promise *general* rather than *specific* benefits to voters. People's expectations of what government can do have therefore been raised. Once in office, however, party politicians have been obliged to focus on the provision of specific benefits. Honoring specific promises to one group often means penalizing another group, a point discussed later.

A large part of this chapter is devoted to explaining why the American party system has taken the particular shape it has. Although this system has retained its two-party, largely nonideological status through history, it has by no means been static or unchanging. In organization and function, the parties have changed dramatically over the past 200 years—and indeed have changed considerably since the late 1960s. To understand these changes, it is first necessary to discuss the functions that political parties normally play in political systems.

The Functions of Parties

Although often abused by politicians and publics alike, political parties perform vital functions in every political system, and in countries with democratic traditions, they are an indisputably necessary part of the democratic process. In the American context, parties perform at least five major functions.[1]

Aggregation of Demands

In any society, social groups with particular interests to promote or defend need some means whereby their demands can be aggregated and articulated in government. Traditionally, political parties have performed this function—hence the association of party with particular social groups, regions, or religions. In the United States, parties have acquired just such associations, although as noted to a lesser extent than in some other countries. Hence, the Democrats became the party of Southern interests quite early in U.S. history, although by the 1930s the Democrats had also become the party of Northern industrial workers. The Republicans emerged from the Civil War as the party of national unity and later became identified as the party most interested in defending free enterprise and corporate power, an identification that remains today.

But generally, parties in the United States have not been exclusively identified with one social group or class or one geographical region. Instead they tend to be coalitions of interests, aggregating demands on behalf of a number of social groups and regional interests. Given the relatively low level of ideological division and conflict in the United States (see Chapter 2), this coalition-building feature is, perhaps, unsurprising.

Conciliation of Groups in Society

Even in the most divided society, some conciliation among competing or conflicting interests must occur if government is to operate efficiently. Political parties often help this conciliation process by providing united platforms for the articulation of diverse interests. Indeed, there has hardly been a major U.S. political party that has not performed this function. In recent history, for example, the Democrats have attempted to reconcile (and until 1964 largely succeeded) a rural segregationist South with the interests of the urban industrial North.

In specific elections, the particular coalition of support established is uniquely determined by contemporary issues and candidates. Thus in 1960 Democratic presidential candidate John F. Kennedy managed to appeal both to the Catholic voters of the North (Kennedy was himself a Catholic) and Southern Protestants. In 1968 and 1972, the law-and-order issue cut across regions and classes and helped bring victory to Richard M. Nixon, the Republican candidate. By 1980 the Republicans had forged a new coalition consisting of a regional component (the West and the South), a religious-moral component (the Christian right), and an economic-ideological component (the middle class and supporters of a "return" to free enterprise). By conciliating such diverse groups and offering a common program, Republican candidate Ronald Reagan was assured victory. In 1988 George Bush managed to retain the loyalty of sufficient numbers of these same groups to win. In 1992 Bill Clinton was successful in reviving at least parts of the old New Deal coalition by appealing to industrial workers, minorities, women, and many middle-class voters on the issue of economic revival. His appeal in 1996 was slightly different, based as it was on a vote for the status quo. As in 1992, however, Clinton managed to form a complex coalition of support based on gender, ethnicity, and region (the West and the industrial North).

Clearly, political parties have to appeal to a number of competing and potentially conflicting interests if they are to succeed in a country as diverse and complex as the United States. As a result, parties have tended to move toward the middle of the ideological spectrum, avoiding those more extreme positions likely to alienate potential supporters. Noting this tendency toward moderation, political theorists have produced a general model of party behavior. This model assumes that if parties are rational and really want to win elections, they will always move toward the center, for only in this way can they ensure majority electoral support.[2] Whatever its merits in other countries, this theory seems particularly apt in the United States, where with rather few exceptions (of which more later) parties have remained remarkably moderate.

Staffing the Government

In a modern, complex society, parties are a necessary link in the relationship between government and people. According to social-contract theory, governments must be held accountable for their actions. If they are perceived to be failing, then the people can always replace them at election time. Unfortunately, accountability and responsiveness can never be continuous or complete except in very small societies or communities. Given this elusiveness, parties provide the public with a focus for accountability.

Once elected, a president appoints government officials to fill the major posts in the new administration. Not only departmental chiefs (members of the cabinet) but also the top civil service positions are filled in the main through party linkages (see Chapter 11). When judging the performance of the government, therefore, the public can look to the record of an administration united by a common party

label and, presumably, a common set of policies. Because the party is
rooted in society via party organizations, staffing the government
through party helps to ensure an intimate link between the implementation of policies and public preference. This at least is the theory of how party should operate in government, though the practice
is rather different. One serious practical problem occurs when party
organization, rather than reflecting the interests of social groups or
regions, is instead merely the vehicle for the promotion and election
of a particular candidate. Another problem, discussed next, occurs
when different branches of government have different constituencies
and therefore distinct party organizations.

Coordination of Government Institutions

As previously noted, American government is uncommonly fragmented. The national legislature is separated from the executive,
and the judiciary is independent of both. Federalism adds further
fragmenting influence by giving state (and through the states, local)
governments considerable independence from the federal authorities. In centralized systems with cabinet government, parties actually dominate institutions. In Britain, for example, powerful political party organizations nominate candidates, fight elections, and, if
successful, form the government out of a majority in the House of
Commons. By exercising control over the party organization, governments (or oppositions) can usually ensure the obedience of individual members of Parliament. In this sense, party is not needed as
a coordinating influence, because a system of *party government*
prevails. In marked contrast, America's separated powers and federal arrangements greatly aggravate problems of coordination, and
as numerous American political scientists have pointed out, party is
the main means by which disparate institutions can coordinate the
formulation and implementation of policy.[3]

So, even if state and local government, Congress, and the president have different constituencies, a common party label can provide a means of communication and coordination. In fact, Democratic governors, mayors, and members of Congress normally do
have more in common with Democratic presidents than with Republican presidents—although as discussed later, they often do not.
Indeed, there have been periods in American history when relations
between Congress and the president have been greatly aided by political party ties. During the Jeffersonian period, for example,

something approaching party government prevailed. More recently, Presidents Franklin Roosevelt and Lyndon Johnson (both Democrats) used party ties greatly to enhance their relations with Congress and thus erect major new social programs. During the periods 1969–1977 and 1981–1993, Republican presidents faced a Congress dominated by Democrats, although the Republicans held the Senate between 1981 and 1987. Divided government of a very different sort prevailed after 1994 when the Republicans controlled Congress and the Democrats the presidency. Government coordination became particularly difficult during these years.

At the state and local levels, the coordinating function of party has taken a rather different form. In the decades immediately following the Civil War, municipal and, to a lesser extent, state governments proved less than adequate in dealing with successive waves of immigrants from Europe. Hopelessly divided and fragmented institutionally and politically, local governments could do little to improve transportation, housing, and other urban facilities, or even to ensure a reasonable degree of public order. Political parties filled this void through the creation of the political machine—an informal "government" based on patronage, bribery, and corruption.[4] Machines depended on tightly knit grassroots organization, with the party providing ordinary citizens with direct access to the political authorities. Officials in the legitimate government gained through patronage and bribes, and the party was given a guarantee of political power in return. Although hardly welfare organizations, the urban machines of the late nineteenth and early twentieth centuries did at least keep government functioning in the great cities by providing an essential buffer between the immigrant masses and a hostile economic and political environment.

Promotion of Political Stability

Parties do not always promote political stability. In many countries, parties mobilize movements against existing regimes and are a major force in bringing about regime change. Moreover, if *governmental* (as opposed to regime) stability is the measure, it is clear that the multiparty systems of Western Europe do anything but promote stability, as the Italian and other systems testify (Italy has had more than twenty-five governments between 1970 and 2000). In "mature" democracies, however, parties do help socialize citizens into an acceptance of the regime, if only by legitimizing national parliaments and assemblies and facilitating the peaceful transfer of power from one government to another.

For reasons to be discussed later, America's two-party system has proved remarkably resilient, with the result that the country has never suffered the problems associated with a proliferation of organized parties. Although the causal lines are blurred, it is reasonable to argue that American political parties have helped promote political stability. Quite frequently, for example, political movements outside the mainstream of American political life have had their policies preempted by one of the leading parties. This happened to the Populists during the 1890s, when much of their program was adopted by the Democrats, and to a number of left-wing parties and movements during the early New Deal period.

Moreover, the two most significant third parties of the twentieth century, the Progressives and the American Independent Party, grew out of existing parties and were eventually reincorporated into them. In each case, the breakaway was led by a single charismatic figure— Theodore Roosevelt led the Progressives in 1912, George Wallace the American Independent Party in 1968. In fact, George Wallace effectively *was* the party, and without him it simply disappeared. But the crucial point is that the issues that inspired both movements— dispute over the federal government's role in the economy and society and the racial integration of the South—and that the existing parties could not accommodate did not lead to a permanent shift in party alignments. Instead, either the Democrats and Republicans adapted to the new demands, or the movements themselves were reincorporated into the mainstream once the protest had been made. In a rather different context, Ross Perot's strong showing as a third candidate in 1992 (19 percent of the vote) showed disillusionment among voters with the Republican and Democratic Party candidates. Significantly, however, it did not lead directly to the emergence of a third party. Indeed, Perot's second challenge to the two-party system in 1996 proved much less effective, when he managed only 8 percent of the vote.

The constantly impressive ability of American political parties to absorb potentially destabilizing social movements has no doubt contributed to the stability of the system, although the more inquiring mind could note that the two major parties have been able to perform this function only because there have been so few deep divisions in American society. A more divided society could not possibly sustain such a monopoly of power shared by two such amorphous and adaptable parties. This premise is clear when the United States is compared with deeply divided societies such as Northern Ireland or Belgium. In both cases, religious cleavages are such that they are faithfully reflected in the party system.

Crisis and Change in the American Party System

At least since the early 1950s, political scientists have bemoaned the decline of American political parties. The "crisis" has been identified mainly in terms of a constant erosion of the five functions just listed. In what is already a highly fragmented political system, the decline of these functions has, so the argument runs, led to inefficient government and to an erosion of the legitimacy of institutions.

In order to understand this critique, it is necessary to be familiar with the development of American political parties. Table 5.1 provides a schematic outline of their history by identifying five distinct stages of development. Such a brief summary of the parties' growth must oversimplify somewhat. In particular, the outline implies that the parties have mobilized different regions and social groups in a coherent way throughout history, but this has never been the case. With the notable exception of the Civil War period, the parties have always represented broad coalitions, and they have almost always eschewed appeals to those class-based ideologies that exploit social divisions in society.

Until the early years of the nineteenth century, parties were considered useful only as temporary expedients, or as "factions" necessary to mobilize political power in response to particular crises. As was emphasized in Chapter 3, the Constitution and the political culture generally in the new republic reflected deep suspicion of political parties and their implied threat of government by factions, tyrannical majorities, and mass political action. Significantly, when mass parties did develop (under the guidance of Andrew Jackson and Martin Van Buren) they did so in a way that largely avoided the dangers foreseen by the founding fathers. The new Democratic Party appealed to broad principles of political equality (at least for white males) rather than to narrow class and sectional interests. It also transformed the party into a highly *instrumental* organization. For the first time, the idea that working for the party could bring specific rewards for the individual became influential. Party membership and loyalty brought rewards or political "spoils," of which

TABLE 5.1 The Development of American Political Parties

	Majority Party	Minority Party
1789–1800	*Federalist:* A coalition of mercantile and northern land-owning interests led by Alexander Hamilton, George Washington, and John Adams.	*Republican* (the first Republican party): A coalition of farmers and planters based in the central and southern states and led by Thomas Jefferson.
1800–1856	*Democratic-Republican:* The original Republican coalition was consolidated in this period under James Madison. Later, under the leadership of Andrew Jackson and Martin Van Buren, the party broadened its mass appeal and was renamed the Democratic Party.	*Federalist* then *Whig:* Federalists, Whigs, and a number of smaller parties failed to challenge the Democratic-Republican ascendancy. Victories by the conservative Whigs in 1840 and 1848 were temporary exceptions and led to the rather inauspicious presidencies of William Harrison and Zachary Taylor, both of whom died in office.
1856–1932	*Republican:* The Civil War produced a second Republican Party championing the unionist cause under Abraham Lincoln. Following the war, a coalition of industrialists, bankers, and northern and western farmers, and some industrial workers proved formidable. Apart from Abraham Lincoln, only Theodore Roosevelt (1901–1909) proved a memorable president. The era of strong local and state party organizations and machine politics.	*Democratic:* Democratic strength remained firmly rooted in the South where poor whites and larger landowners supported the party (those blacks briefly enfranchised after the war supported the Republicans). The four Democratic victories of 1884, 1892, 1912, and 1916 were greatly aided by splits in the Republican ranks.
1932–1964	*Democratic:* The era of the New Deal coalition, with the South, the unions, the big cities, ethnic groups, and intellectuals providing a near-permanent	*Republican:* Republican victories in 1952 and 1956 were attributable to the charismatic appeal of Dwight Eisenhower. Main Republican support came from

majority in the House and the Senate. Franklin Roosevelt, Harry Truman, John Kennedy, and Lyndon Johnson were notable presidents.

rural areas, big business, middle-class suburbanites, the West, and New England.

Republican:

With victories by Richard Nixon in 1968 and 1972, the Republicans exploited divisions in the Democratic Party. They also made major inroads into the South. Their association with the Watergate scandal (1973–1977), however, led to an overwhelmingly Democratic Congress in 1974 and indirectly helped the defeat of President Ford in 1976.

1964–1980

Democratic:

Period of the breakdown of the New Deal coalition. The South first voted for segregationist candidate George Wallace and then increasingly for Republican candidates. Vietnam and social issues split the traditional blue-collar, industrial-worker Democratic vote, some of which defected to the Republicans. The Democrats remained the majority party in Congress and in state and local government but managed only one presidential election victory, in 1976.

No Clear Majority Party

Republican:

With three presidential election victories and success in Congress after 1994, there was much talk of a Republican realignment. Although this was true of the South, the West and the North and East remained highly competitive at the state, local, and national levels. The Republicans did, however, redefine themselves as the party of fiscal rectitude, moral or family values, and a transfer of power from the federal level to state governments. Generally, public identification with the two parties declined, which was reflected in lower electoral turnout and increasing disillusionment with political institutions.

1980–

Democratic:

Although the Democrats won the 1992 and 1996 presidential elections, their support was gradually eroded during these years. They lost the Senate 1981 to 1987 and both houses of Congress after 1994. Generally their support collapsed in the South, and they were no longer the dominant party at the state and local levels. Their appeal remained high among women, minorities, and in the Northeast of the country, however.

patronage was the most important. Clearly, delivering the vote and distributing patronage required organization, and it was during this period that local and state parties acquired permanent organizations. The unifying element in these new party organizations was a simple belief in equal opportunity for white males (and a concomitant opposition to aristocratic political values) and in the party as a distributor of spoils. Beyond this the party represented little that was tangible. Great local and regional variety was encouraged rather than tolerated.

A party based on equality and democracy (achieved mainly through the extension of the franchise) and that adopted a new instrumentalism in organization was unlikely to undermine the republicanism and constitutionalism that the founding fathers so feared would be threatened by mass parties. From the very beginning, therefore, mass political parties in the United States built their electoral competition not by appealing to class, ethnic, or religious division but rather by adapting their programs to what was always a broad base of support for individualism and democracy. In this context, the parties were also able to aid the presidential nomination process by limiting competition and providing truly national constituencies.

This new party system was far from being completely successful. Southern Democrats were determined to champion their exclusive sectional interests, and the Civil War effectively destroyed the first mass party system. There emerged after the war a dominant Republican Party (Table 5.1), which again depended on a broad coalition of support.

Furthermore, during the latter half of the nineteenth century, parties became associated with corruption and the growth of the large urban political machine. Much has been written about the machine, although nobody quite captured the spirit of the period as did George Washington Plunkitt, the notorious boss of New York's Tammany Hall. His comment that "you can't keep an organization together without patronage. Men ain't in politics for nothin'. They want to get somethin' out of it" gives some of the flavor of the time.[5] Milton Rakove has characterized the machine in slightly more academic terms: "An effective political party needs five things: offices, jobs, money, workers, and votes. Offices beget jobs and money; jobs and money beget workers; workers beget votes; and votes beget offices."[6]

It follows that if one party controls all the offices, it effectively controls the politics in that jurisdiction. Just such a pattern

FIGURE 5.1   Party Organizational Structure

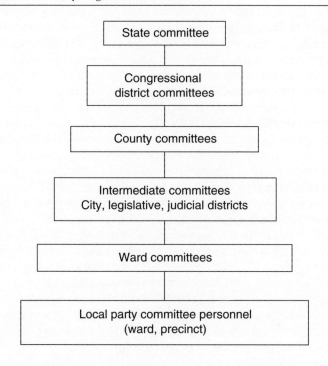

State committee

Congressional
district committees

County committees

Intermediate committees
City, legislative, judicial districts

Ward committees

Local party committee personnel
(ward, precinct)

emerged in numerous nineteenth-century towns and cities (and in a modified form in some states). Scholars have cited a number of reasons for the spread of machine politics, the most important being the growing need for an institution capable of integrating a diverse and ever increasing number of urban immigrants into American society. With state and local authorities unwilling or unable to provide immigrants with good government, political machines stepped in to fill the gap. The new Americans, confused, intimidated, or exploited by employers, landlords, or the police, could turn to party precinct captains or ward bosses for help. In return, the machine demanded electoral loyalty.

Machine politics permeated party systems from the lowest ward and precinct level up to city and in some cases state committees. Figure 5.1 shows the basic party organizational structure that emerged during this period and that still holds true in most states today. As will be developed later, this structure once was very much a "bottom up" affair, with the committees at county level and below as the key organizational units.

In spite of the emergence of a largely middle-class reform movement intent on cleansing the cities of machine politics, the machine remained an important part of the American scene until well after World War II. But some of the reforms introduced in the late nineteenth and early twentieth centuries did have a significant and lasting effect on American politics. A major concern of the reformers was to remove the partisan element from the electoral process. Accordingly, most of the proposed changes involved weakening the link between parties and electors. Party labels were removed from voting lists; elected mayors were sometimes replaced by city managers appointed by the local assembly; candidates were elected "at large" or from a list covering the whole city rather than on a ward-by-ward basis; and, most significant, *primaries* were introduced in order to deny the party machines control over nominations for office. Instead, voters were given a direct say in who was to be nominated through an intraparty primary election. These and other reforms hardly transformed the American party system. At best they had a limited effect in certain areas and regions, particularly in the more populist mountain and western states. Local party machines were, in any case, the main target of the reformers; it was in the burgeoning industrial cities that the most corrupt regimes had developed.

Primary elections, however, soon affected national parties as an increasing number of states adopted them for presidential elections. By 1916 twenty states required the parties to go directly to the voters to decide the selection of delegates to the national nominating convention (see Table 5.2) rather than rely on party machines with party bosses deciding among themselves who should go to the convention pledged to a particular candidate.

In fact, between the 1920s and the 1960s, this democratizing trend in American political parties received little fresh impetus. On the contrary, this period witnessed something of a return to old-fashioned party politics. Presidential primaries declined (to a mere sixteen or seventeen in 1968) as the nominating power reverted to the state party caucuses. At the local level, parties often found ways of bypassing the institutional obstacles to party hegemony.[7] However, it would be misleading to characterize these trends simply as a return to the old model. In many ways they were profoundly different from the late-nineteenth-century structure. Above all, after 1932 the Democratic Party emerged as the "majority" party constructed around

TABLE 5.2 Number of Presidential Primaries and Percentage of
Convention Delegates from Primary States, by Party, 1912–1996

	Democratic[a]		Republican	
	Number of Primaries	Percentage of Delegates from Primary States[b]	Number of Primaries	Percentage of Delegates
1912	12	32.9	13	41.7
1916	20	53.5	20	58.9
1920	16	44.6	20	57.8
1924	14	35.5	17	45.3
1928	17	42.2	16	44.9
1932	16	40.0	14	37.7
1936	14	36.5	12	37.5
1940	13	35.8	13	38.8
1944	14	36.7	13	38.7
1948	14	36.3	12	36.0
1952	15	38.7	13	39.0
1956	19	42.7	19	44.8
1960	16	38.3	15	38.6
1964	17	45.7	17	45.6
1968	17	37.5	16	34.3
1972	23	60.5	22	52.7
1976	29[b]	72.6	28[b]	67.9
1980	31[b]	74.7	35[b]	74.3
1984	26	62.9	30	68.2
1988	34	66.6	35	76.9
1992	39	78.8	38	80.4
1996[c]	37	83.5	41	85.9

[a] Includes party leaders and elected officials chosen from primary states.

[b] Does not include Vermont, which holds nonbinding presidential preference votes but chooses delegates in state caucuses and conventions.

[c] Based on preliminary primary and caucus schedules as of April 1995.

SOURCE: Stephen J. Wayne, *The Road to the White House, 1996* (New York: St. Martin's Press, 1996), table 6.2.

a seemingly invincible coalition consisting of the South, northern industrial workers, ethnic minorities, and an increasingly insecure middle class. Local, state, and even national Democratic Party organizations were greatly strengthened by this enduring coalition, which scored victory after victory at every level of politics. But unlike during the nineteenth century, these party organizations did not primarily function as intermediaries between the authorities and urban masses. By the 1930s, welfare and Social Security reforms reduced the dependence of the poor on party workers, and government officials themselves became increasingly professional and less susceptible to bribery and corruption. Instead, parties developed into modern organizations performing, albeit imperfectly, many of the functions previously described. The parties also became markedly more ideological, with the Democrats clearly emerging as the party of the left and the Republicans as the party of the right. Indeed, almost all the major social and economic reforms in the 1933–1968 period were initiated by Democratic administrations. Although hardly socialist in conception or outcome, these forays have resulted in a greatly increased role for the federal government in society.

But even by the 1940s there were signs that the New Deal coalition was not completely secure. The South, in particular, found unpalatable the hesitant steps taken by the Truman administration on civil rights, and by the 1968 election, the Democratic-led integration of the South resulted in open revolt, with George Wallace leading a breakaway Southern party intent on preserving racial segregation. As important, the considerable—and, in historical terms, highly atypical—ideological cohesion of the Democratic Party began to crumble as suburbanization, affluence, and a changing occupational structure slowly transformed the political agenda. The relationship between these changes and voting is detailed in Chapter 6, but how these shifts affected political parties needs brief explanation here.

Obviously, if parties are to perform their functions competently, they must have some internal cohesion. Within Congress, a party label must mean something more than mere nomenclature. If a common party is the major means whereby Congress and the president can cooperate, then the president and legislators must have at least some shared policies and perspectives. When a president staffs the executive branch, he must assume that his appointees broadly share his philosophy of government. Such party cohesion must have roots in the broader society; in effect, some form of party organization must exist to facilitate the exchange of ideas and to mobilize electoral support and nominate candidates. The apparent erosion of cohesion and party organization from the mid-1960s worried many commentators. Three major questions were raised: What was the nature of party decline? What could explain it? More controversial, does such decline really matter—especially given recent evidence of revival in the state and national parties?

Party Decline?

In *The Party's Over,* published in 1971, journalist David Broder argued that American parties were in a process of disintegration, with their main functions being replaced by special-interest groups and media images.[8] Since then, claims that the parties are declining have never been far from the surface, and by many measures, parties are much less influential now than they were in earlier eras. There are a number of ways of measuring party decline, the most common of which are membership; party identification; organization and control over candidate nominations; ideological cohesion; the role of party in government; and, of course, voting patterns, including electoral turnout.

Party membership is not a meaningful measure in the United States because it is equivalent in most states to the simple act of registering (usually as a Democrat or Republican) to vote. In other words, people do not join and pay dues in the European manner.

Party identification—the psychological attachment individual voters have to particular parties—weakened steadily from the 1960s, with the number of independents clearly on the rise, at least until the late 1970s. Weaker party identification produces a more fickle electorate prone to sudden shifts in loyalty, to ticket splitting, and to voting for individual candidates or issues rather than according to traditional party ties.

Measuring changes in party organization is rather more difficult. Certainly the party machine model no longer applies. Recent research has shown that even in what used to be archetypal machine cities such as Chicago or Philadelphia, elected officials no longer expect party loyalty and service in return for the patronage they dispense.[9] But the typical party organization described earlier still applies even if individual activists' motivations have changed.

Party organization has always been loose in the United States, and formerly it was the case that the higher the level of committee, the looser it became. Much of the essential work of fundraising and campaigning occurs at the precinct level, with the counties also playing a major role in some states. State parties vary in organizational strength. In some states (mainly in the West), state parties are quite powerful in such areas as fundraising and slating statewide candidates. Unfortunately, there is no consistent pattern; much depends on the history and tradition of individual states.

Until the 1970s it was normal to characterize the national party committees as little more than very loose ad hoc organizations that emerged every four years to help arrange the national conventions. They are much more than this today, however. The Republican National Committee (RNC), in particular, has acquired a range of new resources and powers since the 1970s, including a capacity to run direct-mail campaigns on behalf of candidates at the national and the state levels. The RNC also provides staff and technical services (polling, breakdowns of local and regional voting patterns) for candidates. Much of the impetus for this new role came from RNC chairmen William E. (Bill) Brock (1977–1981) and his successor, Frank Fahrenkopf (1981–1988), both of whom realized the potential for a national role in what had become a much more ideologically unified Republican Party. The staff of the RNC grew from a mere 30 in 1972 to 600 in 1994, and by then it had a budget of more than $100 million. In addition, the Republican committees responsible for helping House and Senate candidates also grew in strength and influence. Under the leadership of Bill Paxon of New York, the national Republican Party played a key role in the famous midterm congressional victories in 1994. The Democratic National Committee (DNC) got off to a slower start than did the Republicans, but by the late 1990s it was rivaling the Republican committee in size and influence.

Perhaps the greatest change in the role of the national committees concerns the growth of "soft money" contributions to the various national committees. "Soft money"—donations not tied to any particular candidate's campaign—is essentially unregulated by national campaign finance law. It can be used for generic advertising and issue advocacy and can be transferred to state parties, which in turn can use it to boost the election chances of state and local candidates. The rising strength of the national committees has, therefore, also helped revive state party committees. In the 1995–1996 campaign, the Republicans received more than $138 million and the Democrats $124 million in soft money. These sums represented a threefold increase for the Democrats from 1991–1992 and more than a doubling for the Republicans.

Until the 1990s, one of the most important functions performed by the DNC was the initiation of a series of inquiries into the presidential nominating process, including how the party chose delegates to the national convention. The first of these, the McGovern-Fraser Commission (1969), recommended that state parties change their rules so as to allow greater participation by minorities, women, and young people at the convention. Two subsequent inquiries, the Mikulski Commission (1972–1973) and the Winograd Commission (1975–1978), further refined these rule changes. Subsequently, the Hunt Commission (1981–1982) and the Fairness Commission (1984–1985) moved the party in a quite different direction, requiring increased representation of party regulars and elected officials (the so-called superdelegates). The background to these changes is discussed in the next section.

With regard to party activists, only about 2 percent of American adults are active participants in party organizations, almost all of which are locally based. Since the 1970s, these activists have become more candidate- and issue-oriented, with one of their primary motivations being to promote a particular candidate or to fight for one special issue. Critics argue that these trends have weakened party organization and coherence even further.

One area where the role of party organization can be accurately measured is control over nominations. At the presidential level, at least, the trend was unequivocal until 1980, by which time primaries had spread to such a degree that around 75 percent of Democratic and Republican delegates to the national conventions were chosen or bound by primary elections (Table 5.2). In quite dramatic fashion, therefore, the intraparty means of choosing delegates (party caucuses and conventions, use of which increased between 1916 and 1968) were rejected, and this key decision was left to the mass of voters. After 1980 concern in the Democratic Party in particular that it was losing control of nominations led to a partial return to the caucus method. However, even caucuses are more open to popular pressure than old-style party meetings. By 1988 the trend toward the use of primaries was reestablished, and by 1996 more than 83 percent of delegates to the conventions were chosen by this route. These particular changes have had particularly significant consequences for the state of the modern presidency.

The evidence is also strong that intraparty cohesion is weakening. Several surveys have shown how, since the mid-1960s, the issues that bound the New Deal coalition together—and that provided a convenient target for the Republicans—have either receded in importance or have been diluted by the emergence of other, less class-based issues. Until the mid-1970s, the major change involved the decline of economic issues in relation to "social" (race, gender, public morality) issues. In 1975, Walter Dean Burnham characterized this shift in the terms shown in Figure 5.2.

FIGURE 5.2   Cross-Cutting Issues in the Late 1960s and Early 1970s

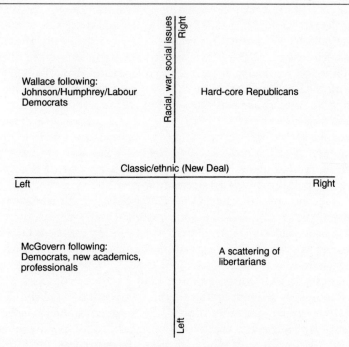

SOURCE: Adapted from William Nisbet Chambers and Walter Dean Burnham (eds.), *The American Party Systems: Stages of Political Development,* 2d ed. (New York: Oxford University Press, 1975), p. 340. Reprinted with permission.

Burnham was describing what social scientists call "cross-cutting cleavages," or the fact that individuals and social groups often lack ideological coherence across all issues. Hence in the late 1960s, many industrial workers and labor union members remained left wing on economic or class issues while finding themselves on the right of the political spectrum over racial questions and the Vietnam War. Although Figure 5.2 is now out-of-date, the phenomenon of cross-cutting cleavages is still very alive. Figure 5.3 is an attempt to characterize the divisions of the mid-1980s.

Although not shown by these two figures, which give no indication of the *distribution* of support for these issues, the major shift from the earlier period was the emergence of a more ideologically coherent right, organized around the presidency of Ronald Reagan. In the early 1970s, the majority party Democrats were in disarray,

FIGURE 5.3   Cross-Cutting Issues in the Early 1980s

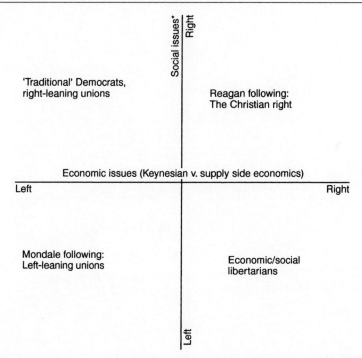

NOTE: "Social issues" include affirmative action, abortion, civil liberties, the environment.

their support split between the two left-hand segments of Figure 5.2. By the early 1980s, this division continued to affect the Democrats, and a number of commentators were claiming that the Republican right was fast assuming the status of majority party. But the Reagan victories were not to be repeated at the congressional or state levels, and by 1988 Democratic presidential prospects improved, even though George Bush was the eventual winner.

Clearly this recovery was related to the personalities of the respective candidates, but it was also related to issues. As shown in Figure 5.4, by the late 1990s it was possible to make distinctions according to the public's and candidates' association with (1) economic and welfare-state issues and (2) social-policy issues. The former refer to such matters as job security (providing a minimum notice of dismissal for laid-off workers), education, training, relief for

FIGURE 5.4   Cross-Cutting Issues in the Mid-1990s

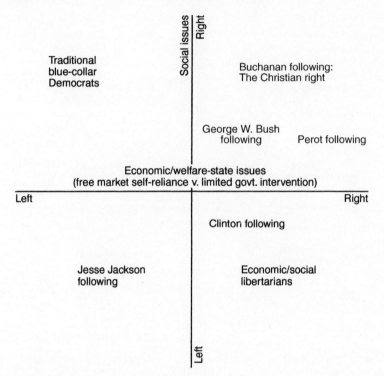

NOTE: "Social issues" include affirmative action, abortion, civil liberties, the environment.

economically distressed regions, and health care and welfare reform. The latter refer to issues of conscience and gender (abortion, civil liberties, prayer in public schools), affirmative action (civil rights enforcement), the environment, consumer protection, occupational safety, and child care. In the 1996 campaign, the three presidential candidates were closer together on the economic-welfare dimension than was the case in the 1970s and 1980s. Today, social issues are the main source of division between the parties or at least among politicians.

Indeed, as the electorate has become more volatile and a politics of personalities rather than issues has developed, so it has become increasingly difficult to characterize the parties in terms even of a loose ideological profile. Ever more complex cross-cutting issues are leading the system further and further away from the relative ideological cohesion associated with the New Deal. Such an analysis helps explain the success of Ross Perot in 1992, an independent candidate who stood as a protest candidate in opposition to traditional party politics.

In addition, the divisions in society may be so complex that they cannot be expressed in terms of two simple dimensions. Former House Speaker Newt Gingrich would look properly placed in the top right-hand segment of Figure 5.4. However, on one crucial issue, the U.S. role in the world economy, Gingrich is a "liberal"— he believes in free trade and multilateral financial organizations such as the International Monetary Fund (IMF). On this issue he is very different from fellow rightist Pat Buchanan, who opposes free trade and the IMF.

The rise of split-ticket voting provides additional evidence of a public less committed to one party or another. This topic is discussed in later chapters, but in brief, split-ticket voting and the consequent phenomenon of divided government have become the rule rather than the exception in American government.

In conclusion, political parties are now much weaker both as vote mobilizers and in terms of their ideological cohesion among the electorate. Paradoxically, however, the influence of parties *in government* has by some measures increased since the 1980s. Following the election of Ronald Reagan in 1980, the Republicans managed to forge a new unity organized around reform of the economy and conservatism on moral issues. By the mid-1990s, this new agenda was the centerpiece of the Republican electoral victories in Congress and engendered an unusual degree of ideological cohesion among House (and to a lesser extent, Senate) Republicans. This new ideological cohesion was not part of a dominant social movement rooted in the electorate in the manner of the New Deal of the 1930s. Democrats continued as the majority party among the electorate, and the dramatic Republican congressional advances in 1994 were to be partly reversed in 1996 and 1998.

Explaining Party Change

Reference has already been made to the social and economic shifts usually invoked to explain party change. Affluence, increasing levels of education, and suburbanization have produced less "solidaristic" communities, as the sociologists put it. In other words, a political life based on an individual's place of work or neighborhood has become increasingly irrelevant as the mobile service-sector worker living in a sprawling suburb or semirural area replaces the blue-collar inner-city industrial worker as the "norm" in American society. This new, essentially middle-class citizen has acquired a political life defined in terms not only of occupation or geographical location but also of individual characteristics, preferences, prejudices, and particular interests. In response to this more complex and less classifiable voter, the parties have themselves changed, becoming less programmatic and ideological. But in trying to be all things to all citizens, parties have at once raised public expectations of government while proving less adept at meeting specific demands. It stands to reason that an ideology- (or class- or region- or religion-) based party can have instant attraction to voters whose lifestyles and occupational interests coincide closely with those represented by party policies. A more amorphous, nonideological party is rarely as appealing and risks alienating a particular segment of society should it commit itself to a specific policy. Should one party decide to commit to a single position or grouping—much as did George McGovern on the left in 1972 and, to a lesser degree, as did the congressional Republicans on the right after 1994—it risks a hostile reaction by the electorate.

This sociological analysis is not universally applicable. Many groups—in particular, ethnic and racial minorities—remain solidaristic, concentrated as they are in ghettos and in lower-paid manual jobs. At the other end of the political spectrum, the Republican right has shown an impressive ideological cohesion on a range of issues. More important, this analysis suggests some simple past when American political parties represented "left" and "right" in society with reasonable coherence. But as previously noted in this chapter, this clear-cut division has never been the case. Parties have always been essentially nonideological, and even the New Deal Democratic Party was marked by a degree of internal dissension and compromise over policies that would be unusual in European class-based parties.

A related explanation for the decline of parties in the electorate concentrates less on societal changes and more on the performance of government itself. Hence, the "overload" thesis argues that the increasing democratization of American society has placed an excessive burden on what is in any case a complex decisionmaking system. Unable to cope with the array of competing demands placed on them, institutions have increasingly come under fire from a disenchanted public. Indeed, during the early 1970s, a burgeoning litera-

ture on declining trust in government hinted that public disillusionment with political institutions posed a threat to democracy itself.[10]
Although this particular argument is now largely discredited, parties
continue to take much of the blame for public disenchantment with
politics. To repeat the critics' point, the failure of parties to provide
coherent programs, to staff the government, and to help smooth relations between Congress and the president accounts for the apparently growing gap between public expectations of government and
the ability of political institutions to satisfy them.

Paradoxically, attempts within the parties to improve their performance may have aggravated the situation. By the late 1960s, activists in both parties, but particularly from within the ranks of the
Democrats, became increasingly disillusioned with the undemocratic nature of intraparty decisionmaking. Both parties were dominated by age cohorts recruited during the New Deal period—male,
white, middle-aged, and middle-income (upper-middle-income in
the case of the Republicans). The new activists, most of whom were
strongly committed to the "new" issues of the 1960s—social reform
in the case of the Democrats, economic liberalism with the Republicans—slowly but surely began to take over local and state party organizations. In doing so, they insisted on more open decisionmaking
structures and better access by underrepresented groups—within
the Democratic Party, African Americans, women, the poor, and
younger people. This quite virulent intraparty reform movement
paved the way for the spread of primary elections and for new rules
at nominating conventions favoring delegates from underrepresented groups (as recommended by the 1969 McGovern-Fraser
Commission). As previously mentioned, the spread of primaries
weakened both parties as the crucial power of control over nominations passed directly to the voters. And more open conventions led,
in the case of the Democrats, to party opinions and policies seriously out of tune with those supported by the "typical" Democratic
voter. Hence, the now famous 1972 Democratic convention was
dominated by new "social issue" delegates (see bottom left quad-
rant of Figure 5.2) whose nominee, George McGovern, had little
support from traditional "economic issue" Democrats.

Since 1972, the Democrats have modified the party rules to permit a less rigid selection of delegates and to ensure some representation of party regulars and elected officials (the so-called superdelegates), but in one important sense the change was permanent, for
the events of the late 1960s and early 1970s reduced the influence

of regular activists in myriad state and local parties. In their stead, a new breed of party volunteers took over many party organizations. Paradoxically, these new activists were more middle-class than the people they replaced, despite the fact that the rule changes were inspired by calls for equal opportunity and greater representation of the poor and minorities. The explanation is simple: People who *volunteer* their services and who care about issues are usually educated, competent, and well informed. They are also more committed to particular issues or causes. Thus party activists who support pro-life candidates in the Republican Party or pro-environment candidates in the Democratic Party are likely to hold more "extreme" positions on these issues than are typical Republican or Democratic voters.

In contrast, many of the old-style party workers were recipients of party patronage or had become active during the 1930s and 1940s when the relationship between party and class was clearer. As a result, the old-style Democratic activists, although white, male, and middle-aged, were decidedly less well educated and generally of lower socioeconomic status than the new-style party workers who replaced them. They also tended to hold generally moderate opinions on the issues of the day.

Unraveling cause and effect when explaining party change is difficult. The rise in the importance of social issues from the 1960s through the 1990s resulted in large part from changes in American society. Parties and political institutions were profoundly affected by these changes and, once affected, in turn influenced the public's perception of the performance of government. This complex interaction of institutions and society is, of course, a continuous process, and it may well be that, not only in the United States but also in other mature democracies, the age of the highly organized and effective political party is over. A crucial question is raised by this prospect: Can liberal democracy function properly without strong political parties?

Toward the Millennium:
A New Role for Political Parties

To pessimistic observers, the fact of party decline is incontrovertible. Pointing to the indicators just discussed, they reluctantly accept the demise of the parties, warn of the deleterious consequences, and plead, somewhat forlornly, for party revival, or more "consensual" institutions.[11] In essence, weak parties erode the vital five functions discussed earlier. Presidential-congressional liaison becomes difficult; presidents have few cues to guide them when appointing officials; a presidential nominating process outside the control of party boosts "media-created" candidates who may be skillful at campaigning and winning primaries but rarely make good presidents. Above all, loose amorphous parties are obliged to make general promises to the electorate rather than offer to satisfy specific demands. As a result, the public's regard for parties has declined, and the gap between public expectations of government and the ability of politicians to meet these expectations has widened.

This critique should not be accepted in full, however, without noting the following. First, amid all the furor over disintegrating parties, not a single third party has emerged with even a semblance of electoral strength. Third-party *candidates* have sometimes done well, but they represent more of a protest vote than some discernible social movement. Such was certainly the case with John Anderson in 1980 and Ross Perot in 1992 and 1996. The institutional obstacles that hinder third parties in the United States are well known and continue to apply.[12] But a much more significant obstacle is the continuing distaste among the American electorate for parties based on class, region, religion, ethnicity, or a single ideology. Second, it is important to stress again that the parties have *not* declined in the sense that they have ceased to be important *in government* or to be an indicator of electoral behavior. Instead they have *changed* and today perform rather different functions or perform traditional functions in a different manner. As already noted, state and national party organizations have been strengthened in recent years, and the influence of party in Congress has undoubtedly increased since the 1980s.

The very forces that precipitated the reforms of the early 1970s also set in motion a period of soul-searching that continues today. Notwithstanding the Democrats' inquiries into the presidential nominating process, disquiet with the ways in which Democratic candidates are selected remains (see Chapter 7). National parties are now stronger, but their authority in part depends on the support of incumbent presidents. This is one reason the Republican National Committee was able to achieve so much during the 1980s compared with its Democratic counterpart. With Bill Clinton as president, the Democratic National Committee experienced a revival during the 1990s.

Recent party revival is not equivalent to the party strength associated with smoke-filled rooms and party machines, but more, not fewer, people are now actively involved in party organizations. Party activists may be motivated more by issues or candidates than by party loyalty—which is not a new feature in American politics—but the labels "Democrat" and "Republican" continue to mean something to most Americans. This association is amply demonstrated by the continuing importance of party label in congressional elections—very few candidates dare to call themselves independents. Research has also revealed that voters, rather than being *alienated* from the parties, increasingly view them neutrally. They continue to see important differences between them but, crucially, find it difficult to link these differences to the policies of particular candidates.[13] Thus, the parties have not so much disintegrated as they have become even looser coalitions of diverse interests. In some ways, they have gained organizational strength, particularly at the national level. But their control over candidates and nominations has weakened.

The preceding analysis implies that should politics again crystallize around a few central issues, the parties are poised to resume the role they played during the New Deal period. They are not about to disappear. In the meantime, parties appear set to remain imperfect vehicles for the articulation of the complex and diverse interests and ideologies that today make up American society.

Notes

1. This list of functions—although not the discussion of them—is taken from Gerald M. Pomper, "Party Functions and Party Failures," in Gerald M. Pomper et al., *The Performance of American Government: Checks and Minuses* (New York: Free Press, 1972), pp. 46–63.

2. Anthony Downs, *An Economic Theory of Democracy* (New York: Harper and Row, 1957).

3. This has been a recurring theme among critics of the separation of powers at least since the time of Woodrow Wilson, who wrote on this subject as a political scientist before becoming president (1913–1919).

4. The classic account of the political machine is by Harold F. Gosnell, *Machine Politics: Chicago Model* (Chicago: University of Chicago Press, 1937).

5. William Riordan, *Plunkitt of Tammany Hall* (New York: E. P. Dutton, 1963), p. 63.

6. Milton Rakove, *Don't Make No Waves, Don't Back No Losers* (Bloomington: Indiana University Press, 1975), p. 42.

7. The city of Chicago, for example, was "reformed," but the mayor retained his position as "boss" through control of the Democratic Party in Cook County, which includes the city.

8. David Broder, *The Party's Over* (New York: Harper and Row, 1971).

9. For a general discussion of party decline, see Martin P. Wattenberg, *The Decline of American Political Parties, 1952–1994* (Cambridge, MA: Harvard University Press, 1996).

10. See, in particular, the tenth anniversary edition of *The Public Interest*, No. 41, Fall 1975.

11. An eloquent essay on this theme is Samuel P. Huntington, *American Politics: The Promise of Disharmony* (Cambridge, MA: Harvard University Press, 1981).

12. The American electoral system puts additional burdens on third parties, for all states require a minimum number of registered voters to sign a petition before a party can field a candidate. Also, acquiring strength in one state or region—the usual pattern for American third parties—is rarely enough to ensure national impact. Victory in a presidential election is achievable only via mass national support, and without at least the prospect of winning at this level, third parties cannot hope to be taken seriously.

13. See Martin P. Wattenberg, *The Rise of Candidate-Centered Politics* (Cambridge, MA: Harvard University Press, 1991).

Further Reading

An excellent account of the origins and changes in the party system is provided by John H. Aldrich, *Why Parties? The Origin and Transformation of Political Parties in America* (Chicago: University of Chicago Press, 1995). The best historical (but analytical) account of American parties is William Nisbet Chambers and Walter Dean Burnham (eds.), *The American Party Systems: Stages of Political Development* (New York: Oxford University Press, 1975). See also David R. Mayhew, *Placing Parties in American Politics* (Princeton, NJ: Princeton University Press, 1986). A good recent account of party decline is Martin P. Wattenberg, *The Decline of American Political Parties, 1952–1994* (Cambridge, MA: Harvard University Press, 1996). One of the better textbook treatments of parties is William J. Keefe, *Parties, Politics, and Public Policy in America*, 8th ed. (Washington, DC: Congressional Quarterly Press, 1998). L. Sandy Maisel's *The Parties Respond: Changes in American Parties and Campaigns* (Boulder, CO: Westview, 1998) is a good collection of essays on changes in the party system.

6

Political Participation
and Electoral Behavior

Elections commit the people to a sense of responsibility for their own betterment . . . It seems clear that they are essential to us as props of the sentiment of legitimacy and the sentiment of participation.

—W.J.M. Mackenzie

There is currently a widespread sense, shown by public opinion surveys and complaints by informed observers, that the American electoral system is in trouble. Some believe that this trouble is minor and can be dealt with through moderate reforms; others think it goes deep and requires extensive political surgery, perhaps accompanied by sweeping changes in the larger social order.

—A. James Reichley

America's claim to status as a democratic country depends almost entirely on the nature and extent of public participation in political life, and from the earliest years of the republic, there has been dispute and controversy over what, precisely, participation means. To the educated eighteenth-century man, "democracy" was equivalent to a republican form of government that limited electoral participation to those with an established stake in society—white men of property. Any further extension of participation raised the specter of rule by the mob and the eventual breakdown of civil society. In contrast, many artisans and small farmers, especially in New England, were imbued with a more egalitarian brand of democracy that implied participation by a much wider electorate. Slowly, during the nineteenth and twentieth centuries, this egalitarian spirit gained ascendancy over the more elitist views of the founding fathers.

Today, the degree of electoral participation would truly shock an eighteenth-century observer. Measured in terms of the number of public offices open to electoral choice, democracy is at its fullest in the United States; some 530,000 posts are elected, from the humblest local officials to local and state judges, mayors, council members, governors, and legislators to the vice-president, president, and members of the U.S. Congress. In addition, many Americans vote in primary elections to nominate which party candidates will stand in the election proper. Many states and localities have also introduced a number of devices associated with populism or direct democracy. Hence, some citizens vote in referenda or in initiative and recall elections, all of which are designed to give the voter a direct say in policymaking.[1] Further, there no formal barriers to the participation of any particular social group. Property and tax-paying restrictions were abolished by the 1830s, effectively enfranchising all adult white males. Women won the right to vote in national elections following the adoption of the Nineteenth Amendment in 1920. Formal restrictions on southern blacks' electoral participation were swept away by the 1965 Voting Rights Act and by a number of Supreme Court decisions. Finally, the Twenty-sixth Amendment, ratified in 1971, reduced the minimum voting age to eighteen.

The simple measure of electoral access, therefore, attests to the democratic nature of the American system. Yet as the discussion of political parties revealed, participation entails far more than mere access to elections. More important are questions of *choice* and *control* over government policy. Many people ask whether the United States can be "truly" democratic when electoral turnout is so low and when the choice offered by elections is often so narrow. Others probe further and argue that the rhetoric and commercialization typical of U.S. elections serve to raise public expectations of what politicians can do. When they fail to deliver, disillusionment and cynicism result. The remainder of this chapter is devoted to these and related questions. The first section focuses on electoral behavior—why Americans vote as they do, what sort of choice they are offered by the electoral process, and how patterns of behavior have changed over time. The second section introduces a discussion of nonelectoral participation that will be continued in later chapters.

Patterns of American Electoral Behavior

Basic Questions

Observers of voting behavior usually first ask the simplest and most obvious question: "Who has voted for which party?" Thus, findings from opinion polls indicate that support for a particular party has risen or fallen or that some region, ethnic, or social group has shifted its allegiance away from or toward a party. Survey or poll data have helped to establish some very general norms or expectations about people's voting behavior. The data in Table 6.1, showing the distribution of votes by social group in the 1996 presidential election, confirm tendencies that apply in most democratic countries: White voters and those of higher socioeconomic status tend to be more conservative (i.e., voted for Dole) than younger, lower-status, ethnic minority voters. Table 6.1 also reveals patterns that may be peculiarly American: The South appears markedly more conservative than the East; women are more prone to vote Democratic than are men.

But even these general trends provoke a number of deeper questions. What, precisely, is meant by "conservative" and "liberal" in the American context? To what extent does the *party* as opposed to candidates and issues determine voting behavior? It must be that the balance of influence shifts quite markedly among the three, for some candidates manage to overcome party ties and attract voters from the other party—hence the phenomenon of the "Reagan Democrats" during the 1980s when many traditional Democratic voters switched their allegiance to the Republicans. Other questions arise. Why are African Americans so overwhelmingly Democratic in their loyalties? What accounts for the regional variations in voting behavior? These questions are examined in detail later, but for now it should be noted that American voting behavior seems considerably more complex than electoral participation in other countries. In many European countries, for example, class, regional, ethnic, or religious divisions are quite clearly defined and can act as accurate predictors of voting intentions. In the United States, however, because the political parties are loose coalitions and ideological and other social cleavages are relatively weak, analyzing who votes for whom and why becomes more difficult.

In broad terms, the Democrats can be categorized as the liberal or even "left" party and Republicans as the conservative or "right" party, but when the range of candidates in each party is examined, numerous exceptions to these generalizations are evident. To complicate matters further, federalism and the separation of powers have spawned myriad elections and distinctive levels of government, each with a different constituency. At the national level, this diversity shows itself most graphically in the relationship between

TABLE 6.1 Distribution of the 1996 Presidential Vote by Social Group and Issues (percent)

	Clinton	Dole	Perot	Total
Sex and race				
Men	44	44	10	48
Women	54	37	7	52
White men	39	48	11	48
White women	49	42	8	52
White	44	45	9	83
Black	83	12	4	10
Hispanic	72	21	5	4
Age				
18–29	53	34	11	16
30–44	49	40	9	32
45–59	48	41	9	26
60 plus	49	43	7	25
Income				
<$30,000	56	33	10	35
30–49,000	48	40	10	28
50–74,999	49	45	7	21
>75,000	42	50	6	18
Region				
East	55	34	9	22
Mid-West	48	40	10	26
South	47	46	7	30
West	49	39	8	22
Political ideology				
Liberal	78	11	7	20
Moderate	57	32	9	47
Conservative	20	71	8	33
Condition of the economy				
Excellent/good	64	30	5	56
Not so good/poor	32	52	14	42
Most important issues and qualities				
Medicare and Social Security	67	26	6	15
Taxes	18	73	7	11
Economy and jobs	61	27	10	21
Federal deficit	28	51	19	12
Shares my view of government	42	45	10	20
Is honest and trustworthy	9	84	7	20
Has vision of the future	77	12	9	16

SOURCE: *Washington Post* exit poll as reported in *The Washington Post*, November 6, 1996, p. A5.

presidential and congressional elections. Individual members of Congress are beholden to their own constituents, whose interests may be quite separate from those of the national electorate responsible for electing the president. In earlier eras, the successful party at the presidential election would also be at least partly successful at the congressional level, but in recent years voters have increasingly split their tickets and voted for one party at the congressional level and the other at the presidential level. In 1972, for example, the near-landslide victory of a Republican president, Richard Nixon, was not accompanied by any significant inroads by his party into the Democratic majorities in both houses of Congress. The pattern was similar in 1984, 1988, 1992, and 1996. In 1996, Bill Clinton won the presidency for the Democrats, but the Republicans retained control of both houses of Congress.

A second question raised in any simple description of voting behavior is, who actually votes? A wealth of social science and professional opinion poll research has enabled analysts to make quite accurate assessments of electoral participation patterns. Very generally, people of higher socioeconomic status (a combination of income, occupation, and education) vote and participate in other political activities to a much greater extent than people of lower socioeconomic status.[2] The relationship between voting and age is more complex, with participation rising from a low at age eighteen to a peak during middle age and then declining slightly in later-middle and old age.

Until the late 1960s, one of the most dramatic differences in participation was between black and white Americans. Until the civil rights legislation of the mid-1960s, very few southern blacks were able to register to vote (for example, in 1964 a mere 7 percent in Mississippi), and among those registered, actual turnout was low. Since the 1965 Voting Rights Act, however, registration has steadily increased, and by 1990 the percentage of African Americans registered to vote was only 8 percent below the figure for whites. Black turnout remains generally below that of whites but mainly because a disproportionate number of blacks are of lower socioeconomic status.

Finally, turnout among women is slightly higher than for men. However, the gap is small (around 2 percent), and compared with differences based on socioeconomic status and age, voter participation rates of men and women are comparatively close.

A third basic question is, how many of the people actually vote? In the United States, turnout is notoriously low for all elections. Even the contest perceived by most people as the most significant—electing the president—does not inspire a high level of mass participation. Since 1960 turnout has been declining and now rarely exceeds 55 percent for presidential elections and 50 percent for congressional contests (see Table 6.2). In 1996 turnout sank to 48.4 percent—the lowest for a presidential election since 1924. At the state and local levels, turnout is even lower and can fall as low as 20 percent.

This seeming political apathy has long puzzled and disturbed American political scientists. Explanations usually fall into one of two categories—institutional and noninstitutional. The institutional barriers to voting are, in fact, considerable, although claims that the formidable *number* of elections reduces turnout are probably erroneous. After all, turnout at presidential elections remains low in spite of their relative infrequency and the disproportionate amount of publicity and attention paid to them by political parties and the media.

More significant are America's voter registration laws. Under the laws of individual states, voters must themselves make the decision to register, and most states apply minimum residency requirements. Although for presidential elections this requirement has been reduced by Congress to only thirty days, the fact remains that in a mobile, open society, many people fail to register or to register in time. Unlike most European countries, the United States has no automatic nationally organized compulsory registration system, and recent studies have shown that were such a system introduced, turnout might increase by between 10 and 12 percent. In 1993 Congress passed the "motor voter" law, which encouraged states to allow people to register to vote whenever they applied to renew their driver's license. Although by some estimates this measure increased the number of citizens registered to vote by 9 million by 1996, there is little evidence that these new registrants actually voted. Indeed, 1996 exit polls showed that the percentage of first-time voters (of all those voting) dropped from 11 percent to 9 percent.[3]

Nonvoting may also be linked to the fact that the United States has a simple-majority, single-member-district electoral system rather than one based on proportional representation (PR). By closely relating votes cast to representation in legislatures, PR "wastes" few votes. Under a single-member-district system, however, voters know that in many constituencies, their vote will make no difference because of the large majority enjoyed by one party. Their incentive to vote is, therefore, reduced. In fact, if turnout is measured in terms of

128

TABLE 6.2 Voter Turnout in Presidential and House Elections,
1930–1998 (percent of voting-age population)

	Presidential Elections	House Elections
1930	—	33.7
1932	52.4	49.7
1934	—	41.4
1936	56.9	53.5
1938	—	44.0
1940	58.9	55.4
1942	—	32.5
1944	56.0	52.7
1946	—	37.1
1948	51.1	48.1
1950	—	41.1
1952	61.6	57.6
1954	—	41.7
1956	59.3	55.9
1958	—	43.0
1960	62.6	58.5
1962	—	45.4
1964	61.9	57.8
1966	—	45.4
1968	60.9	55.1
1970	—	43.5
1972	55.4	50.9
1974	—	36.1
1976	54.4	49.5
1978	—	35.1
1980	53.4	48.1
1982	—	37.7
1984	53.3	47.4
1986	—	33.4
1988	50.1	44.7
1990	—	33.0
1992	55.2	50.8
1994	—	36.0
1996	49.0	47.0
1998	—	38.0

SOURCE: Norman J. Ornstein, Thomas E. Mann, Michael J. Malbin, Allen Schick, and John F. Bibby, *Vital Statistics on Congress,* 1991–92 ed. (Washington, DC: American Enterprise Institute), table 2.1. Data for 1998 from http://cnn.com/allpolitics.

TABLE 6.3   Voter Turnout by Voting-Age Population and Registered
Voters, Selected Countries

Vote as a Percentage of Voting-Age Population			*Vote as a Percentage of Registered Voters*		
1	Italy	94.0	1	Belgium	94.6
2	Austria	89.3	2	Australia	94.5
3	Belgium	88.7	3	Austria	91.6
4	Sweden	86.8	4	Sweden	90.7
5	Portugal	85.9	5	Italy	90.4
6	Greece	84.9	6	Iceland	89.3
7	Netherlands	84.7	7	New Zealand	89.0
8	Australia	83.1	8	Luxembourg	88.9
9	Denmark	82.1	9	W. Germany	88.6
10	Norway	81.8	10	Netherlands	87.0
11	W. Germany	81.1	11	*United States*	86.8
12	New Zealand	78.5	12	France	85.9
13	France	78.0	13	Portugal	84.2
14	United Kingdom	76.0	14	Denmark	83.2
15	Japan	74.4	15	Norway	82.0
16	Spain	73.0	16	Greece	78.6
17	Canada	67.4	17	Israel	78.5
18	Finland	63.0	18	United Kingdom	76.3
19	Ireland	62.3	19	Japan	74.5
20	*United States*	52.6	20	Canada	69.3
21	Switzerland	39.4	21	Spain	68.1
			22	Finland	64.3
			23	Ireland	62.2
			24	Switzerland	48.3

NOTE: U.S. data are for presidential elections.

SOURCE: Adapted from Nelson W. Polsby and Aaron Wildavsky, *Presidential Elections,* 8th ed. (New York: Free Press, 1991), tables 5.3 and 5.4.

the number of people who are registered, the picture is very different (Table 6.3). Nonetheless, Americans remain concerned about their rate of voter participation. The U.S. data in Table 6.3 are for presidential elections. Turnout for House and Senate elections—which are, after all, for national offices—is low by international standards. Moreover, an increasingly educated population should lead to an improvement in turnout. However, 1992 excepted, the opposite has been the case.

Very broadly, two schools of thought have attempted to explain low voter turnout: public-choice theory and the sociological view.

Public-choice theorists argue that it is simply not rational to vote when the choice offered by parties is so limited. The relative absence of well-defined and deep-rooted social cleavages articulated by class, ethnic, or regionally based parties reduces the direct and immediate interest voters have in ensuring that their preferred party is represented in government. American parties and candidates rarely promise social revolution, nor do they often promise to defend well-defined sectional, class, religious, or ethnic interests. Moreover, recent research has shown that citizens often vote *retrospectively*, or they decide to vote for party A rather than party B by judging an incumbent's past performance—usually in terms of whether the party's period in office has increased the voter's real income. As Morris Fiorina and others have shown, it is increasingly difficult to make this calculation when party programs are so diffuse and when the appeal to voters is by individual candidates rather than parties.[4]

This more atomized, individualized politics may account for the decline of voting among all social groups since 1960. Interestingly, voter turnout went up slightly in 1992 following a period when many voters' real incomes had declined. Many people voted against President Bush on economic grounds and instead put their faith in Clinton (or Perot) as a vote for economic change. By way of contrast, turnout declined in 1996 in the context of a relatively healthy economy. Although the very low turnout of that year (48.4 percent) could be interpreted as voter apathy or even alienation, it could also be that most voters were relatively happy with their economic lot and therefore saw little point in voting for change. Among those who did vote, the appeal of the candidates rather than programs and policies may have been paramount.

The sociological school argues, simply, that citizens who are poorer and less well educated vote less than those who are richer and better educated. The data certainly confirm this, with more than 50 percent of manual workers apparently excluded from voting altogether.[5] Again, this is a uniquely American phenomenon. In other democracies, the (usually much smaller) number of nonvoters is drawn from all social groups, with few citizens caught in a pattern of permanent nonvoting. Nonvoting among members of lower-status groups can also be linked to rational expectations. Their sense of political effectiveness tends to be lower because they are poorer and, as important, they find it difficult to identify with a party that fails to appeal to voters on class lines. Significantly, since 1968, the party that formerly projected such an appeal, the

Democratic Party, moved further away from class-based politics and toward issue- and candidate-based politics.

Concern about nonvoting in the United States is compounded by the fact that an increasingly educated and sophisticated population should have led to increased rather than decreased electoral participation. This phenomenon, above all, confirms political scientists' claims that voters cannot easily make rational decisions when faced by inchoate parties and a politics based on individual officeholders unable to offer effective programs of social and economic change.

"The American Voter" Model and the New Deal Coalition

During the 1950s and early 1960s, a number of published studies established a "model" of American voting behavior. (The seminal work was *The American Voter*, published in 1960.)[6] The unique contribution of this work was to explain the voting of individual citizens in terms of *psychological* orientations. By asking survey respondents how they felt about parties, candidates, and issues and then relating these sentiments to political behavior, researchers built up a cognitive picture of how individuals thought about politics. The results were surprising, to say the least. In a more recent study, Nie, Verba, and Petrocik summarized the findings thus:

> The American public had a remarkably unsophisticated view of political matters characterized by an inability to consider such matters in broad abstract terms. . . . Citizens had inconsistent views when one looked across a range of issues. . . . Most Americans had strong, long-term commitments to one of the major political parties and this commitment served as a guide to their political behavior. . . . Citizens felt relatively satisfied with the political system and relatively efficacious.[7]

Very few respondents—a mere 2.5 percent—in the sample studied in *The American Voter* were categorized as ideologues, or people who thought about politics in abstract terms. Most evaluated candidates and parties in terms of the benefits they brought to social groups (42 percent) or in terms of the "nature of the times" (24 percent). In other words, most voters had little sense of "left" and "right" or the role that parties and candidates might play in moving society in a particular direction. Instead, immediate or recent events or simple promises by politicians to lower taxation, say, or to increase social spending influenced voters. Reinforcement of this analysis was provided by studies showing that voters were often inconsistent in their views across issues. Some citizens favored increased social spending but also wanted a reduced role for government in society; anti-Communists did not always approve of an increased role for the United States as international police force. Most important, when attitudes on all issues were examined, researchers could not identify any pattern consistent with a coherently thought-out ideology, whether liberal, conservative, socialist, or other.[8]

The image projected, therefore, is one of a rather ill-informed voter who does not think about politics to a significant degree. However, in one important respect, American voters were found to be consistent—in their attachment to political parties, voters displayed enduring loyalties. Labeling this phenomenon *party identification,* voting analysts discovered that people acquired a positive or negative psychological attachment to a party early in childhood that remained with them throughout their lives.

In essence, citizens were *socialized* by family and other social cues into thinking of themselves as Democrats or Republicans, a factor that may explain why 78 percent of respondents to a 1958 survey had the same party identification as their parents. Not all voters were found to be strong party identifiers. Some identified less clearly with a party, while others considered themselves either independent or independently supportive of one or the other of the parties.

The data presented in Table 6.4 for voting in presidential elections raise an interesting question: How did the Republicans manage to win in 1952, 1956, 1968, 1972, 1980, 1984, and 1988, given the built-in Democrat majority implied by the preponderance of Democratic identifiers (Figure 6.1)?

In answering this question, political scientists at first stressed that party identification was very much a psychological orientation to politics. There may be elections when voters deviate from their normal identification because of the particular appeal of the candidate (as was the case in the 1950s with Dwight Eisenhower) or because of the importance of certain issues (for example, law and order in 1968). Obviously, however, the Democratic majority must come from somewhere; it cannot be purely psychological. The answer is that there have been certain periods in American history when rapid social and economic changes have forged new political coalitions. During these periods, orientations toward parties

TABLE 6.4 Presidential Election Results, 1928–1996

	Candidates	Party	Electoral College Vote	Popular Vote	Percentage Share	Number of States Won[a]
1928	Herbert Hoover	Republican	444	21,392,190	58.2	42
	Alfred E. Smith	Democratic	87	15,016,443	40.8	6 (all Southern)
	Norman Thomas	Socialist	0	267,420	1.0	0
1932	Franklin D. Roosevelt	Democratic	472	22,821,857	57.3	42
	Herbert Hoover	Republican	59	15,761,841	39.6	6 (all Northeastern)
	Norman Thomas	Socialist	0	884,781	2.2	0
1936	Franklin D. Roosevelt	Democratic	523	27,751,597	60.7	46
	Alfred M. Landon	Republican	8	16,679,583	36.4	2 (Maine and Vermont)
	Norman Thomas	Socialist	0	187,720	0.5	0
1940	Franklin D. Roosevelt	Democratic	449	27,244,160	54.7	38
	Wendell L. Wilkie	Republican	82	22,305,198	44.8	10
	Norman Thomas	Socialist	0	99,557	0.2	0
1944	Franklin D. Roosevelt	Democratic	432	25,602,504	52.8	36
	Thomas E. Dewey	Republican	99	22,006,285	44.5	12
	Norman Thomas	Socialist	0	80,518	0.2	0
1948	Harry S. Truman	Democratic	303	24,179,345	49.5	32
	Thomas E. Dewey	Republican	189	21,991,291	45.1	12
	J. Strom Thurmond	States' Rights Dem.	39	1,176,125	2.4	4 (all Southern)
	Henry A. Wallace	Progressive	0	1,157,326	2.4	0

(continues)

TABLE 6.4 (continued)

	Candidates	Party	Electoral College Vote	Popular Vote	Percentage Share	Number of States Won[a]
	Norman Thomas	Socialist	0	139,572	0.2	0
1952	Dwight D. Eisenhower	Republican	442	33,936,234	55.2	40
	Adlai E. Stevenson	Democratic	89	27,314,992	44.5	8 (all Southern)
1956	Dwight D. Eisenhower	Republican	457	35,590,472	57.4	41
	Adlai E. Stevenson	Democratic	73	26,022,752	42.0	7 (all Southern)
1960	John F. Kennedy	Democratic	303	34,226,731	49.9	23[b]
	Richard M. Nixon	Republican	219	34,108,157	49.6	26
1964	Lyndon B. Johnson	Democratic	486	43,129,484	61.1	46
	Barry M. Goldwater	Republican	52	27,178,188	38.5	5 (Southern and Arizona)
1968	Richard M. Nixon	Republican	301	31,785,480	43.3	32
	Hubert H. Humphrey	Democratic	191	31,275,166	42.7	14
	George C. Wallace	American Independent	46	9,906,473	13.5	5 (all Southern)
1972	Richard M. Nixon	Republican	520	47,169,911	61.3	49
	George McGovern	Democratic	17	29,170,383	37.3	2 (DC and Massachusetts)
	John G. Schmitz	American	0	1,099,482	1.4	0

Year	Candidate	Party				
1976	Jimmy Carter	Democratic	297	40,830,763	50.1	24
	Gerald R. Ford	Republican	240	39,147,973	48.0	27
	Eugene J. McCarthy	Independent	0	756,631	1.0	0
1980	Ronald Reagan	Republican	489	42,951,145	51.0	46
	Jimmy Carter	Democratic	49	34,663,037	41.0	5
	John B. Anderson	Independent	0	5,551,551	7.0	0
1984	Ronald Reagan	Republican	525	54,450,603	59.2	49
	Walter Mondale	Democratic	13	37,573,671	40.8	2 (DC and Minnesota)
1988	George Bush	Republican	426	47,917,341	54.0	40
	Michael Dukakis	Democratic	112	41,013,030	46.0	11
1992	Bill Clinton	Democratic	370	44,908,233	43.0	32
	George Bush	Republican	168	39,102,282	37.4	18
	Ross Perot	Independent	0	19,741,048	18.9	0
1996	Bill Clinton	Democratic	379	47,401,504	49.2	31
	Bob Dole	Republican	159	39,197,350	40.7	19
	Ross Perot	Independent	0	8,085,285	8.4	0

a From 1960 includes Alaska and Hawaii. From 1964 includes Washington, DC.

b 15 electoral college votes were cast for segregational candidate Harry F. Byrd, including eight in Mississippi, which he effectively "won."

FIGURE 6.1 Party Identification in the United States, 1952–1996

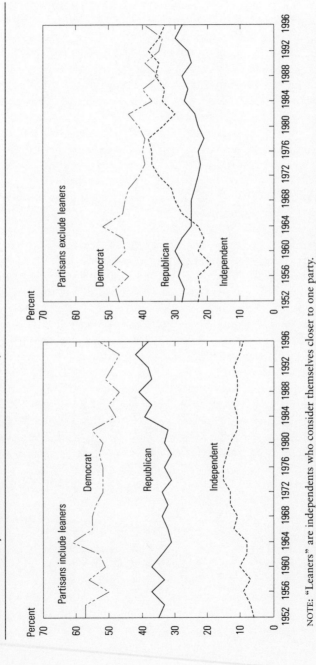

NOTE: "Leaners" are independents who consider themselves closer to one party.
SOURCE: Calculated from National Election Studies by Harold W. Stanley and Richard G. Niemi, *Vital Statistics on American Politics, 1997–1998* (Washington, DC: Congressional Quarterly Press, 1998), figure 3.1.

change as the parties themselves come to represent an emergent social group or region. By implication, during these years of turbulence, the voter is indeed guided by the issues and by objective economic and social circumstances.

Political scientists have called such transition periods of *realignment* when new electoral majorities are built. Between 1896 and 1928, the Republican Party reigned supreme. Urbanization, depression, the naturalization and integration of new immigrant groups, and the emergence of an organized working class transformed party politics during the 1920s and early 1930s, however, and culminated in the resounding Democratic victory of 1932 (Table 6.4). From the late 1920s, the Democrats became the party associated with the urban working class, trade unions, and the underprivileged. The nearly invincible New Deal coalition was assured because of the support guaranteed by the traditionally Democratic South. By the mid-1930s, the intellectual establishment and many members of an insecure middle class had joined the coalition, and this grouping produced the *maintaining* elections of 1936, 1940, 1944, and 1948. Not until incumbent Democrats (most notably Harry Truman) began to support civil rights for southern blacks did the first cracks in the majority appear (in 1948).

The Republican victories of 1952 and 1956 were, according to the scholars, *deviating* elections. In other words, the Democrats remained the "natural" majority party, but the specific circumstances of these elections allowed the Republicans to triumph. Eisenhower was an avuncular, charismatic war hero; in contrast, Adlai Stevenson, the Democratic candidate, projected an aloof, intellectual, and narrow eastern-establishment image. This personality contrast was, above all, responsible for the Republican victories. Significantly, these successes were only partly repeated at the congressional level. Republicans had victories in 1946 and 1952, but after 1954 Congress was firmly controlled by the Democrats.

Decline of Partisanship and of the New Deal Coalition

This neat and appealing theory of electoral behavior seemed to be reinforced by the 1960 and 1964 presidential elections. Democratic victories returned, with the Republicans reverting to their normal status as the minority party. However, from about 1964 to the late 1970s, a number of developments appeared that collectively presented a rather serious challenge to the accepted theory.

Lessening of Partisanship.   A popular interpretation of Richard
Nixon's victory in 1968 was that it heralded a new Republican majority.[9] More citizens were suburban, middle class, and conservative, so the Republicans should have found themselves ascendant.
Moreover, the South, so long solidly Democratic, could no longer
tolerate the integrationist policies of Democratic presidents.

Superficially, the 1972 election seemed to reinforce these trends
(Table 6.4). Yet 1968 and 1972 were not classic *realigning elections*
like 1932. The number of Republican Party identifiers did not increase but instead decreased slightly during these years (see Figure
6.1), and the Democrats retained their dominance of Congress.
Likewise, at the state level, there was little evidence of an unstop-
pable Republican surge.

However, Democratic Party identification also declined during the
1960s. This fact, together with the rise of independent identifiers, led
some commentators to speculate that what was occurring was party
dealignment, or the slow demise of party identification as a key indicator of political preference. By 1976, this process of dealignment
seemed to have stabilized (Figure 6.1), but at the same time, neither
party had recaptured center stage in the way the Republicans did
after 1896 or the Democrats did after 1932.

Another indicator of declining partisanship is "ticket splitting,"
or the tendency of voters to divide their loyalties between candidates of different parties. As can be seen from Table 6.5, ticket
splitting rose sharply from 1952 to 1980. By that year, some 34
percent of voters split their tickets between presidential and House
candidates. A similar picture emerged for statewide offices (elections for senators, governors, state legislatures) in a number of
states and regions.

Increase in Candidate and Issue Voting.   A natural corollary to a
decline in partisanship is that citizens (or at least citizens who vote)
are using some other criterion when deciding for whom to vote.
Candidates and issues had always played some part in the voting
calculus, of course, but from the 1960s they began to play a much
more prominent role. It follows that if people are voting for individual candidates or for particular issues, the electorate is much
more sophisticated than implied by *The American Voter* model. Indeed, in their 1976 work, *The Changing American Voter,* Nie,
Verba, and Petrocik discovered that from about 1964 voters
showed a significantly increased consistency in their views on do-

TABLE 6.5 Key Indicators of Dealignment, 1952–1988

	1952	1956	1960	1964	1968	1972	1976	1980	1984	1988
Percentage identifying with a party	75	73	75	77	70	64	63	64	64	63
Percentage splitting their ticket between president and House	12	16	14	15	26	30	25	34	25	25
Percentage splitting their ticket between Senate and House	9	10	9	18	22	23	23	31	20	27
Percentage neutral toward both parties	13	16	17	20	17	30	31	37	36	30
Percentage positive toward one party and negative toward the other	50	40	41	38	38	30	31	27	31	34

SOURCE: SRC/CPS National Election Studies, reproduced from Martin P. Wattenberg, *The Rise of Candidate-Centered Politics* (Cambridge, MA: Harvard University Press, 1991), table 2.2.

mestic and foreign policy issues. Unlike the unthinking citizen portrayed by *The American Voter,* the public appeared more able to see the connections among issues, parties, and candidates and to view the world in terms of broad ideological categories such as "liberal" or "conservative."

Certainly, presidential elections took on a more ideological stance after 1964. The Goldwater-Johnson contest of that year was clearly a conflict between conservative and liberal, as were the later contests among Humphrey, Nixon, and Wallace (1968) and, more especially, between McGovern and Nixon (1972). In 1976 there was a marked decline in ideological voting, almost certainly because the two candidates projected rather bland images and few issues clearly divided them. A return to a clear-cut choice came in 1980, however, with the conservative Ronald Reagan facing an incumbent president, Jimmy Carter, identified—albeit reluctantly on his part—with the liberal cause. The 1984 election also presented a clear-cut choice, with Ronald Reagan appealing directly to the right and Walter Mondale to liberals and the left. In 1988, however, the two candidates were much closer together on basic issues—so much so, in fact, that George Bush worked hard to label Michael Dukakis a "liberal" so as to secure the conservative vote. George Bush found his identification with conservative policies a liability in 1992, however, when the electorate called for new economic policies following a period of recession. Bob Dole tried to learn this lesson four years later in 1996 when he worked hard to capture the middle ground. Incumbent Bill Clinton also moved to the center, and in the context of a healthy economy, this was sufficient for him to win reelection.

Twilight of the New Deal Coalition. Declining partisanship and the rise of what has been called "issue voting" raise a number of questions. An important issue was addressed in the last chapter—the failure of the political parties to exploit the new interest in politics by providing the electorate with coherent and ideologically consistent programs. Indeed, to many foreign observers, the combination of more ideological voters but declining parties and partisanship should be slightly baffling. Shouldn't parties surely be stronger in such a context? But as has been pointed out in earlier chapters, the complexity of the issues dominating the political agenda and the recent changes in American society have made it impossible for the parties to know what to say and to whom. Recall that in order to win, American political parties have to build broad coalitions of support. And research has shown that although there has been a rise in ideological thinking among some of the electorate, it hardly dominates.

The price of presenting to voters an unequivocally ideological program was revealed in 1972, when George McGovern's evangelizing liberalism was rewarded by a landslide victory for his Republican opponent. In sum, rather than parties and issues coinciding and thus strengthening partisanship, the opposite has been happening. Issues and individual candidates have gained importance independently of parties and have often done so in a way that seriously damages a party's fortunes. Hence in 1968 and 1972, Vietnam and social issues —a combination of law and order, civil rights, and civil liberties— dominated. Liberals within the Democratic Party found themselves seriously at odds with some of the traditional Democratic supporters on these issues. Southerners were conservative on civil rights, and a large number of blue-collar workers were consistently conservative on Vietnam and social issues. This combination helps explain Richard Nixon's victories in 1968 and 1972. Nixon's success seemed to herald the beginning of the end for the New Deal coalition. At the level of presidential elections, the South was moving rapidly into the Republican camp, and the now dominant social issues divided rather than unified the Democrats.

Some have argued that Ronald Reagan's 1980 and 1984 victories were in a different category. He won, so the theory goes, because his economic policies coincided nicely with what the electorate wanted. Disillusioned with high levels of public spending and inflation, the public had acquired an *ideological* aversion to big government. Ronald Reagan's promise of a new prosperity based on free-market principles offered an irresistible alternative. Concomitant with the success of this issue appeal came a revival of the Republican Party, and because the party became identified with "Reaganomics," some commentators claimed that a permanent realignment was under way.

Yet, as shown in Figure 6.1, the number of Republican identifiers did not increase markedly either in 1980 or in 1984. Moreover, the public's attitudes on economic issues were not as unambiguously ideological as the more optimistic of the Republican supporters claimed. Everyone wants a healthy economy, of course, but if the price of low inflation—the major objective of Reagan's program— was high unemployment, then large sections of Republican support were likely to fall away. This is exactly what happened during the 1982 midterm elections when Republican candidates associated with the administration's economic policies fared particularly badly. President Reagan's 1984 victory was no doubt attributable to a number of factors, including his personal popularity. But few commentators doubt that the rapid recovery of the economy in 1983 and 1984 was crucial.

These electoral results suggest that 1980 and 1984 were far from being realigning elections. Much the same could be said for the 1988 contest, when the Democrats made further inroads into the House and Senate while once again losing the presidency. In 1992, the Democratic victory was achieved in the context of what was widely perceived to be a damaging recession. The incumbent, George Bush, was accordingly punished by the voters. Efforts by Bush to appeal to the Christian right on a range of moral issues actually harmed his cause—even among some Republicans—because most voters felt much less strongly on these issues than they did about the economy. A revived economy and a move to the center ground of American politics by Bill Clinton ensured his reelection in 1996.

Dealignment, Realignment, and the Modern American Voter

Although the presidential election results of 1992 and 1996 suggest there is no realignment of American voters toward the Republican Party, some evidence of the beginnings of a realignment does exist. In particular, the Republican congressional victories in 1994 and 1996, together with major advances by the party at the state and local levels, led many commentators to believe that a "real" realignment was under way.[10]

Such claims are boosted by the changing pattern of party identification since 1990. As can be seen from Table 6.6, although in 1994 the Democrats remained the largest party in terms of identifiers, the Republicans were catching up fast. Note also the decline in the number of independents during the 1976–1996 period. Since 1994, however, the Democrats have recovered slightly, and the number of Republican identifiers appears to have stabilized at around the 40 percent level, which implies that old-style party is far from dead. In an important book published in 1992, a group of scholars based at the University of California, Berkeley, and at Brigham Young University argued that the decline of party voting

TABLE 6.6 Party Identification by Election Cycle, 1976–1996 (percent)

	1976–1978	1980–1982	1984–1986	1988–1990	1992–1994	1994–1996	Change
Democratic	54	54	50	50	48	53	1
Independent	14	12	12	11	11	8	–6
Republican	32	34	38	39	41	39	+7
Total	100	100	100	100	100	100	

NOTE: Percentages based on average of presidential election year and following midterm election year.

SOURCE: American National Election Studies, Inter-University Consortium for Political Research, University of Michigan, various years.

in the United States has been greatly exaggerated.[11] Most people who in surveys call themselves independents do in fact have some allegiance to one of the major parties. The number of *pure* independents has changed little since the 1970s (Table 6.6).

Notwithstanding these data, there can be no dispute about the rise of split-ticket voting or about the number of voters whose strength of commitment to one or the other of the major parties has weakened over recent years. The parties continue to find it difficult to present coherent programs to the electorate, and as the Ross Perot phenomenon in 1992 demonstrated, disillusionment with parties or their candidates can persuade voters to defect to an independent candidate. Perot's 19 percent of the vote was the highest scored by a third-party candidate since Teddy Roosevelt's Progressive vote in 1912. Perot's showing does not seem indicative of third party strength.

Political scientists and others have long expressed concern that these developments present a problem for democratic theory. It is at least feasible to expect parties presenting coherent programs of change to be held accountable by the electorate. The voter can, after all, test the party's performance in government against electoral promises. Individual candidates, however, cannot be held to this test. If they are elected on personality and appearance alone, no programmatic element can exist. If candidates do take stands on issues, then at most levels of government they cannot directly translate issue promises into policy changes. What difference can one member of Congress make in the rate of inflation, for example? Only presidents (and possibly governors) can be expected to deliver electoral promises, but most recent presidential candidates deliberately have avoided taking clear issue stands because they knew the electorate was divided on most issues in highly complex ways.

In 1992 it briefly seemed that a return to old-style politics was possible. George Bush lost because he was blamed for an economic recession, and Bill Clinton promised bold new federal programs to stimulate economic growth. In any event, these promises came to little, and during his first term, Clinton moved rapidly toward the center ground of politics. By 1996 both candidates were vying for this center ground, and on the most important issues of the day—including the deficit, law and order, welfare reform, and foreign policy—there was little discernible difference between Clinton and Dole.

Although the general problem of the tenuous link among parties, candidates, and voters continues to apply, the electorate is not a broad undifferentiated mass; changes in voting alignments continue to occur, the most important of which are listed next.

1. A "gender gap" has emerged among voters in presidential elections. In the five elections in the period 1980–1996, more women voted Democratic than should have been expected from national trends. This applied with particular force in 1996, when women split their vote 54-37 percent between Clinton and Dole, compared with a 44-44 percent margin for men. This gender gap seems if anything to be growing. In 1992 only 46 percent of women voted for Clinton compared with 41 percent of men. Younger, educated, and single women are especially prone to vote Democratic, reflecting, perhaps, an antipathy toward the tendency of Republican candidates to be conservative on a range of issues that resonate with women (abortion, child care, gun control, education, affirmative action).

The gender phenomenon has other interesting aspects. One, women seem to find the personal behavior of candidates less important then their stand on the issues. The scandals surrounding Bill Clinton, for example, including his admitted dishonesty over his sexual affairs, seemed to do him little electoral harm among women. Two, foreign policy issues have virtually disappeared as a gender-related cue for voters. During the 1980s, one of the explanations of the gap was the distaste many women had for the more aggressive and warlike stance of Republican candidates—hence the contrast between Reagan and Carter or between Bush and Michael Dukakis, the 1988 Democratic candidate. By 1996, however, "strength abroad" as an electoral issue had all but disappeared from the campaign agenda, yet the gender gap actually increased. This trend suggests that domestic rather than foreign policy issues are the driving force behind many women's preference for Democrats.

2. Major changes in the regional pattern of voting have occurred since the 1960s. During the first half of the twentieth century, the South was solidly Democratic, and until the 1930s New England was solidly Republican. Today the South is markedly more Republican than Democratic, not just at the presidential but increasingly at the state and local levels as well. The region is far from being as solidly Republican as it used to be Democratic, however, even if it is conservative. In 1996, Bill Clinton, himself very much a southerner, won five of the south and border states to the seven secured by Bob Dole.

The West also tends to be Republican and conservative, although this applies only erratically in the Pacific states (Washington, Oregon, and California), where the personality of particular candidates is often a better indicator of their success than is their ideological position. Indeed, in 1996 Bill Clinton won all three states. States in the mountain and prairie regions now look firmly committed to the Republican camp, with victories for that party in the 1980–1996 five presidential elections and an increasingly large congressional representation.

Northern and northeastern states are more Democratic and liberal—as should be expected from their industrial past. Bill Clinton managed a near sweep of these regions in both 1992 and 1996. Nevertheless, they cannot with certainty be labeled Democratic. At the congressional, state, and local levels, the Republicans remain quite strong in many of the northern states, and voter preference at the presidential level has as much to do with the attractiveness of individual candidates as with party label.

3. Finally, of significance is the high and consistent support for the Democrats among African American and some other minority voters. In 1984 a staggering 90 percent of blacks voted Democratic, 4 percent up from 1980 and against the national trend. In 1996, 83 percent voted for Clinton and a mere 12 percent for Dole. Two conclusions can be drawn from these figures. Either the vast majority of blacks perceive themselves to be the direct beneficiaries of Democratic policies, or they display a remarkable sense of group solidarity. On the former point, Democrats are more supportive of the civil rights and welfare policies from which many African Americans benefit. But by no means are all blacks direct beneficiaries of these policies, and the high support for the Democrats implies that the party is always unambiguously in favor of welfare and civil rights, which is certainly not the case. Indeed, the Clinton administration has supported draconian reforms to the welfare system involving reductions in welfare benefits for mothers with dependent children (see Chapter 14). More feasible is that most blacks feel a strong sense of racial solidarity and vote Democratic because they know that many among them are more likely to benefit from Democratic policies than from Republican measures. No other social group of significant size shows such solidarity, which speaks volumes for the special and troubled status of blacks in American history and present-day society.

In conclusion, then, most minority groups apart, the behavior of the American electorate is now much more volatile and difficult to predict than during the 1950s and 1960s. Voters are also more sophisticated, are better informed, and make their electoral choices according to rational criteria—such as where candidates stand on issues. In the main, however, the political parties are less able to provide voters with clear choices based on coherent programs of social and economic change. This combination is crucial to understanding the gap between increased public expectations and the inability of politicians to meet these expectations.

Nonelectoral Political Participation

As earlier implied, elections must by their very nature represent limited means of control over those forming and implementing policy. A considerable degree of centralized political power is necessary even for a relatively low level of economic efficiency and social justice. With centralized power, individual citizens casting their votes in periodic elections can only hope to exercise an occasional veto influence over those at the apex of the constitutional system. This principle applies even in elections at the state and local levels, where voters, although closer to the officeholders, are still several steps removed from day-to-day decisionmaking.

But elections are only one means whereby citizens can influence the decisionmakers. As Table 6.7 shows, participation extends to a number of other activities, particularly those associated with the local community. Historically, the local community was the primary focus of political life, with both formal and informal access to local officials being the very essence of American democracy. In many respects this holds true: Some 34 percent of a sample of citizens worked on community problems and 24 percent contacted a local official on a particular issue in 1987 (Table 6.7). For most Americans, then, nonelectoral participation involves contact with local officials or community leaders over such questions as school management, zoning, public works projects, and law enforcement. This is a continuing, constantly changing, interactive process. It is also perceived by all parties to be highly legitimate, and local policies *are* created, modified, and vetoed through citizen involvement.

Of course, this process is not equivalent to direct or pure democracy. Biases against participation by lower-income groups, women, and ethnic minorities remain, and virtually no apparently

TABLE 6.7 Citizens Engaging in Fourteen Acts of Participation, 1967
and 1987 (percent)

Specific Activity	1967	1987	Absolute Change	Relative Change
Voting				
Regular voting in presidential elections	66	58	–8	–12
Always vote in local elections	47	35	–12	–26
Campaign				
Persuade others how to vote	28	32	+4	+14
Actively work for party or candidate	26	27	+1	+4
Attend political meeting or rally	19	19	0	0
Contribute money to party or candidate	13	23	+10	+77
Member of political club	8	4	–4	–50
Contact				
Contact local officials: issue-based	14	24	+10	+71
Contact state or national official: issue-based	11	22	+11	+100
Contact local official: particularized	7	10	+3	+43
Contact state or national official: particularized	6	7	+1	+17
Community				
Work with others on local problem	30	34	+4	+13
Active membership in community problem-solving organization	31	34	+3	+10
Form group to help solve local problem	14	17	+3	+21

SOURCE: Sidney Verba, Kay Lehman Schlozman, and Henry E. Brady,
Voice and Equality: Civil Voluntarism in American Politics (Cambridge,
MA: Harvard University Press, 1995), table 3.6.

local policy issue is entirely local today. Federal and state funding of local programs ensures that local political activity is but one of a number of influences at work. Nonetheless, the importance of local community activity should not be underestimated, especially in the light of the high percentage of citizens (17 percent in 1987) who have directly helped form a group or organization to solve a local community problem (Table 6.7).

Table 6.7 provides further fascinating data on the trends in participation over a twenty-year period. As earlier noted, voting rates have declined, but almost all other forms of participation have increased. Contacts with elected officials in particular have increased, which suggests that many Americans become involved politically when they are concerned about particular *issues*. Indeed, the study from which these findings are drawn confirms that although people may vote less than they used to, they are nonetheless often deeply involved in a range of political issues.[12] This participation almost certainly reflects the fact that those citizens who feel strongly about issues, and whose demands have not been met through voting, decide instead to become directly involved in such issues as abortion, education, or environmental protection.

The same study shows the continuing strong relationship between income and education on the one hand and participation on the other. It should come as no surprise, then, that ethnic and racial minorities, who tend to be poorer than better-off whites, participate much less in politics (Table 6.8). Latino Americans and, in particular, noncitizens have the lowest participation rates. This lack of political activity reflects the fact that many people among these groups are recent arrivals in the United States and therefore have had less opportunity to become involved in community affairs.

In comparative context, American levels of nonelectoral political participation are very high. As can be seen from Figure 6.2, Americans may not be inclined to vote in elections, but they are much more involved in community work than are the citizens of comparable countries, and they also contact officials more frequently. Again, this involvement relates to dissatisfaction with electoral politics where the public's demands often go unfulfilled.

There are two further varieties of political participation that Table 6.7 either excludes or refers to only obliquely. The first involves the activities of national interest groups. As discussed in Chapter 11, almost no aspect of economic or social life escapes influence by interest groups. How representative or democratic these groups are is a

TABLE 6.8 Political Activities by Race (percent active)

Activity	Anglo-Whites	African Americans	Latinos	Latino Citizens
Vote	73	65	41	52
Campaign work	8	12	7	8
Campaign contributions	25	22	11	12
Contact	37	24	14	17
Protest	5	9	4	4
Informal community activity	17	19	12	14
Board membership	4	2	4	5
Affiliated with a political organization	52	38	24	27

SOURCE: Sidney Verba, Kay Lehman Schlozman, and Henry E. Brady, *Voice and Equality: Civil Voluntarism in American Politics* (Cambridge, MA: Harvard University Press, 1995), table 7.9.

point covered later, but as earlier implied, membership in and loyalties to them do cut across party allegiances, so their activities must be considered an additional part of the representative process.

Second are all those political actions usually viewed as external to the established channels of political access: demonstrations, marches, boycotts, and, more rarely, acts of political violence and terror. Clearly the latter are evidence of the breakdown of democratic processes, and at the national level, at least, such acts have been remarkably rare in the United States. In recent U.S. history, they have largely been confined to the actions of isolated individuals (assassinations, hijackings) or have been precipitated by a single, sometimes ephemeral issue (the Vietnam War).

At the local level, the picture is somewhat different. Until the 1960s, political violence was a relatively common feature of some parts of southern society, with blacks becoming the victims of systematic intimidation and random violence. Rarely, however, has local political violence been motivated by a desire for regime change. More often the motivation has been the assertion of authority over a politically and socially subordinate minority group. Often, these illegal acts were implicitly endorsed by the legitimate authorities.

One partial exception to this generalization is the "survivalist" and militia movements of the 1990s. Although for the most part these fiercely antigovernment groups are nonviolent, there have-

FIGURE 6.2   Comparative Political Activity Rates in Five Countries
(percent)

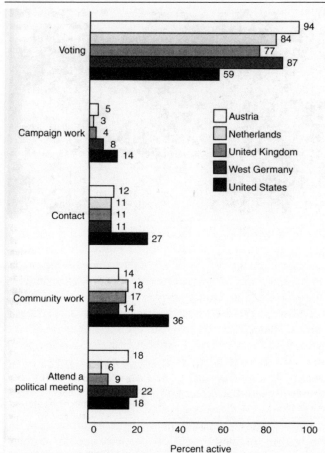

SOURCE: Sidney Verba, Kay Lehman Schlozman, and Henry E. Brady, *Voice and Equality: Civil Voluntarism in American Politics* (Cambridge, MA: Harvard University Press, 1995), table 3.5.

been some notable exceptions. The bombing of the federal building in Oklahoma City in 1996 that killed 164 people is generally attributed to one of the more extreme of these groups. It is easy to exaggerate the size and importance of such organizations, however. They represent a tiny fraction of Americans, and they lack ideological and organizational coherence.

More difficult to evaluate are acts of political protest—demonstrations, marches, boycotts, political strikes. These are very much a part of American life and at certain times have played a crucial role in politics. Starting in the 1940s and reaching a crescendo in the early 1960s, these were precisely the methods successfully employed by the civil rights movement—a fact that must help explain the greater proclivity for the African American community to partake in this type of political activity today (Table 6.8).

Other than civil rights, however, it is difficult to find an issue about which protest is successful and broadly accepted as legitimate, and even the civil rights movement helped inspire the urban riots of the 1960s that aroused bitter controversy and, eventually, a backlash from many whites. This is not to deny that protest has been influential. In many instances—over unemployment in the 1930s and the Vietnam War in the 1960s—clearly it has. But it is almost impossible to *measure* its influence, or in some cases, to judge whether it in fact helped or hindered the cause in question.

In sum, protest is very much a last resort. Only when the unambiguously legitimate means of access are either unavailable or exhausted do individuals and social groups take recourse to protest. In some cases they have had no choice, as was true for southern blacks in the 1950s and early 1960s because within southern states normal channels of access were closed to them. But even in this example, the movement needed and received vital support from established political actors and institutions in northern states. In other cases—protest over the Vietnam War, nuclear energy, and abortion, for example—some critics have argued that direct political action was illegitimate because normal channels of access were available and the democratic process took its course. This last point demonstrates nicely the problems involved in discussing political participation. As emphasized, "the democratic process"—whether electoral or through interest-group activity—must always be an imperfect representative mechanism. Some individuals and social groups will win or lose more than others; some have disproportionately greater access and hence greater political power than others.

What is perhaps remarkable about the American system is that in spite of its obvious biases in favor of certain interests and classes, there is a broad acceptance of basic constitutional arrangements. Protest and political violence are comparatively rare. Most Americans accept the legitimacy of the established channels of political access—elections and the activities of interest groups. Although these premises hold true, falling turnout and evidence of increasing cynicism with political institutions suggest that for many voters, the electoral system is far from being a perfect mechanism for the translation of public demands into public policy. As the next three chapters will show, this dissatisfaction relates closely to the failure of legislators and presidents to live up to the high expectations of American voters.

Notes

1. Recalls enable the electorate, following the presentation of a minimum number of signatures, to hold a special election to recall an official from office. Initiatives are similar devices enabling the electorate by petition to vote directly on a proposition (such as a tax change), thus bypassing the state or local legislature. Referenda are proposed by legislatures and present to the electorate the opportunity to vote directly on an issue. Referenda—but not recalls and initiatives—are increasingly common in Europe to legitimize constitutional changes such as the peace agreement in Northern Ireland or membership in the European Union.

2. See, in particular, Sidney Verba and Norman H. Nie, *Participation in America: Political Democracy and Social Equality* (New York: Harper and Row, 1987).

3. Quoted in *USA Today*, November 8, 1996, p. 3A.

4. Morris P. Fiorina, *Retrospective Voting in American National Elections* (New Haven: Yale University Press, 1981).

5. See Walter Dean Burnham, "The Turnout Problem," in A. James Reichley (ed.), *Elections American Style* (Washington, DC: Brookings Institution, 1987), table A4.

6. Angus Campbell et al., *The American Voter* (New York: Wiley, 1960).

7. Norman H. Nie, Sidney Verba, and John R. Petrocik, *The Changing American Voter* (Cambridge, MA: Harvard University Press, 1979), p. 42.

8. Philip Converse, "The Nature of Belief Systems in Mass Publics," in David E. Apter (ed.), *Ideology and Discontent* (New York: Free Press, 1964), p. 543.

9. Kevin Phillips, *The Emerging Republican Majority* (New York: Doubleday Anchor, 1970).

10. Walter Dean Burnham, "Realignment Lives: The 1994 Earthquake and Its Implications," in Colin Campbell and Bert A. Rockman (eds.), *The Clinton Presidency: First Appraisals* (Chatham NJ: Chatham House, 1996).

11. Bruce E. Keith et al., *The Myth of the Independent Voter* (Berkeley and Los Angeles: University of California Press, 1992).

12. Sidney Verba, Kay Lehman Schlozman, and Henry E. Brady, *Voice and Equality: Civil Voluntarism in American Politics* (Cambridge, MA: Harvard University Press, 1995).

Further Reading

The best analysis of political participation in the United States is Sidney Verba, Kay Lehman Schlozman, and Henry E. Brady, *Voice and Equality: Civic Voluntarism in American Politics* (Cambridge, MA: Harvard University Press, 1995). For a discussion of changes in electoral behavior, see Bruce Keith et al., *The Myth of the Independent Voter* (Berkeley and Los Angeles: University of California Press, 1992); Martin P. Wattenberg, *The Rise of Candidate-Centered Politics* (Cambridge, MA: Harvard University Press, 1991). The classic statement of the voter as rational actor is Morris P. Fiorina, *Retrospective Voting in American National Elections* (New Haven: Yale University Press, 1981). Presidential elections are fully covered by Nelson Polsby and Aaron Wildavsky, *Presidential Elections,* 9th ed. (New York: Scribner's, 1996), and by Stephen J. Wayne, *The Road to the White House 1996: The Politics of Presidential Elections* (New York: St. Martin's Press, 1996).

7

U.S. Legislators and Their Constituents

Because [members of Congress] are vulnerable, they go to prodigious lengths to protect themselves. Like workers in nuclear power stations, they take the most extreme safety precautions. The fact that the precautions are almost entirely successful in both cases does not make them any the less essential. As David Mayhew remarks of the American Congress in a frequently quoted passage: "If a group of planners sat down and tried to design a pair of national assemblies with the goal of serving members' electoral needs year in, year out, they would be hard pressed to improve on what exists."

—Anthony King

The U.S. Congress is usually—and accurately—referred to as the most powerful legislature in the world. Whereas a common trend in other democratic countries has been the rise of powerful executives and the relative decline of assemblies and parliaments, Congress has been remarkably successful in maintaining its independence from executive influence. This is not to deny that the powers and functions of Congress have changed over time. Clearly they have, and the particular way in which the institution operates today is very different even from in the 1980s. But throughout its history, Congress has remained an essentially autonomous institution. Even during periods of executive ascendancy—most recently during the Johnson and Nixon years—Congress never became the mere instrument of presidents.

The independence of Congress derives in part from its constitutionally defined powers and in part from the particular way in which the American party system has evolved. Constitutionally, Congress was given three main powers, all of which remain important today. First, all legislative power is vested in the House of Representatives and the Senate, and within this broad function, Congress is given special powers to appropriate moneys, to raise armies, and to regulate interstate commerce. Second, Congress has a constitutionally established right to declare wars and ratify treaties. Finally, the Senate is specifically empowered to ratify treaties and approve appointments by the president to the judiciary and the executive branch. The House can impeach executive judicial officers for wrongdoing, and the Senate is charged with the responsibility for trying impeached officers. In addition, from very early in its history, Congress established the right to oversee and investigate the behavior of the executive. In total, these powers are impressive, especially when it is remembered that originally Congress was expected to be the major initiator as well as approver of legislation. As with other legislatures around the world, Congress has partly (although by no means entirely) forfeited to the president the responsibility for initiating legislation. Unlike most other assemblies, however, Congress retains an independent power to approve legislation, appropriate moneys, and generally oversee the executive branch.

The simplest explanation for this autonomy is the distinctive constituency base that individual members of Congress enjoy. In contrast to parliamentary systems, the electoral fortunes of presidents and legislators are not directly linked. Presidents can, and often do, face a legislature dominated by a party other than their own. But this constitutional arrangement has been reinforced by the nature of the American party system. It is certainly possible to imagine a system characterized by bicameralism and the separation of powers in which political party ties are strong and the electoral fortunes of legislators are interdependent with those of the executive. Only rarely has this been the case in the history of the United States. Much more common is a very loose party relationship between the president and members of Congress, with the legislators remaining essentially independent.

Representation and Congress

The sort of party government associated with parliamentary systems greatly restricts the representative function of individual legislators. In Britain, for example, the individual member of Parliament (MP) is largely tied, through party discipline in the House of Commons, to the policies of either government or opposition. Crucially, the member's electoral survival depends on an official party endorsement.[1] MPs may exercise some independent pressure on party leaders or governments, but it is limited. Clearly, this close organic link between executive and legislator limits the representative function of MPs. The electorate may benefit, at least in theory, from the coherent programs and policies that party government produces, but the interests of individual constituencies tend to become subordinated to national policy objectives. Curiously, British MPs are quick to insist that they come closest to what is called "trustee" representatives—that is, they are elected by the people on trust to exercise their judgment. They are not delegated to carry out a specific program, to the letter, and without discretion. In reality, they are closer to being party delegates than trustees.

Members of Congress are patently not delegates in the sense either of being slaves to a party program or of being mandated by their constituents to carry out specific policies. Indeed, the idea of a representative being a direct delegate of the people has relatively few applications in modern industrial societies. In small communities—and possibly in early New England town meetings—such a concept has meaning. But no member of Congress can accurately and continuously carry out the wishes of diverse and volatile electorates. Even if he or she knew what the electorate wanted, the individual member of Congress has but limited powers to influence what is a complex national policy process.

In truth, members are much closer to being trustees of their electorates. They are elected on the promise that they will exercise their judgment on behalf of their constituents' interests. And should they fail in the opinion of the electorate to defend and promote these interests, they are punished in subsequent elections. If members of Congress are not delegates, neither are they representative in the microcosmic sense (representative of the general population in ethnic and socioeconomic terms). By this measure, in fact, they could hardly be less representative. An overwhelming majority of senators and representatives are white, college educated, middle-aged, middle class, and male. In the 106th Congress (1999–2000), only 56 women were elected out of the total 435 members of the House, and only 9 of 100 senators were women. No African American senators and just 35 black representatives were elected (Table 7.1). Lawyers and businesspeople are greatly overrepresented among the

TABLE 7.1   Characteristics of the 104th, 105th, and 106th Congresses (1995–2000)

	104th	105th	106th
House			
Democrats	197	206	211
Republicans	235	228	223
Independents/vacant	3	1	1
Women	48	49	56
Men	385	386	379
Blacks	38	37	35
Hispanics	17	18	19
Asian/Pacific Islander	3	3	3
Senate			
Democrats	47	45	45
Republicans	53	55	55
Women	8	9	9
Blacks	1	1	0
Hispanics	0	0	0
Asian/Pacific Islander	2	2	2
Native American	1	1	1

SOURCE: Library of Congress web pages. http://lcweb.gov/global/legislative/congress.html.

members in both houses, although there has been a dramatic decline in the number of lawyers in the House since the 1970s (Figure 7.1). In the occupational category "other," educators and representatives with government backgrounds predominate.[2]

To claim that members most closely approximate a trustee form of representation is accurate but indicates little about the precise linkages among legislators, constituency, and party and how these have changed over time. A common assertion, for example, is that since the 1970s, party has weakened its influence on members even further, with constituency pressures in the ascendant. At the same time, many voters have grown disillusioned with what they believe are members who put their self-interest first and the public interest second. The remainder of this chapter is devoted to the ways in which the representative system raises public expectations of what members of Congress can do for citizens. At the end of the chapter is a preliminary discussion of the links between constituency influences on members of Congress and their work within the House and the Senate.

FIGURE 7.1   Occupations of House Members in Twelve Selected
Congresses

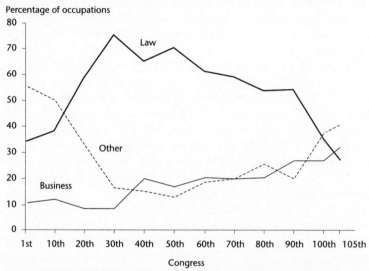

SOURCE: Roger H. Davidson and Walter J. Oleszek, *Congress and Its
Members*, 6th ed. (Washington, DC: Congressional Quarterly Press,
1998), figure 7.1.

Congressional Elections

Representatives are elected every two years, senators every six (with
one-third elected every two years). This simple fact helps account for
what are some starkly contrasting trends in the electoral dynamics of
the two houses, but there are also some common trends.

Spread of Direct Primaries

As with presidential elections, primaries are now the major means
whereby members of Congress win their party's nomination for office. One major consequence of the demise of party conventions (the
standard nineteenth-century form of nomination) has been to weaken
the role of political parties in the nomination process. By being able
to appeal directly to the electorate, the senator or representative now
owes much less allegiance to local and national party figures.

Rise and Decline of Democratic Dominance

Until 1994 it was widely believed that Democratic dominance of the House of Representatives was a nearly permanent feature of American politics. As can be seen from Table 7.2, the Democrats managed to maintain a large majority in the House for many years. They were also strong in the Senate and controlled that house for all but six years in the 1961–1995 period. In the midterm election of 1994, however, the Republicans swept the board, winning back both the House and the Senate and leading many commentators to conclude that an era of Republican dominance was about to begin. However, in the 1996 presidential election, the Republicans' majority was reduced, and in 1998 they suffered a further small loss in the House. The 1998 loss is highly significant because the party in control of the presidency almost always loses seats at midterm. The 1998 result (a four-seat loss in the House and no change in the Senate) was the worst result for the nonpresidential party at midterm since 1934.

Nonetheless, the 1994 turnaround was regarded as representing a major change in American politics, and it raised two important questions. Why did the Democrats manage to maintain their grip on Congress for so long—especially as the Republicans actually won most of the *presidential* elections during this period? Second, what accounts for the Republican victories in 1994? As for the first question, undoubtedly the Democrats benefited from being the majority party—more Americans identified with the Democrats than with the Republicans. The Democrats also benefited from being the majority party in another sense: In single-member-district, simple-majority electoral systems, majority parties usually score more constituency victories than would be expected from their aggregate popular vote. Democrats also dominated state legislatures, which are responsible for drawing up the boundaries of congressional districts. Although the courts have been active on the question of malapportionment (see Chapter 12), a considerable amount of discretion remains—especially over the shape of constituencies rather than the balance of population among districts. As Gary Jacobson has pointed out, at least as far as the House is concerned, Democrats were actually better campaigners and politicians than their Republican counterparts. They were used to winning and to delivering the goods. As a result, they continued to win.[3]

By the mid-1990s, most of these advantages had eroded. The number of people identifying with the Democrats declined, and the

TABLE 7.2 Composition of Congress, by Political Party, 1961–2000

			House			Senate		
	Party and President	Congress	Majority Party	Minority Party	Other	Majority Party	Minority Party	Other
1961	D (Kennedy)	87th	D-263	R-174	—	D-65	R-35	—
1963	D (Kennedy)	88th	D-258	R-174	—	D-67	R-33	—
1965	D (Johnson)	89th	D-295	R-140	—	D-68	R-32	—
1967	D (Johnson)	90th	D-247	R-187	—	D-64	R-36	—
1969	R (Nixon)	91st	D-243	R-192	—	D-57	R-43	—
1971[a]	R (Nixon)	92nd	D-254	R-180	—	D-54	R-44	2
1973[a, b]	R (Nixon)	93rd	D-239	R-192	1	D-56	R-42	2
1975[c]	R (Ford)	94th	D-291	R-144	—	D-60	R-37	2
1977[d]	D (Carter)	95th	D-292	R-143	—	D-61	R-38	1
1979[d]	D (Carter)	96th	D-276	R-157	—	D-58	R-41	1
1981[d]	R (Reagan)	97th	D-243	R-192	—	R-53	D-46	1
1983	R (Reagan)	98th	D-269	R-165	—	R-54	D-46	—
1985	R (Reagan)	99th	D-252	R-182	—	R-53	D-47	—
1987	R (Reagan)	100th	D-258	R-177	—	D-55	R-45	—
1989[e]	R (Bush)	101st	D-259	R-174	—	D-55	R-45	—
1991[e]	R (Bush)	102nd	D-267	R-167	1	D-56	R-43	—
1993[e]	D (Clinton)	103rd	D-259	R-175	1	D-57	R-43	—

(continues)

TABLE 7.2 (continued)

	Party and President	Congress	House			Senate		
			Majority Party	Minority Party	Other	Majority Party	Minority Party	Other
1995[e]	D (Clinton)	104th	R-235	D-197	1	R-53	D-47	—
1997[e]	D (Clinton)	105th	R-227	D-207	1	R-55	D-45	—
1999[e]	D (Clinton)	106th	R-223	D-211	1	R-55	D-45	—

D = Democratic, R = Republican. Data for beginning of first session of each Congress. Excludes vacancies at beginning of sessions. — represents zero.

[a] Senate had 1 independent and 1 conservative Republican.
[b] House had 1 independent-Democrat.
[c] Senate had 1 independent, 1 conservative Republican, and 1 undecided (New Hamsphire).
[d] Senate had 1 independent.
[e] House had 1 independent.

SOURCE: U.S. Congress, Joint Committee on Printing, Congressional Directory annual; beginning 1977, biennial.

number of Republican identifiers increased (Chapter 6, Figure 6.1). The Democrats' hold on the state legislatures also weakened. By the mid-1990s, the two parties controlled roughly the same number of state legislatures, and the Republicans held a handsome majority of the state governorships. As was established in the last chapter, these changes were greeted by many as evidence of a Republican realignment. More likely is that a changing political agenda resounded to the Republicans' advantage but not to the extent that they became in any sense the dominant or majority party. As for the congressional elections, the Republicans benefited from public support for lower taxes, a balanced budget, an enhanced role for state governments, welfare reform, and tougher law-and-order policies. But many issues on which the Democrats had the advantage—education-, gender-, and race-based issues; the environment; gun control; and the protection of Medicare and Social Security—remained very important to many voters. In this sense, these election results are a likely forecast of much more competitive congressional elections in the future.

Regional Change

At the congressional level, the Democrats continue to show strength in the North and the East, but they have lost the solid support they once had in the South. Because the electorate is now more volatile, most regions cannot be labeled as unequivocally Republican or Democratic. This said, the South is now effectively a Republican region, as are states in the mountain and prairie regions. The old industrial Northeast remains primarily Democratic; in the Pacific and midwestern states the Republicans have the edge. Even these generalizations can be misleading. At any time, a Democrat can win many southern districts and a Republican many northeastern districts. Much depends not only on the socioeconomic and ethnic makeup of the district in question but also on the personal appeal and financial resources of the candidate running for office.

The Importance of Money

For both senators and representatives, money has become a crucial resource in congressional elections. With voters acting in response to the appeal of individual candidates rather than to parties, both incumbents and challengers must ensure that the voters know who

FIGURE 7.2   Average House Campaign Expenditures by Incumbency
and Party, 1978–1996

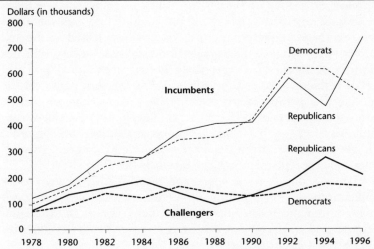

SOURCE: Roger H. Davidson and Walter J. Oleszek, *Congress and Its Members*, 6th ed. (Washington, DC: Congressional Quarterly Press, 1988), table 4.2.

they are and what their record is. This translates into buying television time for advertisements as well as spending money on mailings, meetings, and other attention-seeking devices.

At one time, the personal efforts of candidates in raising money were less important than winning the party endorsement or the endorsement of the big corporations and labor unions. Large donations from such sources could help clinch the election of a particular candidate. However, with declining partisanship and the passage of the Federal Election Campaign Act (FECA) in 1974, candidates have been forced to rely increasingly on their capacity to raise funds or to persuade others to contribute to their campaigns. FECA was designed to reduce candidate dependence on money, but in fact the very opposite has happened. As can be seen from Figure 7.2, campaign spending soared between 1978 and the early 1990s. The increases generally leveled off thereafter, though there was a strong increase in spending by House Republican incumbents, particularly after 1994 when they controlled the House.

What accounts for the increasing importance of money? In part it is because the Supreme Court struck down a central provision in

FECA that limited contributions from candidates' own funds, and in part because the law encouraged the growth of political action committees (PACs). Although PACs are limited to giving $5,000 per candidate per campaign, they contributed 45 percent of all campaign financing to Democrats in 1990. Individuals are limited to $1,000 per candidate, but there are no limits on what candidates themselves can spend on their campaigns.

Figure 7.2 shows only part of the picture, because under FECA, the rules for national party contributions "on behalf of" candidates—that is, not going directly or exclusively to a particular candidate's campaign—are much looser than for individual or PAC contributions. There are limits on this so-called coordinated spending (often called "soft money"), but by exploiting the law to the full, national party committees can contribute up to $73,620 to a House candidate and $1.73 million to a senator from the most populous states. These loopholes can give well-organized Republicans an enormous advantage. In 1994, for example, Representative Newt Gingrich mobilized the Republican national congressional committees to sponsor candidates supporting his "Contract with America," which itemized his program of change for the United States.

Until quite recently, it was common to contrast the advantages of incumbency in the House and the Senate. Of incumbents seeking reelection to the House in 1990, a remarkably high (and generally rising since) percentage were reelected (90 percent in that year).[4] The contrast with the Senate used to be considerable—in 1980 only 73 percent of those seeking reelection were successful. In the last several elections, however, the incumbency advantage has also been enjoyed by senators—in 1996 only one incumbent seeking reelection was defeated.

Despite this advantage, there is little doubt that congressional elections are becoming more competitive, because although incumbents usually win, they believe that unless they raise a large amount of money and organize and campaign well, they are in danger of losing. Indeed, House incumbents virtually never cease to campaign. With elections every two years and the ever present threat of an aggressive challenger, they cannot afford to let down their guard. One consequence of this stressful environment is an increase in the number of vacant seats. Many representatives decide to quit after a few terms and to seek alternative careers. When this happens, the "out" party is likely to build an impressive campaign organization in order to win the seat. As Burdett Loomis has noted:

Only open seat candidates build organizations that resemble an incumbent's enterprise (with no accounting for congressional staff, district offices, communications capacities, and travel expenses). In the end, that is what much of the struggle for open seats is all about—to obtain the resources of incumbency for the future. One measure of the Republicans' 1994 success is that they won twenty-one open seats previously held by House Democrats and six such seats in the Senate.[5]

Senators are, of course, more secure by virtue of their six-year term. Challengers rarely manage to amass the money and staff to match incumbents (Figure 7.2)—although there are often celebrated exceptions to this rule. In 1996, for example, incumbent John Kerry of Massachusetts narrowly held off a challenge by the Republican governor, William Weld. In the same election, conservative Republican incumbent Larry Pressler of South Dakota was defeated by Democrat Tim Johnson.

Given the personalized nature of congressional electoral politics, tension exists between how members reconcile their commitment to campaigning and winning reelection on the one hand and their obligations to public policymaking on the other. The following analysis deals with the work of members and, in particular, the sort of strategic choices they face when seeking election or reelection.

Legislators as Rational Actors

The determined efforts of a senators or representatives to get elected or reelected involve an interaction between the candidate and the constituency. Although not unimportant, party ties and contacts have long since ceased to dominate the nomination and campaign process. But this electoral interaction is not simply one of candidate projection and media promotion. Members are also required to tend to the needs and interests of their constituencies—a job that in the American context is both complex and demanding. In no other comparable political system are legislators so electorally vulnerable as to have to devote themselves wholeheartedly to this task. In most other systems, members of lower houses are relatively secure from immediate electoral pressures (Table 7.3). They do not have to compete in primary elections; they depend on party identities and financial support rather than personal campaign fundraising at the time of their election; voters tend to use national rather than local cues when voting; and the life of the typical parliamentary session is longer than in the United States.

TABLE 7.3 Legislators' Electoral Vulnerability in Nine Countries

	Maximum Legal Life of Largest House of National Legislature (years)	Average Actual Life of Largest House of National Legislature 1960–1994 (years)	Percent of years 1960–1994 Taken up by Legislatures That Lasted 3.5 Years or More[a]	Level of Use of Primaries for Selection of Party Candidates for National Office	Level of Candidate-Centered, as Distinct from Party-Centered, Voting Among Electorate[b]	Level of Member-Centered, as Distinct from Party-Centered, Voting in National Legislature[c]	Level of Individual Candidate's Reliance on Own Fund-Raising Efforts[d]
Australia	3	2.3	0.0	Nonexistent	Low	Low	Low
Britain	5	3.3	94.3	Nonexistent	Low	Low	Low
Canada	5	32.9	72.3	Nonexistent	Low	Low	Low
France	5	3.5	76.7	Nonexistent	Low	Low	Low
Germany	4	3.2	83.3	Nonexistent	Low	Low	Low
Italy	5	3.2	85.6	Nonexistent	Low	Medium	Low
Japan	4	2.8	31.4	Nonexistent	Medium	Low	Medium
New Zealand	3	2.8	0.0	Nonexistent	Low	Low	Low
United States	2	2.0	0.0	High	High	High	High

SOURCE: Anthony King, *Running Scared* (New York: Free Press, 1997), table 1. (See original table for explanation of footnotes.)

Political scientists have attempted to characterize these efforts in terms of rational-choice analysis. David Mayhew, for example, in his stimulating and influential book *Congress: The Electoral Connection*,[6] argued that members of Congress primarily have a single motivation: reelection. Almost all their behavior inside and outside Congress is shaped by this simple drive. A major a priori assumption is that members can affect their reelection chances. Although Mayhew accepts that there are limits to what representatives or senators can do to please their constituents—no single legislator can, after all, banish unemployment or solve the drug abuse problem—he does identify three broad strategies that can improve reelection chances. First, candidates can advertise by spreading their name and reputation and generally creating a favorable image. Exposure on television and in the local press can be important, and unlike the Washington and New York press, local newspapers are generally sympathetic to members of Congress. Sometimes members go to unusual lengths in their efforts at self-promotion. Mayhew cited examples: Charles Diggs Jr. (Democrat, Michigan) ran a radio program with himself as "combination disc jockey–commentator and minister," and Daniel Flood (Democrat, Pennsylvania) apparently was "famous for appearing unannounced and often uninvited at wedding anniversaries and other events."[7]

Claiming credit—convincing constituents that the member has "delivered the goods"—formerly was the key motivation of members. Indeed, "pork-barrel" politics is part of American folklore. Pork-barrel politics almost always involves particular rather than collective benefits to constituents. It would be very difficult for an individual member of Congress to claim credit for having balanced the budget, which benefits everyone. Credit is more likely to inure to a member who helps to direct federal investment to his or her constituency (investment such as a military installation or community development project, for example). As discussed later, the internal structure of power in Congress—not least the absence of strict party discipline—facilitates just such distributions.

Finally, members benefit from position taking or being identified positively in the minds of constituents with a particular policy position. Constituencies that are predominantly Roman Catholic or Christian right would be gratified by their congressional members' public pronouncements or legislative action against abortion. New York's large Jewish community would expect its members of Congress to take a pro-Israeli stance, and so on. Legislators have also formed caucuses to promote or defend a particular constituency interest. Typical examples are the House Automobile Task Force and the Steel Caucus, both of which have striven to counteract economic decline and foreign competition in these industries.

Senators and representatives have always tended their constituencies, but in recent years the pressures to do so have increased considerably. The changing nature of political party influence is one potentially major bulwark against an intimate constituency-legislator relationship. Less obvious is the impact of a number of political and technological changes on the information flow between the electorate and member. On the members' side, free mailing privileges, together with computerized mailing lists, enable legislators not only to send out a vast volume of letters (Senate offices, for example, send out about 1 million letters a month) but also to target mail to particular groups of constituents. Thus, legislators who want to publicize their antiabortion stand to all Roman Catholics and pro-life Christians in their district can do so. They can even narrow the target group to a particular neighborhood or block.

On the constituents' side, interest groups and political action committees increasingly "rate" the legislative voting record of individual members. These ratings enable groups and, via publicity back home, constituents to identify their legislators as liberal, conservative, and for or against such matters as environmental protection, labor, and affirmative action. In addition, issue groups spend "soft money" on television campaigns to support or criticize particular candidates. Often, with such issues as gun control, penal policy, and abortion, these soft-money campaigns result in giving the voters the impression of an electoral conflict more polarized than it in fact is.[8]

Predictably, compared with representatives, senators are less exposed to such highly focused pressures, but Mayhew contends pressures are just as instrumental in senators' quest for reelection as they are for House members. There is undoubtedly a great deal of validity to the rational-choice approach. Any observer of the Washington scene would have to concede that members are increasingly preoccupied with constituency matters. Richard Fenno, who spent several months with members of Congress as a participant observer, dubbed these activities "home style."[9] Fenno also noted another phenomenon, however, that casts some doubt on the rational-actor thesis. The longer House members remained in Congress, the more concerned they became with Washington affairs and the less diligent they became in their pastoral constituency work. The implication is that there are forces at work in the lives of members of Congress other than the simple drive to win reelection. It may be, of course, that these other forces complement rather than compete with constituency pressures. Most voters have very little knowledge of what representatives and senators actually do in Washington. And given that the electorate is not so naive as to expect an individual member to transform society, a steady flow of positive messages linked to advertising, credit claiming, and position taking may be enough to convince voters that "their" representative or senator is doing a good job.

Undoubtedly there are a number of activities important to legislators that do not seriously conflict with constituency duties. On some issues—especially foreign policy or technical financial questions—constituents do not have well-formed opinions. Yet if members devote themselves to such issues, possibly they are at least indirectly neglecting their reelection chances by not putting their time to the most effective use. The rational-choice theorists' answer is simple: Members devote time to nonconstituency questions because the internal dynamics of the House (or Senate) demand it. As separate and individual political actors, they can achieve very little for the voters. So in order (say) to ensure the siting of a federal installation in their constituency, they are obliged to form coalitions with other members. Naturally, coalition formation involves give-and-take. A legislator must spend time on apparently nonrelevant legislative activity in order to win support on issues that are directly relevant. This "logrolling"—political slang for the bargaining, vote trading, and exchange of favors—has long been a characteristic of Congress.

Logrolling occurs principally in any one of the more than 100 work groups (committees and subcommittees) in the Senate and 150 in the House that dominate day-to-day legislative business. It is important to stress, however, that although persuasive, the rational-choice view of the work of Congress has its limitations. It assumes that legislators can know the interests of their respective constituencies. Often this is difficult. Some districts are socially, ethnically, and economically diverse. A senator from Washington State may not need any prompting when voting on legislation affecting lumber, aerospace, and software—three industries that dominate that state. But it is much more difficult for senators from California, representing diverse and politically volatile populations, to respond in this way. Even the Washington senator would have to think twice about always serving the lumber industry given the size and the influence of the environmental lobby in that state.

Moreover, as is elaborated in the next chapter, it has become increasingly difficult for members to deliver in terms of traditional pork-barrel politics. With almost all politicians in agreement on the need for fiscal rectitude, the pork barrel has been reduced in size in recent years. Instead, members are more likely to play their part in providing programs and policies that benefit most or all of their constituents—lower taxes, tougher policing, a return to family values, and so on. In such a context, members are better advised to indulge in *general* position taking than in claiming credit for *particular* constituency benefits.

More serious is the implication in the rational-choice approach that members of Congress are mere automatons responding to constituency demands and that there is no place for ideology, party, or individual preferences. Yet a wealth of empirical evidence exists to suggest that at one point or another in a legislator's life, all of these can be—and usually are—important. As suggested, party influences are weak by European standards, but that does not mean they do not exist. Democrats have some policy positions and perspectives in common, as have Republicans. The next chapter will show, indeed, how party leadership within both House and Senate can be crucial in determining the outcome of legislation.

Furthermore, there is considerable evidence of party solidarity— at least among Republicans in the House. In the 104th Congress, Speaker Newt Gingrich managed to persuade his Republican troops to vote the party line most of the time. Even more dramatic was the almost solid party-line voting in the impeachment trial of President Clinton in 1999. Similarly, appeals by a president to fellow party members in Congress can be effective. Lyndon Johnson used the Democratic majorities in the House and Senate to great effect when pushing through his Great Society social and civil rights programs. More recently, Ronald Reagan appealed directly to party solidarity when endeavoring to persuade the Republican Senate to support his economic reforms in 1981 and 1982. He was assured of Republican minority support in the House, and victory there was sealed by the additional support of conservative Democrats.

The existence of "conservative" and "liberal" groupings shows the importance of ideology. In itself, ideological labeling need not be significant—members may after all be simply mirroring their constituents' views—but constituencies are not always easily labeled conservative or liberal, and it is not uncommon for an established conservative or liberal member to represent a constituency that cannot accurately be described as either. Legislators are also influenced by other members and by their staff. In other words, in the context of a legislative process that is both fragmented and complex, they are exposed to a number of pressures and influences. Constituency demands may be on the ascendant, but this does not mean the role of legislators should be reduced to vote-getting machines as implied by some political scientists.

In sum, members are exposed to many influences. Given the importance of their constituents' preferences in deciding their electoral survival, it is unlikely that members will do anything directly to antagonize the voters. And, if particularly vulnerable or in a marginal seat, they may indeed devote all their energies to reelection. For some, and particularly for members of the Senate, however, political life becomes much more complex, with constituency, party, committee, interest-group, and ideological pressures competing for the members' favor.

The Work of Members of Congress

A useful way to link discussion of the activities of members outside and inside the legislature is to examine the typical workload of legislators and the support in staff, offices, and other services provided for them.

Clearly, representatives and senators are not "lobby fodder" or bound by party discipline to follow a particular line, as British MPs are often labeled. Members of Congress have little choice but to take note of the needs and demands of their constituents and to act on them. Part of this function involves formulating and monitoring a mass of complex legislation. Given the sheer volume of legislation (some 10,000 bills are introduced every session, but fewer than 1,000 become law), most members specialize in a particular policy area, often but not always related to their constituents' interests. Senator William Fulbright, for example, was for many years chairman of the Senate Foreign Relations Committee. In this job he took a predominantly liberal stance, especially on the conduct of the Vietnam War—not a strategy linked in any obvious way to the interests of his rural and conservative constituency, Arkansas.

Most of the crucial legislative work is conducted in the committees and subcommittees, yet as shown in Table 7.4, members spend

TABLE 7.4 Activities, Actual and Ideal, of Members of Congress (by percent)

Activity	Members Actually Spending Time				Members Preferring to Spend More Time
	Great Deal	Moderate Amount	A Little	Almost None	
Representation					
Meet with citizens in state/district	68	30	1	0	17
Meet in Washington with constituents	45	50	5	0	17
Manage office	6	45	39	10	13
Raise funds for next campaign, for others, for party	6	33	45	16	7
Lawmaking					
Attend committee hearings, markups, other meetings	48	46	6	0	43
Meet in Washington on legislative issues	37	56	6	0	43
Study, read, discuss pending legislation	25	56	6	0	31
Work with informal caucuses	8	43	36	13	25
Attend floor debate, follow it on television	7	37	44	12	59
Work with party leaders to build coalitions	6	33	43	18	42
Oversee how agencies are carrying out policies/programs	5	22	43	29	53
Give speeches about legislation outside state/district	5	23	49	23	16

NOTE: A total of 161 members of Congress (136 representatives, 25 senators) responded to this survey, conducted in early 1993 under the auspices of the Joint Committee on the Organization of Congress. This series of questions elicited responses from 152 to 155 members.

SOURCE: U.S. Congress, Joint Committee on the Organization of Congress, *Organization of Congress, Final Report*, H. Rept. 103-413 (103d Congress, 1st sess., Dec. 1993), vol. 2, pp. 231–232, 275–287. Reproduced from Roger H. Davidson and Walter J. Oleszek, *Congress and Its Members*, 6th ed. (Washington, DC: Congressional Quarterly Press, 1998), table 5.2.

relatively little of their heavy workloads directly on committee work. The remainder is devoted to a number of tasks, in particular consulting with interest groups, meeting with constituents, and preparing legislation. To assist the legislator perform all these functions, Congress has voted for itself a quite extraordinary number of services.

Office space, furnishings, stationery, and postal allowances are generous. All communication with constituents, primarily by mail, is free for senators, and representatives are given generous mailing privileges. All of these benefits pale compared with the provisions made for congressional staff. In 1997 a staggering 24,000 people worked for Congress, including 9,830 staffers in the House and 6,732 in the Senate. Each representative has approximately 17 workers on staff, and each senator enjoys the assistance of no fewer than 38 aides. This support is vastly greater than in comparable legislatures, including the Japanese Diet and the British and Canadian Houses of Commons. Some positions are secretarial, but many workers are professionals, including some (about two for each member in the House and five in the Senate) directly assigned the job of drafting and amending legislation. In addition, 2,000 staffers work for House committees and more than 1,200 for Senate committees. The number of congressional staff has increased exponentially since 1950 (Figure 7.3).

Between the early 1970s and 1995, there was also a rapid increase in the number of subcommittees, reflecting both an increase in the legislative workload and the increasing independence of members of Congress. Committee staff numbers rose correspondingly. However, as the incoming Republican Speaker in 1994, Newt Gingrich reduced the number of subcommittees and their staffs (discussed in Chapter 8).

Finally, members benefit from the work of a number of support agencies, such as the Library of Congress (more than 5,400 staff) and the General Accounting Office (5,300). Of course, these support agencies are rarely directly involved in legislation, but their presence does reinforce the claim that, uniquely among world assemblies, Congress has acquired a formidable permanent bureaucracy.

Conclusion

There is no question that the typical member of Congress is a man or woman under pressure. Members are constantly campaigning—

FIGURE 7.3   Staff of Members and of Committees in Congress, 1891–1997

SOURCE: Norman Ornstein, Thomas Mann, and Michael Malbin (eds.), *Vital Statistics on Congress, 1997–1998* (Washington, DC: Congressional Quarterly Press, 1998), figure 5.2.

raising money, appearing on television, taking carefully prepared stands on a range of issues. At the same time, they are increasingly obliged to seek the lowest-common-denominator issue stance in order to please the largest number of constituents and displease the fewest. Often this strategy results in constituents' specific demands remaining unsatisfied. In this sense, the feverish pace of constant campaigning may have contributed to an increasing disillusionment with Congress among the voters. Few members of the public have high confidence in Congress, while the number having low confidence has risen rapidly since the early 1980s. To understand the full dynamics of representation and in particular how it interacts with those aspects of the job that are only remotely related to constituency pressures, it is necessary to examine how Congress actually influences the policy process. Are the laws made in a responsible and representative manner? To what extent does Congress check executive power? In sum, to what extent does Congress defend and promote the public interest?

Notes

1. Only in exceptional cases do British MPs survive the removal of party endorsement; they may survive on personal appeal for one election but rarely longer.

2. Congress has 435 members of the House of Representatives, 100 Senators, 3 delegates (District of Columbia, Guam, and Virgin Islands), and a resident commissioner from Puerto Rico. The latter four cannot vote on the floor but can serve as committee members.

3. Gary C. Jacobson, *The Electoral Origins of Divided Government: Competition in U.S. House Elections, 1946–1988* (Boulder, CO: Westview Press, 1990).

4. For a discussion of this point, see Gary C. Jacobson, *The Politics of Congressional Elections*, 4th ed. (New York: Addison-Wesley, 1996).

5. Burdett A. Loomis, *The Contemporary Congress* (New York: St. Martin's, 1996), p. 108.

6. David Mayhew, *Congress: The Electoral Connection* (New Haven: Yale University Press, 1986).

7. Both quotes from Mayhew, *The Electoral Connection*, p. 51.

8. A compilation of ratings can be found in Michael Barone and Grant Ujifusa, *The Almanac of American Politics, 1996* (Washington, DC: Barone and Co., 1997).

9. Richard E. Fenno, *Home Style: House Members in Their Districts* (Boston: Little, Brown, 1978).

Further Reading

David Mayhew's *Congress: The Electoral Connection* (New Haven: Yale University Press, 1986) remains the classic statement on the electoral connection. *Home Style*, by Richard E. Fenno Jr. (Boston: Little, Brown, 1978), is rich in anecdote on the same theme. See also Roger H. Davidson and Walter J. Oleszek, *Congress and Its Members*, 6th ed. (Washington, DC: Congressional Quarterly Press, 1998), Part 2. Congressional elections are examined in Gary C. Jacobson, *The Politics of Congressional Elections*, 4th ed. (New York: HarperCollins, 1996), and in James A. Thurber and Candice J. Nelson, *Campaigns and Elections American Style* (Boulder, CO: Westview Press, 1995). Two textbook treatments of Congress are provided by Michael Foley and John E. Owens, *Congress and Presidency: Institutional Politics in a Separated System* (Manchester: Manchester University Press, 1996), and Burdett A. Loomis, *The Contemporary Congress* (New York: St. Martin's, 1996). An excellent comparative analysis of the electoral connection is Anthony King, *Running Scared: Why America's Politicians Campaign Too Much and Govern Too Little* (New York: Free Press, 1997).

8

Congress as Policymaker

Let me say this about Congress. . . . A Congress is not a President. . . . A Congress should not be a President. . . . A Congress should be nothing more, nothing less than what it is: a reflection of the will of our people and the problems that disturb them and the actions they want taken. The Congress ought to improve its ability to serve that function.

—Senator Edmund S. Muskie

It is impossible for either the internal or the foreign policy of great states to be strongly and consistently carried out on a collegial basis. Collegiality unavoidably obstructs the promptness of decision, the consistency of policy, the clear responsibility of the individual, and ruthlessness to outsiders in combination with the maintenance of discipline within the group.

—Max Weber

As was stressed in Chapter 3, Congress was originally intended to be the key institution in the federal government. Only through Congress were the people given a direct control over policy. Members of the House of Representatives were directly elected. Senators, president, and vice-president were not. Moreover, Congress was meant to formulate and pass laws; the president's primary job was merely to implement them. Popular control of government was, of course, limited by the presidential veto and the territorial base of appointed senators. But the House of Representatives controlled the purse strings, and Congress as a whole stood, as legislature, at the apex of the constitutional system.

The institution never quite functioned as intended. During the first thirty years of the nineteenth century, state legislatures voted to adopt what became effectively the direct election of the president, and as the country grew and demands on government increased, president and executive took on the major responsibility for formulating legislation. This trend has occurred in nearly every country and is an almost inescapable consequence of the vast information and power resources available to modern executive bureaucracies but not to legislatures. Yet unlike most national legislatures, Congress retains formidable power. It remains an indisputably important actor in the policy process. It is also an institution whose powers and internal operations are constantly changing. The main purpose of this chapter is to analyze the nature and significance of these changes so that an accurate understanding of the policymaking role of Congress at century's end can be achieved. Particular attention is paid to the *responsiveness* of the institution and how this relates to the growing gap between public expectations and the ability of Congress to meet these expectations.

Functions of Congress

As indicated in Chapter 7, the first and most general function of Congress is representation. At its simplest, this means that members of Congress are held accountable for their actions through the electoral process. In complex societies, the citizen-representative relationship must necessarily be limited, however, so the concept "representative function of Congress" actually refers to a number of different functions, most of which are at least one step removed from the direct influence of the voters. Thus, the business of formulating and passing laws—the legislative function—involves constant interaction among members and staff, interest groups, executive officials, the courts, and the media. Clearly, the individual voter's influence in this process is limited, although the constant threat of electoral defeat does oblige U.S. legislators to tend to the general pastoral needs of their constituencies.

A second major function of legislatures, and especially the Congress, is to oversee the executive branch. Constitutionally and by convention, Congress has a number of established oversight powers. It controls finance, so appropriations bills originate in the House of Representatives and have to be approved by both houses. As discussed later, the president initially produces the annual budget, so the appropriations process is an opportunity for Congress to approve, modify, or criticize the executive's spending plans and also to monitor them during implementation. The Senate also approves presidential appointments and treaties, and both houses have power to investigate inefficiency or wrongdoing in the executive branch, including power to impeach executive officers (the House impeaches and the Senate tries).[1] Finally, Congress has the power to approve all administrative reorganizations in the executive branch. Before these functions are described in detail, it is necessary to outline the formal structure of power in the two houses.

Structure of Power in Congress

Committees

Of the two major foci of power—committees and party leadership—committees have always been central to the business of legislation in Congress, and their importance has increased over the years. The standing committees listed in Table 8.1 are distinguished by function, and as government has become more complex, so the number of committees and subcommittees has tended to increase. Consolidation and reorganizations do occur—indeed, the Republican 104th Congress (1995–1996) managed to reduce the number of subcommittees substantially (Table 8.2). Nevertheless, both the House and the Senate have a large number of working groups—especially in comparison with other legislatures. Both internal and external pressures are at work to maintain this need. Internally, individual legislators build reputations by specializing in a particular subject. Often this specialization is linked to constituent needs. Moreover, Congress's bureaucracy has had to match developments in the executive branch, and as its departments and agencies have increased in number and function, so Congress has been obliged to respond. Often this is a two-way street. Members' career and constituency needs may benefit from executive fragmentation that legislation often encourages.

Distinctions are drawn in Table 8.1 between policy committees concerned primarily with *general* policy and committees devoted mainly to servicing constituencies. In addition, the House has what might be called "prestige" committees that are primarily concerned with money—an area where the House has special responsibilities—or with parliamentary procedure.

TABLE 8.1   House and Senate Committees Listed by Preference
Motivations of New House Members and Senators, 106th Congress
(1999–2000)

House	Senate
Prestige committees	Policy committees
Appropriations	Budget
Budget	Foreign Relations
Rules	Governmental Affairs
Ways and Means	Judiciary
	Health, Education, Labor,
	and Pension
Policy committees	Mixed policy/constituency
	committees
Banking and Financial Services	Armed Services
Education and the Workforce	Banking, Housing, and
International Relations	Urban Affairs
Government Reform	Finance
Judiciary	Small Business
Constituency committees	Constituency committees
Agriculture	Agriculture, Nutrition, and
Armed Services	Forestry
Resources	Appropriations
Transportation and	Commerce, Science, and
Infrastructure	Transportation
Science	Energy and Natural Resources
Small Business	Environment and Public Works
Veterans' Affairs	Indian Affairs
Unrequested committees	Unrequested committees
House Administration	Rules and Administration
Standards of Official Conduct	Veterans' Affairs

SOURCE: Steven S. Smith and Christopher J. Deering, *Committees in Congress,* 2d ed. (Washington, DC: Congressional Quarterly Press, 1990), pp. 87 and 101. Updated from Library of Congress web site: http://lcweb.gov/global/legislative/congress.html.

The committees handle the business of framing, amending, and rejecting legislation. Most committees *authorize* legislation, while others provide funds to *finance* programs. Hence the Appropriations, House Ways and Means, Senate Finance, and the Budget Committees are concerned with approving income (taxation) and expenditure bills. (The budgetary process is examined in more detail in

TABLE 8.2   Number of House and Senate Subcommittees,
Selected Congresses, 1955–2000

	84th (1955–1956)	90th (1967–1968)	94th (1975–1976)	100th (1987–1988)	104th (1995–1996)
House subcommittees	99	154	172	160	77
Senate subcommittees	105	126	174	93	70

SOURCE: *Vital Statistics 1993–1994: Congressional Quarterly's Players, Politics, and Turf of the 104th Congress,* special issue of *Congressional Quarterly,* March 25, 1995. Updated from Library of Congress web site: http://lcweb.gov/global/legislative/congress.html.

Chapter 15.) By no means are all committees equal in power. The above-named finance committees are particularly prestigious and influential, especially so in the case of the House Appropriations Committee (which is the source of all appropriations bills), the House Ways and Means and Senate Finance Committees (which are responsible for tax bills), and the Budget Committees. Of the authorizing committees, the Senate Foreign Relations is of central importance in foreign policy, and the Agriculture, Banking, and Judiciary Committees are prominent in both houses. An equivalent hierarchy applies to most subcommittees; for example, the House Appropriations Subcommittee on Defense is markedly more important than the Military Construction Subcommittees.

Because the House of Representatives is a larger and, by tradition, a more formal body than the Senate, a number of complex rules have been formulated to govern day-by-day business. The Rules Committee is responsible for interpreting these regulations and in particular for helping to decide which bills, and in what form, come before the floor of the House. This power to withhold bills or to allow them to proceed only if certain amendments or provisions are omitted or included gives the Rules Committee considerable political clout. Indeed, during the late nineteenth and early twentieth centuries, the Rules Committee was at the very center of congressional power. Today, although it continues to perform a gatekeeper function, it is less powerful, in part because the House is less formal than it was (of which more later) and in part because it tends to be the voice of the majority party leadership rather than an independent source of power in Congress.

Clearly, membership on committees is an important determinant of the status and influence of individual representatives and senators, and accordingly the processes by which members are selected to sit on committees and eventually selected as chairpersons have long been the subject of debate and controversy. The most basic rule is that the party with a majority in the chamber automatically achieves a majority in the committees, with the minority party represented in rough proportion to its delegation in the chamber as a whole. Committee and subcommittee chairpersons are drawn exclusively from the majority party. In the House, members are allowed to sit on a maximum of two standing committees, although House members assigned to the important Rules, Ways and Means, and Appropriations Committees are not normally permitted further assignments. Typically, senators sit on three standing committees.

In both houses, party committees selected by party caucuses (meetings of all party members in each house) choose the members of the standing committees. This process is predictably political, with seniority, experience, reputation, and connections being the main determinants of assignments. Since the late 1950s, the Senate has ensured that all freshman (new) senators are given at least one major committee assignment (the so-called Johnson Rule introduced under the influence of the then Senate majority leader, Lyndon Baines Johnson). By winning prestigious committee jobs, members can enhance their institutional reputations, gain access to legislative programs of direct interest to their constituents, and, occasionally, attract national attention.

During the first two years of the 1981–1985 Reagan administration, for example, Representative James R. Jones (Democrat, Oklahoma) assumed a pivotal position as chairperson of the House Budget Committee. Although he opposed many of the administration's economic policies, Jones was able to straddle party positions by proposing alternative, but by no means opposite, policies and by maintaining a friendly relationship with Pete Domenici, the Republican chairperson of the Senate Budget Committee.

Status is no less important within individual committees and subcommittees, with the chairperson of each work group at the very top of the pecking order. Both rank within committees and chairpersons' assertion of power over committee members are largely determined by seniority. Until the early 1970s, the seniority rule was condemned by liberals because of the enormous advantage it gave to the solidly Democratic—but conservative and often racist—one-party South. Indeed, the caricature of elderly white-haired Southerners lording over all and sundry on Capitol Hill was not far from the truth, as evidenced by such figures as Richard Russell of Armed Services, Russell Long of Finance, and James Eastland of Judiciary in the Senate and Carl Vinson of Armed Services and Howard Smith of Rules in the House.

Since the 1970s, there have been three distinct waves of reform affecting committee power. Until the mid-1970s, chairpersons were particularly powerful because of their control of the agenda. They could decide the order in which bills were discussed, the timing of committee meetings, the frequency of public hearings, and the management of bills on the floor of the House. They also had a major say in the number and composition of subcommittees, together with the selection of subcommittee chairs. During the 1970s, the Democrats instituted reforms that removed committee chairs from the very pinnacles of power. Their control of the work and membership of subcommittees was weakened. Moreover, seniority was removed as the only criterion for advancement within committees. In 1975 the House Democratic caucus, caught up in a general atmosphere of reform, removed three of the most powerful committee chairpersons at a stroke (Wright Patman of Texas, Banking and Currency; W. R. Poage of Texas, Agriculture; and F. Edward Hébert of Louisiana, Administration). In fact, seniority remained central to any promotion within committees. From 1975 to 1994, chairpersons were obliged to treat subcommittee chairs (and committee members generally) more as equals than as feudal vassals. This restructuring was part of a general democratization and dispersal of power in both the House and (to a lesser extent) the Senate.

This decentralization of power led many commentators to conclude that Congress was incapable of making quick decisions. Worse, decentralized committees were likely to pander to particular (or constituency) rather than general (or the public) interest. Republican presidents and congressional opposition spokespersons pointed to the fact that the Democrats' apparently permanent control of the House made it impossible to cut the budget deficit or to pass needed reforms in such areas as health care and the economy.

These criticisms were almost certainly exaggerated, but they helped inspire a second major wave of reforms instituted by the Democratic leadership in the 1980s that were designed to relocate power away from the committees and return it to the leadership. Although subcommittee powers were reduced (especially in the

Senate), the Democrats were less than successful in transforming the system. However, following the Republicans' capture of Congress in the 1994 midterm elections, Newt Gingrich, the new House Speaker, and Dick Armey, the new majority leader, were determined to push through the legislative program outlined in their "Contract with America." As a result, they persuaded the Republican Conference (the committee representing all the House Republicans) to push through a number of changes in committee operations.

The major objective of these reforms was to strengthen party control over the committees. In light of the Republicans' success in passing most of the Contract with America legislative program (although much of it was eventually defeated in the Senate or by presidential veto), this objective seems to have been achieved. However, the reforms produced changes in the "folkways" of the House that may have had negative rather than positive consequences. Also, the enthusiasm and determination of the Republican leadership in the 104th Congress began to flag after the Democratic advances in the 1996 and 1998 elections.

In addition to the standing committees in each house, a number of other work groups exist, including the conference committees. These are ad hoc bodies created to reconcile differences that arise in the House and Senate versions of the same piece of legislation. Membership is drawn from those members in each house who have been most closely involved with the legislation (usually the relevant committee members), who then vote en bloc so as to represent the wishes of their chamber. A great deal of politicking goes on in conference, with bills often amended considerably, and not always in line with the wishes of the House or Senate as a whole. Conference decisions can, however, be rejected by a subsequent vote on the floor of each chamber and sent back to the committee.

In addition, ad hoc committees can be formed by the Speaker of the House to reconcile standing committees with overlapping jurisdictions, and select committees appointed by presiding officers can be created in either house to expedite a particular problem, often in association with a congressional investigation. In recent years, for example, select committees on aging and intelligence have been formed in both houses. Such committees must be renewed every two years, and they cannot report legislation to the floor. In most cases, select committees emerge as a forum for airing currently controversial issues.

Party Leadership

The second focus of power in Congress is the party leadership. In the House, the key figures are the Speaker and the minority leader, and the key groups are the party caucuses, in particular the majority party caucus (in 1999, the Republican Conference). The Speaker of the House formerly had substantial formal powers. Until 1911, he was also chair of the Rules Committee, and he appointed committee chairpersons. This combination enabled Speakers to control the flow of legislation to the floor. Concentration of such power in the personage of one particularly assertive Speaker, Joseph Cannon, led to a revolt in the 1910–1911 Congress that resulted in the removal of the Speaker's control of the Rules Committee and of committee assignments.

Nevertheless, the Speaker retains considerable authority. He continues to help control the flow of legislation, recognizes who is to speak on the floor, can create ad hoc committees, gives advice on assignments to conference and select committees, helps in assigning bills to committees, and votes in the event of a tie. The Speaker has the greatest formal power of any individual in the House, but his potential informal power is much greater. As both leading parliamentarian and party leader, he can become a crucial link between other centers of power—in particular, committee chairpersons—as well as be the person most able to muster often disparate party forces behind a particular bill or the program of a president. Whether these powers are utilized to the full depends on the personality, capabilities, and political skills of the incumbent.

Since the 1940s, for example, the office has come full circle as incumbents have changed. Between 1940 and 1960, the office was dominated by the forceful and highly political Sam Rayburn (with breaks in the 1947–1948 and 1953–1954 sessions when the Republicans had a majority in the House). During the period 1961–1978, first John McCormack and then Carl Albert became Speakers, neither of whom had the skills or the charisma of Rayburn. Between 1978 and 1986, the highly partisan and politically astute Thomas (Tip) O'Neill partly returned the office of Speaker to its former glory. O'Neill's personality was ideally suited to the brokerage politics of the House, and he was aided by the 1975 reforms that gave the Speaker the power to appoint Democratic members of the Rules Committee and to the Democratic Steering Committee, which assigns new committee members within the

party. Given the Democratic dominance of the House, these powers were considerable. On his resignation in 1986, O'Neill was replaced by Jim Wright of Texas, a longtime O'Neill supporter and
until 1986 Democratic House majority leader. In June 1989,
Wright was forced to resign after allegations of financial irregular-
ities were brought against him by the House minority whip, Newt
Gingrich. Wright was replaced by Tom Foley, who had a more accommodating style than the often feisty Wright.

Following the 1994 midterm Republican victory, Speaker Newt
Gingrich took on a legislative leadership role unprecedented since
the days of Joe Cannon. In addition to the committee reforms, Gingrich's formal powers were enhanced. Because he was also widely
perceived as partly responsible for the Republican victory, he had
built up considerable political capital with House members. His
dominance was dented, however, when in 1996 he was accused of
a number of ethics charges, and he was only narrowly reelected
Speaker in early 1997. As a result, during the 105th Congress
(1997–1998), his parliamentary position was weakened, and some
power was returned to the committee chairpersons. Gingrich resigned after the Republicans' poor showing in the 1998 midterm
elections. His eventual successor (the first choice, Bob Livingston,
was forced to withdraw after admitting to extramarital affairs) was
Dennis Hastert of Illinois, who was elected by the Republican caucus January 6, 1999. Hastert proved to be much less combative
and more collegial in his approach than Gingrich.

After the Speaker, the most important offices are the majority
and minority floor leaders, who are elected by the party caucuses
and whose main job is to monitor and organize party business on
the floor of the House. In fact, the minority leader is often a more
crucial figure than the majority leader, largely because the Speaker
is the effective majority spokesperson. Dick Gephart saw his position and importance as minority leader increase in the context of
Clinton's 1996 victory and the difficulties encountered by Speaker
Gingrich between 1996 and 1998.

Finally, both parties appoint whips to help control floor business.
These are in no way equivalent to British parliamentary whips;
they have no effective sanctions at their disposal to oblige members
to toe the party line. Instead their job is to persuade, negotiate, bargain, and cajole members into broad agreement on particular items
of legislation.

The party caucus meets infrequently and then usually to agree on procedure rather than to discuss substantive policy issues. As important today are the informal caucuses that have emerged since the 1980s. These are usually organized around a particular interest group, such as the Democratic Black and Hispanic caucuses, or around an ideological orientation, such as the Democratic Study Group representing liberal causes or the conservative Republican Study Group. In the late 1990s, the typical House member belonged to sixteen caucuses and the typical senator to fourteen.

Leadership in the Senate roughly parallels that in the House, but there are some important differences. Unlike in the House, the Senate's presiding officer—formally the vice-president of the United States—is an honorific position carrying with it few powers, the main one being to vote in event of a tie. Nor does much power rest with the president pro tempore, which goes by tradition to the longest-serving senator from the majority party. On a day-to-day basis, the members of the majority party preside over the chamber on a rotating basis. Real power lies with the majority and minority leaders, although even they can often do little to control the behavior of 100 fiercely independent senators. Again, much depends on the personality of the incumbents. Some majority leaders, such as Lyndon Johnson (1956–1961), built reputations as power brokers, as did Republican Howard Baker, whose management of the Republicans' fragile majority 1981–1985 showed great political skill. Robert Dole of Kansas, who succeeded Baker in 1985, had to use all his political skill to hold together an even narrower Republican majority until the Democrats regained control of the Senate in 1986. In contrast to Johnson and Baker, some recent leaders such as Mike Mansfield (1961–1978) have either been unwilling or less able to assert authority over fellow party members. Following the Republican victory in 1994, Bob Dole became majority leader. Although a skilled parliamentarian, Dole had his energies diverted by his race for the presidency in 1996. His replacement, Senator Trent Lott of Mississippi, was more in the mold of an old-style party leader. A strong partisan devoted to good organization, Lott was able successfully to exploit the more ideological agenda that came to dominate Congress by the late 1990s.

The preceding discussion about the formal powers of committees and party leaders indicates little about the dynamics of the policy-making process, however, and how Congress as an institution can be assessed in terms of its performance and effectiveness. One way to examine these questions is first to assess the validity of the criticisms directed at Congress over recent years and then to analyze the reform measures adopted in response to these criticisms.

Congress Under Fire

At least since World War II, Congress has been the subject of sometimes intense criticism. Very generally, these criticisms fall into two broad categories—those that are historically specific and those that identify structural features of Congress that persist through time. Of course, the two sets of critiques are related, especially as the institution is constantly changing, but this simple distinction does facilitate a more subtle understanding of how the institution works.

Fragmentation and Unresponsiveness

Perhaps the most common and persistent criticism is that Congress is fragmented and unresponsive—that it is not a coherent policymaking body but instead a forum for the defense and promotion of disparate, unrelated interests. That the policymaking process in Congress is fragmented cannot be disputed. Power is dispersed to committees and subcommittees, and the legislative process itself is cumbersome. When a bill is introduced, it faces a formidable number of potential veto points before it becomes law, and this is true even of those bills that are part of the president's program, have substantial support in Congress, and are recognized as important public issues.

The major obstacles that confront any bill introduced into Congress are identified in Figure 8.1. Committee action is the most difficult stumbling block, with only about 10 percent of bills actually reported out of committee. The presidential veto was formerly a rare barrier, but since the advent of divided government, it has been exercised more frequently on important items of legislation (see Chapter 10). Even less common are successful attempts to override a veto. The president can also exercise a pocket veto by failing to sign a bill passed within the last ten days of a legislative session.

Not listed in Figure 8.1 is the Senate *filibuster*—a debating device that has ended the life of several controversial bills. Filibustering is the practice, allowed only by Senate rules, of speaking in unlimited debate and eventually forcing the opposition to back down. During the 1950s and 1960s, many civil rights bills were killed by this

FIGURE 8.1   How a Bill Becomes Law: The Obstacle Course for Legislation in Congress

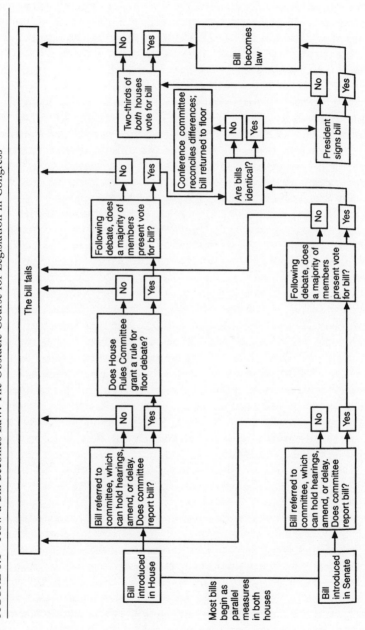

method, with segregationist Southern senators speaking for many hours against the reform measures. A device does exist for ending a filibuster; known as a *cloture* (or closure) rule, this can be invoked to end debate if three-fifths of the senators agree. Between 1917 (when the cloture rule was introduced) and 1996, 437 cloture votes were taken, of which 147 were successful. Since the 1970s, cloture has been voted much more frequently and is now successful in about 30 percent of cases. During the 103rd Congress (1993–1994), the Republicans as the minority party managed to produce 42 filibusters, many of which thwarted President Clinton's legislative measures. After 1994, when the Republicans were in the majority, the Democrats returned the favor, fighting as they were to prevent enactment of the Republican's Contract with America program.

In the House, the Rules Committee can constitute a further barrier to the passage of a law. Until 1975, Southerners dominated the committee and frequently refused to grant rules to bills they disliked, irrespective of the support the measures may have won in the legislative committees. Again, liberal and, especially, civil rights legislation was the victim. In 1975, however, the Democratic caucus voted to give the Speaker the power to appoint Rules Committee members. As a result, although the committee can still stop bills, it acts more in accordance with the general wishes of the House—and particularly those of the relevant legislative committee—than before. Interestingly, debate on the floor once was an insignificant aspect of the legislative process, for by the time a bill reached this stage, it was already roughly in its final form. Recent reforms, however, have increased floor activity, with individual legislators now more able to attach riders and amendments to bills. Floor votes can also be crucial, of course.

Figure 8.1 gives the slightly misleading impression that bills either proceed past a number of legislative hurdles or are simply killed off. The reality is that most bills are nonstarters because they lack the support of key members—although some are initiated simply to attract public attention to an issue—and the remainder embark on a course beset with problems and pitfalls. But these difficulties do not always involve the possibility of a sudden death. As likely are the possibilities of amendment and delay. Delay can occur at almost any stage of the process, but committees are where bills most often become buried, sometimes never to reappear. Given that Congress has a heavy workload and is constantly under pressure, delaying a bill is often an expedient course to follow. For a bill's supporters, including presidents, this tactic can be highly frustrating.

Few bills emerge from Congress in the precise form that they entered. They are amended—sometimes dramatically—from their original form, and this amendment process is the very essence of congressional politics, for it is by changing the detailed provisions of bills that members can indulge in logrolling, or the exchange of favors that is so crucial to their electoral survival. Thus, items are added to or deleted from bills in accordance with bargains struck between key legislators, usually within or between committees. Committee hearings, open to public scrutiny, also allow organized interests to air their views and generally to advertise particular points of view. And of course executive departments and agencies usually have a crucial interest (with positions to defend or promote) in the detail of legislation. Finally, committees may compete one with the other, for as can be inferred from the list of committees in Table 8.1, there are a number of areas where overlapping jurisdictions occur.

When all these influences are at work, as they are in major items of legislation, the potential for delay, obstruction, and even confusion can be appreciated. A classic example of what can happen to a vital piece of legislation is provided by President Clinton's health care reforms introduced in Congress in 1993. Given the enormous complexity of the bill—a result of the need to consolidate a large number of existing federal health and welfare programs—it was assigned to multiple committees. Two of these, the House Education and Labor and the Senate Labor and Human Resources, agreed on a reform package but one too liberal for the Congress as a whole to accept. In addition, the key Finance Committee chairs found it difficult to win sufficient committee support for the reforms. As Burdett Loomis has noted, these failures reveal a great deal about congressional power given that the chairs of the committees involved included some truly formidable legislators—Representatives John Dingell (Energy and Commerce) and Dan Rostenkowski (Ways and Means) and Senator Daniel Patrick Moynihan (Finance). In the end, Congress found it impossible to reconcile all the conflicting bureaucratic, health care, and insurance company interests in a way that would produce a coherent legislative package. The bill died a year later during the 1994 midterm election campaign.[2]

There have, in fact, been remarkably few occasions when a major legislative package has not been delayed or obstructed by Congress.

The early New Deal (1933–1935) and Great Society (1965–1966) periods are usually mentioned as the notable exceptions (see Chapters 14 and 15). Some analysts have argued that the first two years of the Reagan administration were also characterized by a responsive and responsible Congress, but the president by no means had it all his way, and by the end of 1982, Congress began to assert a more independent position, especially on economic policy. Similarly, the much publicized reform program of the Republican 104th Congress achieved much less than the Republicans desired—partly because President Clinton was able successfully to exercise the veto power.

Perhaps, indeed, Congress should assert its independence. How else, after all, could it be responsive to the demands of public opinion and voters? There are two answers to this question. The first, which is highly controversial, is the simple fact that in a complex and pluralistic society beset with urgent domestic and international problems, democratically elected executives should not have to face open resistance from the legislative branch. Executives in most Western European countries are relatively free from such pressures and may be, as a result, more able to respond effectively to crisis. This contentious point is explored in later chapters.

The second response is more relevant to the argument in this section: Fragmentation of power in Congress, multiple veto points, and open access by myriad interests to centers of power render the institution *inefficient*. In other words, it cannot be responsive because its decisionmaking structure is clumsy, slow, and confused. When it does appear to "work," it works to resist change and to pander to special rather than collective or public interests. This brief survey of the legislative process suggests that there is considerable truth to this charge. Certainly several generations of House and Senate members have been aware of it, for they have repeatedly attempted to reform the institution.

Lack of Oversight

Another criticism is that Congress has failed to perform the oversight function effectively. In addition to passing legislation, Congress is charged with the job of overseeing the executive, or holding the president, executive departments, and agencies accountable for their actions. The appropriations process (see Chapter 15) in part involves this responsibility. In addition, Congress is responsible for monitoring executive appointments and holding formal investigations into the executive branch; as a last resort, it has the authority to impeach executive officers.

The Constitution requires the Senate to approve presidential appointments, but it has not used this power in the strictly "moral" sense—that is, to root out inefficient, incompetent, or corrupt appointees. As often, senators are concerned with ensuring that incumbents in the more than 1,500 major posts subject to Senate confirmation are men and women who are sympathetic to the legislators' political or constituency interests, or who are likely to defend an organized interest (such as labor or business) with which senators are known to identify. In short, the appointment process is not unlike the legislative process—highly politicized and subject to similar constituency and interest-group pressures. Only rarely are nominations withdrawn, and even more rarely are they rejected. Between 1987 and 1996, for example, only two nominations were rejected out of more than 400,000 submitted—although around 1,200 were withdrawn.[3]

Thus, Congress is accused of two failings with respect to appointments. First, it favors many appointees not because they are likely to serve the public interest but because they will support particular or special constituency and group interests. Second, and independent of this problem, Congress has failed to root out some of the more obvious and colorful examples of incompetent presidential nominations. The Nixon administration was littered with such cases. But even the Carter presidency had Bert Lance, the budget director who was eventually obliged to resign following exposure of illegal banking practices. More recently, the first Clinton administration also had its share of dishonest or incompetent appointees, with accusations leveled at a number of cabinet secretaries, including Secretary of Housing and Urban Development Henry Cisneros and Commerce Secretary Ron Brown.

Although such cases have occurred, Congress does examine the records of the most senior nominees more carefully now than in the past. This is particularly true of Supreme Court nominees, who have the potential to shift the ideological complexion of the Court on a range of sensitive issues. Such perceptions certainly applied to Robert H. Bork, Reagan's 1987 nominee to the Court, who was opposed by the wide margin of 58 to 42 senators. Reagan's second nominee for the vacant position, Douglas H. Ginsberg, was obliged to withdraw following an admission that he had smoked marijuana while at law school. Eventually the president nominated a "safe" candidate, Anthony Kennedy, who was quickly confirmed by the Senate. George Bush had fewer difficulties with his appointees, although his nomination of Supreme Court Justice Clarence Thomas was confirmed by the narrow margin of 52-48 following allegations of sexual harassment against the judge. In addition, Bush's first choice as defense secretary, John Tower, was forced to withdraw following allegations that he was personally unsuitable for the job.

Most commentators agree that in the context of divided government, presidents have experienced more partisan and ideological objections to their appointees. In particular, President Clinton's efforts to make the U.S. District and Appeals Courts look "more like America" in terms of gender and ethnicity were partly thwarted by the Senate Judiciary Committee's delays on his nominations. Fearing that the Clinton appointments would lead to a more activist (i.e., liberal) judicial branch, the committee tied up many of the Clinton nominations for many months during both of the president's two terms.

The investigative power of Congress consists of investigations by the standing committees, the work of special or select committees created for the specific purpose of inquiring into a particular problem, and the work of the General Accounting Office (GAO). GAO auditing of executive spending is a continuous process, and its findings are reported to Congress. Congress can also require the GAO to investigate a particular program or agency at any time. Standing committee investigations involve public hearings into alleged executive inefficiency or wrongdoing. One of the most famous was the Army-McCarthy hearings by the Senate Government Operations Permanent Investigations Subcommittee into Communist influence in the U.S. Army, the Central Intelligence Agency (CIA), and the Department of State. Subcommittee Chairman Joseph McCarthy became notorious as a red-baiter in this role, and his unfair and intimidating methods led eventually to his censure by the Senate in 1954.[4]

More typical are the several instances when Congress has created a select committee specifically to investigate a subject of public concern. In recent years, for example, the Senate Select Committee on Campaign Practices—known popularly as the (Sam) Ervin Committee after its chairperson—won great public attention through its inquiries into the Watergate scandal. This in turn spawned further investigations into the security agencies (FBI, CIA, Defense Intelligence), the legality of whose activities had been questioned during the Watergate exposures. In 1987 the Reagan administration was also investigated by congressional select committees set up in each house to investigate the origins and management of the Iran-Contra affair. In this case, the House and the Senate decided to conduct joint hearings, and the investigation led directly to a number of indictments and prosecutions, including the prosecution of former Defense Secretary Caspar Weinberger. Weinberger and four other former officials were pardoned by President Bush in late 1992. Congress also has investigated the involvement of President Clinton and first lady Hillary Clinton in the Whitewater property company that operated in Arkansas during Bill Clinton's tenure as governor. Other notable congressional investigations include inquiries into racketeering in trade unions, safety in nuclear power stations, the conduct of the Vietnam War, and standards in the pharmaceutical industry.

Not only federal government activities come under congressional scrutiny, although investigations into the executive branch usually arouse the most feeling and controversy. The reason for this is simple: Investigations (and oversight generally) raise awkward questions about where executive power begins and ends. With the rise of big government and the vast bureaucracy that accompanies it, Congress has found it increasingly difficult to perform the oversight function because it has limited access to exactly what goes on within the executive. Information is a valuable commodity and one jealously guarded by presidents and their bureaucrats. Even though Congress can subpoena witnesses and documents, presidents have repeatedly refused or been extremely reluctant to hand over information. In recent years they have claimed "executive privilege" to certain information. Unfortunately, this concept has no clear constitutional status, so the legality of withholding information remains an open question. Since Watergate and Richard Nixon's unprecedented reluctance to furnish evidence to congressional committees (he withheld information at least nineteen times on matters unrelated to Watergate), presidents have been more compliant. But as the Iran-Contra affair confirmed, the executive continues to hold the trump card, because the sheer volume and technical complexity of documentation often make it difficult for a hard-pressed committee even to know what to ask for.

Finally, Congress has the power to impeach executive officers. Impeachment is a formal accusation of wrongdoing as determined by the House of Representatives; the Senate then tries and convicts impeached officials. But on only thirteen occasions has the House used this power, and on only four has the Senate convicted. One president, Andrew Johnson, was formally impeached, although the Senate failed to convict (by one vote), and the House Judiciary Committee voted articles of impeachment against Richard Nixon, who resigned before further action could be taken.

The most famous case, of course, was the impeachment of Bill Clinton in 1998 and the subsequent Senate trial in 1999. Clinton's impeachment demonstrated both the advantages and disadvantages of the impeachment process. On the one hand, the House vote for articles of impeachment (258 to 176 with 31 Democrats voting against the president) was widely regarded as a hasty and partisan interpretation of the "high crimes and misdemeanors" established in the Constitution as grounds for impeachment. On the other hand, the Senate trial, though also partisan, was conducted with great dignity. In any event, the president was acquitted of both charges—on the perjury count, 55-45 for acquittal, on obstruction of justice, 50-50. With a two-thirds vote needed for conviction, neither vote came close to removing the president.

The Clinton impeachment undermined one of the main criticisms of the impeachment process—that it is so cumbersome and formalized that it is rarely used. However, the case bolstered one of its advantages—that it is very difficult to secure a conviction unless the offenses are truly a threat to the integrity of the office and the Constitution.

In addition to these structural criticisms, Congress is at any one time criticized for its specific failure to deal with a contemporary crisis or problem. Or, observers infer that a structural feature of the institution is permanent when it is only temporary. In the decade after World War II, it was common to accuse Congress of excessive partisanship. And indeed the red-baiting committees of the late 1940s and early 1950s did in part represent Republican attempts to indict the activities of past or present Democratic administrations. By the late 1950s and early 1960s, the charge was somewhat different: Congress was dominated by conservative, segregationist Southerners. Since the reforms of the 1970s, the criticism has shifted once again. Now the accusation is that Congress is the creature of increasingly vocal and influential special- and public-interest lobbies—or simply that members serve their own rather than the public interest.

Recent events seem to confirm this view in the minds of the American public. In 1989, five senators were found to have intervened in favor of Charles Keating of the Lincoln Savings and Loan

Association. In 1991, the Senate Ethics Committee found evidence of wrongdoing by Senator Alan Cranston of California, and the other four were reprimanded. During the 103rd Congress (1993–1994), 267 House members were found to have used an interest-free overdraft facility from a bank set up specifically for use by members of Congress. The public outcry at the extensive use of these "rubber checks" was considerable. Finally, in early 1997, Speaker Newt Gingrich was formally reprimanded and fined by the House for illegally using income from college courses he taught for partisan purposes. Although he was reelected, this unprecedented action against a sitting Speaker weakened his position as House leader, and Gingrich eventually resigned in 1998.

Reform and Change in Congress

The major criticisms of Congress prevalent in the late 1960s and early 1970s stressed two failings: Legislative business was dominated by a few senior committee chairpersons; and in its dealings with the executive, Congress was failing to provide either realistic policymaking alternatives or to check the burgeoning growth of executive power. Commentators had long noted that if these problems were to be solved, political party organizations in the two houses would have to take the lead.

Indeed, in terms of centralizing and decentralizing influences, party and party leadership are clearly centralizing forces, whereas the committee structure essentially disperses power. Party voting has never been as strong as during the 1890–1910 period, when over half the roll calls (votes on the floor) involved 90 percent of one party voting differently from 90 percent of the other. As shown in Figure 8.2, even by the weakest measure of party unity—the percentage on which a majority of voting Democrats opposes a majority of voting Republicans—party voting has not exceeded 75 percent since 1970. Note, however, the general trend toward more party voting—especially in the House. These figures are high in comparison with the mid- and late 1960s when the Democratic Party, in particular, was alive with sectional and ideological conflict.

Frustrations resulting from these conflicts were often centered on the ways in which a few conservative chairpersons dominated committee business and the legislative agenda. By the early 1970s, this frustration had reached such a point that a number of sweeping reforms were introduced, and these reached a crescendo in 1975 fol-

FIGURE 8.2   Party Unity Scores by Chamber, 1954–1998

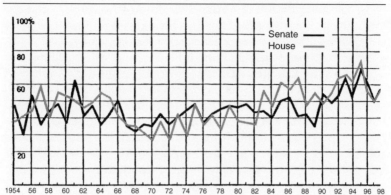

SOURCE: *Congressional Quarterly Weekly Report,* January 9, 1999, p. 79.

lowing the election of the unusually liberal post-Watergate Congress in 1974. The major changes were as follows:

1. In 1970 the House ended nonrecorded teller voting and switched to electronic voting on all roll calls. As a result, the number of roll calls increased dramatically, from 177 in 1969 to 541 in 1978.
2. In 1973 all bill drafting in committee was opened to public scrutiny, thus exposing to organized interests and constituents the precise policy preference of members.
3. The Democratic caucus in the House voted in 1971 to permit ten or more members to demand a special vote on a disputed committee chairperson assignment. In 1975 all nominees for chairperson were subject to an automatic secret ballot by caucus members.
4. Also in 1975 the caucus voted to give the Speaker the power to appoint Rules Committee members, subject to caucus approval.
5. Since 1973 all Democratic House members have been guaranteed a major committee assignment, and since 1974 committee assignments have passed from the Ways and Means Committee (traditionally dominated by Southerners) to the party's Steering and Policy Committee.
6. Subcommittees were greatly strengthened and increased in number by several measures, beginning with the 1970

Legislature Reorganization Act. In 1973 the subcommittees were provided with a "Bill of Rights" that gave to the full committee caucus the power to set subcommittee jurisdictions and select chairpersons. Subsequently, subcommittees were allocated extra staff.

7. Although the number of formal changes in the Senate were fewer than in the House, reforms took the same general direction and in some cases were quite radical. Committee meetings were opened to the public, the Democratic caucus's power was strengthened in relation to the nomination of committee chairpersons, and it became much easier to end a filibuster than it was in the early 1970s. Also, the committee structure was rationalized with the number of committees reduced and some overlapping jurisdictions eliminated.

All these reforms were designed to speed up the legislative process and to weaken the entrenched power of committee chairpersons. Through these measures, members hoped to make Congress a more effective policymaking body and therefore to enhance its position in relation to the executive. In fact, in the wake of the abuse of executive power represented by the conduct of the Vietnam War and Watergate, Congress passed a number of laws specifically designed to curb such excesses and to strengthen the legislative branch. The two most important of these measures were the following.

1. The 1973 War Powers Act: Overriding a presidential veto, Congress acted in 1973 to limit the president's ability to conduct war without the prior approval of Congress. Under this law, the commitment of U.S. armed forces could occur only if Congress declared war or authorized the use of forces or if the president acted in a national emergency. During emergency actions, presidents were required to win congressional support after sixty days, and a further thirty days could be granted. After the ninety-day period, Congress could act to stop the use of troops through a law that is not subject to presidential veto.

2. The 1974 Budget and Impoundment Control Act: A perennial complaint of Congress watchers in the post–World War II period was the failure of the institution to match the executive's budget-making capacity. Presidents presented annual budgets, which had effectively become national policy programs. Congress, in contrast, seemed unable to see the budget as a coherent whole. Indeed, Con-

gress dealt with finance in an incremental, piecemeal way, reflecting the fragmentation characteristic of bicameralism and the appropriations process. The 1974 legislation attempted to compensate for these problems by creating budget committees in each house and a Congressional Budget Office to provide specialized technical information for both chambers and allow Congress to compete with the president as budget maker.

At the time these reforms were being adopted, analysts expected them to have little effect. By the early 1990s, however, these measures had helped to contribute to what are now recognized as profound changes in the institution, as suggested by scholars in such books as *The New Congress, The Decline and Resurgence of Congress,* and *Legislative Leviathan.* The primary changes can be summed up quite simply: Power in Congress remained dispersed, but the institution was more professional, more concerned with the details of the legislative process, more ideological, and more focused on oversight of the executive. Finally, Congress was still essentially a conservative body—although not in the same ways as before.

The reform movement was fueled by two main forces: (1) members' increasing electoral independence from party and regional ties that a more rapid turnover of members and other changes had produced and (2) the already noted disillusionment with the institution's ability to deal with executive power. As previously described, constituency pressures had increased greatly, and electoral success came to depend less on traditional party organization and more on personal resources. In order to "deliver the goods" to constituents, members needed two things: more control within Congress over legislation and more control over the executive policymaking process. Although the reforms went a long way toward the achievement of both objectives, they also had the unintended effect of weakening party leadership in Congress.

During the early 1990s, Democratic congressional leaders were only too aware that their control over members was all too limited. The experience of the 103rd Congress (1993–1994), when much of President Clinton's program died in a Democratic Congress, persuaded them of the need for further reform. However, given the entrenched power of large numbers of Democrats in Congress, reform had to await the arrival of a new cohort of Republican members in early 1995. As was mentioned earlier, the new Speaker, Newt Gingrich, was intent on reform, which would strengthen party leadership. His own powers were enhanced, and serious efforts were made to weaken committee power in relation to party influence. The major changes were these:

1. A one-third reduction in staff;
2. The control of all staff by the chair;
3. A three-term limit for committee and subcommittee chairs;
4. A limit of five subcommittees for most committees, and an overall reduction from 118 in the 103rd Congress to 77 in the 104th;
5. Abolition of the District of Columbia, Merchant Marine and Fisheries, and Post Office and Civil Service Committees;
6. Limiting most members to serving on two committees and a total of four subcommittees;
7. Requiring that all committee votes be published and no proxy voting be allowed;
8. Requiring that most committee meetings be open and allowing coverage of television and radio, if requested;
9. Requiring that the Speaker no longer refer bills to multiple committees simultaneously (with modest exceptions).[5]

Although in total these reforms constitute a shift away from committee power, the committees remain the focal point of activity in Congress. Moreover, any weakness in the party leaders is likely to result in some return of authority to the committees. Although parallel moves have occurred in the Senate, reforms there have been less extensive. As has always been the case, power in the Senate tends to reside in the influence of individual senators rather than be determined by parliamentary rules and procedures. Although the Gingrich reforms seem a sensible rationalization of decisionmaking, they have been criticized for undermining cross-party civility in the institution and thereby accelerating a lack of public confidence in Congress.[6] Moreover, a more partisan Congress in the context of divided government works against the sort of bargaining and compromise that, historically, has been necessary for the legislative and executive branches to cooperate effectively. Indeed, following the poor electoral showing of the House Republicans in 1996 and 1998 and the public's generally hostile response to the way the Republicans handled the impeachment of President

FIGURE 8.3   Public Bills in the Congressional Workload, 80th–104th
Congresses, 1947–1996

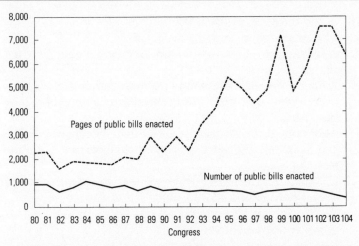

SOURCE: Norman Ornstein, Thomas Mann, and Michael Malbin (eds.),
Vital Statistics on Congress, 1997–1998 (Washington, DC: American
Enterprise Institute, 1998), figure 6.3.

Clinton, moves back to cooperation and away from confrontation
were evident in the 106th Congress (1999–2000).

Increased partisanship in Congress can largely be explained by
two factors. First, the number of Southern Democrats has declined.
These members were conservative and often voted with the Republicans rather than their party. Second, congressional politics has
generally become more conflictual and ideological since the 1980s.
Often this means confronting presidents of another party in ways
that were rare during the 1950s and 1960s. This point is developed
in the next chapter, but a more abrasive executive-legislative environment has undoubtedly increased partisanship on all sides.

In one sense, Congress is more efficient—for although the number
of bills passed has not increased, those that are passed tend to be
more complex and comprehensive (Figure 8.3). In addition, committees expedite bills more rapidly than before. But these changes to the
institutional rules have not transformed the essentially slow and
cumbersome nature of the legislative process. In other words, Congress remains an institution where blockages, delays, and vetoes can
occur at several stages in the legislative process. As a result, Congress

retains a built-in conservative bias—it is easier to kill legislation than to be proactive and pass bills. The increase in the number of "omnibus" bills (see Figure 8.3 for the increase in page count) represents an attempt to please as many members as possible. But each of these bills is passed only after members have spent an enormous amount of time and effort on them.

In short, coalition building—always a defining characteristic of Congress—has assumed an even greater importance since the 1980s. Partly as a result of this institutional characteristic, although also because of the electoral changes outlined in Chapter 7, a conservative coalition continues to exercise considerable influence. Until the early 1970s, this group consisted of Southern Democrats and Northern Republicans. During the 1980s, it included Southern Democrats and Republicans from every region. Since 1994, virtually all Republicans and a sizable minority of Democrats have formed this coalition.

Conclusion: Can Congress Lead?

In some respects, Congress reflects the moods and wishes of the nation more accurately now than it has for many years. This is a direct result of a new, more intimate legislator-constituency relationship and the easier access to legislators that organized interests now enjoy. Since the 1980s, public opinion has moved to the right, and Congress has accurately mirrored this trend. But the American electorate is highly volatile, and issues are much less susceptible to a simple identification on a left-right political continuum than they used to be. In addition, scandals involving members and the decline of cross-party civility on the Hill have almost certainly undermined public confidence in the institution. Approval ratings fell particularly low during the 1990s (Figure 8.4). In spite of recent reforms, therefore, many Americans continue to view Congress as self-serving rather than as a responsive and responsible institution.

The assumption should not automatically be made, however, that because Congress appears to be self-serving and pandering to particularistic interests in American society (individual constituents and organized interests) rather than to the public interest, it is always incapable of effective collective action. On rare but important occasions, it has shown unexpected resolve. In 1985 both houses passed the Gramm-Rudman-Hollings Deficit Reduction Act that bound the president and Congress to successive reductions in the

FIGURE 8.4   Approval of Congress, 1974–1997

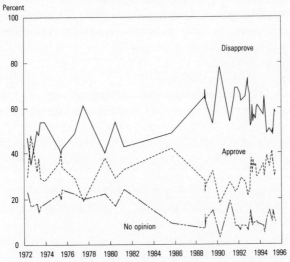

NOTE: Question: "Do you approve or disapprove of the way the U.S. Congress is handling its job?"

SOURCE: Harold W. Stanley and Richard G. Niemi, *Vital Statistics on American Politics, 1997–98* (Washington, DC: Congressional Quarterly Press, 1998), figure 3.6.

budget deficit (although the Supreme Court struck down the compulsory provisions in the act—for details see Chapter 12). A year later Congress passed the most sweeping overhaul of the American tax system in modern history. Moreover, against all expectations, the budget deficit was eliminated in the late 1990s.

Clearly, the House and Senate can respond to outside pressures or to perceptions that the collective interest must take precedence over particular interests. Unfortunately, however, collective action of this sort is rare. In its everyday business, special and particular interests dominate, because the central dilemma for Congress today is, in fact, the same dilemma it faced in the 1950s and 1960s: Building coalitions in a highly fragmented institution involves many trade-offs, with costs in terms of time, coherence, and efficiency mounting steadily as the legislative process lumbers on. And although reforms have been initiated through party mechanisms, political party influence on legislation remains relatively weak. Given the serious economic and international problems confronting the United States, the need for decisive and coherent policymaking is as great as ever. If Congress can contribute relatively little in this area, then this role must be played by that institution traditionally associated with national leadership—the presidency.

Notes

1. Impeachment is a formal act of accusation similar to indictment. The impeachment process involves the gathering of evidence. If sufficient evidence of wrongdoing is found, the Senate then tries the impeached person.

2. Burdett A. Loomis, *The Contemporary Congress* (New York: St. Martin's Press, 1996), chap. 10.

3. Harold W. Stanley and Richard G. Niemi, *Vital Statistics on American Politics, 1997–98* (Washington, DC: Congressional Quarterly Press, 1998), table 6.10. See also G. Calvin Mackenzie, *The Politics of Presidential Appointments* (New York: Free Press, 1981), table 8.1.

4. The institution of red-baiting, if not the actual practice, continued with the House Un-American Activities Committee (later the Internal Security Committee) until its abolition in 1975.

5. Loomis, *The Contemporary Congress,* p. 81.

6. Richard F. Fenno Jr., *Learning to Govern: An Institutional View of the 104th Congress* (Washington, DC: Brookings Institution, 1998).

Further Reading

A good textbook treatment of Congress is Burdett A. Loomis, *The Contemporary Congress* (New York: St. Martin's Press, 1996). A comprehensive treatment is also provided by Roger H. Davidson and Walter J. Oleszek, *Congress and Its Members,* 6th ed. (Washington, DC: Congressional Quarterly Press, 1998). The reforms of the 1970s and 1980s are covered by James L. Sundquist, *The Decline and Resurgence of Congress* (Washington, DC: Brookings Institution, 1981), and Roger H. Davidson (ed.), *The Post-Reform Congress* (New York: St. Martin's Press, 1992). The classic work on committees is by Richard Fenno Jr., *Congressmen in Committees* (Boston: Little, Brown, 1973). A current and comprehensive account of the institution with an emphasis on presidential relations is provided by James E. Thurber (ed.), *Rivals for Power: Presidential-Congressional Relations* (Washington, DC: Congressional Quarterly Press, 1996). Facts and figures on the institution can be found in Norman J. Ornstein, Thomas E. Mann, and Michael J. Malbin, eds., *Vital Statistics on Congress 1997–98* (Washington, DC: American Enterprise Institute, 1998).

9

Presidential Power

The modern Presidency of the United States, as distinct from the traditional concepts of our highest office, is bound up with the survival not only of freedom but of mankind. . . . The President is the unifying force in our lives. . . . The President must possess a wide range of abilities: to lead, to persuade, to inspire trust, to attract men of talent, to unite. These abilities must reflect a wide range of characteristics: courage, vision, integrity, intelligence, sense of responsibility, sense of history, sense of humor, warmth, openness, personality, tenacity, energy, determination, drive, perspicacity, idealism, thirst for information, penchant for fact, presence of conscience, comprehension of people and enjoyment of life—plus all the other, nobler virtues ascribed to George Washington under God.

—*Nelson A. Rockefeller*

The saddest life is that of a political aspirant under democracy. His failure is ignominious and his success is disgraced.

—*H. L. Mencken*

These two quotations pinpoint the central dilemma of the modern presidency: In the American political system, the president is the only national unifying force. Only the president is elected by a single national constituency, and all executive power is vested in the office. He has, therefore, both great responsibilities and great power. Because the chief executive is so centrally placed, public expectations of the office are high.[1] But in recent years, few incumbents have possessed the qualities necessary to carry out the job efficiently and responsibly.

Every president between the mid-1960s and 1992 was associated to a greater or lesser extent with failure. Lyndon Johnson was broken by the Vietnam War, and Richard Nixon by Watergate. Gerald Ford was little more than a caretaker president, and Jimmy Carter was judged indecisive and politically inept. Ronald Reagan will probably not be deemed one of the great presidents given his involvement in the Iran-Contra affair and the consequences of his economic policies (see Chapters 15 and 16). George Bush lacked the charisma and authority associated with great presidents and, after one term, achieved the dubious distinction of being beaten by a larger margin than any incumbent president since Herbert Hoover in 1932. And although it is too early to pass judgment on Bill Clinton, his ambitious first-term legislative program came to little, and at midterm, the Republicans captured both houses of Congress for the first time since 1952. The Republicans maintained their majority status for the whole of his second term, which was, of course, marked by the only impeachment of a sitting president in the twentieth century.

Curiously, this association of the office with mediocrity and the abuse of power is comparatively recent. Most texts on the American presidency written during the 1950s and 1960s saw little wrong either with the nature of the office or with recent incumbents.[2] In retrospect, the midcentury presidents—Franklin Roosevelt, Harry Truman, Dwight Eisenhower, and John Kennedy—do seem impressive figures. So what has happened since?

There are three possible answers to this question, which will constitute the major part of discussion in this chapter. First, it could be that public expectations of the office have increased in recent years just as the ability of presidents to satisfy these expectations has declined. Second, the process whereby presidents are recruited may have changed in ways that preselect inappropriate presidential candidates. Third, it could be that, independently of the selection process, different—and inappropriate—personality types have occupied the office in recent years. These claims require further examination, but first it is necessary briefly to outline the formal and informal sources of presidential power and to trace the growth of the modern presidency.

Formal Sources of Power

To an outside observer, one of the most remarkable features of the American political system is the concentration of governmental functions in one institution, the presidency. The Constitution is

partly responsible for this, for it assigns to the presidency the roles
of chief executive (Article 2, Section 1), commander-in-chief of the
armed forces (Article 2, Section 2), chief diplomat (or the power to
make treaties, Article 2, Section 2), chief recruiting officer to the
executive and courts (Article 2, Section 2), and legislator (by making recommendations to Congress, Article 2, Section 3, and by exercising the veto power under Article 1, Section 7). As was emphasized in Chapter 3, the framers did not expect the president also to
become *chief* legislator, but over the past century, he has assumed
this crucial function. Finally, the president is head of state, so must
carry out all those diplomatic and ceremonial duties normally performed by constitutional monarchs (in Britain, the Netherlands) or
presidents (in Israel, India, and Italy).

Given this panoply of powers, it is understandable to think of periods in American history in terms of incumbent presidents. The first
years of the republic are inseparable from the personality and influence of George Washington. Andrew Jackson's presidencies are
closely associated with the democratization of American politics and
the rise of a modern two-party system. Abraham Lincoln's personal
conduct of the Civil War effectively shaped a whole era in American
history, while Woodrow Wilson was the first president to elevate the
United States onto the world diplomatic and military stage. Since the
New Deal period—itself synonymous with the personage of Franklin
D. Roosevelt—every president has made a lasting imprint on American and world politics.

Of course, presidents are constrained, sometimes seriously, by a
number of domestic and international forces, but within the United
States, the chief executive is the natural and immediate focus of attention. As noted in Chapters 7 and 8, it would be difficult to consider Congress a natural leader or decisionmaker. If anything, the
opposite is true. Federalism fragments political power and authority even further, leaving the presidency (and on rather rare occasions, the Supreme Court) as the sole unifying and centralizing influence in the system.

During the nineteenth and early twentieth centuries, the constitutionally assigned powers in military, foreign, and diplomatic policy tended to raise the visibility of the office. Indeed, through exercising these powers, some presidents greatly expanded and even
exceeded the constitutional authority. In 1803, Thomas Jefferson
authorized the purchase of the Louisiana Territories from France
(see Map 2.1) without consulting Congress. Abraham Lincoln's

conduct of the Civil War was almost authoritarian, involving as it did a blockade of the South, the suspension of habeas corpus, and unauthorized increases in the size of the army and navy. Much later, Woodrow Wilson asked for, and was given, broad powers under the 1917 Lever Act to seize factories and mines and fix prices to help the war effort. But government, and especially the federal government, played a relatively minor part in economic and social life during this period. An assertive Congress could, and often did, dominate the political agenda. Without the vast bureaucratic and logistical resources of the modern executive, those presidents lacking political skills or unfortunate enough to preside over particularly difficult domestic events, such as the recriminations and confusion characteristic of the post–Civil War period, were truly secondary political figures. From the New Deal period onward, no president has been able to stay backstage, because the demands of the office have multiplied so dramatically.

Since World War II, the role of commander-in-chief has often meant control over several million men and women under arms and literally the power of life and death over humankind. As chief executives, modern presidents are responsible for numerous programs and policies affecting every aspect of society. As chief legislator, the president takes to Congress a package of programs, together with budget requests, that effectively mold the national political agenda. As was cataloged in Chapter 4, the rise of federal regulations and grant programs has meant that even local governments—those bodies so free from central control in the early republic—now depend in part on the president's policies. Of course, the president is constrained when performing these functions, and every industrial country has been required to centralize power in executives and greatly to expand the role of government.

No Western country, however, has acquired such formidable military and strategic power as has the United States, and in none has the role of state been transformed in quite the way as in America. In the United States, after all, government has traditionally been weak in relation to society, and the market has been considered the most appropriate mechanism for distributing resources. Yet by the 1990s, more than 30 percent of national income was accounted for by government spending, and in some areas of economic and social life, the federal government had become a major source of income and support for large numbers of individuals, subnational governments, and corporations.

It could be argued that American institutional arrangements, especially federalism and the separation of powers, are ill-suited to the sort of efficient and effective policymaking needed in a modern industrial society. If this premise is valid, the pressures on the executive are increased even more, because only the president has a truly national constituency and only the president is the natural coordinator and organizer of national policy. Put another way, for many Americans, the president is the embodiment of the federal government. It is not surprising, then, that the public's ambivalence about the role of government should often show itself as hostility to the office of the president.

Informal Powers

Because of the president's position at the apex of the constitutional system, the office has also attracted a number of informal powers or influences in addition to those constitutionally assigned. These include the president's roles as party leader, agenda setter and national leader, and world leader. All three can provide presidents with valuable extra resources, but they can also burden the office with extra duties and responsibilities.

Party Leader

Once elected, presidents become the de facto leaders of their political party. This position carries with it both advantages and disadvantages. One advantage is that the opposition party has no equivalent position. Even when another party controls the Congress (as in the late 1990s), there is no "natural" leader of the other party. Thus, incumbent presidents have a great advantage over opposition opponents in the race for a second term (U.S. presidents are limited to two terms). Although being party leader certainly sounds grandiose and impressive—and in the British system, for example, being prime minister and party leader is indeed a great political advantage—American political parties are fragmented and weak. Only very rarely in recent history have presidents been *guaranteed* party support in Congress, and lucky is the president who knows he can count on the support of governors, mayors, and other party leaders in the federal system.

This accepted, weak party ties are almost certainly better than none at all, and presidents do use party connections to rally support (if not always successfully) during elections. Party is also the vital cue available to presidents when they make appointments to the executive branch. Without the myriad party contacts at congressional, state, and local events, it would be difficult to fill all the 50,000-plus jobs that are nominated annually. Presidents also use this process to repay debts for electoral and other services rendered.

Agenda Setter and National Leader

Americans expect something more than the efficient execution of policy from their presidents; they also expect them to embody the spirit of the nation or, in Clinton Rossiter's term, to be the "voice of the people."[3] It should not be forgotten that the United States has relatively few symbols of national unity, such as the monarchy in Britain, or a long-established culture rooted in language and custom, as in France. In some respects, the institution of the presidency helps fill this gap by providing Americans with a sense of national identity. When at press conferences an aide announces the entrance of "The President of the United States," he or she is presenting a national symbol as well as chief executive, and the simple words of the announcement carry with them a level of respect that is notably missing when a British prime minister or German chancellor appears in public.

Related is the expectation that the president will set the national political agenda. This means more than simply sending a legislative program to Congress in the State of the Union address. The public looks first to the president to shape the terms of debate for national legislation and national action. Presidents are *expected* to be responsible for the economic and social well-being of the country and are held accountable at the polls should they fail to deliver. In 1992, for example, George Bush was blamed for economic recession and lost the election to Bill Clinton. In addition, during crises and natural disasters, the public looks first to the president for leadership, action, and moral support. Hence, after such tragedies as the Oklahoma City bombing in 1995 or the mass high school shooting in Littleton, Colorado, in 1999, it has been the president who addresses the nation and pronounces on the need for better security in federal buildings or for stronger gun-control legislation.

World Leader

In recent years, the president's role as a national leader has been reinforced by America's emergence as a world power, a fact amply demonstrated by President Kennedy's famous speech at the time of the Cuban missile crisis:

> Let no one doubt that this is a difficult and dangerous mission on which we have set out. No one can foresee precisely what course it will take or what costs or casualties will be incurred. Many months of sacrifice and self-discipline lie ahead—months in which both our patience and our will will be tested, months in which threats and denunciations will keep us aware of our dangers. But the greatest danger of all would be to do nothing. The path we have chosen for the present is full of hazards, as all paths are; but it is the one most consistent with our character and courage as a nation and our commitments around the world. The cost of freedom is always high—but Americans have always paid it. And one path we shall never choose, and that is the path of surrender or submission.[4]

Such stirring rhetoric may seem inappropriate at century's end, but presidents continue to project themselves as world leader, as an examination of George Bush's speeches on the Gulf War or Bill Clinton's on Kosovo would show. In other words, presidents attempt to portray themselves as defenders of the *national interest*. In contrast to the fragmentation and particularism of Congress and the federal system, the president alone claims to see foreign policy in terms of what is in the interest of the whole country. In this sense, presidents attempt to elevate themselves above party, special interests, and even ideology. Of course, they do not always succeed—indeed, few recent presidents have even come close to succeeding—but they are constantly striving for this very special status, and almost certainly American citizens expect their presidents to play this part. Indeed, surveys consistently show that the public is dramatically more aware of the presidency (including the vice-president) than other public offices, and this consciousness is acquired early in life.

As world leaders, some recent presidents have had to attenuate their styles and rhetoric in line with the changing nature of American power. But they retain a special status in the international system. Certainly, presidents' words and actions are significantly more important than the speeches and deeds of British and Japanese prime ministers, German chancellors, and French presidents. This crucial international status adds yet another dimension to presidential power—and also to the pressures of the office.

In sum, because presidents are considered the embodiment of the federal government, they are the focus of myriad public demands. Expectations of the office are, therefore, very high. At the same time, public disquiet over the role of government in economy and society is often focused directly on the incumbent in the office of the presidency.

The Presidency in Crisis

Presidential Selection

In answer to the questions posed at the beginning of this chapter about presidential quality, it seems reasonable to hypothesize that the crisis of the modern presidency is one of recruitment. It may be simply that the wrong people are being selected for the job. What is the nature of the presidential nomination process? And why is it now the subject of such criticism? Presidential elections have four distinct phases: preprimary, primary, convention, and campaign.

The Preprimary Phase. It is often quipped that no sooner is a president elected than he has to start running for his second term. Although an exaggeration, this is not so far from the truth, for any candidate with even the slightest hope of winning nomination must plan his or her campaign several years ahead. In his buildup for the 1976 campaign, Jimmy Carter cultivated newspaper editors and political commentators more than a year before the convention. His strategy was simple: He had to raise his public visibility in order to neutralize the "Jimmy who?" reaction whenever his name was uttered. Ronald Reagan announced himself more than two years before the 1980 election, and by late 1982, former vice-president Walter Mondale was already grooming himself for the 1984 contest. In 1985, Vice President George Bush was beginning to build an organization to be ready for 1988, and Bill Clinton made no secret of his ambition to run for president many years before he formally announced his candidacy in October 1991. By the beginning of Clinton's second term, Vice President Al Gore was carefully positioning himself for the contest in 2000. Merely announcing early guarantees nothing, of course. Much depends on the political resources, reputation, experience, and skill of the candidate.

The times are also important. Jimmy Carter's extraordinary journey from obscurity to president between 1972 and 1976 owed much to the prevailing disillusionment with "Washington" and established party candidates. More typically, candidates must win the support of key political figures if they are to have any chance. In 1980, Ronald Reagan was endorsed by many of the leading Republicans and "king-makers" of the political right; Gerald Ford notably lacked such support and was well advised to make an early retreat from the race. Edward Kennedy, in contrast, failed to win the unequivocal endorsement of the Democratic establishment but soldiered on nonetheless. In 1992, Bill Clinton did win support from established sections of the Democratic Party that almost certainly helped him to create the image of front-runner early in the campaign. An incumbent president naturally enjoys a huge advantage in winning the party's nomination, and there is no instance in recent years of a president who wants to stand failing to secure nomination.

Curiously, few incumbent vice-presidents have been elected president in American history. George Bush was to prove an exception, in part because he won the support of many leading Republicans early in Reagan's second term. In 1992, however, he had to fight hard to win over the Republican right and eventually won only their grudging support.

The Primaries. There was a time when a candidate with strong intraparty support could avoid the primary circuit. In 1968, for example, only 49 percent of the votes cast by delegates at the Democratic convention were decided by primary election; the remainder were in the pocket of party caucuses. By 1976 this figure had risen to 75 percent, which made it essential for candidates to run in the primaries. Thus, Hubert Humphrey's strategy of depending on his very considerable Democratic Party connections was successful in 1968 but suicidal just four years later when he entered the primaries late and was effectively beaten before the convention. Following reforms in the Democratic Party, the number of primaries was reduced in 1984 but increased again in the 1990s, so that no candidate now can afford to ignore them.

Today, there are thirty-seven primaries in the Democratic Party and forty-one in the Republican (figures are for the 1996 presidential election). The primary season remains lengthy, running from February to June, but most of the important primaries, including those of California, New York, and Texas, are held in March. Unfortunately, the precise technicalities of primaries defy simple description because each state decides the timing, voter eligibility, and general organization of its primary elections. The most important formal distinction is between *closed primaries,* operative in most states, which are open only to registered party members, and *open primaries,* in which voters can vote for either party, but not both, by asking for that party's ballot at the polling station. They do not, in other words, have to be registered as Democrats or Republicans to vote in that party's election.

In those states without primaries for presidential nominations (all states have some form of primary for statewide elections), party caucuses or meetings decide delegate selection. Since the 1980s, primaries have become more important, not only because they have increased in number but also because changes in party rules have had the effect of binding delegates more closely to candidates. Moreover, the partial switch back to caucuses in the Democratic Party in 1984 did not signal a return to "old-style" party politics. Most of the new caucuses were very open and were as binding on delegates as primaries. So open were some of the caucuses—in many, almost anyone could participate—that some were replaced by primaries in the 1990s. In previous eras, bargaining on the convention floor resulted in delegates switching their allegiances, thus making the convention a key decisionmaker in the nomination process. Today the primaries and caucuses proper play this role.

Because candidates cannot afford to bypass the primaries, they must have the political, financial, and even physical resources to endure the long series of campaigns involved. They must also have the time, for staging a series of primary campaigns is effectively a full-time job. As will be developed later, this fact alone may preselect certain sorts of candidates. Recent elections have also shown how important it is for candidates to make a good start. Through what might be called a "media bandwagon effect," a particular candidate is identified as a winner, and this in itself provides an essential impetus to that person's campaign. This factor may constitute a disadvantage for candidates with key support in those large industrial states where primaries come relatively late—although the primary season is shorter than it used to be. Some commentators have even gone so far as to claim that Iowa (an early party caucus state) and New Hampshire (the first primary) hold the key to the fortunes of candidates—and these are hardly representative areas of the United States. Certainly, Jimmy Carter did well in early contests in 1976 and 1980, which helped him to head off opponents with support in larger states. And in 1980, George Bush's late vic-

tories in such states as Michigan meant little when Ronald Reagan
had already won most of the early primaries and therefore had accumulated a formidable number of delegate votes. Even if candidates do not win all the early primaries, they must at least enter
and perform reasonably well. Such was the case with the successful
nominees in 1988, George Bush and Michael Dukakis. In 1992,
Bill Clinton bucked the trend of winning early primaries. He lost
the New Hampshire primary to Paul Tsongas, the South Dakota
primary to Bob Kerrey, and the Colorado primary to Jerry Brown.
Not until March 10, with the "Super Tuesday" series of southern
primaries, did he establish a lead.

The Nominating Conventions.   To foreign observers, nothing better represents the sheer theater of American politics than the nominating conventions. During the summer before the election, several
thousand party delegates meet to choose their presidential and
vice-presidential candidates in an apparently crazy few days of
party festival. Although policy is discussed at conventions, they are
more of a media event, where candidates and their supporters
strive to achieve maximum public exposure. There was a time
when the conventions actually chose candidates for the general
election, with several ballots required before a majority (until 1936
two-thirds in the Democratic convention) of all the delegates could
agree on a candidate. During this period, conventions were an accurate reflection of the vote trading and coalition formation typical
of American politics generally. They were, in other words, highly
political, involving deals, bargains, and periodic deadlocks as party
bosses switched their blocks of delegate votes or opted for a compromise candidate. In recent elections, however, the winning candidate is identifiable before the convention begins because the primaries effectively decide the contest.

The spread of primaries was part of a general party reform
movement prevalent in the late 1960s and 1970s. In the case of the
Democrats, calls for reform were greatly aided by the events at the
1968 convention in Chicago when an old-style party organization
nominated Vice President Hubert Humphrey, a candidate associated with organized labor and Lyndon Johnson's conduct of the
Vietnam War. But this was the period when social issues (the war,
minority rights, the liberalization of society) were in the ascendant,
and traditional Democratic Party organizations were notably unsympathetic to the new movement. After violent scenes outside the

convention hall when young people, radicals, and other excluded groups demonstrated against the old-style machine politics, the party was plunged into a turmoil of recriminations.[5] The upshot was the appointment of a commission (the McGovern-Fraser Commission) to recommend changes in delegate selection. Since then the party has never been free of commissions, reforms, and debate on how best to organize itself.

McGovern-Fraser resulted in two major changes. From 1972, representation at conventions from minorities and underrepresented groups—blacks, women, youth—was greatly increased. Second, a system of proportional representation was recommended for primary elections. Previously, the person winning the primary took all the delegate votes ("winner takes all"). McGovern-Fraser recommended that the delegates given to a candidate should be in proportion to his share of the vote. Between 1972 and 1984, the rules were modified further following the advice of more commissions, most notably the Hunt Commission's report in 1982. From 1980, a minimum 20 percent cutoff point was established in the primaries to discourage frivolous candidacies. (It has since been set at a minimum of 15 percent.) The original McGovern-Fraser idea of quotas for underrepresented groups was replaced with affirmative-action requirements, and beginning in the early 1970s, the rules governing selection of delegates to party caucuses were gradually modified to open meetings and committees to rank-and-file members.

Very generally, these reforms (which were paralleled in an attenuated form in the Republican Party) involved the struggle (discussed in Chapter 5) between old-style party professionals and a new breed of party activists. The new party activists generally prevailed, yet it would be misleading to argue that somehow party influences are stronger as a consequence. In fact, the opposite is true. Because delegates are now mainly chosen in primaries and are almost always tied to particular candidates, the voters, not party activists, decide the nomination. And given the rise of candidates' vote-getting organizations, this shift of power effectively relegates political parties to a lesser position in the nominating process.

The drive for more democratic procedures in party nominations not only has weakened the influence of party, but it also has failed to correct the nonrepresentativeness of convention delegates. In 1972, the delegates were certainly younger and more radical than in 1968, but in ideological and programmatic terms they were not typical of the average Democratic voter.[6] By 1980, Democratic delegates were markedly more female and black than before, but they were also more middle class, had fewer links with industrial trade unions and traditional Democratic Party organizations, and had stronger links with the growing public-sector unions. Aware of this, the Hunt Commission also recommended the creation of "superdelegates" to the convention, or regular party-elected or -appointed officials. It was assumed that state legislators, governors, and members of Congress would be more moderate in their views and would inject an element of peer-group review into the selection process. In 1984 and again in 1988, about one-seventh of all delegate spots to the convention were reserved for party and public officials, and caucuses replaced primaries in several states.

Most observers agree that these changes did little to alter the fundamental nature of the nomination process. Although a "traditional" candidate, Walter Mondale, was nominated in 1984, Gary Hart, a "new-style" candidate, very nearly beat him. And the candidacy of civil rights activist Jesse Jackson, who did well in many primaries, showed how the system was basically unchanged since 1980. In 1988, neither of the two front-runners was an old-style party candidate. Jesse Jackson's impressive showing in the primaries and caucuses came to nothing, not because Michael Dukakis had won the support of the party regulars (which he had), but because Dukakis won more primaries and caucuses than Jackson and therefore came to the convention with enough delegate votes to ensure victory.

By 1992 the number of superdelegates was increased to nearly one-fifth of the total, but again, there is no evidence that their presence made any difference. For one thing, superdelegates are not necessarily more moderate than the typical Democratic voter. For another, it is difficult to imagine how, in a media-infused process, they could make a difference. As Walter Dean Burnham has put it: "They're little more than window dressing. There's not a lot of room for peer review in the television era ... there's just no way super delegates can exercise a credible veto."[7] On the other hand, by the late 1980s almost all important party officeholders were at least attending the Democratic conventions (see Table 9.1), even though their influence was not easy to measure.

The Hunt Commission also recommended that the primary season be shortened and that more primaries be held on the same days. The primary season was shortened slightly (state law, not party rules, dictates the timing of primaries, although the courts have given the parties the right to decide who is eligible to vote in

TABLE 9.1 Representation of Major Elected Officials at National Conventions, 1968–1992 (percentages)

	1968	1972	1976	1980	1984	1988	1992
Democrats							
Governors	96	57	44	74	91	100	96[a]
U.S. senators	61	28	18	14	56	85	81[a]
U.S. representatives	32	12	14	14	62	87	88[a]
Republicans							
Governors	92	80	69	68	93	82	81
U.S. senators	58	50	59	63	56	62	42
U.S. representatives	31	19	36	40	53	55	30

NOTE: Figures represent the percentages of Democratic or Republican officeholders from each group who served as delegates.

[a] Unpledged delegates (i.e., "superdelegates") only, not including those officeholders who went to the Democratic convention by other means.

SOURCE: Figures provided by the Democratic and Republican National Committees, as reproduced in Stephen J. Wayne, *The Road to the White House 1996: The Politics of Presidential Elections* (New York: St. Martin's Press, 1996), table 4.6.

primaries). Since 1988, most southern states have voted on the
same day (the so-called Super Tuesday, usually in early March).
This last innovation did little to help southerner Al Gore in 1988,
but it gave southerner Bill Clinton an essential boost in 1992. Finally, in 1996 California and a number of other states moved their
primary dates from May and June back to March. As a result, the
winning candidate in future primaries likely will be known by the
end of March.

The Campaign.   Before the campaign proper starts, nominated
candidates must choose their vice-presidential running mates. Until
recently this decision was taken at the convention. Today, however,
nominated candidates choose their running mates some weeks before the convention. Nominees use the opportunity to heal political
wounds or to balance the ticket geographically or ideologically. In
1960, John Kennedy's choice of Lyndon Johnson helped to smooth
relations between the two main contenders for the nomination; it
also balanced the ticket between the urbane Catholic from the
Northeast and the more populist Protestant from the South. The
choice is a crucial one, for although the office of vice-president is
not the top position, five of the ten vice-presidents who served during the period 1945–1988 eventually became president themselves
(Harry Truman, Lyndon Johnson, Richard Nixon, Gerald Ford,
and George Bush).

Occasionally, vice-presidential choices create major difficulties.
George McGovern's initial choice of Thomas Eagleton in 1972 had
to be changed with indecent haste after it was revealed that Eagleton
had once received psychiatric treatment. In 1980, Ronald Reagan's
first preference, Gerald Ford, proved politically tactless when Ford,
not unsurprisingly, laid down certain conditions for acceptance, including a demand that the vice-president should be more of an executive partner than a subordinate. In 1984, Democratic vice-presidential candidate Geraldine Ferraro was constantly dogged by
revelations of her husband's financial wrongdoings. George Bush's
choice in 1988 of Dan Quayle, the junior senator from Indiana, was
greeted with surprise and incredulity among Republicans and Democrats alike. Quayle apparently did little to balance the ticket in geographical or ideological terms. In addition, he proved an inept and
inexperienced campaigner. After a few weeks, the Bush organization
was obliged to shunt Quayle off onto political sidings where any
damage he might do would be kept to a minimum. In stark contrast,

Bill Clinton chose Tennessee Senator Al Gore as his 1992 running mate. Although Gore did not balance the ticket—he was close to being a political clone of Bill Clinton—he did add to Clinton's image of youth, moderation, and vigor.

Both the preconvention and postconvention campaigns are expensive. Advertising, and in particular television advertising, takes the lion's share of campaign funds. Indeed, spending on television has risen almost exponentially since the first major exposure of candidates during the 1960 campaign, when John Kennedy confronted Richard Nixon in live debates. What effect television advertising has on the voters is, however, an open question. Some evidence exists to suggest that it has little effect; most voters apparently acquire positive or negative impressions toward candidates quite early on, and then their perceptions are based on performance rather than image.[8]

Nevertheless, advertising and the presidential debates almost certainly *reinforce* public perceptions of candidates. In 1988, for example, the Bush campaign's efforts to label Dukakis as a liberal who was soft on law and order almost certainly confirmed in the minds of many voters—Republican, Democratic, and independent—what they had suspected. Similarly, in 1996, Bill Clinton's constant reference to "building a bridge to the twenty-first century" contrasted with Bob Dole's references to the values of the past and helped reinforce his appeal as the candidate of youth and of the future. Thus, candidates can never afford to drop their guard, and television is widely perceived as important even if its effects are difficult to measure.[9] In 1992, Ross Perot used television to quite remarkable effect. By July he was polling approval ratings as high as those of the party candidates. His subsequent withdrawal and reentry reduced his support, but he still managed to win 19 percent of the vote.

For most candidates, a high level of public exposure is maintained by constant travel, usually by air, but a candidate still may hire a train to reenact the famous whistle-stop tours of an earlier era. Incumbent presidents standing for reelection are usually less eager to engage in constant public-image building. They do, after all, enjoy the advantages of incumbency and can exploit their established positions as statesmen. In 1972, for example, Richard Nixon appeared in public infrequently and relied instead on the prestige of the presidential office when appealing to the voters. Whatever the campaign strategy, all candidates continue during the last two or three months before the election to build political bridges and to strengthen the coalition of support they must already have established to have won the nomination.

To non-American observers, the campaigns are remarkably free from reference to specific programs and policies. Indeed, candidates score points against opponents or make reference to very broad issues and ideological labels. Michael Dukakis was condemned by George Bush as inexperienced and incapable of upholding American power and prestige abroad. Dukakis in turn criticized Bush for his insensitivity to the needs of ordinary citizens. Attacking opponents may not be the only focus. Reagan promised in 1980 to "get America back to work." Richard Nixon in 1968 pledged that he would pursue "peace with honor" in Vietnam. In 1992, Bill Clinton repeatedly made references to the state of the economy and the need for change. George Bush steered away from the issues and emphasized the allegedly weak character of his opponent. In the context of a continuing economic recession, Bush's strategy proved ineffective. In 1996, Clinton made few specific campaign pledges and instead relied on his record and on building bridges to the next century. Republican candidate Bob Dole's specific promise to reduce income tax by 15 percent backfired. Few economists—or for that matter, voters—believed it was possible to achieve such a large reduction and balance the budget at the same time.

In sum, the entire campaign, pre- and postconvention, has increasingly become an exercise dependent not on traditional party organization but on *personal* party organization and, in some cases, simply on personal followings. Again, this emphasis demonstrates the general trend toward essentially nonpartisan elections, the implications of which are discussed later.

Flaws in Presidential Selection

Many of the criticisms of the type of person who today is likely to end up as the Democratic or Republican candidate for president relate to party and campaign finance reforms, most of which have weakened candidates' ties with party organizations. Under the 1971 and 1974 Federal Election Campaign Acts, primary candidates receive matching federal funds (financed by a $3.00 checkoff on all income tax returns). In 1992, Clinton and Dole combined received $23 million. In addition, around $11 million was available for each party for its party convention. During the campaign proper, a further subsidy is available provided candidates do not spend more than this from money raised from other sources. In 1996, Clinton and Dole collectively spent $120 million in public money. National and state local party committees can also spend a limited amount on the campaign.

Crucially, candidates must raise most of this money from large numbers of individual contributors. Voters can contribute no more than $1,000 to candidates per election (primary and general election), and only $250 of this qualifies for matching funds. Pursuant to a 1976 Supreme Court decision *(Buckley v. Valeo)*, no limit exists on what candidates can themselves spend on their campaigns. In 1992, independent candidate Ross Perot spent only personal funds, and in 1996 Republican candidate Steve Forbes spent a staggering $37 million of his own money. Although these reforms have reduced dependence on a few large contributions, they have also reduced candidate dependence on grassroots party activists and organizations. Thus, according to the critique, candidates are out of touch with the "real" world of party organization and with day-to-day governmental activity.

Ronald Reagan and (in 1976) Jimmy Carter were "unemployed," middle-aged (or even elderly) men with no experience of Washington and the wider international community. In 1988 and 1992, both Michael Dukakis and Bill Clinton were incumbent governors, but again both lacked any Washington experience. They owed their success to undisputed political acumen devoted to winning their party's nomination. This strategy involved mobilizing a personal party following and exploiting the uniquely open—even populist—nature of the "new" American nomination process. As critics bluntly assert, such a system encourages the candidacy of a breed of politicians—the "unemployed," ambitious, and instrumental (and often wealthy)—who are much less likely to make good presidents than those tested by peer-group pressures and the rigors of many years' experience in high office.

There is, without doubt, a great deal of truth to these charges. Certainly, few successful European leaders have assumed office with as little experience of the world of high politics as did Ronald Reagan or Bill Clinton. But to extrapolate from so small a sample would be overreaching; the same accusation would, after all, be difficult to level at the three "failures" among recent presidents—Lyndon Johnson, former Senate majority leader and vice-president; Richard Nixon, former House member, senator, and vice-president; and Gerald Ford, former House minority leader and established party man. In 1988, the American people elected a man of very broad experience, for George Bush had not only been vice-president for eight years but had also been a member of Congress, chief of the CIA, and U.S. ambassador to the United Nations. And whereas the inexperienced small-state governor Bill Clinton won the Democratic nomination, the 1996 Republican nomination went to the vastly experienced former Senate majority leader, Bob Dole.

Of course, at least four old-style party candidates (Hubert Humphrey, Gerald Ford, Walter Mondale, and Bob Dole) did *lose* elections, which may vindicate the charges, but so too did George McGovern in 1972 (very much a nonparty candidate) and Jimmy Carter in 1980 (an incumbent president with all the advantages that should bring). In 1992, an incumbent president was beaten by what at first blush seemed another "outsider" candidate—the governor of Arkansas, a very small, poor, southern state. But in many respects, Bill Clinton was an unusual outsider: He was well connected with the Democratic Party establishment, was widely traveled, and had received an elite education at Yale and Oxford. In fact, he had all the attributes of the ideal late-twentieth-century candidate—his main advantage lay not in long-established party contacts and experience in government but in the fact that he was a brilliant campaigner.

In sum, the American presidential selection process is far from ideal and has no doubt contributed to a succession of less-than-impressive presidents. But the considerable problems associated with the office in recent years also have their origins in forces beyond the technicalities of the selection process, and these factors are the next focus.

The Presidency in a Changing America

As suggested, reforms in the selection process reflect deeper changes in the party system and in American society generally. It could well be argued that, almost irrespective of the quality of president, these and other developments have together made the job of chief executive much more difficult than ever before. Three such developments have added to the burden of the office.

Decline of Party and the Rise of Issue Politics. In one sense, condemnation of recent presidential candidates because they have lacked close party ties and have failed to subject themselves to party peer-group review is unfair, for if traditional party organizations have declined, candidates cannot be expected to have pursued this particular route to nomination. Once the winner is in the White House, however, the real problems of trying to govern in the absence of unifying party forces become painfully apparent. Of the functions of political parties listed in Chapter 5, among the most important are the provision of institutional cohesion and a means to staff the government. Jimmy Carter is usually cited as the classic case of a president who failed on both counts—largely because he came to Washington with very limited executive experience (as governor of Georgia) and with few connections in the traditional world of the Democratic Party (the unions, urban interests, elite universities, the Northeastern establishment). As a result, so the argument runs, his liaison with Congress was poor, and his ability weak to fill key posts with the right men and women.

Certainly, Carter had a rough time with Congress and was not personally inclined to create and nurture relationships with congressional leaders. But he was not unique in experiencing difficulties with Congress. All presidents have had such problems, including John Kennedy and even Franklin Roosevelt, both of whom had strong party contacts and support. In his first two years in office, Clinton enjoyed the advantage of a Democratic Congress and was undoubtedly more politically skillful than Jimmy Carter. Nonetheless, he achieved little in the way of enacting his legislative program.

An additional problem is that the political vacuum left by the parties has in part been filled by "issue politics," or the mobilization of political resources around particular issues and ideas. This phenomenon is examined in more detail in Chapter 11, but even the most casual observer of the American political scene will be aware of the rise of the minority caucuses, pro- and antiabortion leagues, women's caucuses, the environmental lobbies, the Christian Coalition, and so on. Each of these movements has its congressional supporters and advocates within administrations and state governments.

Issue politics has had a more subtle effect on the political agenda, however. When policy is defined in terms of discrete issues or one-dimensional ideologies (such as "conservatism"), the effect is to fragment decisionmaking throughout the political system. Within the executive departments and agencies, each issue or position has its supporters, and this alignment compounds the already problematical business of getting bureaucrats to implement policy (of which much more later). In sum, in the absence of strong party linkages, presidents increasingly lack ideological and organizational "connective tissue" when performing their duties. At the same time, the expectations of the office remain high—indeed, they have almost certainly increased. These developments place even more of a premium on the skills and political acumen of individual incumbents.

Nationalization of Politics and Society.   With improved communications and the spread of governmental responsibilities, the United States has become a much more centralized society since the 1960s. Information is disseminated centrally by the three major television networks (NBC, CBS, ABC), by the news services and syndicated columns of major newspapers, and by cable TV networks. Economically, society is more centralized and nationalized, with giant corporations providing the same goods and services uniformly throughout the country. It follows that the demands on local, state, and national governments have been centralized, with Washington increasingly the focus of political activity. The discussion in Chapter 4 of intergovernmental relations showed how state and local governments have become more interdependent with the federal government in recent years. The same is true of corporations, farmers, and almost all those interests in society affected by federal government spending, regulation, and arbitration. Naturally, the president is a major focus of all this attention, for he frames most major laws, draws up the budget, and has the responsibility for implementing all laws. As chief executive, the president has to manage the vast bureaucracy responsible for these tasks, a bureaucracy that, in terms of powers and complexity, has grown considerably.

Changing Nature of U.S. Economic and Political Power.   Although not always true, it seems reasonable to assume that governing is easier when a country's economy is growing in real terms and its status and power abroad are in the ascendant. Both applied in the case of the United States between 1942 and 1965. Between 1965 and the 1980s, American international economic and military might experienced relative decline—although it is difficult to argue that this development continued as a trend through the 1990s. Perhaps it is not entirely coincidental that the earlier period is associated with the era of "successful" presidents, whereas the latter has witnessed the incumbency of executive "failures." It would be foolhardy to accept this argument in full—was Harry Truman, after all, a "success," and was Ronald Reagan a "failure"?—but there is no question that the management of the economy and the exercise of military and diplomatic power abroad are more likely to be difficult during periods of relative decline or when there is little consensus on management of the economy or on America's role abroad.

The Vietnam War was the first major demonstration of the limits to American military power, and it effectively broke one president (Lyndon Johnson) and led another (Richard Nixon) to commit a series of illegal acts, including the secret bombing of Cambodia and the unauthorized surveillance of opponents of the war. Subsequently, Jimmy Carter's handling of the Iranian hostage situation dominated the final year of his presidency and provided a poignant reminder of the limitations of American might.

For recent presidents, ventures abroad have been problematical, for nothing increases presidential popularity more instantly than successful—or even unsuccessful but bold—military and diplomatic forays overseas. John Kennedy's popularity soared during the Cuban missile crisis, as did Jimmy Carter's following the signing of the Begin-Sadat-Carter Camp David accords in 1979, and Ronald Reagan's after the U.S. invasion of Grenada and the bombing of Libya. George Bush's successful execution of the 1990–1991 Gulf War led to approval ratings of over 80 percent, and in 1998 Bill Clinton's strong stand against Saddam Hussein's obstruction of UN resolutions raised his popularity even amid allegations about sexual wrongdoing in the White House. When the United States is apparently "humiliated" abroad—as eventually occurred with Vietnam and the hostage incident in Iran—pressure increases on presidents to do something about it. Whether the resulting actions are in the public interest or in the interests of world peace are, of course, another matter.

At home, managing the many distributional questions that are the very essence of the chief executive's job is obviously more difficult when the economy is stagnating or when, even if the economy is growing, there are numerous demands on the government's budget. Even so, no single individual is more centrally placed to make these distributional decisions than is the president. He is responsible for producing an annual budget amounting to over $5 trillion and for ensuring that this money is properly spent on literally thousands of programs. Congress is, of course, also involved in this process, and when it comes to contested distributions, the courts become key actors. But neither Congress nor the courts are as politically visible as

is the president. Only the president is perceived as national leader
and defender of the public interest. It is small wonder, then, that recent presidents have experienced budgetary difficulties, both in domestic policy and with defense spending; the latter, of course, naturally affects the sums available for domestic programs.

Add to this problem the increasingly strident demands of the single-issue lobbies, and the potential for conflict and failure can be
appreciated. Thus until 1998, no recent president was able to balance the budget (in 1986, Ronald Reagan, a fiscal conservative,
presided over a deficit of more than $80 billion) or has come any-
where near to satisfying the demands of social groups. For example, Ronald Reagan's 1981 tax-cut measures, as passed by Congress, had a number of divisive consequences. They gave those
earning $15,000–$20,000 a year (a majority of wage earners) only
$6 extra a week. But for the rich, the benefits were sizable—$90 a
week for those earning $100,000 a year, $257 a week for the su-
perrich in the $200,000-plus class. Organized labor was offended
by this apparently unfair package, especially because it was accompanied by cuts in welfare and Social Security benefits. Together
with tax cuts on corporate profits and increases in defense spending, this combination obliged Reagan to recoup some of the cuts
with tax hikes during 1983. Thus the president's radical changes,
which had been central to his 1980 electoral platform, ended up
satisfying almost nobody.

Between 1983 and 1988, the dramatic recovery of the American
economy certainly helped Ronald Reagan's popularity, but the basic
distributional problem remained of how to cut expenditures and not
offend almost everybody. This dilemma was amply demonstrated by
the experience of the Bush administration. When the economy
started to slow in 1990, the budget deficit began to grow, reaching
$300 billion by 1992. With the economy in recession, pressure to in-
crease expenditures proved irresistible. At the same time, tax increases were politically as unpopular as ever. In any event, George
Bush did go along with a tax hike in 1991 that almost certainly contributed to his subsequent defeat in 1992.

During his period in office, Bill Clinton was fortunate to enjoy a
growing economy that, combined with controls on federal spending, resulted in a meaningful reduction in the federal deficit (see
Chapter 15). After 1994, however, Republican control of Congress
resulted in a serious deadlock over the fiscal 1996 budget and a
temporary shutdown of some federal government activities. And

even when, as occurred in 1998, the president presented to Congress a balanced budget for the first time since 1969, the distributional questions did not go away. Instead the debate shifted to conflict over how best to spend any surplus. Should it go for lower taxes (the Republican position) or for improved health and education programs (the president's position)?

Indeed, the achievement of a balanced budget may actually aggravate distributional problems. If, as seems likely, politicians from all parties vie with one another to maintain balanced budgets, then satisfying public demands for more and better government services without increasing taxes will become that much harder. Reagan managed to "have his cake and eat it"—lower taxes *and* increased spending (mainly on defense)—but at the price of a ballooning deficit. Future presidents are unlikely to enjoy this luxury. Instead they will be obliged to reconcile the apparently irreconcilable—satisfying high public demands and expectations while preaching and practicing the merits of limited government.

Presidential Abuse of Power and the Congressional Response

In effect, these changes in society and politics have made the United States less easy to govern. Public expectations of the central institutions of government have increased, but the ability to respond effectively has been weakened. For the presidency, this unfortunate combination has been particularly serious and helps explain the waxing and waning of presidential power during the last third of the twentieth century.

The era of the "imperial presidency" coincided with America's postwar dominance in economic and military affairs and, of course, with the incumbency of two especially imperious presidents. By the mid-1960s, the office had grown enormously in power, and the pressures imposed by the Vietnam War and a declining economy tested the office to the full. The potential for the abuse of power was considerable. Unfortunately for the American people, Lyndon Johnson and, in particular, Richard Nixon fell to this temptation. The real importance of the Nixon period is not that the president, along with many of his aides and cabinet officers, broke the law, but that the chief executive wielded power in such a way that raised very serious questions on where, exactly, presidential power began and ended.

Richard Nixon impounded funds appropriated by Congress for programs he disliked (impoundment is the setting aside by the executive of funds appropriated by Congress). Toward the end of his presidency, he was exercising the veto power extensively, and few of his vetoes were overridden by Congress. He invoked executive privilege to justify the withholding of information from congressional investigative committees, and he nominated a number of men to official posts who were unqualified or otherwise unsuitable.

Even before Watergate, Congress began to fight back, notably by rejecting two of his more outrageous Supreme Court nominees. In 1972, Congress attempted to control the president's discretion to make executive agreements—in effect, treaties with foreign powers that could be concluded, sometimes in secret, without consulting the Senate. Under the Case Act, all such agreements must be submitted to Congress. More far-reaching was the 1973 War Powers Act passed by Congress over a presidential veto that put limits on the president's power to commit troops overseas. In 1973, Congress also insisted that the president's director and deputy directors of the vital Office of Management and Budget be subject to Senate confirmation.

After Watergate, Congress asserted its power even more vigorously—in part because Watergate had precipitated a landslide victory for the Democrats in the 1974 midterm elections. The Budget and Impoundment Control Act of 1974 obliges the president to report "rescission" to Congress when funds appropriated remain unspent. Congress then has to approve rescission within forty-five days. The same law created the Budget Committees in Congress to enable the legislature to play a more constructive part in the budget process.

As can be seen from Table 9.2, Gerald Ford exercised the veto on major bills frequently and was overridden by Congress on seven occasions. Note also the general tendency for the veto to be applied more frequently and in particular to appropriations and foreign policy bills that, in the past, almost never attracted the presidential veto. This shift reflects the more difficult environment in which today's presidents have to work. Sometimes this means facing a Congress controlled by the opposition's party. Equally often it means that there are fundamentally irreconcilable interests represented by a fragmented Congress on the one hand and the president on the other. During his first two years in office, Bill Clinton did not use the veto power, but he certainly did so thereafter and,

TABLE 9.2 Major Bills Vetoed, 1933–1998

President	Total	Number Involving Appropriations	Number Involving Foreign and Foreign Economic Policy	Major Vetoes per Year in Office	Number Overridden
Roosevelt	2	0	0	0.16	2
Truman	6	0	0	0.8	5
Eisenhower	2	2	0	0.25	1
Kennedy	0	0	0	0	0
Johnson	0	0	0	0	0
Nixon	13	10	1	2.4	4
Ford	11	10	1	4.4	7
Carter	5	2	2	1.3	1
Reagan	15	7	5	1.9	5
Bush	15	4	5	3.7	1
Clinton	15	9	3	2.5	1

SOURCE: David McKay, "Presidential strategy and the veto power: a reappraisal," *Political Science Quarterly*, 1989, table 5. Updated from *Congressional Quarterly*.

by so doing, successfully thwarted the Republicans' attempt to pass much of their ambitious legislative program in 1995 and 1996. Clinton continued to use the veto through to the end of his presidency, including a 1999 veto of Republican plans for tax cuts funded by the budget surplus.

In 1976, Congress put limits on the president's power to declare emergencies and assume special powers. Under the National Emergencies Act of 1976, Congress can terminate a declaration of emergency, and all declarations must be reported to Congress, together with legal justifications for them.

Finally, Congress in 1978 passed the Ethics in Government Act that allowed the naming of an independent counsel (sometimes called a special prosecutor) to investigate alleged wrongdoing in the executive branch. Between 1979 and 1998, eighteen independent counsels were appointed to investigate a wide range of allegations. In some cases, such as the Iran-Contra affair, indictments and convictions ensued. By the second Clinton term, the legislation came under increasing criticism, as independent counsel Kenneth W. Starr was perceived by many to have exceeded his authority when investigating the involvement of President Clinton in the Whitewater real estate scandal and related matters while he was governor of Arkansas. As is well known, the most serious of the eventual charges related to Clinton's affair with White House intern Monica Lewinsky and to his untruthful attempts to conceal the affair for an eight-month period from January to August 1998. The ensuing impeachment and trial of the president and the damage done to President Clinton and the presidency over what was, at least at first, a private matter led many to question the scope and methods of the inquiry.

Following the adoption of all these measures and the incumbency of an unusually unassertive president, Jimmy Carter, presidency watchers began to talk of the decline of presidential power and the resurgence of Congress. As previously discussed, there is no doubt that Congress has become more, rather than less, difficult for presidents to deal with. Presidents retain an enormous fund of resources on which to draw, however. The next section concentrates on those resources not covered in earlier sections and on the ways in which successive presidents have adapted to the pressures and problems associated with the office. Two main resources can be identified—the public and the presidential bureaucracy—to which a third, conceptually distinct resource, personality, can be added.

Presidential Resources

The Public

It may seem paradoxical in the light of the foregoing discussion to view the public as a resource. Yet under many circumstances it can be just that. As national leaders, presidents can make direct appeals to the public through press conferences and special televised announcements. In some instances, this approach amounts almost to a limited form of direct democracy. In 1981 and 1982, for example, Ronald Reagan made specific appeals to citizens via television that they should write to their members of Congress expressing support for the president's economic policies. Both the tax and spending cuts were passed by narrow margins, and it seems reasonable to assume that Reagan's pleadings had some effect—especially because many members cannot afford to ignore a sudden influx of constituency mail. More recently, Bill Clinton appealed to the public to oppose efforts by the Republican 104th Congress (1995–1996) to cut Medicare and Social Security benefits. His appeals were successful, not only in the sense that the harshest cuts were not imposed but also in that he could invoke this experience as evidence of Republican hard-heartedness in the 1996 presidential campaign.

Appeals to the public are not always successful, of course, as Richard Nixon's sometimes painful public attempts to hide his guilt over Watergate demonstrated. But earlier in his presidency, Nixon made highly effective use of this resource through his carefully constructed public lectures on American disengagement from Vietnam.

Although still a potentially powerful weapon, the public-appeal resource is beset with problems and pitfalls. As was established in Chapter 6, the American electorate is now highly volatile. Together with a growing cynicism about public institutions, not least the presidency,[10] this unpredictability has made the president's public appeals riskier than they used to be. During Ronald Reagan's first two years, the public was willing to provide support during what was effectively a "honeymoon" period. Following the midterm elections when the Democrats made deep inroads into the conservative coalition in the House, such support became more grudging, with the balance of public opinion shifting to the Congress rather than to the president. Although highly popular during the Gulf War when he made numerous public appeals, George Bush could do nothing to boost his popularity during the ensuing economic recession. In short, the popularity of presidents has waxed and waned over recent years (see Figure 9.1).

This state of flux accepted, no other national institution—Congress, party, courts—can use the media quite like the president. He is, after all, just one person with a special national status. Given all the problems of governing, presidents will continue to make direct appeals to the public, for it is one of the few, if imperfect, means whereby the fragmenting influences in American politics can be overcome. This cohering influence was demonstrated very well during the impeachment and trial of President Clinton in 1998 and 1999. Despite all the adverse publicity surrounding the president, not to mention his admission of guilt, he was able to retain a semblance of dignity and authority, and he continued to use the public as a valuable political resource. Certainly his popularity did not wane during this very difficult period.[11]

Most commentators agree that the three most important indicators of presidential performance are the state of the economy, the extent of American involvement in foreign wars, and the public's approval of the president. As can be seen from Table 9.3, these indicators can be closely associated—a weak economy and/or American soldiers dying abroad helped defeat the incumbent party in 1952, 1968, 1980, and 1992.

Bureaucracy

As the job of president has become more demanding, so incumbents have adapted their administrative resources accordingly. Every president has had a cabinet composed mainly of departmental heads at his disposal, but the cabinet is but one of a number of administrative devices available, most of which were introduced during the twentieth century to help presidents formulate and execute policy. In 1921, the Bureau of the Budget (now called the Office of Management and Budget) was established to help the president prepare the budget and coordinate spending policies.

As can be seen from Figure 9.2, other agencies have since been created that collectively are known as the Executive Office of the President (EOP) (formally established by Congress in 1939). Quite distinct from the cabinet, the EOP consists of about 2,000 individuals directly accountable to the president. This figure includes about 500 people who work in the White House as personal aides to the president (the White House Office in Figure 9.2). How presidents use the

FIGURE 9.1 Presidential Approval, 1977–1997

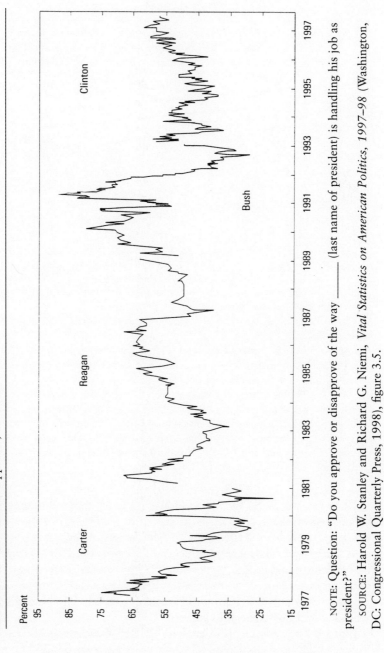

NOTE: Question: "Do you approve or disapprove of the way _____ (last name of president) is handling his job as president?"

SOURCE: Harold W. Stanley and Richard G. Niemi, *Vital Statistics on American Politics, 1997–98* (Washington, DC: Congressional Quarterly Press, 1998), figure 3.5.

TABLE 9.3   Three Indicators of Presidential Performance

	Real Growth in GNP in the Year Before the Election[a]	Number of Deaths in a Major War During the Election Year[b]	Approval Rating in the Summer Before the Election[c]
1952	2.30	4,437	30
1956	1.35	0	70
1960	2.22	0	59
1964	5.35	205	74
1968	4.34	16,588	39
1972	5.52	640	58
1976	4.03	0	45
1980	−1.94	0	33
1984	5.63	0	54
1988	3.84	0	51
1992	2.11	0	36
Range	7.57	16,588	44
Average	3.16	1,988	50

[a] Real growth in GNP was measured from the third quarter of the preceding year to the third quarter of the election year.

[b] Figures on war deaths are based on Combat Area Casualties file in the National Archives.

[c] Approval ratings were taken from Gallup Polls conducted during June and July of each election year. When more than one survey included the presidential approval question, the results were averaged.

SOURCE: GNP data are taken from the U.S. Department of Commerce, *National Income and Product Accounts* (multiple years), as reproduced in William G. Mayer, "Changes in Elections and Party System: 1992 in Historical Perspective," in Bryan D. Jones, *The New American Politics: Reflections on Political Change and the Clinton Administration* (Boulder, CO: Westview, 1995), table 2.6.

EOP, and in particular the White House staff, has aroused bitter controversy since the 1980s. A major criticism, inspired mainly by Watergate, has concerned the extent to which the staff has grown in recent years and has increasingly insulated presidents from public opinion and political reality. A related theme centers on whether any personal bureaucracy can be an adequate administrative tool against the vast resources of executive departments and agencies and against a fragmented but powerful Congress.

Indisputably, some presidents have used their staffs unwisely. Richard Nixon, in particular, relied heavily on a mere handful of per-

FIGURE 9.2   The Executive Office of the President

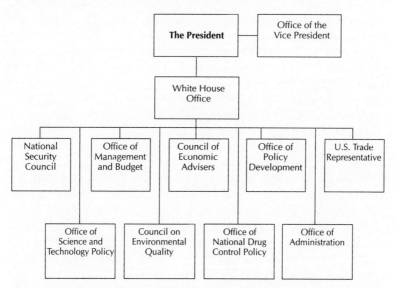

SOURCE: James P. Pfiffner, *The Modern Presidency*, 2d ed. (New York: St. Martin's Press, 1998), p. 88.

sonal aides, eschewing most cabinet officers and congressional and party leaders. Three of his closest aides, John Ehrlichman, Robert Haldeman, and Ron Ziegler, became so effective in acting as the president's mouthpieces that they earned the sobriquet "The Berlin Wall." In the Carter presidency, Stewart Eisenstadt, the domestic policy adviser, almost assumed the status of policy initiator and spokesperson. During the second Reagan administration, Donald Regan guarded his position as chief of staff jealously and used it to limit access to the president by other administration officials. Faced with the open hostility of the first lady, Nancy Reagan, and criticism over his role in the Iran-Contra affair, Regan was eventually forced to resign. George Bush's first chief of staff, John Sununu, was also widely regarded as imperious and insensitive. He, too, was forced to resign following allegations of misuse of government resources, including presidential jets. Bill Clinton's problems with staffers were no less serious, although in his case the criticisms were directed at a group of presidential "cronies" rather than at the chief of staff. The twentieth century had at least three other instances of staffers assuming national prominence and even notoriety as "the powers be-hind the throne."[12] Critics have argued that the considerable power of personal staffs is undemocratic—they are, after all, unelected, and few are subject to Senate confirmation.

Personal staffs—and all modern presidents have domestic, eco-nomic, and foreign policy advisers; a press secretary; legal counsel; and staff responsible for liaison work with Congress—often overlap with members of other agencies within the EOP. Hence, the presi-dent's national security adviser is also a member of the National Se-curity Council, a body consisting, among others, of the president, vice-president, and defense and state secretaries that was set up by Congress in 1947 to help the formulation of foreign policy and to aid crisis management. In some instances, the national security ad-viser becomes more important than the secretary of state, as was clearly the case with Henry Kissinger before he "deposed" the in-cumbent, William Rogers, and assumed the office of secretary of state himself during Nixon's second term.

Similarly, the director of the Office of Management and Budget (OMB) can become a key figure, for the OMB is responsible for monitoring the spending of the various executive departments. In 1980, Ronald Reagan's choice of director, David Stockman, a bright young former member of Congress, was designed to ensure that the OMB director would have direct responsibility for handling the bud-get and the cuts to be imposed on many of the departments and agencies. (Significantly, since 1973, the director of OMB has been subject to Senate confirmation.) In this sense, the OMB and its di-rector resemble (although they are by no means identical to) finance ministries and ministers in other political entities such as the British Treasury and Chancellor of the Exchequer.

How presidents use the EOP and especially their personal staff varies greatly from administration to administration. Until Water-gate, it was common to note how Franklin Roosevelt's style of cre-ating an atmosphere of constructive competition, with aides deliber-ately positioned to provide contrasting information and advice, differed from Eisenhower's tendency to delegate responsibility and Kennedy's emphasis on intelligence and esprit de corps.[13]

Since Watergate, however, evidence indicates that whatever man-agement strategy is adopted by presidents, they will experience se-rious command problems. Certainly, presidents have felt obliged to innovate and have reorganized the executive branch to improve management. As noted, most presidents have adopted a "chief of staff" specifically to help management of the White House—for example, Haldeman served for Nixon, Regan for Reagan, and Sununu for Bush. During his first term, President Reagan relied on a triumvirate of staffers for policy guidance and political advice: Chief of Staff James Baker, President's Counsel Edwin Meese, and Deputy Chief of Staff Michael Deaver. All three had left the White House by 1985, however, when former Treasury Secretary Donald Regan took over as chief of staff.

After Regan resigned in 1987, he was replaced by the more politically astute Howard Baker, former Senate majority leader. Indeed, Reagan's use of the EOP changed dramatically between his first and second terms. In his first term, he relied on at least three chief advisers, and in his second, just one (apart from his wife, who played an active role throughout). Although praised for his management style in the first term, Reagan was condemned for his failure to oversee the detail—and sometimes even the main thrust—of policy in the second. The Iran-Contra debacle resulted in part from this failing.

Criticisms of George Bush's management style were of a different order. Although John Sununu was supposed to play the "bad cop" to Bush's "good cop"—to be the president's hit man—it soon became obvious that neither man was fully aware of the policy position of the other. As a result, an impression of drift and indecision pervaded the Bush presidency. Sununu's replacement, Samuel Skinner, did little to help because he proved to be a gray, almost anonymous figure.

Bill Clinton's experience with staffers was also fraught with difficulties. His first choice as chief of staff, Mack McLarty, was accused of being an Arkansas crony and was replaced during the first term with the tougher and more political budget director, Leon Panetta; in his second term, Clinton selected Erskine Bowles. None of these men took on a major executive or gatekeeping role, however. Clinton surrounded himself with numerous confidants, some of whom had little formal authority. Indeed, it could be argued that some of the most influential people in his first term were in this category. They included first lady Hillary Clinton, staffer Dick Morris, and personal confidant Vernon Jordan. Perhaps unsurprisingly, as the 1996 election drew closer, Clinton increasingly relied on the advice of political consultant Dick Morris, who urged him to move toward the center ground of politics and thereby secure victory.

A more radical ploy has involved attempts to institutionalize the delegation of power through strengthening the cabinet. Although every president has had a cabinet, the Constitution unambiguously assigns executive power to the president, so whether the device is used or not is a matter of great discretion. Its membership consists of the heads of the executive departments plus individuals assigned by the president. Reinvigorating the cabinet is a natural option for presidents to choose, because a major part of executive leadership involves control and management of the vast federal bureaucracy. Much of the work of personal staff involves liaison with this bureaucracy, and the closer the communications and the finer the line of command, the better. Presidents Nixon, Carter, and Reagan pledged that they would strengthen their cabinets. Nixon patently failed to do this, but Carter did in fact use the cabinet quite frequently, as did Ronald Reagan. Indeed, during his first year in office, Reagan convened his cabinet thirty-seven times, a high figure in historical perspective. It is doubtful that this smoothed relations between the White House and the executive departments. As discussed in Chapter 10, a natural antipathy exists between the two, largely because departments and agencies have constituencies and interests of their own.

Whatever the promises, presidents generally resort to using their own (usually reliable) staff rather than risk giving real power to departmental secretaries, and recent history is littered with examples of conflict between powerful staffers or EOP members and departmental heads. During his first term, Bill Clinton was no exception to this rule. As already indicated, he acquired an inner circle of advisers. Interestingly, this group contained cabinet secretaries, including Commerce Secretary Ron Brown and HUD Secretary Henry Cisneros. But they were involved as friends and confidants rather than as spokespersons for their departments. (Secretary Brown was subsequently killed in a plane crash over Bosnia. Secretary Cisneros resigned following allegations of sexual and financial misconduct.)

The need to reorganize extends to other areas. A major reorganization of the EOP was undertaken by Jimmy Carter, who eliminated seven of the office's administrative units. Also, Jimmy Carter and Ronald Reagan promised to make greater use of their vice-presidents. Traditionally, the position has meant little in itself, or "about as useful as a cow's fifth teat" as Harry Truman colorfully put it. Walter Mondale was, however, accorded a more central position in the Carter administration than many previous vice-presidents, and George Bush was given an unusual degree of public visibility. Similarly, Al Gore was accorded a special status in the Clinton White House. Gore not only assumed the mantle of heir apparent but also became active in a number of policy initiatives.

All these efforts demonstrate the increasingly difficult political environment in which presidents have to work. Public expectations of the office remain high just as the ability of presidents to meet these expectations has diminished. Together with the nationalization of political life, this tension has forced presidents to manage numerous centers of political power, each with its own semiautonomous policy network. As Hugh Heclo has emphasized, staff and other administrative assistance are helpful, but they cannot solve the central dilemma of the office:

> Whoever the President and whatever his style, the political and policy bureaucracies crowd in on him. They are there in his office to help, but their needs are not necessarily his needs. Delegation is unavoidable; yet no one aide or combination of aides has his responsibilities or takes his oath of office. However much the President trusts personal friends, political loyalties, or technocrats, he is the person that the average citizen and history will hold accountable.[14]

Personality

Although no one could deny the importance of changes in the nomination process and the political environment as determinants of change in the nature of the presidency, some observers stress that the most crucial element in the office is the personality of the incumbent. With so much discretion attached to the job and such a premium on leadership skills—persuasion, manipulation, coercion, insight, charisma—personality is undoubtedly important. Indeed, even the most casual student of American politics has a cognitive picture of certain presidents—Truman as confrontational and combative, Eisenhower as wise and avuncular, Kennedy as inspirational, Reagan as reassuring, and above all, perhaps, Richard Nixon as devious and insecure.

Borrowing heavily from psychology, one political scientist, James Barber, has attempted to formalize the "presidential character" by classifying presidents by personality type.[15] Barber's two dimensions are active-passive and positive-negative. To simplify somewhat, the former describes how much effort presidents put into the job, and the latter how much enjoyment or satisfaction they get from it. The key types are "active-positives," representing individuals who receive enormous satisfaction from being active in the job, and "active-negatives," who put in intense effort but get little emotional reward for their pains. Beware, says Barber, of the active-negatives, who are likely to dig in when under pressure and display a sometimes paranoid inflexibility. Active-positives, in contrast, enjoy the cut and thrust of a highly demanding job and are likely to show that spirit of compromise and adaptability so essential to the politics of coalition formation.

As with all simple psychological theories, Barber's typology is open to criticism.[16] Events often mold personality rather than the other way round. Who, after all, would have judged Lyndon Johnson "inflexible" before he became so fatally obsessed with the war in Vietnam? And in many respects, Richard Nixon, the epitome of the active-negative type according to Barber, was pragmatic and adaptable. Unlike Woodrow Wilson and Lyndon Johnson, Nixon had little moral commitment to causes or higher ideals. Moreover, to put Ronald Reagan in the same category as Warren Harding and William Taft seems misguided, for every modern president has to be "active." This may not mean working eighteen-hour days, but it must at least mean being psychologically active or aware of events and political priorities. Although there is no doubt that George Bush was active, some doubt exists as to whether he drew great satisfaction from the job. Certainly, by the end of his term, he displayed an element of weariness and resignation that was not typical of an active-positive.

In sum, Barber's categories are not very useful guides to presidential quality. Highly successful and "failed" presidents are put in the same category (Franklin Roosevelt and Jimmy Carter as active-positives, Dwight Eisenhower and Calvin Coolidge as passive-negatives), and the political and historical changes earlier analyzed, especially those associated with presidential selection, appear to bear little or no relationship to Barber's idea of presidential quality.

Nevertheless, the typology does provide a way to analyze the impact of personality on the office. There is no disputing that some men have been more suited to the job than others, and that this fact holds true irrespective of events, changes in the selection process, and shifting trends in American society. All the evidence suggests, for example, that Ronald Reagan enjoyed being president and had a talent for handling people around him that most other recent presidents have lacked. This does not guarantee that history will judge him a great president or even that his record in dealing with Congress and the public will be deemed successful. His casual style and willingness to delegate undoubtedly helped lead to the Iran-Contra affair in 1985 and 1986. But having a personality apparently suited to the job must at least help the incumbent come to terms with what possibly is the most demanding executive position in the modern world.

All the indications are that Bill Clinton, too, enjoyed the business of being president. He was a naturally gregarious and extrovert personality who liked, and was liked by, most of the people who worked with him. During his first term, he perhaps became frustrated at the glacial progress of his legislative program and his party's subsequent defeat at the midterm congressional elections, but in response to these events he did not become depressed and introspective. On the contrary, they inspired him to renewed enthusiasm during the last two years of his first term, an enthusiasm devoted not to legislation but to what Clinton did best—campaign for reelection.

During his second term, the trials and tribulations of the myriad accusations of personal wrongdoing leveled at the president did not deflect him from the job at hand until the publication of the Starr report in August 1998 elevated the issue to the center of the political stage. During the subsequent House impeachment hearings and Senate trial, the president continued to maintain his composure, even amid what were the gravest of proceedings. Given the narrow majority enjoyed by the Republicans in the Senate, Clinton was never in serious danger of being convicted and removed. Nonetheless, he appeared to maintain control of his administration throughout. By spring 1999, the crisis in Kosovo and other matters soon diverted public and political attention away from the impeachment saga.

Remarkably, the public's regard for the way in which Clinton was doing his job remained high throughout these extraordinary events. In contrast to Richard Nixon, who resigned before the House of Representatives could vote articles of impeachment, Clinton in fact saw his popularity increase during the period of the scandal (Figure 9.3). Most of this difference must be due to the very different contexts of the two scandals, but some must also stem from the ways in which the respective incumbents handled the crises. Nixon was embattled, insecure, and politically isolated;

244

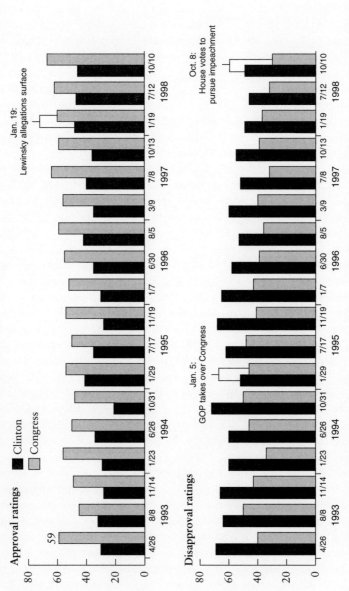

FIGURE 9.3   Clinton and Congress in the Polls

NOTE: These charts show how the approval and disapproval ratings of President Clinton and Congress have fluctuated since 1993 in the polls conducted for the *Washington Post*. The questions asked were: "Do you approve or disapprove of the way Bill Clinton is handling his job as president?" and "Do you approve or disapprove of the way the U.S. Congress is doing its job?" The latest results based on telephone interviews of 802 adults conducted Oct. 6 following the House vote to open an impeachment inquiry, have a margin of error of plus or minus 3 percentage points.

SOURCE: *Washington Post*. Reproduced from *Congressional Quarterly Weekly Report*, October 17, 1998, p. 2796.

Clinton was confident, relaxed, and continued to command the support of his aides and confidants.

Assessing Presidential Power at Century's End

When Richard Neustadt described presidential power in 1960 as the "power to persuade," he accurately captured the need for presidents to be successful bargainers, negotiators, and manipulators.[17] Coalition building, in other words, is the very essence of the president's job, and incumbents must have the personal capacity not only to appreciate this fact (as Jimmy Carter constantly said he did) but also to act accordingly (as Jimmy Carter repeatedly failed to do). Coalition-building skills are necessary at every level—within the White House and in relations with executive departments, Congress, the media, interest groups, and the public. Neustadt's famous essay was designed to show that formal command was not sufficient; that, indeed, it was sometimes quite limited, unless supplemented by the more subtle political skills involved in the art of persuasion.[18]

To reduce most of the president's job to bargaining skills is, of course, to oversimplify. Constitutionally, the chief executive has immense power of command—not least as commander in chief—that he can exercise without a finely honed aptitude for bargaining. The presidencies of Lyndon Johnson and Richard Nixon are proof enough of this. Yet both presidents are now considered less than successful, and since the early 1970s, the number of power centers and policy networks in the American system has increased considerably. Moreover, changes in the selection process, although perhaps not preselecting certain personality types among candidates, have certainly affected the nature of their party and political contacts and hence their access to major bargaining resources. Add to this the increased expectations of the office on the part of the public and it is easy to appreciate why so many commentators complain of the office being "overloaded."

In such a context, the premium on bargaining and leadership skills is greatly increased, but there is also the danger that, under such enormous pressures, presidents will resort to confrontation or to clandestine and possibly illegal acts simply to get things done. Such was the case with the later years of the Nixon administration. Later, in the Iran-Contra affair, it was not the president but his subordinates who initiated illegal acts in order to overcome congressional opposition.

As noted in this chapter, the veto power is now used more often than in the past, and presidents are also prone to go over the heads of congressional leaders with appeals made directly to the American people. One thing is certain: No matter how difficult the job becomes or how recent presidents are judged by an increasingly fickle and demanding electorate, the position of president of the United States will continue to attract enormous attention both at home and abroad. Alone in a highly fragmented political system, the presidency is the natural coordinating institution of national leadership. The president has at his command, therefore, the vast resources of the American federal government. And although all recent presidents have preached the virtues of limited government, none has meaningfully reduced the size of the federal bureaucratic machine. Domestic and foreign demands on the office are such that all presidents are obliged to use the resources of this behemoth— even as they extol the merits of smaller government.

Notes

1. Because there is no historical example of a female president (or candidate), the presidency will be referred to in the masculine throughout this chapter. Things may, of course, well change early in the twenty-first century.

2. For a review of this "textbook" view of the presidency, see Thomas Cronin, *The State of the Presidency* (Boston: Little, Brown, 1990), chap. 2.

3. In the heady optimism of the late 1950s, Clinton Rossiter, in his famous essay *The American Presidency* (New York: Harcourt Brace, 1960), pp. 4–25, listed five informal powers that continue to resonate today: (1) voice of the party; (2) voice of the people; (3) protector of the peace; (4) manager of prosperity; (5) world leader.

4. Quoted in Robert F. Kennedy, *Thirteen Days: A Memoir of the Cuban Missile Crisis* (New York: Norton, 1971), p. 37.

5. For a graphic description of these harrowing events and the contrast with the Republican convention of that year, see Norman Mailer, *Miami and the Siege of Chicago* (New York: Donald I. Fine, 1986).

6. See Jeane Kirkpatrick, *The New Presidential Elite* (New York: Russell Sage/Twentieth Century Fund, 1976).

7. Quoted in *Congressional Quarterly*, July 4, 1992, p. 18.

8. Thomas E. Patterson and Robert D. McClure, *The Unseeing Eye: The Myth of Television Power in National Elections* (New York: Putnam, 1976).

9. For an account of presidential communications, see Roderick P. Hart, *The Sound of Leadership: Presidential Communications in the Modern Age* (Chicago: University of Chicago Press, 1987).

10. Both during and immediately after Watergate, public rating of the office sank to a new low, with only 13 percent of Americans in 1974 expressing a great deal of confidence in the executive branch. Since the mid-1970s, public confidence in the office has increased a little, but the ratings of individual presidents have tended to be low. Comparing Reagan with his predecessors after twelve months in office, around 55 percent of the public approved of the way he was handling his job, versus 68 percent for Eisenhower, 77 percent for Kennedy, 69 percent for Johnson, and 61 percent for Nixon. Both Ford (46 percent) and Carter (52 percent) fared badly by comparison. Reagan's ratings improved with the recovery of the economy through 1986, only to decline with the revelations of the Iran-Contra affair. His ratings subsequently recovered but not to pre–Iran-Contra levels. Bush started his term with higher ratings than his competitors; his popularity then fell, only to rise in spectacular fashion to over 80 percent with the invasion of Kuwait. Economic recession then reduced his ratings to below 40 percent by the time of the 1992 elections. Bill Clinton's ratings followed an equally unusual path. Three months after his election, his ratings dipped below 50 percent—a historic low. However, economic recovery and peace abroad helped to boost his popularity to over 60 percent— a level he maintained through mid-1999.

11. For a comprehensive account of how presidents use the public resource, see Sam Kernell, *Going Public*, 3d ed. (Washington, DC: Congressional Quarterly Press, 1997).

12. Colonel House with Woodrow Wilson, Harry Hopkins with Franklin Roosevelt, and Sherman Adams with Dwight Eisenhower.

13. For an excellent account of how different presidents have used their staffs, see John Hart, *The Presidential Branch*, 2d ed. (Chatham, NJ: Chatham House, 1994).

14. Hugh Heclo, "The Changing Presidential Office," in Arnold J. Meltsner (ed.), *Politics and the Oval Office* (San Francisco: Institute for Contemporary Studies, 1987), p. 177.

15. James David Barber, *The Presidential Character*, 4th ed. (Englewood Cliffs, NJ: Prentice-Hall, 1992).

16. For a good critique, see Alexander L. George and Julliete L. George, *Assessing Presidential Personality and Performance* (Boulder, CO: Westview Press, 1998), chap. 5

17. Richard E. Neustadt, *Presidential Power* (New York: Wiley, 1960).

18. Neustadt showed how the commands of presidents on three occasions—Truman's sacking of General MacArthur, his decision to seize the steel mills in 1953, and Eisenhower's decision to send federal troops to Little Rock, Arkansas, in 1954—were as much a demonstration of failure rather than success, for they represented the failure of persuasion or the bargaining skills so crucial to the office. *Presidential Power*, chaps. 2 and 3.

Further Reading

An up-to-date textbook treatment of the presidency is provided by Thomas E. Cronin and Michael A. Genovese, *The Paradoxes of the American Presidency* (New York: Oxford University Press, 1998). The classic statement on the president's power to persuade is provided by Richard E. Neustadt, *Presidential Power and the Modern Presidency* (New York: Free Press, 1993). For an account of the increasingly public nature of the office, see Samuel Kernell, *Going Public*, 3d ed. (Washington, DC: Congressional Quarterly Press, 1997). Presidential elections are covered in Nelson W. Polsby and Aaron Wildavsky, *Presidential Elections: Contemporary Strategies of American Electoral Politics*, 9th ed. (New York: Free Press, 1995), and in Stephen J. Wayne, *The Road to the White House, 1996: The Politics of Presidential Elections* (New York: St. Martin's, 1996). For an impressive historical sweep through the presidency, see Stephen Skowronek, *The Politics Presidents Make: Leadership from John Adams to George Bush* (Cambridge, MA: Harvard University Press, 1993). A recent study of the presidential bureaucracy is John Hart, *The Presidential Branch* (Chatham, NJ: Chatham House, 1994). An interesting comparative perspective on the presidency is Richard Rose, *The Post-Modern President: George Bush Meets the World* (Chatham, NJ: Chatham House, 1991).

10

The Federal Bureaucracy

The fully developed bureaucratic mechanism compares with other organizations exactly as does the machine with the non-mechanical modes of production. Precision, speed, unambiguity, knowledge of the files, continuity, discretion, unity, strict subordination, reduction of friction and of material and personal costs—these are raised to the optimum point in the strictly bureaucratic administration.

—Max Weber

Our Government has no special power except that granted it by the people. It is time to check and reverse the growth of government which shows signs of having grown beyond the consent of the governed. It is my intention to curb the size and influence of the federal establishment . . .

—Ronald Reagan

Our principles are clear. The government service is a noble calling and a public trust. . . . There is nothing more fulfilling than to serve your country and fellow citizens and to do it well.

—George Bush

Reinventing government requires ending overregulation and micromanagement. That implicitly demands that Congress give up its penchant for tinkering with bureaucracy and leave more of management to the managers.

—Report of the National Performance Review [on Reinventing Government], 1993

Few areas of federal government activity come in for as much opprobrium as does the bureaucracy. As the Weber quote suggests, bureaucracies are supposed to work efficiently. Hierarchy, order,

FIGURE 10.1   Trends in Political Alienation Indicators

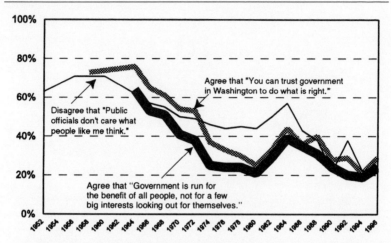

SOURCE: University of Michigan's Survey Research Center, Center for Political Studies, National Election Studies.

responsibility, and professionalism are implied by the model of the "rational" bureaucrat, yet, according to public folklore, typical federal administrators are the very opposite of this. They are over-paid, inefficient, and wasteful. Worse, they are often the creatures of special interests, and occasionally they are simply corrupt. Surveys have shown, indeed, that the federal government is considered easily the most inefficient of all the major institutions in American society. Moreover, the public's regard for Washington and public officials has been steadily declining since the 1960s (Figure 10.1).

Although some of the more colorful charges leveled at the federal bureaucracy more closely resemble caricature than accurate portrait, the executive branch does seem unusually inefficient, fragmented, and complex—indeed, so much so that every president has pledged to simplify the executive branch and to root out wasteful and unnecessary programs. Promises of this sort are popular with the electorate, and no doubt presidents genuinely believe that they can actually rationalize the bureaucracy. In spite of some changes, however, the complaints—and frustrated attempts at reform—continue. This issue raises a number of questions. Why is it that the executive branch attracts so much criticism? Is the criticism justified? To what extent can the federal bureaucracy be controlled and reformed in ways that make it more responsive to public demands? It may be that the structure and behavior of the executive departments and agencies reflect other forces in American government that would have to be changed as a prelude to bureaucratic reform. Analysis of these issues first requires an understanding of some basic facts about the federal administration in the United States.

The Federal Bureaucracy: Organization and Function

The annual *United States Government Manual* contains an organizational chart of the government of the United States (Figure 10.2). Although such charts can be misleading—they imply a hierarchical simplicity and equality among units at the same level that is far from reality—they do reveal the bare bones of the system.

The most important distinctions are among the fourteen executive departments, the independent establishments, and the government corporations. Executive or cabinet departments are responsible for the major federal programs, and their chiefs, the departmental secretaries, are directly answerable to the president or to agencies within the Executive Office of the President such as the Office of Management and Budget. Given the growth in government since the 1940s, cabinet departments have not proliferated as might have been expected. In 1999, only seven of the fourteen departments were creations of the modern era, and of these, one (Defense) grew out of older departments. In fact, successive presidents have worked hard to reduce the number of departments or to rationalize existing ones. In 1949, the Departments of War, Army, Navy, and Air Force were combined in one Department of Defense. In 1971, President Nixon proposed "the most far-reaching reorganization of the executive branch that has ever been proposed by a President of the United States"[1] by amalgamating seven cabinet departments into four new ones. His plan was rejected by Congress, but Jimmy Carter and Ronald Reagan continued the campaign to simplify the departments. Ronald Reagan went so far as to label the Departments of Education and Energy unnecessary, and during 1982, bills were introduced into Congress proposing their abolition. Both were created by Jimmy Carter—the former because the existing Department of Health, Education, and Welfare was so large and cumbersome, and the latter as a direct response to the nation's energy crisis. By 1988, they were still in existence, however, demonstrating Congress's resistance to major rationalizations. In any event, Reagan presided over an expansion of the cabinet de-

252

FIGURE 10.2 The Government of the United States

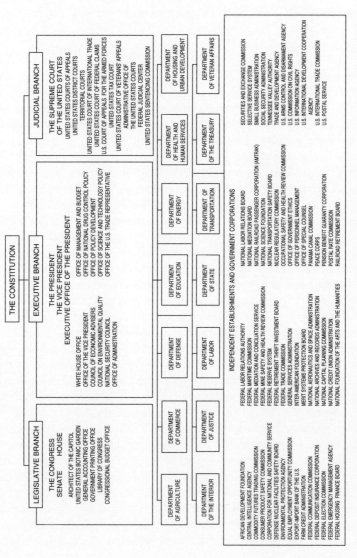

SOURCE: *United States Government Manual, 1998–99* (Washington, DC: US Government Printing Office, 1998), p. 22.

partments with the creation of the Department of Veterans Affairs in 1988.

Most presidents prefer a small, compact cabinet to facilitate smooth policymaking. Yet the number of departments for which they are responsible is but one of a number of management problems they face. Another involves the complexity characteristic of each department. This can be formidable, for, with the possible exception of the Department of State (responsible for the foreign service and foreign policy), each department is itself a collection of different agencies and services, each with its own interests and constituents. For example, the Department of Health and Human Services (HHS) was created in 1979 following an earlier incarnation as the Department of Health, Education, and Welfare, which was itself a loose collection of disparate agencies.

HHS's apparently simple hierarchical structure (Figure 10.3) belies a reality of considerable complexity and competition—although the sheer number of different programs does give some sense to the complexity of the department. In almost all cabinet departments, there is a horizontal division of responsibilities and a vertical division organized geographically. Thus, much of the day-to-day work of HHS is carried out at the regional and area levels. There are ten standard federal regions and, within these, a number of area offices, usually based in large cities.

Figure 10.3 also illustrates some distinction among different sorts of bureaucrats. In the American system, a crucial distinction exists between the *competitive* service, which includes officials recruited by examination or on the basis of technical qualifications determined by the Office of Personnel Management, and the *excepted* service, in which appointment is decided, again mainly on merit, directly by such agencies and departments as the FBI, the Postal Service, and the State Department. The excepted service includes the Senior Executive Service (SES) created by the 1978 Civil Service Act. SES appointees are the supergrade officials who can, in theory at least, be moved across agencies and given merit pay awards. The excepted service also includes political appointees, who constitute about 3 percent of the total. In Figure 10.3, the secretary, deputy secretary, assistant secretaries, and top officials in each of the subunits would be *political* appointees. Other very senior officials would be part of the SES, while the bulk of the remainder would be part of the competitive service. As will be developed later, the whole question of the role of political appointees has been highly controversial since the 1970s.

FIGURE 10.3   Department of Health and Human Services

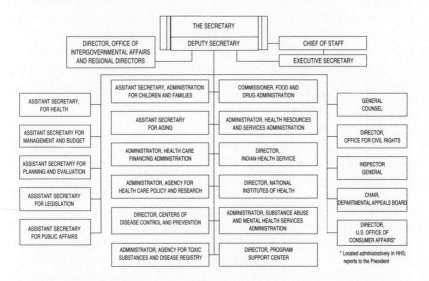

SOURCE: *United States Government Manual, 1997–98* (Washington, DC: U.S. Government Printing Office, 1997), p. 272.

The independent establishments and government corporations (Figure 10.2) include a vast number of agencies performing numerous functions. A very general distinction can be drawn between government corporations (broadly equivalent to state-owned industries in other countries), which include the U.S. Postal Service, and the regulatory agencies. But there are other institutions that fall into neither category, including the General Services Administration and the Office of Personnel Management that deal, respectively, with the provision of buildings, equipment, and other services for the whole executive branch, and the recruitment of staff to the cabinet departments. It is somewhat misleading to label all of these institutions "independent"—the chief administrators (or in a few cases the boards of governors) are appointed by the president, subject to confirmation by the Senate. The president is also a key figure in helping decide the size of their budgets, and in some cases he or the cabinet secretaries take a very direct interest in their activities. Such involvement is patently the case with the Central Intelligence Agency (CIA) and with the U.S. Information

Service (the latter effectively functions as a propaganda service for the State Department).

The regulatory agencies are genuinely more independent, however, because most of them were originally established by Congress to function as nonpartisan organizations responsible for monitoring, controlling, or regulating various aspects of economic and social life. Three waves of reform in American politics correspond to the three generations of regulatory agencies that exist. Between 1887 and 1915, a rising tide of reform sentiment led to the creation of agencies designed to tame the unacceptable economic and social activities of large corporations and natural monopolies, in particular the railroads. Thus, during this period, the Interstate Commerce Commission and Federal Trade Commission came into being. During the 1930s, most of the reforms were inspired by the Depression and its consequences. Hence, the Federal Deposit Insurance Corporation underwrites bank deposits to protect the public against bank failures, the Securities and Exchange Commission regulates the stock market, and the National Labor Relations Board helps regulate industrial relations.

The final wave of reform, during the 1960s and 1970s, was inspired by, among other things, concern about environmental pollution (leading to the Environmental Protection Agency, which is, incidentally, not an independent agency but a cabinet-level organization), civil rights (the Equal Employment Opportunity Commission), election malpractice (the Federal Election Commission), and consumer protection (the Consumer Protection Safety Commission). These agencies have sometimes been given formidable powers by Congress to exercise administrative, legislative, and judicial powers over corporations, unions, and the public at large. Until the 1960s, a common criticism was that they were anything but independent in the use of these powers. Instead the "regulated controlled the regulators," or, to cite two celebrated cases, the Food and Drug Administration was in the hands of the drug companies, and the Interstate Commerce Commission was deferential to the needs of the truckers and railroads.

Although the criticism is sometimes exaggerated, there is little doubt that many of the regulatory commissions established a *symbiotic* relationship with what had become their clients. They needed each other—the clients for guidance on how best to operate in (or dominate) the market, and the regulators to ensure political independence and to justify their bureaucratic raison d'etre.[2] During the

1960s and 1970s, increasing public concern about the abuse of corporate power led the newer agencies (such as the Environmental Protection Agency) to establish a more *adversarial* relationship with the regulated.[3] This approach, limited reforms in the older agencies, and a general increase in the amount of regulation in American life—especially of corporations—have led to a backlash by the corporate world and their political allies, the Republicans.

Contrary to popular belief, the burgeoning responsibilities of the federal government, together with greatly increased expenditures, have not been matched by dramatic increases in the number of federal employees responsible for implementing programs and policies. As can be seen from Figure 10.4, the number of federal employees has remained roughly the same since the mid-1960s and in the early 1990s actually declined. The major increases in total government employment have been accounted for by state and local governments. Indeed, starting with the Carter administration and continuing under President Reagan, the absolute number of federal-civilian employees fell—although the decreases were modest.

These reductions were part of the continuing campaign against big government, but that factor does not entirely account for the general failure of federal employment to rise in the postwar period. Another reason, at least until the early 1980s, was the rapid increase in the number and size of grants-in-aid programs to state and local governments. As noted in Chapter 3, a fair percentage of the general increase in federal spending derives from this source. Devolved programs increase employment at the lower, rather than federal, level. Second, increased expenditure does not necessarily require more federal employees—although it has almost certainly led to a considerable expansion of the number of professionals in federal employment. Professionals are the middle-grade employees, often scientists, or the highly trained personnel who have been increasingly recruited to help run more complex programs, old and new. In fact (the Post Office excluded), the federal government employs relatively few less qualified workers. State and local governments employ most of the lower grades (transportation, hospital, municipal employees) and lower-middle grades (teachers, social workers, police, and firefighters). A more professional civil service is harder to control because it can more easily fall back on technical and highly specialized information when challenged by the public, Congress, or the president. Finally, a recent trend in all government bureaucracies, including the federal government, has been to con-

FIGURE 10.4   Number of Federal, State, and Local Government
Employees, 1929–1995

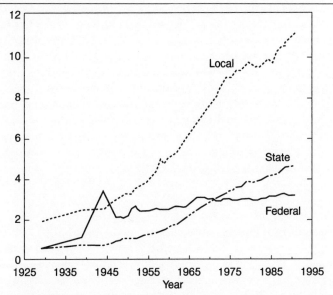

SOURCE: Harold W. Stanley and Richard G. Niemi, *Vital Statistics on American Politics, 1997–98* (Washington, DC: Congressional Quarterly Press, 1998), figure 8.1.

tract out services to the private sector. Although progress has been slow in this area, privatization obviously reduces the number of federal employees and is likely to become more important in the future.

The Bureaucracy: How Uncontrollable?

Students of administrative behavior are quick to identify certain characteristics of bureaucracy that are present whatever the political system involved or governmental function being performed. Some of these characteristics are labeled "undesirable"—usually because they greatly reduce the accountability of bureaucrats to elected officials—and as government becomes larger and more complex, so these undesirable features multiply. There is, of course, no reason to suppose that the United States is exempt from these trends. It is not, and that is problem enough. But critics go much further and argue that the U.S. government, and particularly the federal bureaucracy,

has a number of additional, uniquely American features that make
the problem of accountability a particularly serious one.

Unfortunately, unraveling cause and effect is difficult in this area,
especially in a country where "federal government" and "bureaucracy" often hold negative connotations. With so many Americans
deeply prejudiced against what they see as big government, it is important to treat with caution some of the more colorful critiques
leveled against bureaucracy, regulation, "Washington," and the
civil service. The objective in the remainder of this chapter, therefore, is to outline the major criticisms directed at the federal bureaucracy, to assess their validity, and to record the ways in which
presidents, Congress, the courts, and the public have attempted to
increase their control over administrators.

The Inherent Power of Bureaucracy

Simple theories of constitutional government and of administrative
behavior assign little or no independent power or discretion to administrators. Their job is to implement laws. The legislature passes
the laws, and the chief executive is responsible for managing and
directing the administrators in the implementation process. According to classical theories of administration, bureaucrats can do
this effectively if they operate in line with certain basic principles—
hierarchical command, specialization, and delegation of duties.
The elected chief executives are at the apex of this system; they
alone give commands. Bureaucrats may advise them, but it is not
their job to give orders. Reality is, of course, very far from this
ideal type. In most systems, bureaucrats have two main powers,
both of which can give them considerable control over the policy
system.

Information.   Bureaucrats function as administrative gatekeepers.
When laws are being framed, whether it be by legislatures or executives, it is essential to determine what is achievable and what is
not. A new law on lead levels in gasoline, for example, needs to be
carefully informed about a host of technical questions, including
the efficiency of internal combustion engines, pollution levels, the
automakers' ability to compete internationally once their products
are adapted, and so on. Politicians are obliged to heed the advice of
their officials on such technicalities, and the officials themselves
can, up to a point, select and organize information according to

their own preferences and prejudices, or in favor of one interest rather than another. They may, for example, advise the politicians that certain options are simply not possible for technical reasons.

Examples of administrative gatekeeping in highly technical areas may sound understandable and possibly exceptional. But most law-making and implementation processes in modern industrial societies are technical and complex. From housing to transportation to law enforcement to social security and defense, technical questions are paramount. No single president or cabinet secretary can possibly absorb all this information—even with the assistance of professional staffs. They have to rely on their bureaucrats.

Clientelism. "Clientelism" is the word used to describe the sort of symbiotic relationships between bureaucrats and their customers referred to earlier. Again, it is not unique to American politics; to a greater or lesser extent, it occurs everywhere. It is also an entirely understandable phenomenon. Consider the case of defense agencies and defense contractors. In those Western countries with sizable defense industries (Britain, Germany, France, the United States), intimate relations exist between contractors and officials in defense departments. Defense officials have, therefore, a continuing interest in particular corporations and defense systems—and also, perhaps, in ensuring that defense spending remains at certain levels. These interests may or may not be the same as those of the administrators' political masters. But there can be no doubting the independent political influence of officials in this context. Information is, again, the crucial resource, but it is not merely technical information; it is this plus all the advantages that daily personal contact and shared values give to the official and that are often denied to the politicians.

As government has increased in size and scope, so clientelism has spread. In modern societies, all bureaucracies have their customers whose interests and needs must be tended to, whatever the government in power or the values and preferences of elected politicians.

The Bureaucratic Hydra: A Uniquely American Phenomenon?

Scholars of comparative government often refer to the extent to which different political systems are characterized by "strong" or "weak" states. Almost invariably, the United States is categorized as a weak state. In other words, rather than government being unified, resolute, and separated from the rest of society, it is fragmented, indecisive, and infused with social influence. The aforementioned clientelism is a good indicator of the power and autonomy of the state. Although it exists everywhere, clientelism is likely to be more pervasive in weak-state systems. In addition, weak states are likely to be characterized by competition among different parts of the administrative process. Thus, subunits—individual departments and agencies—display a marked degree of *autonomy* from the center. They serve different interests, and their officials do not all share the same values and policy objectives. This analysis does not refer to the absolute *size* of government. As noted, in terms of expenditure and function, American government is large by any standards. Rather, the focus is the extent to which American government is fragmented and simply not amenable to central direction and control.

Much of recent criticism centers on this fact. Critics usually do not put the particular American situation in comparative context, but there is good reason to believe that the United States is different from many other countries; that certain institutional relationships make it especially difficult to exercise central control over public policy. Three basic critiques of American bureaucracy have been made since the mid-1960s; these pertain to "iron triangles," "issue networks," and the concept of "public choice and principal-agent."

Iron Triangles.   Starting with books written by Douglass Cater and Leiper Freeman in the mid-1960s came accusations that subgovernments working as iron triangles—with each triangle composed of congressional subcommittee, administrative bureau, and special interest—were the dominant actors in American politics.[4] The analysis was simple: Congressional subcommittees provide the money and monitor regulations, the bureau hands over the money or enforces the regulation, and the special interest is the beneficiary. All parties need one another, and the system would break down without equal participation by all—hence the "iron triangle" metaphor. Empirical confirmation of subgovernments of this sort was readily at hand, especially in public works, defense, agriculture, and water policy. Agriculture became a particularly appealing example, with a bureau in the Department of Agriculture handing out subsidies to farmers who, in turn, had established intimate links with members of the several agricultural subcommittees. The triangle was "iron" because it was impenetrable. The combined political clout of the leading subgovernment actors was formidable, with no individual president, public-interest lobby, or congressional leader able to break the pattern of distribution and public expenditure the triangle had molded.

The empirical validity of this case was convincing for certain sorts of public policy, but it was clearly inappropriate in other areas. Appreciating this fact, Ripley and Franklin refined the thesis in an important book first published in 1976.[5] They pointed out that, in what they called "redistributive" domestic policy (in which resources are taken from one group or class and given to another, as in social welfare programs), presidents and top-level (politically appointed) officials, as well as Congress as a whole, play an important part. And in some regulatory policies, bureaucracy and administration play a relatively small role. Other, more sophisticated refinements were added by the authors to the subgovernment theory, all of which demonstrated that the American administrative and political process is indeed unduly complex and often not amenable to simple, single-model characterizations.

Issue Networks. A conceptually much simpler, yet almost certainly more accurate, picture of administrative politics in America has been drawn by Hugh Heclo. Heclo has argued that as government programs have grown in size and scope, so they have generated new lobbies, interests, and, simply, a larger number of active participants in the policy process. Moreover, the networks of politicking and lobbying that develop as a consequence are constantly adapting and changing. Thus it is very difficult accurately to categorize where the policy system begins and ends: "The notion of iron triangles and sub-governments presumes small circles of participants who have succeeded in becoming largely autonomous. Issue networks, on the other hand, comprise a large number of participants with quite variable degrees of mutual commitment or of dependence on others in their environment; in fact it is almost impossible to say where a network leaves off and its environment begins."[6]

As a result of this much more open and volatile system, no erstwhile secure subgovernment can afford to be complacent. The cozy relationships established between corporations and bureaucrats have been challenged by environmentalists, consumer-protection advocates, and other public-interest lobbies (a point developed in the next chapter). The subgovernments continue to exist, of course, but they are increasingly buffeted by competing centers of power. Heclo does not view these developments as entirely negative—indeed, there may be greater scope for executive leadership when the system is more open. But he does view with alarm the increasing complexity of government and the fact that direct democratic accountability is difficult to achieve when the "real" decisions are taken not by the president and members of Congress but by numerous additional political actors, including bureaucrats, lobbyists, the media, and political consultants.

Public Choice and the Principal-Agent Problem.   Neither the iron-triangle nor the issue-network approach offers definitive *solutions* to the problem of bureaucracy. From the 1970s to the 1990s, however, a number of economists and political scientists argued that the central problem of bureaucracy related to the sort of personal incentives available to the bureaucrats themselves. Public-choice theory assumes that all actors in the political process (politicians, voters, officials, interest groups) are self-interested and seek to maximize benefits, whether these be votes, income, or power. Officials do this by maximizing their budgets so as to accumulate personal benefits (promotion, salary, status). Given this tendency, in the traditionally organized bureaucracy, some overprovision will occur and will result in unit costs higher than those that would prevail if the services were provided by the market.

Even in private firms, there remains what some economists have called the principal-agent problem. This concept assumes that the principal (for example, the owner of a firm) cannot always be sure that his managers (the agents) are not shirking or are operating at a level that optimizes profits. The concern is that because employees receive the same salary irrespective of effort, they have little incentive to work hard. In bureaucracies, the problem is even more serious, because government officials rarely produce anything that can be measured. If, for example, an FBI agent makes no arrests, is this because he or she is shirking or because there is no crime? Also, what is the equivalent of the private-firm owner in bureaucracy? In a sense, all the managers, including those at the very top, have little incentive to perform.

Two possible solutions exist to reduce or eliminate this problem. First, services can be privatized so that the discipline of the market is imposed. Second, if full privatization is not possible, the institutional rules and procedures can be changed in ways that alter officials' incentive to maximize spending. This can be done by creating quasi-independent agencies run by managers on fixed contracts under instructions to meet predetermined cost and performance targets. As a result, officials will see a common interest between improvements in efficiency and their own career and pay prospects.

Bureaucratic Critiques in Perspective

Interestingly, these critiques of bureaucratic power are comments not only on administrators and administrative agencies but also on the entire policymaking system. Many make the a priori assumption that more government is, by definition, a bad thing and that increasing public disenchantment with government derives from the constantly expanding volume of legislation and special regulations. Regardless of the normative question of whether more government is good or bad, it is obviously the case that government, by whatever definition (number of employees and policies, volume of regulations, amount of public expenditures), has increased in all modern industrial societies since the 1970s. Criticism of big government has occurred in other countries, but it has been particularly vocal in the United States—a country where, as a percentage of GNP, government, though large, is not at the top of the international-league table. No doubt this disparity can partly be explained in ideological terms. One factor, of course, is the long-established American tradition of antagonism to government. But there are also important institutional differences between the United States and most other countries that underlie both academic and popular critiques of government in general and bureaucracy in particular.

Easily the most important difference is the independent role of Congress. Iron triangles and issue networks depend at least in part on an autonomous legislature and, within Congress, little legislatures (committees and subcommittees). Although this feature has long been appreciated—for example, in 1970 Harold Seidman noted that "meaningful improvements in executive organization and in the management of the Federal system . . . will depend in the final analysis on reorganization of the congressional committee structure"[7]—it seems to have been partly forgotten amid all the talk of special-interest politics, political action committees, and the generally more complex and confusing pattern of government typical of the 1990s. Although it could be argued that autonomous legislative power increases accountability, it also greatly facilitates the sort of volatile issue-network politics in which no single actor in the policy process can ever fully understand what is going on, let alone control events. Arguably, this result is the very antithesis of accountability. As discussed later, successive governments, including the Clinton administration, have recognized this problem, but few have been able to do much about it.

A second unique feature of the American system is its openness. Access to Congress and members of Congress, as well as to officials at all levels, is remarkably easy compared with most other countries. Multiple players have exploited this fact, and Washington has become a political consultants' and lobbyists' paradise. No interest, whether economic (corporations, unions), public interest (environment, consumer protection), or governmental (state and local governments), can afford to drop its guard by failing to make full use of the availability of policymakers. Again, openness is at least partly a function of the proliferation of centers of autonomy or power. With subcommittees, bureaus, agencies, and even individual officials competing with one another over particular areas of public policy, they are usually only too ready to make use of any resource that will enhance their autonomy further; in essence, this means organized interests (together with their technical advisers, lobbyists, and consultants) and the media. A more open system received fresh impetus from the cathartic effects of the Watergate scandal. Freedom of information became a major public issue during the late 1960s and early 1970s, and the formal legal access of groups and individuals to government files and information was greatly strengthened as a result.[8] But these formal changes were almost certainly not as important in producing greater access as were the changes in Congress, the party system, and American society generally that earlier chapters have chronicled.

Reform Attempts

Perhaps the most common recent response to the problem of big government and bureaucratic power is simply to propose a reduction in the size and complexity of government. This has been the aim of three recent presidents. In his 1982 State of the Union message, Ronald Reagan declared: "Together, we have cut the growth of new federal regulations in half. In 1981, there were 23,000 fewer pages in the Federal Register, which lists new regulations, than there were in 1980. . . . Together, we have created an effective federal strike force to combat waste and fraud in government. In just six months it has saved the taxpayers more than two billion dollars—and it's only getting started."

As noted earlier, the number of federal employees declined during the late 1970s and early 1980s, steadied through to the mid-1990s, and has dipped slightly since (Figure 10.4). Does this mean that presidents are winning the battle against bureaucracy? Not necessarily. Federal employment may not have risen rapidly, but numbers are only loosely related to complexity and autonomy. Similarly, Ronald Reagan's reductions in new regulations did nothing to alter the fact of already established regulations, together with their policy networks. "Waste and fraud" in the federal government undoubtedly exist, but this condemnation is more of a populist rallying cry than an attack on the central problems of complexity and autonomy.

Several presidents have attempted to reorganize the executive branch, the most dramatic proposal being Richard Nixon's 1971 plan to create four "superdepartments"—Natural Resources, Human Resources, Community Development, and Economic Affairs. Other, less ambitious reorganizations have been attempted, some successfully, others not. Sometimes these involve the creation of new departments (Housing and Urban Development [HUD] in 1965, Health, Education, and Welfare [HEW] in 1953, the Department of Energy in 1977, the Department of Education in 1979, Veterans Affairs in 1988). More common are internal reorganizations usually aimed at simplifying administration and reducing overlapping jurisdictions. Although well intentioned, reorganization is almost always a less than adequate reform measure. For one thing, Congress is reluctant to approve reorganizations that affect its internal distribution of power and accordingly has vetoed the more far-reaching reforms. Committees and, increasingly, subcommittees have vested interests in the continuing autonomy of departments, bureaus, and agencies. Second, internal reorganization often involves "shuffling the same old drones into new hives," as Robert Sherrill has put it, so no real change occurs.

In fact, Ronald Reagan eschewed the reorganization device, opting instead for more direct *political* control of the executive branch. He did this in two ways: through control of agency and departmental rulemaking and through the appointment power. In 1980, Congress passed the Paperwork Reduction Act, a law fa-

vored by the Carter administration and designed to simplify federal
regulations. The act established an Office of Information and Regulatory Affairs (OIRA) within the Office of Management and Budget (OMB). Although this new unit was not in itself very significant, the Reagan administration used it, in combination with two executive orders, to screen new agency regulations. In effect, this procedure required the executive departments and agencies to submit any changes in policy to OMB. In turn, OMB rejected any rules considered not in line with administration policy. Not surprisingly, this strategy particularly affected those agencies that, in the past, the administration had considered too progressive in such areas as environmental protection, affirmative action, occupational safety and health, welfare, education, and social security. These centralized gatekeeping efforts provoked a storm of protest in Congress and almost certainly led to a loosening of regulations in a number of areas. As a number of commentators have noted, however, these changes did not amount to a fundamental shift in policy.[9]

The Reagan administration's use of the appointment power attracted a great deal of publicity because it represented a thoroughgoing attempt to politicize the executive branch. In addition to placing Reagan supporters in the cabinet departments and regulatory agencies, the administration centralized the appointment, transfer, and promotion of members of the Senior Executive Service. Utilizing the provisions of the 1978 Civil Service Act, the Office of Personnel Management, under direct instructions from Ed Meese in the White House, promoted, rewarded, and transferred Reagan loyalists while punishing those considered liberal or disloyal. At the cabinet level, some of the Reagan appointees were so out of tune with their departments and with public opinion that they were forced to resign (Anne Gorsuch at EPA; James Watt at Interior). Lower down, the politicization strategy was also controversial and led to falling morale and frequent resignations among civil servants.

Again, limits exist as to what can be achieved from such a strategy. If Congress establishes an Environmental Protection Agency, its job is to protect the environment. Officials recruited to the EPA will support this basic objective. Changing senior managers can undermine this policy but cannot transform it. Congress, moreover, is ever vigilant and keen to exercise its oversight function. This extends to the appointment power, and, as noted, several Reagan appointees were rejected or obliged to resign (including the director of the Office of Personnel Management, Donald Devine).

Other oversight resources have been utilized by Congress in its attempts to control the bureaucracy. The General Accounting Office has been more rigorous in providing an information base for evaluation of whether the criticism is politicization or not. There has even been some flirtation with "sunset" legislation. Another symptom of the populist revolt against big government, sunset laws require agencies or programs to be renewed annually. If they are not fulfilling their purpose, they simply cease to exist. Such measures have not so far been adopted on a significant scale.

As the third quotation at the beginning of the chapter suggests, George Bush was much more sympathetic to the federal bureaucracy than was Ronald Reagan. Bush had served as an official ambassador to the UN and China and as head of the Central Intelligence Agency, and one of his first acts as president was to invite all the top officials to a reception labeled "A Salute to Public Service." His appointments were noticeably less ideological than Reagan's, although as a Republican, he too favored the "core" departments whose values and functions are close to the Republican ethos: State, Defense, Justice, Treasury.

On coming to power, Bill Clinton had two major objectives in terms of administrative reform. First, he wanted to reverse what he saw as the Republican bias toward employing older white males in senior positions in the executive branch. Second, he was intent on further streamlining the civil service to make it more responsive to the public and less enmeshed in red tape and regulations. There is no doubting that he achieved a much greater degree of ethnic, racial, and gender diversity than his Republican counterparts. Indeed, in his search for diversity, he was not always able to find appropriate appointees and was accused of being inordinately slow in his appointment process. Most of the new appointees were what might be called "New Democrats," or pragmatic, rather than ideological, reformers. Notably absent were "Great Society liberals" who believe that the answer to most of society's problems lies in bigger and better federal programs.

The values of these new appointees fit well with the administration's infatuation with the "reinventing government" movement. *Reinventing Government* was the title of a book by David Osborne and Ted Gaebler, who argued that the public sector could be transformed by applying market principles and the entrepreneurial spirit to the public sector. This involved, among other things, "empowering" employees by decentralizing decisionmaking within the civil service, cutting red tape, reducing costs, and "putting customers first."[10] These proposals, though very much in the public-choice tradition of reform, generally did not involve an *ideological* agenda of the Reagan variety that was designed to meet the objectives of the "new right." Instead, making bureaucracy more efficient and responsive were the key objectives.

In line with these principles, President Clinton commissioned a National Performance Review (NPR) chaired by Vice President Al Gore. The resulting report recommended 384 major changes affecting 27 agencies and departments. Most of these involved reducing the number of rules and regulations and decentralizing power within individual departments and agencies. It should be stressed, however, that it was never Clinton's intention to *weaken* executive power. Rather, the aim was to make the executive branch more *efficient and responsive*. In this sense, the president was continuing the trend begun by Jimmy Carter in the 1970s. Nevertheless, as the quote from the NPR report at the beginning of the chapter suggests, Clinton's initiative in fact achieved little, because wholesale change can occur only if Congress agrees to cooperate.

Reinventing government means making it more autonomous. This means weakening Congress's grip on the executive branch. In fact, Congress produced its own initiative for "downsizing" government—the Government Performance and Results Act (GPRA) of 1993. By requiring federal agencies to set goals and reach performance targets, this legislation was in much the same mold as the NPR. However, by the end of 1998, the results were highly uneven. Significantly, the one attempt to give the NPR legislative teeth—the creation of performance-based organizations (PBOs)—was defeated by Congress in 1996.

In sum, although both Congress and the Clinton administration supported administrative reform, they did not act in concert in this crucial area. This is the major reason why, with some exceptions, most of the major moves toward the market in the United States, including most privatizations, have occurred in state and local rather than in the federal government. In such countries and Britain and New Zealand where executive power and party discipline are more unified, moves toward market-type reforms in national bureaucracies have been far more extensive.

Conclusion

The foregoing review confirms that the system is characterized by numerous and highly volatile issue networks. These are not impenetrable, because a more open policy system allows new forces and interests to influence even the most established relationships. These networks remain autonomous, however, not because they constitute closed policy systems but because they have proved not to be easily amenable to central control. Even a determined president with great public support like Ronald Reagan, who was intent on imposing radical changes in bureaucratic behavior, could achieve only limited results. More recently, public disquiet with the federal bureaucracy has impelled both presidents and Congress to downsize the federal bureaucracy through devolution, the contracting-out of services, and other reforms. However, the two branches have generally failed to act in concert on this issue.

Quite apart from executive-legislative difficulties, downsizing does not always have positive results. For example, the number of HHS employees was reduced by almost half in the three years 1993 to 1996. But this was because many medical services were contracted out to the very same personnel removed from the HHS. Whether this will make the agency more "accountable" and "responsive" remains to be seen. The experience of other countries suggests that downsizing government sometimes results in less rather than more public confidence in such programs as health and education.[11] In sum, the currently popular reforms, most of which are influenced by the public-choice critique of bureaucratic power, may reduce costs and make government more accountable, but they may not satisfy the expectations of the public.

Notes

1. Quoted in Otis L. Graham, *Toward a Planned Society: From Roosevelt to Nixon* (New York: Oxford University Press, 1976), p. 209.

2. See Murray Edelman, *The Symbolic Uses of Politics* (Urbana: University of Illinois Press, 1964), for a good analysis of this point.

3. For a selection of case studies on regulation, see James Q. Wilson (ed.), *The Politics of Regulation* (New York: Basic Books, 1980).

4. Douglass Cater, *Power in Washington* (New York: Vintage, 1964); J. Leiper Freeman, *The Political Process* (New York, Random House, 1965).

5. Randall B. Ripley and Grace A. Franklin, *Congress, the Bureaucracy, and Public Policy* (Homewood, IL: Dorsey Press, 1976, 5th ed., 1991).

6. Hugh Heclo, "Issue Networks and the Executive Establishment," in Anthony King (ed.), *The New American Political System* (Washington, DC: American Enterprise Institute, 1978), p. 102.

7. Harold Seidman, *Politics, Position, and Power: The Dynamics of Federal Organization* (New York: Oxford University Press, 1970), p. 285.

8. Under the 1966 and 1974 Freedom of Information Acts, Americans have the right to inspect all federal records. Certain information (for example, relating to criminal investigation, defense, or interoffice memos) can be denied, but citizens who are refused information can appeal in the courts. The substantive freedom of access in the United States is dramatically greater than in most comparable countries and especially than in the United Kingdom.

9. For a review, see David McKay, *Domestic Policy and Ideology* (Cambridge: Cambridge University Press, 1989).

10. David Osborne and Ted Gaebler, *Reinventing Government: How the Entrepreneurial Spirit Is Transforming the Public Sector* (New York: Penguin, 1993).

11. For a review of the British public's reactions to such reforms, see Ian Budge et al., *The New British Politics* (New York: Addison-Wesley; Longman, 1998), chaps. 10 and 26.

Further Reading

Randall B. Ripley and Grace A. Franklin provide a fascinating insight into the world of subgovernments in *Congress, the Bureaucracy, and Public Policy*, 5th ed. (New York: Dorsey Press, 1991). A good textbook treatment of the subject is James Q. Wilson, *Bureaucracy: What Government Agencies Do and Why They Do It* (New York: Basic Books, 1989). On reinventing government, see David Osborne and Ted Gaebler, *Reinventing Government: How the Entrepreneurial Spirit Is Transforming the Public Sector* (New York: Penguin, 1993). Also see Al Gore, *Common-Sense Government Works Better and Costs Less* (Washington, DC: U.S. Government Printing Office, 1995). For an assessment of recent reforms, see Donald F. Kettl et al., *Civil Service Reform* (Washington, DC: Brookings Institution, 1996). A good analysis of public disenchantment with bureaucracy is provided by Joseph Nye, Philip Zelikow, and David King, *Why People Don't Trust Government* (Boston: Harvard University Press, 1998).

11

Organized Interests:
The Real Power?

Suppose you go to Washington and try to get at your government. You will always find that while you are politely listened to, the men really consulted are the men with the biggest stake—the big bankers, the big manufacturers, the big masters of commerce. . . . The government of the United States is the foster child of special interests. It is not allowed to have a will of its own. It is told at every move: "Don't do that; you will interfere with our prosperity."

—Woodrow Wilson

Concededly, each interest group is biased; but their role . . . is not unlike the advocacy of lawyers in court which has proven so successful in resolving judicial controversies. Because our congressional representation is based on geographical boundaries, the lobbyists who speak for the various economic, commercial and other functional interests of this country serve a very useful purpose and have assumed an important role in the legislative process.

—John F. Kennedy

Throughout American history, concern about the power of organized interests has never been far from the surface. Indeed, the growth of the republic can almost be described in terms of successive waves of populist revolt against the undue influence of organized groups and, in particular, private corporations. Woodrow Wilson's characterization (above) came after more than twenty years of public disquiet at the operations of the big companies. During the 1920s, corporate power was regarded more benignly, with capitalism flourishing as never before. The Depression transformed this image, however, and not until the 1950s did the benevolent view of private power return. By the 1970s, the critique returned to the center of the political stage, with popular opprobrium directed at those companies responsible for pollution, consumer exploitation, and discrimination against women and minorities. Even during the boom years of the late 1990s, criticism of corporate power was leveled at HMOs, oil companies, and larger airlines. Criticism of other organized interests—labor, promotional groups—has been more fragmented, although at any particular time a particular group may be the subject of public criticism, as were the labor unions during the 1940s and again during the 1980s.

The critique of corporate power has two related strands. First, large private companies are by their very nature ruthless and exploitative. This mainly populist view considers size to be the main problem. Break up large monopolies and oligopolies, and something approaching "fair" competition will emerge. Second, corporations exercise power without accountability. They are not, in other words, answerable to democratically elected institutions. They can "buy" members of Congress; bribe local, state, and federal officials; and generally manipulate democratic processes in their favor.

These points are explored later, but an overriding feature is noteworthy: The critique of capitalism that historically has been most influential in most other countries and especially in Europe—that the private accumulation of wealth in business is *by definition* exploitative—has been quite rare in the United States. Recently, the criticism has shifted away from attacks on large corporations per se to claims that the sheer volume of interest-group activity at all levels of government has undermined the capacity of governments to articulate the wishes of the public and to get things done. On every issue, lobbies mobilize for and against in ways that make the costs of pursuing a particular policy option very high. Members of Congress, in particular, are electorally vulnerable if they are seen to be taking the "wrong" position on an issue. As a result, it is increasingly difficult for citizens to make a clear connection between their specific electoral demands and the actual policies produced by governments.

The quote by John Kennedy represents the second, quite different judgment on the role of organized interests in America. According to this view, groups are an essential part of the democratic process; far from undermining representation, they aid it. Advocates of this position point to the multiple access points in the American system and the ways in which myriad organized groups are able to exploit these to their advantage. Crucially, because *all* classes, interests, ideological positions, regions, localities, and social groups *can* organize (even if some actually do not) to defend or promote their positions, the potential for fair or just policies is particularly great in the American system.

Much of the comment and discussion in this chapter is centered on these contrasting perspectives and how valid they are in the late 1990s. Particular attention is paid to the link between group activity and the increasingly complex nature of what the public expects from political institutions. First, however, it is necessary to provide some basic information on interest groups in the United States.

Interest Groups and Lobbyists

In all modern industrial societies, citizens band together to form organizations with social, economic, and political aims. American group participation is high in comparative terms, with some 79 percent of the population being members of some voluntary association (Table 11.1). Of this number, many members (about one-third) are inactive, however, and the organizations with the most active membership tend to be "nonpolitical" charitable and social clubs (youth groups, church-related groups, fraternal organizations—Rotary, the Masons, the Lions—and so on); professional societies (representing doctors, lawyers, and the like); and educational groups (parent-teacher associations, school and college fraternities). About 14 percent of adults are active in political clubs and organizations—a similar figure to that for most social clubs. Note the relatively low affiliation rate for labor unions.

In addition to voluntary associations with individual membership, a number of groups exist representing corporate and governmental interests, such as trade, commerce, and manufacturers' associations and state, local, county, and regional government organizations. Finally, a number of single-issue groups exist at any one time, ranging from organizations to outlaw abortion, to proponents of stricter environmental protection, to local groups created to stop the construction of a particular public works project.

All of these organizations do have a political dimension, obviously so in the case of corporate, labor, and ad hoc groups but also with most social organizations. Chambers of commerce and pro-

TABLE 11.1 Types of Organizations and Nature of Affiliation

Organizational Type	% of Respondents Affiliated	Among Those Affiliated		
		% Attend Meetings	% Give Money but No Meetings	% Say Organization Takes Political Stands
Service, fraternal	18	50	35	30
Veterans	16	16	70	59
Religious	12	63	30	27
Nationality, ethnic	4	45	32	61
Senior citizens	12	25	20	61
Women's rights	4	33	52	79
Union	12	52	16	67
Business, professional	23	66	13	59
Political issue	14	20	65	93
Civic, nonpartisan	3	60	21	59
Liberal or conservative	1	20	71	95
Candidate, party	5	39	49	94
Youth	17	42	50	18
Literary, art, study	6	72	15	16
Hobby, sports, leisure	21	52	17	18
Neighborhood, homeowners	12	66	11	50
Charitable, social service	44	14	79	16
Educational	25	50	34	43
Cultural	13	14	71	25
Other	4	32	44	30
All organizations	79	65	55	61

SOURCE: Sidney Verba, Kay Lehman Schlozman, and Henry E. Brady, *Voice and Equality: Civil Voluntarism in American Politics* (Cambridge, MA: Harvard University Press, 1995), table 3.5.

fessional associations, for example, frequently engage in political activity when laws and regulations affecting their members are introduced or existing laws are changed. As local, state, and federal governments have legislated in almost every conceivable area of economic and social life since the 1970s, it is not surprising that many erstwhile social groups and associations have found themselves at the very center of political controversy. The debate on gun control intimately involves the National Rifle Association (NRA); environmental pollution controls involve the Audubon Society and Sierra Club; and education cuts and school district consolidation involve parent-teacher associations.

Political scientists have long been engaged in the business of trying to classify interest groups, and even now no completely satisfactory taxonomy exists. The distinction drawn between voluntary associations with individual members and corporate groups, for example, is not that helpful, because all of these can engage in political activity. For purposes of this discussion, it is more useful to distinguish three broad categories of organized groups—economic, professional, and promotional—and to link these to some added comments on political action committees and lobbying.

Economic Groups

Business

In any discussion of business organizations, it is common to distinguish between the activities of individual corporations and those of peak associations (trade union confederations, employers' and trade associations). In the United States, corporations tend to be both powerful and autonomous, and frequently they exercise political power as independent units. Thus, General Motors, the country's largest automaker, is a political force to be reckoned with, as are such companies as Microsoft, AT&T, the major oil companies, or many of the firms on the Fortune 500 list.[1]

In a famous study of business lobbying published in the 1960s, Bauer, Pool, and Dexter concluded that the lobbying activities of individual firms were not an important influence on public policy.[2] The authors were, however, primarily concerned with Congress rather than with executive departments and agencies. And state and local governments were not the subject of their study. Few dispute that corporations wield enormous influence on lower-level

276 *Organized Interests: The Real Power?*

governments. Land, taxation, labor, and public works policies are often molded by corporate interests within states.

Of course, there is also competition between corporate interests, and between these and other organized groups, but in most locales business is the single most important influence. The precise extent of this power varies from area to area, with some states being effectively dominated by one or two corporations (such as with the Du Pont chemical corporation in Delaware or Boeing and Microsoft in Washington state) or by a few interests (until recently, cattle and oil in Texas); whereas in others (New York, Michigan, California, Massachusetts), individual corporate power is more diffuse and is ameliorated by union and public-interest-group activity.

Moreover, evidence since the 1960s is so overwhelming that individual firms have taken a more active part in public policymaking. Most major corporations now have Washington offices and employ professional lobbyists to advance and protect their interests. The size of business lobbying can partly be explained as a response to the increasingly strident and successful efforts of the new public-interest lobbies devoted to environmental and consumer protection and to affirmative action in employment.[3] Since the mid-1970s, however, a further important spur to corporate political activity has been the rapidly changing economic environment and increasing vulnerability of U.S. corporations to foreign competition. Business now needs to ensure that the federal government provides an amenable climate for investment and growth—although, as Charles Lindblom has pointed out, only business imposes an *automatic* sanction on society should antibusiness policies be pursued, namely, recession and unemployment.[4]

American business (or trade) associations have been labeled "weak" in the past. And certainly the influence of the major single-industry associations (representing automobiles, rubber, textiles, and so on) as well as of the two major cross-industry organizations (the National Association of Manufacturers [NAM] and the U.S. Chamber of Commerce) has historically been weak compared with equivalent organizations in such countries as Germany and Japan. Perhaps this should be expected, given the traditional strength of individual corporations in the United States (noted in Chapter 2). Why, after all, should successful individual firms forfeit some of their independence to a trade association?

Indeed, as recently as the 1950s, both the NAM and U.S. Chamber of Commerce were regarded as a marginal influence in Washington. Both adhered to a sometimes unthinking antiregulation philosophy and were notably less important than the sum of the political efforts of individual corporations. Since then, however, both organizations and some new ones (notably the Business Round Table, which represents the chief executives of the 200 leading corporations) have emerged as more respected spokespersons for corporate interests. This is not to say that American business peak associations have assumed the status of equivalent groups in Germany, Japan, or even Britain, but they are now more important than ever before. Again, this revival is linked to the general increase in group activity characteristic of the United States since the 1980s.

However, caution is necessary in making any comparison between business activity in government during the 1950s and today. As mentioned earlier, the 1950s were an especially benign period in American politics. For much of the 1950s and 1960s, corporations were highly successful and entered the political arena only when necessary. Government policy was favorable toward them, particularly toward the larger corporations. Iron triangles and cozy relations with executive bureaus do not require lobbying as such, with all that this implies in terms of attention seeking and publicity. Only when competing or conflicting interests enter the fray is lobbying of the more visible kind necessary.

Labor Unions

American unions have traditionally been considered a relatively weak influence in the policy process. In comparative perspective, this is undoubtedly true. In the late 1990s, only 15 percent of wage and salary workers were affiliated with a union. The unions do not have the unequivocal support of a major political party, and unlike many union movements in Europe, they lack ideological cohesion. Almost all the powerful union movements in history have been driven by some ideal vision of a new—usually socialist—society. Such is not the case with American unions, which, although by no means nonideological, are significantly more instrumental than their European counterparts. Interestingly, the period when unions were most ideological in the United States (the 1930s and 1940s) coincided with the years of their most rapid growth and greatest political achievements.

Although relatively weak and divided, trade unions as a whole constitute one of America's most important organized interests. The United States is, after all, a highly industrialized country, and the unions represent around 18 million workers. However, the relatively high political visibility of the unions has been achieved only slowly. The first unions in America of any significance were craft- rather than industry-oriented, and they eschewed any active involvement in politics. Known for the advocacy of "voluntarism" or "business unionism," these unions formed the American Federation of Labor (AFL) in 1886 under the leadership of Samuel Gompers. As the name implies, business unionism involved workers perceiving themselves as part of the capitalist environment. The union's job was, therefore, to bargain with employers in line with what employers could or should afford. If a company was doing well, then the workers would benefit. If it was not, low wages and layoffs were to be expected.

With over a million members, the AFL became an important representative of the skilled worker, but its limited approach became very obvious when the Great Depression struck. Industrywide unions (such as the United Steel Workers and United Mine Workers) formed rapidly during the Depression years and banded together in 1935 as the Congress of Industrial Organizations (CIO). In contrast to the AFL, CIO unions saw themselves in an adversarial relationship with employers and were strongly disposed to use political means to achieve better working conditions and higher wages.

Since the 1930s, the CIO (and, following an amalgamation in 1955, the AFL-CIO) has lobbied hard in Washington over the whole range of public policies that affect workers and working conditions—union rights, Social Security, job training, vocational education, occupational health and safety, overseas trade relations, and economic policy generally. Observers generally agree that in terms of organization, staffing, and access, the AFL-CIO—mainly through its political organization, the Committee on Political Education (COPE)—has become one of the most coherent and visible of the Washington lobbies. As suggested in earlier chapters, the unions do have links with the Democratic Party, but formal affiliation has always been avoided (although for the first time in 1984, the AFL-CIO endorsed a presidential candidate, Walter Mondale, early in the campaign). This has almost certainly helped, rather than hindered, the AFL-CIO's public image. In recent years, COPE's political interests have widened to include activity on a number of issues not directly related to members' interests, such as foreign policy and civil liberties. Generally—but by no means always—COPE is identified with a liberal political position.

Although the AFL-CIO's national political activities are important, it would be misleading to give the impression that the United States has a centralized and united union movement. In comparison with unions in many countries, U.S. unions are fragmented. Most union structures are highly decentralized, with local and state units often responsible for bargaining over wages and salaries. Moreover, a few of the biggest and most powerful unions are not even members of the AFL-CIO, including the largest teachers' union (the National Educational Association).

Since the 1980s, there has been much talk about the decline of the unions as a political force. Certainly their membership (as a percentage of the labor force) has been falling, and an occupational structure changing in favor of the tertiary sector has generally weakened the unions, whose strength is traditionally rooted in the secondary (manufacturing) sector.[5] In addition, unions suffered from the generally antilabor policies of the Reagan administration. One indicator of union decline is the extent of strike action. During the 1960s and 1970s, the number of major work stoppages fluctuated between 200 and 400 a year. Since 1984, the number has ranged between 40 and 60.

Nonetheless, the unions remain highly visible in the Washington political scene. Graham Wilson has noted that this very visibility is a symptom of weakness, for the unions have so much to do in the pursuit of their interests that they are obliged to take a highly active part in politics.[6] Although this is probably true, it should also be reemphasized that almost *all* interests have become more active at the national level in recent years. In effect, the nature of the policy process is now such that no one group or sector can afford not to take part in the Washington bargaining and coalition-building game.

Farmers

In most modern industrial countries, farmers occupy a special place in society. For strategic and/or electoral reasons, they often exercise formidable political power, and in recent history American farmers have proved no exception. They are the recipients of subsidies designed to raise their incomes to a point at or beyond that necessary to boost production. As in some other countries (notably within the European Union), this has sometimes resulted in overproduction and the need to destroy or store produce in order to keep prices buoyant. American farms are also among the most efficient in the world, being highly capital-intensive and mechanized. Given the high rate of innovation and the general trend toward urban and suburban living since the 1950s, it comes as no surprise to learn that the farm population declined from over 30 million in 1920 to under 10 million in 1970. Indeed, by 1995, less than 3 percent of American workers were employed in agriculture—a remarkably low figure, given the fact that the United States is easily the largest producer (and exporter) of foodstuffs in the world.

In view of this importance, American farming organizations are perhaps rather less cohesive than would be expected. The largest group, the American Farm Bureau Federation (AFBF), has, until recently, actually preached the merits of disengagement of the state from the economy, including presumably the removal of farm subsidies. The National Farmers Union (NFU) has taken a pro-subsidy line, but its membership is smaller and more geographically concentrated (in the West and Midwest). Nonetheless, the NFU is a lobbying force to be reckoned with and has achieved considerable status in Washington.

As the farm population has declined, so the electoral influence of farmers has fallen. During the late nineteenth and early twentieth centuries, farmers virtually constituted a separate social class in the United States, a fact that helps explain the emergence of farm-based political movements, including the Populists, the Farmers Alliance, and the Grange. However, these parties and organizations failed to establish permanent bases of social support, and most have now passed into history. More recently, farmers' influence in state legislatures has continued, although even here, redistricting and demographic change have produced a steady decline in the agricultural lobby. The same is true of Congress. At one time, many members of Congress were virtually elected by farmers. In most states and districts today, the farm vote is but one small voice among many.

In spite of the general weakness of the farming organizations, it would be misleading to suggest that farm interests are politically weak. A more accurate way to characterize them would be simply to see the larger farmers (or agribusiness, as it is called) as other corporations. Indeed, general industrial and financial corporations own a large number of agribusiness farms. No federal government could af-

ford to see these interests seriously damaged. As with defense industries, food is strategically too important for this to happen.

However, smaller farmers, and especially those working marginal land or producing products susceptible to sharp fluctuations
in price, are genuinely weak—a fact shown by the occasional public demonstrations to which smaller farmers are sometimes obliged
to resort. In 1985, for example, attempts by the Reagan administration to cut agricultural subsidies aroused fierce opposition from
Midwestern grain farmers. Although the Republicans were "punished" in the 1988 presidential election in several farming states
(Minnesota, Iowa, Wisconsin), this was not sufficient to affect the
eventual result. By the late 1990s, agricultural subsidies had been
cut further and by both political parties. As a result, it is not easy
to identify a clear electoral pattern to the farm vote, which in any
case diminishes in size from year to year.

Notwithstanding the increased lobbying activity of the three
major economic groupings, the real growth in interest-group membership has been elsewhere. As Figure 11.1 shows, the number of
trade associations (which includes both business and labor) and
farming groups has increased only slightly since 1960, whereas the
growth in other associations, discussed next, has been spectacular.

Professional Groups

Although receiving much less public attention than business or
unions, professional groups have probably grown and improved
their political status more rapidly than any other of the organized interests since the 1960s. As educational standards have risen and the
premium on expertise in a number of areas—particularly the law,
medicine, and education—has increased, so the professions have
prospered. The role of the main lawyers' organization, the American
Bar Association (ABA), is developed in Chapter 12. The ABA not
only acts as gatekeeper for those practicing law, but it also is a major
source of information on legal standards and procedures. Thus, the
nomination of judges and changes in criminal and civil law depend
in part on the opinions and positions taken by the ABA. With more
than 500,000 lawyers in the United States, the central importance of
the law in policymaking, and the great overrepresentation of lawyers
among state and federal legislators and officials, the ABA's opinions
and interpretations must be taken seriously. As with other professional associations, *expert* opinion gives the ABA its special status.

FIGURE 11.1   Growth of Associations by Type

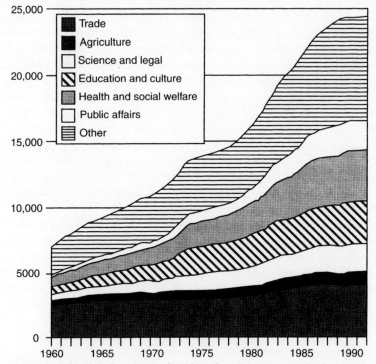

SOURCE: Compiled from *Encyclopedia of Associations* (multiple years), as reproduced by Frank R. Baumgartner and Jeffrey C. Talbert, "Interest Groups and Political Change," in Bryan D. Jones (ed.), *The New American Politics: Reflections on Political Change and the Clinton Administration* (Boulder, CO: Westview Press, 1995) figure 12.1.

Only about one-half of all lawyers belong to the ABA, but its members include the more successful lawyers, whose expert, nonpartisan opinions are highly respected.

The American Medical Association (AMA) performs a similar function for doctors. Again, not all doctors are members, but those who are tend to be among the most politically active. For many years, the AMA was famous for its fight against federal health insurance (or "socialized" medicine), and from the 1940s to the 1960s, it was one of the most vocal and highest spending of the Washington lobbies. It eventually lost the battle with the enactment of Medicare (medical insurance for the old) and Medicaid (medical aid for the poor) in 1965, but it remains a major influence on all legislation affecting health care. Its political action committee (AMPAC) spent more than $4 million in the 1995–1996 campaign and contributed $2.3 million to federal candidates—figures that increase considerably during presidential election years. Generally, the AMA's position has been conservative, although since the advent of federal (and state and local) health programs, it has also sought to improve the position of those members working for governments or receiving government fees.

In recent years, the AMA has been overshadowed somewhat by the rise in importance of groups representing other medical workers and particular medical specialists. As medicine has become more sophisticated and expensive, so the political strength of the specialists has increased. The same applies to hospitals, health maintenance organizations (HMOs), and the insurance companies responsible for most health care coverage. These interests have become major actors in what is a vast and complex health care system. The sheer complexity of this policy system helped contribute to the failure of Clinton's health care plan in 1993. A large number of medical, insurance, and other groups, often with conflicting interests, used their influence with a variety of congressional committees to ensure that no radical change in the health care system occurred. Indeed, the total spending by all groups during this campaign came to an estimated $300 million—vastly more than spent in any one presidential election campaign.

Other leading professional groups include some whose function is more economic than professional (the American Bankers Association, the National Association of Home Builders, the National Association of Realtors). They are no less important for this, of course. The Realtors, for example, contribute large amounts of money mainly to Republican candidates and generally lobby hard to ensure a growing housing market and low interest rates. At the state and local levels, the Realtors are highly active politically—especially in combating what they consider to be any unnecessary regulation of the housing market—whether it be through restrictive zoning laws, building codes, property taxes, or fair housing (antidiscrimination) statutes.

In sum, professional associations often represent the rich and the powerful in American society. This can mean the maintenance of professional standards (as in law or medicine), but it can also mean the advancement of particular economic interests (lawyers, doctors, bankers, Realtors, and so on).

Promotional Groups

By "promotional group" is meant all those organizations devoted
to promoting a particular cause or position. This category can include a wide variety of groups ranging from the National Rifle Association (NRA), which champions the right of Americans to own
firearms; to the National Association for the Advancement of Colored People (NAACP), which represents African Americans; to
Common Cause, one of a newer breed of public-interest groups
that fights for honesty and efficiency in government. Some of these
groups are ad hoc and transitory, as with the several organizations
that emerged in opposition to the American presence in Vietnam,
but most are at least semipermanent.

Such groups exist in all democratic societies, but in America they
are particularly numerous and vocal. Why should this be so? One
reason is undoubtedly the openness of the policy system. Promotional groups know that with enough organization, public support,
and media exposure, they can influence members of Congress, executive officials, and even judges. In the 1960s, for example, well-
known consumer advocate Ralph Nader went about the business
of exposing automobile safety standards with a single-minded determination. Eventually, his methods led to media and later congressional investigations and culminated in stringent new standards
imposed by law. Later, other groups mobilized to launch similar
campaigns on environmental pollution, occupational safety, and
women's rights, and these efforts led to new, often quite far-reaching legislation. Common Cause, the "clean government" public-interest group, has supported the reform of the congressional committee system, the vote for eighteen-year-olds, limits on electoral
campaign spending, rationalizing government organization, and
improvements in voter registration.

Although the sudden blossoming of public-interest groups since
the 1960s has surprised—and even worried—some commentators,
it is not so difficult to explain in historical perspective. Middle-class
reform movements are, after all, hardly new to the United States.
Reformers attempted to "clean up" the cities during the nineteenth
century (Chapter 5), and waves of middle-class moralism have frequently accompanied periods of rapid economic and social change
in American history. The 1960s and early 1970s were just such a
period, characterized as they were by rapid economic growth, so-

cial and political dislocation, and evidence of corruption at the highest level. Moreover, as was chronicled in earlier chapters, this was also a period of party decline and the increasing atomization of political power. In such an environment, coalition building around such particular issues as environmental protection or clean government became that much easier. This was also a policy context with no parallel in other countries, where, although the same issues have been raised to national prominence, they have tended to do so via political parties or through the operation of a consensus between political and economic elites.

Although public-interest groups claim to represent "the public interest," in reality they are not value-free, and the policies they promote hardly have neutral distributional consequences. New environmental standards may help produce cleaner air and water, but they can also lead to higher prices. Reforming government sounds admirable enough, but reforms often have unexpected results, as did the nineteenth-century city reforms and the campaign finance reforms of the 1970s.

By the 1990s, many groups claiming to represent the public interest were as often the champions of special interests. The NRA fights to prevent federal, state, and local governments from passing gun-control laws. In so doing, it claims to represent the public interest, but at the same time, it also serves the interests of the gun manufacturers and dealers. Even more problematical are those organizations whose cause involves moral absolutes. To a "pro-lifer" (an antiabortionist), abortion on demand represents a form of judicial murder that clearly cannot be in the public interest. To pro-choice activists, the free availability of abortion early in a pregnancy represents a basic right of women to exercise control over their own bodies. This position, too, would appear to be in the general or public interest. Clearly the two positions are irreconcilable. Similar dilemmas are raised by such issues as capital punishment, the provision of prayers in public schools, and the identification and treatment of AIDS patients.

In recent years, groups have raised all of these issues to the top of the political agenda, but the mere fact that a particular group is well organized and has access to decisionmakers does not always equal success. As discussed later, certain groups and interests fail repeatedly. The policy system may be open and complex, but it is not neutral.

Political Action Committees

Political action committees (PACs) are organizations set up by corporations, labor unions, and the like specifically to advance a particular political agenda. In the sense that different organized interests have formed Washington committees to fight for or against a particular item of legislation or the electoral success of an individual candidate, PACs are nothing new. Noted earlier were the efforts of the AMA's AMPAC to prevent the passage of Medicare in 1965, for example. Yet since the mid-1970s, PACs have spread to the point where they spent more than $400 million on all political activities in the 1995–1996 election period (Table 11.2). As of January 1, 1999, some 1,567 PACs were active in national politics.

The data in Table 11.3 include sums spent by PACs on individual campaigns and on general efforts to defeat candidates or to support candidates separately from their personal campaign organizations ("independent expenditures" in Table 11.3). The rise of the "electoral" PAC can be explained in the main by changes in campaign finance laws that, by putting restrictions on direct contributions by corporations and unions, have encouraged the big contributors to form committees that in turn can raise money from employees and members, with these funds then passed on to (mainly) congressional candidates. (Federal funding of presidential candidates has reduced direct PAC influence in presidential elections—although not the use of PAC-related "soft money.")

Fearing that PACs would become simply the "fat cat" contributors by another name, Congress has amended the 1974 Federal Campaign Act to put further limits on PAC activity. In particular, each PAC cannot contribute more than $5,000 to any one candidate's primary campaign and a further $5,000 to his or her general election campaign. Although this sum does not seem high, it adds up, as the figures in Table 11.3 show. Moreover, there are no limits on PAC soft-money spending that does not go directly into the campaign coffers of candidates, so PACs can launch their own campaigns against or for particular politicians. For example, it is rare today for any candidate who proposes tighter gun controls not to be attacked in television advertisements paid for by the NRA Political Victory Fund.

As can be seen from Table 11.3, private corporations have donated the largest sums to candidates, followed closely by the labor unions and membership associations (mainly professional groups

TABLE 11.2   Political Spending by Type of PAC, 1977–1996 (millions)

Election Cycle	Corporate	Labor	Trade Membership/ Health	Non-connected	Other connected[a]	Total
1977–1978	$15.2	$18.6	$23.8	$17.4	$2.4	$77.4
1979–1980	31.4	25.1	32.0	38.6	4.0	131.2
1981–1982	43.3	34.8	41.9	64.3	5.8	190.2
1983–1984	59.2	47.5	54.0	97.4	8.7	266.8
1985–1986	79.3	57.9	73.3	118.4	11.1	340.0
1987–1988	89.9	74.1	83.7	104.9	11.7	364.2
1989–1990	101.1	84.6	88.1	71.4	12.5	357.6
1991–1992	112.4	94.6	97.5	76.2	14.1	394.8
1993–1994	116.8	88.4	94.1	75.1	13.7	388.1
1995–1996	130.6	99.8	105.4	81.3	12.9	429.9

NOTE: Figures are in 1996 dollars. Expenditures exclude transfers of funds between affiliated committees for 1975–1984. Detail may not add to totals because of rounding.

a This category combines the FEC categories of cooperatives and corporations without stock.

SOURCE: Harold W. Stanley and Richard G. Niemi, *Vital Statistics on American Politics, 1997–98* (Washington, DC: Congressional Quarterly Press, 1998), table 2.13.

such as the AMA). As noted, however, nonconnected organizations raise large sums of money, much of which is devoted not to particular campaigns but to raising the salience of a political issue or ideological position or to painting a positive or negative picture of a candidate. Of these nonconnected organizations, two ultraconservative groups were notably successful in the early 1980s—the National Conservative Political Action Committee (NCPAC) and the National Congressional Club, the latter of which supports the maverick right-wing senator from North Carolina, Jesse Helms.

Labor PACs contribute mainly to Democratic candidates (predictably), but corporations distribute their largesse more evenly between the two parties (perhaps less predictably). Direct campaign contributions from PACs have generally helped Democrats rather than Republicans, but the overall impact of PAC activity has almost certainly been to help conservatives. This is mainly because conservative PACs are better organized, are generally more professional, and can appeal to the fact that many voters feel very strongly indeed about the moral issues involved.

TABLE 11.3 Contributions and Independent Expenditures by Type of PAC, 1991–1996

Type of PAC	Number[a]	Receipts[b]	Contributed to Candidates[c]		Independent Expenditures[d]	
			Amount	Percentage	Amount	Percentage
1991–1992						
Corporate	1,501	$112,359,989	$68,442,883	61	$47,883	0.0
Labor	254	89,863,124	41,339,090	46	298,497	0.3
Trade/membership/health	625	95,729,703	53,746,146	56	3,422,300	3.6
Cooperative	48	4,798,441	2,981,390	62	0	0.0
Corporations without stock	112	8,713,184	3,983,452	46	385,300	4.4
Nonconnected	531	73,851,846	18,183,052	25	6,276,696	8.5
Total	3,071	385,316,287	188,676,013	49	10,430,676	2.7
1993–1994						
Corporate	1,461	114,978,803	69,581,799	61	31,214	0.0
Labor	255	89,898,089	41,825,927	47	103,743	0.1
Trade/membership/health	628	96,370,355	52,799,649	55	1,767,450	1.8
Cooperative	50	4,377,763	3,042,328	69	0	0.0
Corporations without stock	112	8,848,760	4,071,108	46	509,901	5.8
Nonconnected	500	76,535,445	18,049,730	24	2,307,490	3.0
Total	3,006	391,009,195	189,370,541	48	4,719,848	1.2

1995–1996					
Corporate	1,470	133,793,654	78,194,723	58	387,797	0.3
Labor	236	104,059,450	47,980,492	46	663,400	0.6
Trade/membership/health	650	105,956,146	60,153,725	57	4,633,414	4.4
Cooperative	41	3,897,164	3,006,471	77	4,916	0.1
Corporations without stock	109	8,500,508	4,535,098	53	386,888	4.6
Nonconnected	529	81,165,399	23,960,110	30	4,542,952	5.6
Total	3,035	437,372,321	217,830,619	50	10,619,367	2.4

NOTE: Figures are in 1996 dollars. Data for earlier years can be found in previous editions of *Vital Statistics on American Politics*.

[a] The numbers shown are those PACs that actually made contributions.

[b] Not adjusted for money transferred between affiliated committees.

[c] Figures include contributions to all federal candidates, including those who did not run for office during the years indicated.

[d] Independent expenditures include money spent on behalf of candidates and against candidates.

SOURCE: Harold W. Stanley and Richard G. Niemi, *Vital Statistics on American Politics, 1997–98* (Washington, DC: Congressional Quarterly Press, 1998), table 2.14.

Whatever the merits and demerits of PACs—and Congress and public-interest groups are constantly discussing how they should be reformed—their rise brought out into the open most of the corporate, labor, and association political funding that previously tended to be covert and often illegal. Also, by virtue of their ability to make direct appeals to the public on particular issues, PACs have almost certainly aided the rise of single-interest politics and have helped further to weaken traditional political party organizations.

Perhaps not surprisingly, Democrats have been more vocal in their criticisms of PACs than have Republicans. Indeed, in 1983, both Walter Mondale and Gary Hart announced that they would reject all PAC assistance for their 1984 presidential campaigns. Similar pledges were made by Michael Dukakis and Jesse Jackson in 1988.

The most telling criticism of PAC activity is not so much that they can influence election outcomes but that they can change the nature of public debate in the absence of democratic accountability. Indeed nonconnected PAC advertising on such issues as abortion, gun control, and capital punishment can make election campaigns appear much more extreme and adversarial than they actually are. As a result, many moderate voters can become disillusioned not only with individual candidates but also with the electoral process itself.

The Washington Lobby

The three categories just described—the "traditional" interest groups, promotional groups, and PACs—do not constitute the entirety of the Washington lobby. The executive branch itself lobbies members of Congress for support, as do state and local governments, either individually or through the U.S. Conference of Mayors, Council of State Governments, and other umbrella organizations. Finally, foreign governments lobby Congress and executive alike. The *Congressional Quarterly* lists the Israeli, Cuban-exile, Arab, Korean, and Taiwan lobbies as the most significant in recent years. Given that American foreign policy decisions affect virtually every country and also the openness of the American policy system, the presence of such interests should perhaps be expected.

All of these groups and interests employ consultants and professional lobbyists to collect information and to establish links with the key political actors in the policy system. The result is that Washington is a city alive with political activity, where it is difficult to distinguish between the "insiders" (elected and appointed officials) and the "outsiders" (lobbyists, media consultants, interest-group leaders). Indeed, the presence of policy networks with fluid memberships and constantly shifting agendas means that there are really only "insiders."

If anything resembles pluralistic decisionmaking, then surely this arrangement does. Yet as earlier suggested, openness and accessibility do not necessarily result in neutral policies or a distribution of public benefits that can be considered egalitarian.

Interest Groups: For and Against

The questions posed at the beginning of this chapter make clear why, in a society where economic individualism is much admired, a multiplicity of competing interest groups can be regarded as beneficial. In classical economics, equilibrium is reached when demand and supply match each other in a perfectly competitive market. An analogous situation in politics could prevail when groups (analogous to firms) compete with one another in a completely open political environment. The public interest (equilibrium) is hence achieved by the balancing of different interests. No policy, according to this theory, is likely to be completely against any one interest, because involvement in the system by a group will ensure it modifies or amends policy at least partly in its favor.

These are, in essence, the theoretical assumptions of the "traditional" group theorists, notably Arthur Bentley and David Truman.[7] Government's role in such a context is to *arbitrate* between competing interests. By implication, government exercises little independent power; it more resembles a cipher or sorting mechanism and ensures that actors abide by the rules of the game.

The group theorists never claimed that in reality there was complete *equality* between groups (although that was the ideal), but they did maintain that if the interests of a particular section of society were seriously damaged, its members would mobilize, organize, and, through access to representative institutions, manage to do something to redress the balance. The rise of labor union power in the 1930s is often quoted as an example of such mobilization. Neither were the group theorists so naive as to assume that *all* groups had access, even potentially. David Truman, for example, accepted that the position of American blacks (in the 1950s) was exceptional because they patently lacked access to the policymaking process.

Classical group theory has since been criticized by scholars from almost every school of political thought. Public-choice theorists have stressed the tendency in such a system for public expenditure (or the provision of publicly provided goods) to spiral ever upward. The reasoning here is both simple and familiar. With open access to multiple decisionmaking centers, the potential for logrolling is enormous. Thus, if one group, sector, region, or state or local government is the recipient of a federal program, all the others will be too. Anthony Downs has put this nicely, labeling it the "iron law of political dispersion": "All benefits distributed by elected officials will be distributed to all parts of the constituency, regardless of the economic virtues of concentrating them upon a few parts of the constituency."[8] The result is, in fact, the very opposite of equilibrium or the "optimal" in economics. Governments end up handing out far too much to various interests, which leads to inefficiency and excessive government spending.

This particular critique is popular today. The solution is not to abolish groups but drastically to reduce the role of government in economy and society. Predictably, advocates of this position view with alarm the decline of party and the rise of single-issue and special-interest politics. Such changes have fragmented the system further and therefore increased the potential for logrolling and yet more government programs and regulations. But as already noted in earlier chapters, reducing the size and scope of government is easier said than done, especially given that organized groups and interests are now deeply entrenched in the policy system and that most have some interest in maintaining the present pattern of expenditure.

Efficiency in resource distribution is the main concern of this essentially conservative critique. Critics on the left have been more interested in the consequences of the classical view for political, social, and economic *equality*. They argue that groups are not merely unequal but are grossly unequal. Or, there is a bias in the system that some groups are more able to exploit than others. Business or corporate interests, in particular, are advantaged, whereas labor, the poor, and minorities are disadvantaged. This view harkens back to the populist condemnation of big business mentioned earlier. How much truth is there to this critique?

First should be noted the obvious fact that in terms of its power to move capital, labor, and resources around, business is in a unique position among major organized interests. Only government can exercise remotely equivalent power; none of the other groups can. Instead they are confined to single issues or particular geographical areas, or they exercise influence over only one subgroup of the pop-

ulation. Even labor, with its mass membership and finely tuned lobbying machine, has relatively few resources compared with business.
It is, perhaps, testimony to the power of the corporations that most
of them did not even consider it necessary to engage in overt lobbying until relatively recently, because the policy agenda generally favored them. Whereas the unions and other interests struggled to get
items discussed and legislated, business could often sit back and wait
until it perceived its interests as threatened.

Business is privileged in another sense: It has access to large sums
of money that can be used to "lubricate" the policymaking system to
its advantage. This is also true of unions and some other groups, but
none has access to money in quite the way business has. Revelations
of corruption in American corporate life (ITT, Lockheed, undercover
arms sales to Iraq and other countries) confirm that, quite apart from
legal contributions to candidates, the long-established reputation of
American corporations and business generally for undercover financial deals is still very much extant.

Second, if society is viewed not in terms of discrete groups or organized interests but in terms of social strata, there is very little evidence that the new political openness and accessibility have made
much difference to social and economic mobility. Those groups and
classes at the bottom of the social heap in the 1960s or 1970s are,
in general, still there. Changes in occupational structure have had
some impact, but what many have called a "transformation" of the
political system has had little effect. Indeed, it is often the case that
the more atomized and complex the decisionmaking system, the
lower the potential for redistributive policies. The two great social
reform periods in recent history that laid the foundations of the
welfare state—the New Deal and the Great Society—coincided
with what was virtually the antithesis of the new politics—strong
presidents, pliant Congresses, and a public broadly agreed on the
need for reform.

To be fair, many redistributive policies (counter-recession and
worker-retraining programs, increased Social Security spending) were
enacted during the Nixon and Ford years, and if there is any validity
to the public-choice critique, greater access should result in more
spending, whatever the distributional consequences. This accepted, in
a period of fiscal stress, a fragmented political system almost certainly
leads to resources being more thinly divided among groups, interests,
and classes, and those whose need is greatest are likely to find themselves relatively worse off. By the late 1990s, it was widely accepted

by almost all political interests, including the Clinton administration, that fiscal rectitude (balancing the budget without increasing taxation) was desirable. As such, the potential for redistribution from the haves to the have-nots of society has been seriously reduced.

Finally, the politics of distribution are now multilayered, and it is not always adequate to perceive the system only in terms of social classes or strata. Environmental controls, equal opportunity for women, and improved standards of occupational safety clearly benefit some people more than others, but there is no obvious relationship between the distributional impact of each of these reforms and those produced by traditional "class-based" policies (tax reform, welfare, social security). In fact, much of the assault on corporate power during the 1960s and 1970s involved policies of this sort. Middle-class reformers, outraged at pollution, consumer exploitation, and discrimination, launched the new promotional groups that the corporations were then obliged to engage in battle. Meanwhile, the measures typically used to gauge the living conditions of industrial workers, minorities, and deprived social groups—income, access to housing, and so on—changed very little. Where moral absolutes are concerned—as with abortion and capital punishment—the distributional consequences are also difficult to measure. This accepted, critics of the conservative position on these issues would claim that the "victims" are usually the poor—poor women, African Americans, and other minorities.

The proliferation of groups in recent years has led some commentators to argue that groups are actually becoming weaker as a political force. The reasoning is that because every issue attracts a range of supporters and detractors in a relatively open policymaking environment, decisionmakers are less tied to a particular group or cause. In such a context, the exercise of free choice is easier. Moreover, as constituencies become more complex, so the influence of individual groups in any one constituency is reduced.[9] Of course, another interpretation is that increased group activity actually makes it more difficult for lawmakers to translate individual political demands into public policy. Legislators may not be tied to particular groups as they were to labor or farmers in the past, but now they are bombarded by conflicting opinions and advice from all sides. As a result, they often find it difficult to commit themselves on issues, or if they do, they risk offending many constituents. This dilemma may help explain growing disenchantment with government and the gap between public expectations and the ability of governments to meet these expectations.

Notes

1. *Fortune* magazine produces an annual list of the 500 largest corporations in the United States.

2. Raymond Bauer, Ithiel de Sola Pool, and Anthony Lewis Dexter, *American Business and Public Policy* (New York: Prentice-Hall, 1964).

3. See Graham K. Wilson, *Interest Groups in the United States* (New York: Oxford, 1981).

4. See Charles Lindblom, *Politics and Markets* (New Haven: Yale University Press, 1977).

5. Since the 1960s, however, the level of unionization among government workers (many of them in manual jobs in hospitals and local government services) has increased, as shown by the impressive growth of the American Federation of State, County, and Municipal Employees (AFSCME), which now has over 1 million members. For an account of the changing fortunes of American unions, see Michael Goldfield, *The Decline of Unions in the United States* (Chicago: University of Chicago Press, 1987).

6. Wilson, *Interest Groups in the United States,* chap. 3.

7. Arthur Bentley, *The Process of Government* (San Antonio, TX: Trinity University Press, 1949); David B. Truman, *The Governmental Process* (New York: Alfred Knopf, 1951).

8. Quoted in David McKay, "Industrial Policy and Non-Policy in the U.S." *Journal of Public Policy,* 3, 1983, p. 45.

9. See Robert H. Salisbury, "The Paradox of Interest Groups in Washington: More Groups, Less Clout," in Anthony King (ed.), *The New American Political System* (Washington, DC: American Enterprise Institute, 1990).

Further Reading

Interest groups and lobbying cover such a wide range of political activity that no one book is a completely adequate guide. For a good account of recent developments, see Jeffrey M. Berry, *The Interest Group Society,* 3d ed. (New York: Longman, 1997). More dated but useful is Graham Wilson's *Interest Groups in the United States* (Oxford and New York: Oxford University Press, 1981). Allan J. Cigler and Burdett Loomis have edited a good collection of readings on the subject, *Interest Group Politics,* 4th ed. (Washington, DC: Congressional Quarterly Press, 1995). Grant McConnell's *Private Power and American Democracy* (New York: Alfred Knopf, 1967) remains one of the most stimulating books on groups in America. For an analysis of the power of business, see David Vogel, *Fluctuating Fortunes: The Political Power of Business in America* (New York: Basic Books, 1989). For a discussion of PACs, see Larry Sabato, *PAC Power* (New York: Norton, 1984). A good short account of changes in interest groups in the 1990s is Frank R. Baumgartner and Jeffrey C. Talbert, "Interest Groups and Political Change," in Bryan D. Jones (ed.), *The New American Politics: Reflections on Political Change and the Clinton Administration* (Boulder, CO: Westview, 1995).

12

The Supreme Court
and Judicial Politics

We are very quiet there but it is the quiet of a storm center.
                                                    —*Oliver Wendell Holmes,*
                              Associate Justice of the Supreme Court, 1902–1932

*In a democracy, politics is a process of popular education—the task of
adjusting the conflicting interests of diverse groups, . . . and thereby
the hostility and suspicion and ignorance engendered by group interests . . . toward mutual understanding.*

                                       —*Felix Frankfurter, Associate Justice
                                          of the Supreme Court, 1939–1962*

In all societies, the courts play some political role. In liberal democracies where the independence of the judiciary is regarded as essential to prevent the exercise of irresponsible executive (and sometimes legislative) power, the political role of the courts as
interpreters of the law and as defenders of individual freedoms is
well established. In despotic and one-party states, courts are political in the quite different sense that they are the instruments of a
dominant executive.

However, there are also important distinctions within liberal
democratic states, the most crucial being the presence or absence of
judicial review. As was noted in Chapter 3, judicial review is long
established in the United States, and the Supreme Court is the final
arbiter of the meaning of the Constitution. Hence, all laws passed
by the state and national legislatures, together with all executive

actions, are subject to review by the courts, which judge their compatibility with the Constitution. As the final court of appeal, therefore, the Supreme Court has the legal power to declare any action by any other branch of government unconstitutional.

This apparently formidable power is tempered by a number of factors, but in contrast to many other liberal democracies, the United States has a system that entails enormous potential judicial power. In the United Kingdom, for example, the courts can review executive actions—but only by testing them in relation to the content of acts of Parliament. This can produce sharp rebukes for governments when the courts judge that the government has acted ultra vires (beyond its powers), and the British courts are becoming more active in reviewing executive actions. A British Parliament controlled by the executive can, however, always reverse a judicial judgment, as sovereignty lies not in the Constitution but in Parliament. In the United States, a decision of the Supreme Court involving the constitutionality of a statute or governmental action can be overturned only by constitutional amendment (or by the Court itself, of course), and as was shown in Chapter 3, the amendment procedure is cumbersome and rarely used.

In fact, the Supreme Court uses its power of judicial review quite sparingly, and much of the day-to-day business of the courts is concerned with interpreting the law rather than making solemn declarations on the constitutionality of legislation. Even in nonconstitutional areas, however, American courts are more active than their British equivalents, for the United States is a highly legalistic society. Recourse to the courts for redress of grievances is swift and ubiquitous in American life. Indeed, the country boasts a staggering 650,000 lawyers and judges, and among the occupational backgrounds of American politicians, lawyers constitute a large group.

A number of reasons could be suggested for this legalistic orientation. As has been stressed in this book, the United States is a country with a liberal tradition, and the ideology of economic liberalism implies a society made up of individuals rather than social classes, races, or other social groups. Distinct and separate individuals acting as self-contained economic units are more likely to defend or promote their interests in the judicial marketplace rather than, as in many other countries, fall back on social class, family, ethnic group, or simply custom and tradition for support. There is a danger of making too much of this characteristic, but the tendency for individuals to seek legal redress for poor medical care or a faulty consumer product, or for corporations to sue competitors or suppliers for patent violations or breach of contract, is surely related to a pervasive economic liberalism.

In addition, the United States is infused with constitutionalism. With a written constitution granting certain rights and freedoms to citizens, delineating a separation of powers, and guaranteeing a federal system of government, disputes between individuals and government and between branches and levels of government must be arbitrated. Of course, disputes of this sort must be resolved in any political system, but in few systems are rather rigidly delineated citizens' rights, separation of powers, and federal arrangements married to a strong tradition of legalism and the institution of judicial review.

As far as the political role of the courts is concerned, the presence of judicial review marks the American system as distinctive, and because the Supreme Court is the highest court in the land, its judicial-review function has attracted the most attention. The bulk of this chapter is therefore devoted to this subject. Specifically, the focus is on how the Court has responded to the much more complex political environment of the late 1990s and, in particular, on how judicial decisions relate to the theme of the book—the link between public expectations and governmental performance.

The American Legal System

For the vast majority of Americans, state courts are what matter, for of the approximately 10 million cases tried in the United States every year, the federal courts account for less than 2 percent. State, municipal, county, and other local courts have jurisdiction over state law—which means that in any one state the vast majority of criminal and civil law cases, from muggings to property disputes, from divorce to homicide, are initiated and concluded within the state system. Most of the more sensational criminal and civil cases, such as the O. J. Simpson and Menendez brothers trials, start and end in state rather than federal court.

Most of the time, therefore, the two systems operate independently of one another. As can be seen from Figure 12.1, however, federal courts can play a crucial part in state law, because if a decision by a state's highest court of appeal is controversial and if the case involves a federal question, then it can be appealed to the U.S.

299

FIGURE 12.1 Organization of the U.S. Court System

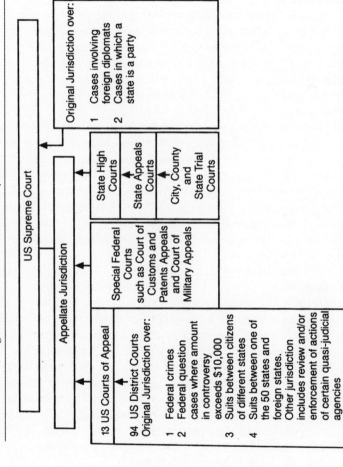

Supreme Court. Effectively, this gives the Supreme Court the power
to interpret and judge state law, for a "federal question" can mean
almost anything that is contentious or controversial. In law it
means any state court decision that is potentially incompatible with
federal law or with the U.S. Constitution. If, for example, a state
high court hands down a decision extending the power of state police to search a suspect's house for evidence, this would have to be
compatible with the Fourth Amendment of the Constitution, which
prohibits unwarranted search and seizure. Only the U.S. Supreme
Court can judge whether the state law is unconstitutional.

In one sense, the Supreme Court's power of judicial review over
state law is its most important function. Without it, the country
would cease to be a united nation-state. Instead, a loose confederacy would prevail, with each state going its own way in economic
and social affairs.

The power to review state high court decisions is part of the *appellate* jurisdiction of the Court. In addition, the Court hears cases
on appeal from within the federal court system. As shown in Figure
12.1, most federal cases originate in the federal district courts (94
in number staffed by 645 judges in 1997) whose decisions can be
appealed to one of the thirteen crucial courts of appeal (staffed by
167 judges), and thence to the Supreme Court. The Court[1] also has
original jurisdiction in a number of minor areas such as cases involving ambassadors.

Most citizens involved in federal litigation, therefore, have contact with the district courts, which are responsible for cases involving federal criminal and civil law. Compared with state law, federal
criminal law is limited to a relatively few areas, the most notable
being bank robbery, kidnapping, currency forgery, drug trafficking,
and assassination. Most of the work of the district courts is in the
area of civil law, with taxation, regulation, and civil rights and liberty cases dominating. Few of these cases are appealed (about 15
percent) and those that are, are usually settled in the federal courts
of appeal, which on a day-to-day basis are the most important judicial policymakers in the country. They are not the key judicial
policymakers, however, because their decisions can always be over-
ruled by the Supreme Court.

As can be seen from Table 12.1, the district courts' caseload
showed an inexorable rise between 1970 and 1985. A greatly expanded federal role in part accounts for this, and although the precise relationship between spreading federal legislation and litiga-

TABLE 12.1 Cases Filed in U.S. District and Appeals Courts and Supreme Court, 1970–1995

	1970	1975	1980	1985	1989	1993	1995
District Courts	87,300	117,300	168,800	273,700	233,500	228,600	239,013
Appeals Courts	11,662	16,658	23,200	33,360	39,734	49,770	49,671
Supreme Court	4,212	4,761	5,144	5,158	5,746	7,786	7,565

SOURCE: *Statistical Abstract of the United States, 1996*, tables 339–342.

tion is hard to establish, there is no doubt that a more active federal government has greatly increased the caseload of both the district courts and appeals courts. By 1978, the overload of the courts had reached crisis proportions, and Congress increased the number of district judges from 281 to 398 and appeals judges from 62 to 97. By 1995, there were almost 600 district judges and more than 150 appeals judges. Since the mid-1980s, the number of cases filed has leveled off at between 230,000 and 270,000 a year, although an increasing number of these cases are now successfully appealed to the courts of appeal (Table 12.1).

As Table 12.1 shows, the Supreme Court also experienced a sharp rise in its caseload until the mid-1980s followed by a leveling off during the 1990s. Increases in the number and use of law clerks (each justice has up to four clerks assigned to him or her) and improved administration of the Court by Chief Justice Warren Burger during his tenure (1969–1985) probably account for the institution's ability to manage. Even so, demands continue for the creation of a National Court of Appeals to screen cases coming before the Court.

As is the case for lower courts, new legislation in civil rights and liberties and in the general area of federal regulation largely account for the new demands on the Court. Thus, as has occurred for Congress and the presidency, an ever expanding federal role has produced new pressures on the Supreme Court that have made its operations more complex and difficult and, crucially, more politically visible.

The Supreme Court's Decisionmaking

Each year about 150 cases are decided by the Supreme Court, and although most of these will be of relatively minor political or constitutional import, some will have profound consequences for the American polity and society. Since 1950, for example, the Court has decided that racially separate educational and other facilities are inherently unequal; that almost exact mathematical equality should be applied to the size of state legislative and congressional districts; that indigent arrested persons should be provided with the services of a lawyer at the government's expense; that tapes of presidential conversations were not so private as to be protected by executive privilege and therefore could be used in court against presidential staff accused of dishonesty; and that the busing of schoolchildren to achieve racial integration is constitutionally required to overcome a historical pattern of legally imposed educational segregation. The very fact that all of these decisions have aroused intense controversy demonstrates their political significance and poses the question of how far and in what ways the Court can hand down decisions that are at odds with public opinion or with the other branches of government. Clearly, *how* the Court makes decisions is important. How does it decide which cases to hear? What criteria does it employ when deciding a case?

It is misleading to talk of *the* Supreme Court. Rather than being a unified organic body, the Court consists of nine individuals each with his or her (in 1981 Sandra Day O'Connor was the first woman to be appointed to the Court) quite distinctive view of law, politics, and society. Justices are appointed by the president with the advice and consent of the Senate. Unlike other executive appointments, they are appointed for life. Once on the Court, then, they are free from the political, financial, and other pressures that insecurity of tenure inflicts on most political actors. Of course, only a small percentage of cases coming before the Court are actually heard; most are denied review, or in the language of the Court, are denied *certiorari*. *Certiorari* is, simply, that act whereby the losing party in the lower court appeals the record of the case to the Supreme Court so that details of the case can be made "more certain." More than 90 percent of cases are appealed in this way; in most of the remainder, the Court is required to hear cases by a statutory appeals process.[2] The granting or denial of *certiorari* is clearly an important decision, and the Court is legally beholden to no one to justify which cases are heard and which are not. From a strictly legal perspective, the criteria for granting *certiorari* are relatively easy to identify. Loren Beth lists seven:

1. How fundamental is the constitutional (or other) issue presented by the case?
2. How many similar cases have been or are being litigated?
3. Is there a conflict of opinion in the lower courts on this particular issue?
4. Does a lower court decision seem to conflict with an earlier Supreme Court decision?
5. Is there a significant individual right involved?
6. Has the lower court departed significantly from the accepted and usual course of judicial proceedings?

7. Does the case involve the interpretation of a statute never
    before construed?[3]

At least four of the nine justices must agree to grant *certiorari*—a
fact that strongly implies the decision is not so clear-cut as the list
suggests. Indeed, not one of the seven criteria is completely unambiguous or not open to serious disagreement or argument. How
many cases in the civil rights and liberties areas—a good proportion
of the total—do *not* involve a significant individual right? Almost
certainly none. Similarly, many cases claim to involve a "fundamental constitutional issue," yet few of these are granted *certiorari*. The
fact is that although the seven points may be a legally correct list of
criteria, they indicate very little about the political context in which
decisions are taken. Why did it take until the 1940s and 1950s before the Court started regularly to hear civil rights cases? Why did it
take to the 1960s for criminal defendants' rights cases to come to
the fore, and until 1973 for the Court to deliberate on the constitutional status of bans on abortion?

There are two possible answers for this delayed activity. First,
the philosophy and outlook of the justices change over time, either
as a result of turnover or because individual justices change their
minds; second, the political and social context in which the Court
operates has changed over time, thus forcing certain issues onto the
judicial policy agenda that were previously excluded. As for the
second point, it is certain that the Court is influenced by the
broader society. In the civil rights area, World War II "nationalized" a number of social issues and brought into sharp focus both
for whites and blacks the injustices of segregation in the American
South. Publicity on conditions in the South was advanced by a
number of interest groups, in particular the National Association
for the Advancement of Colored People (NAACP), which also
acted as a judicial interest group by providing financial and legal
support for litigants involved in civil rights cases.

Although it is impossible to measure the influence on the Court
of the "social and political environment" or of the work of interest
groups intent on promoting a particular cause or defending a special interest, the justices are undoubtedly swayed by such factors, at
least in terms of letting them influence the policy agenda or what
sort of cases are actually heard.

But it would be misleading to leave the impression that the Court
grants *certiorari* only to classes of cases currently subject to public

attention. Many cases are heard when public pressure is minimal or absent. Reapportionment, for example, was not a matter of intense public debate when the Court in the famous 1962 case *Baker v. Carr* found that Tennessee's very unequal state legislative districts could be challenged in the federal courts. Later, in *Wesberry v. Sanders* (1964), the Court directly invalidated Georgia's grossly unequal congressional districts. Finally, in *Reynolds v. Sims* (1964), the Court argued that the equal protection clause of the Fourteenth Amendment should give all citizens an equal weight in elections. Thereafter, all states reorganized their districts according to the general principle of mathematical equality.

Also, the business of getting a case before the Supreme Court is long and hard. It may be years from the time a case is first filed in the district court before it eventually reaches the Supreme Court. Such a process does not always lend itself to instant decisionmaking in response to public or interest-group pressure.

The judicial agenda is also influenced by the philosophies and attitudes of the justices themselves. In general, a decision not to hear a case that in some way does meet one or more of the seven criteria and that is currently controversial is a conservative decision. It can reflect a justice's desire to keep the Court out of the political thicket by leaving a lower court's decision or judicial precedent to settle the matter. The fact that the Court did not hear many civil rights cases in the 1920s and 1930s might be explained in this way, as might the reluctance of the Court to get involved in economic policy during the 1940s and 1950s.

Conclusions should be drawn only with caution, however, for the preceding discussion has been confined to the influences shaping the Court's policy agenda—that is, which cases are heard and which are not. Naturally, the crucial question is how the Court decides those cases granted *certiorari*. Even the most conservative justice would have to recommend the issue of a writ of *certiorari* when a circuit court of appeals had decided a case that fundamentally contradicted judicial precedent as represented by an earlier Supreme Court decision. More interesting are those instances when the Court decides to uphold such a radical departure from precedent or decides that a particular act of Congress or executive action is unconstitutional.

One basic fact must be appreciated when discussing the Court as a political actor: It uses its power sparingly. It exercises *judicial self-restraint* (although sometimes the composition of the Court has affected the degree of restraint). It follows the doctrine of "assumption of constitutionality." In other words, it will use its power of judicial review very selectively, arguing a case on procedural grounds when it can rather than declaring a law unconstitutional. As can be seen from Table 12.2, the Court infrequently invoked its power of judicial review over federal law until 1920. Since then it has been more prone to strike down federal law, and this tendency has increased since 1960. In cases involving state laws, the Court has been more active, especially since the 1960s (Table 12.2).

As noted earlier, the Supreme Court consists of nine individual justices, and the final decision of the Court reflects the interaction of the opinions of these nine people. The formal decisionmaking process is as follows: Once *certiorari* is granted, the justices first receive written and then hear oral argument from the lawyers on both sides of the case. Later a case conference is convened at which the justices, sitting in private, make a preliminary decision. Five justices must be in agreement to constitute a decision, and one of these will be assigned to write the majority opinion. If the chief justice is part of the majority, he or another majority member assigned by him will write the opinion. If the chief justice is part of the minority, the most senior member of the majority will make the assignment.

Once the assignments have been made, the opinion of the Court is written. This can take many weeks to complete, and once the opinion has been published, the names of other members of the majority may be added to it. However, some members, although they may agree with the author of the opinion of the Court, may do so for different reasons, in which case they will write *concurring* opinions. Finally, those in the minority may choose to write a *dissenting* opinion, or even a number of dissenting opinions. Usually members will join just the majority or dissenting opinion, but it is quite possible for the Court to publish up to nine separate opinions: an opinion of the Court, four concurring opinions that may support the Court opinion on four different grounds, and four dissenting opinions that dissent on four different grounds. In the celebrated 1978 *Bakke* decision, which limited the use of racial quotas to discriminate positively in favor of minorities when admitting them to university courses, the Court published six separate opinions. In this case—and this factor often applies when the justices are split—the variety of concurring opinions made it difficult to infer the exact meaning of the Court's decision—an outcome possibly preferred by the Court in this politically sensitive and technically complex area.

TABLE 12.2   Federal, State, and Local Laws Declared Unconstitutional by the Supreme Court, 1789–1996, by Decade

	Federal	State and Local
1789–1799	0	0
1800–1809	1	1
1810–1819	0	7
1820–1829	0	8
1830–1839	0	3
1840–1849	0	9
1850–1859	1	7
1860–1869	4	23
1870–1879	7	36
1880–1889	4	46
1890–1899	5	36
1900–1909	9	40
1910–1919	6	118
1920–1929	15	139
1930–1939	13	93
1940–1949	2	58
1950–1959	5	60
1960–1969	16	149
1970–1979	20	193
1980–1989	16	162
1990–1996	10	45
Total	134	1,233

SOURCE: Harold W. Stanley and Richard G. Niemi, *Vital Statistics on American Politics, 1997–98* (Washington, DC: Congressional Quarterly Press, 1998), table 7.12.

To the more casual observer of the judicial process, how a justice decides in a particular case may seem obvious. Precedent and a careful interpretation of congressional statutes would be the immediate answer. Naturally, the justices do refer to precedent, and they do spend much of their time interpreting legislation. But even reference to precedent can be problematical. What historical precedents were there when the Court first heard cases involving electronic bugging? or genetic engineering? or racial quotas, for that matter? Very few precedents could be considered even vaguely relevant. And interpreting statute law when it involves overruling executive actions can be politically sensitive, to say the least. In both instances, the Court has considerable discretion not only to follow precedent, but also to create it; not only to interpret statutes, but also to direct the executive branch to change policy. When the formidable power of judicial review is added, the discretion available to the Court widens dramatically. Again, the reflex response to the question "What guides the Court when it uses judicial review?" is the Constitution. But there is little in the Constitution that is unambiguous, and the Supreme Court has reversed itself on a number of occasions when interpreting constitutional provisions.

If the justices cannot rely on precedent or the literal meaning of statutes or constitutional provisions, what factors guide their judicial opinions? This is a complex and difficult question. One factor already mentioned is the political and social environment, and there can be no disputing that the Court has been influenced by pressures from public opinion, presidents, and interest groups (discussed later). Partly independently of such forces, however, different Courts and justices have acquired reputations for being "conservative" or "liberal," "active" or "passive." These labels often refer to the jurisprudence or legal philosophy adhered to by different justices.

Certainly, no self-respecting Supreme Court justice would rationalize his or her decision in terms of "political pressures" or "political expedience"—even if these were truly the main influences. Instead, justices would indeed refer to the Constitution and the ways in which the wording of the Constitution should be interpreted. By so doing, they are obliged to look not only at the actual wording of the document but also to the meanings and motives behind the words. If, along with such a "positivist" approach, the justice also believes that the Court has an unbending duty always to "discover" the Constitution's true meaning, then an activist Court is implied. Relating the events in a particular case to the true meaning of the Constitution and then testing whether (say) a law on censorship is reconcilable with the Constitution are steps that invite the Court to declare on the constitutionality of that law.

Such was the approach of the two outstanding jurists of the early twentieth century, Oliver Wendell Holmes and Louis Brandeis. In a number of celebrated cases, both argued that some federal and state laws on internal subversion were incompatible with the First Amendment's general prohibition of laws abridging freedom of speech—although they accepted that absolute freedom of speech was clearly not intended by the framers of the Constitution. In Justice Holmes's famous example, "the most stringent protection of free speech would not protect a man in falsely shouting fire in a theater and causing a panic," the justices argued that if the First Amendment was to mean anything, some principle inherent in the provision must be detected and invoked. By this reasoning, Holmes elaborated the "clear and present danger test," or "the question in every case is whether the words used in such circumstances are of such a nature as to create a clear and present danger that they will bring about the substantive evils that Congress has a right to prevent."

Of course, problems remain in this analysis—discovering exactly when the danger is clear and present must in part be a subjective exercise, perhaps especially so when Congress (or a state legislature) has passed a law attempting to prevent subversion in time of war. Indeed, Holmes and Brandeis sometimes believed there was a clear and present danger, as they did in the *Schenck* case[4] from which the above quotation is taken. But the very fact of attempting to find some principle inherent in the Constitution implies a legal philosophy that is largely independent of the vagaries of social and political pressures prevailing at any one time.

In marked contrast, one of the most prominent jurists of the 1940s and 1950s, Felix Frankfurter, believed that the representatives of the American people—Congress and the president—should be left to interpret the Constitution, and that the Court's involvement should be confined to mediating disputes between the branches or between federal and state governments. Even then, Frankfurter argued, the Court should attempt to *balance* the various competing interests in society rather than search for some "inherent principle" or "higher meaning" behind the wording of the document. Clearly, a passive Court is implied by this approach, or one that steers clear of politics, letting representative institutions sort out conflict in society. The activism of Holmes and Brandeis and the passivity of Frankfurter represent two of the more coherent of a number of philosophical positions taken by the Court, and the labels "active" and "passive," "liberal" and "conservative," usually correspond to the perceived philosophy of the Court at a particular time. This does not mean that different Supreme Courts represent distinct and coherent philosophies. To repeat, nine individuals make the decisions, and each may vary dramatically in outlook.

Some Courts, then, have lacked an identifiable philosophy. More important, it is impossible to separate the decisions of the justices from the political and social environment in which they operate. The "positivism" of Holmes and Brandeis with their search for a consistency and justice inherent in the Constitution, irrespective of political and social pressures, failed to dominate even the Court on which they sat, let alone be the main approach of subsequent Courts. Like any other political institution, the Court has to interact with society and polity. It is subject to a number of pressures and constraints. What makes the institution so interesting, however, is the mix of judicial philosophy and external constraint that has produced an ever changing political role for the Court in American history. This role is the focus of the remainder of this chapter, which includes analysis of the constraints on the Court's power and, in particular, of whether the institution can perform its role to good effect at century's end.

The Court and Political Power

Without question, Supreme Court decisions have political impact. From the momentous *Marbury v. Madison* decision in 1803 when, by declaring Section 13 of the 1789 Judiciary Act unconstitutional, Chief Justice John Marshall effectively established judicial review, through to the landmark civil rights cases decided since the 1960s, the attention of public and polity alike has been concentrated by the political implications of the Court's decisions. But as earlier suggested, this does not mean that these solemn judicial deliberations take place in isolation from society. On the contrary, many observers have argued that the Court rarely deviates from the prevailing weight of political or public opinion; that, in fact, its main function has been to legitimize dominant political influences, and when it has gone against these, it has soon found itself in trouble of one sort or another. In one rather obvious sense, this is always true, for courts depend on their authority rather than naked power. They have no police force or army—or even bureaucrats—to enforce their decisions. For this they have to depend on the other branches of government.

Perhaps the most dramatic example of the dangers inherent in fundamentally disagreeing with the other branches of government was the 1857 *Dred Scott* case. In this decision, the Court declared that African Americans had no right to sue under the U.S. Constitution because they were not "citizens." In addition, the Court declared unconstitutional the 1820 Missouri compromise that gave blacks free status in the territories to the north of the Missouri River acquired in the Louisiana Purchase. If African Americans were to revert to slave status in these Northern and Western territories, a forced extension of the culture and values of the South was implied, a change completely unacceptable to Lincoln and the dominant Republican Party. The decision was never enforced because the Civil War soon followed, as did the Thirteenth and Fourteenth Amendments that specifically granted equal legal status to all citizens.

For the other branches of government simply to ignore the Court is the most serious challenge to its power, for once ignored, its authority and legitimacy are undermined. Without these it loses all influence. After the Civil War, the Court did, in fact, reassert its authority, and it has never been seriously undermined since. But there have been ebbs and flows of judicial power, crises of confidence, and periods of intense controversy. A useful way to study these is to document the constraints or limitations on the Court's power, or to record those instances when the scope and substance of judicial decisions have, in one way or another, been circumscribed.

Constitutional Amendment

Amending the Constitution to overturn the Court is the ultimate legal weapon available to the other branches and to the states. Amendments have been few and far between, however, and only four have been employed to overrule the Court. In one of these— the Twenty-sixth Amendment ratified in 1971 to extend the vote to eighteen-year-olds—the Court's *Oregon v. Mitchell* (1970) decision was overturned. Another (the Eleventh Amendment, which prohibited a citizen of one state from suing the government of another state) has passed into historical obscurity.[5] Only two amendments stand out as changes crucial to preserve the integrity of the union and the smooth running of government—the Fourteenth, which overturned *Dred Scott,* and the Sixteenth, which sanctioned a graduated federal income tax. Ratified in 1913 when the need for increased defense spending was widely perceived as necessary, the Sixteenth Amendment overturned the 1895 *Pollock v. Farmers' Loan and Trust* decision that had declared a graduated or progressive federal income tax unconstitutional.

In recent years, calls for constitutional amendments to overturn Supreme Court decisions have been equally rare, although a movement exists to amend the Constitution to overturn the 1973 *Roe v. Wade* decision sanctioning abortion. In a 1989 decision (*Texas v. Johnson*), the Court struck down a state law banning the burning of the American flag and a year later struck down a federal law on the same issue (*United States v. Eichman*). In response, a movement gathered pace for a constitutional amendment making it a crime to burn the flag. So far, however, Congress has proved reluctant to overturn the Court on what has been an issue of entirely emotional and symbolic importance.

Congressional Control

The Constitution grants remarkably wide discretion to Congress over the composition and organization of the federal judiciary. Article 3 states, quite simply: "The judicial power of the United States shall be vested in one Supreme Court, and in such inferior Courts as the Congress may from time to time ordain and establish." Thus, Congress has the power to determine the size and administration of the federal machinery of justice. Additionally, the Constitution specifically gives to Congress discretion over the Court's appellate jurisdiction and implicitly, at least, over the number of justices and when the Court should actually sit.

Only rarely, however, has Congress exercised these substantial discretionary powers. Easily the most important item of legislation in these areas is the 1789 Judiciary Act, which established the Court's power to review state court decisions denying federal rights to citizens. Apart from this, Congress has regularly increased the number of federal judges and courts in line with population and caseload increases, and the number of Supreme Court justices fluctuated between six and ten until 1870, since when it has remained at nine. During the 1930s, President Roosevelt attempted to increase the size of the Court to overcome opposition to his New Deal legislation, but Congress was disinclined to tinker with the Court in this way. By the 1930s, the figure of nine justices was regarded as almost a part of the Constitution.

If Congress has been reluctant to alter the Court's composition and jurisdiction, it has shown little hesitation in overturning Court decisions via statutory reversals or in legislating to invalidate a particular judicial interpretation of federal law. Between 1946 and 1968, for example, some 111 roll-call votes in Congress reversed Court statutory interpretations. Few of these were of great import, however, and of course Congress cannot touch those decisions that are based on *constitutional* interpretation.

Perhaps Congress's most important function in relation to the Supreme Court is as a forum for public opinion. Senators and representatives quite frequently openly attack the Court or even introduce bills designed to curb its power. During the 1950s and 1960s, for example, Southerners incensed at the Court's desegregation decisions, and conservatives at its civil liberties and reapportionment decisions, regularly did both. More recently, the "pro-life" lobby in Congress has attempted to change the law on abortion, following the Court's liberal *Roe v. Wade* decision in 1973.

Indeed, moral outrage at Court decisions on abortion, obscenity, and school prayer inspired thirty bills designed to curb the Court's jurisdiction during 1980 and 1981. Although such attempts may fail, constant attacks in the national legislature undoubtedly have an effect on the justices. In some contexts, they may well influence the Court, especially if the justices are effectively isolated in their policy position, as was the case in 1937 when few sources of power or influence in American society sided with the Court. Finally, the Senate must confirm all nominations made to the judicial branch by presidents, and the Senate has used this power with increased vigor in recent years.

Presidential Control

Presidents have two main means whereby they can influence the Court: first and more important, via the appointment power; second, by appealing to public or congressional opinion to reinforce their opposition to or support for a particular position. All federal judges are political appointees, and the vast majority nominated by a president share his political party label if not his total political and social philosophy. In the case of district court and, to a lesser extent, appeals court nominations, presidents used to be guided by the advice and influence of the Senate (via the confirmation power) but also by state and local party leaders and dignitaries. Today, however, both lower court and Supreme Court nominations are very much a matter of presidential preference. In general, presidents have appointed judges whose political views are similar to their own. This predilection does not mean that presidents deliberately manipulate an appointment in order to change the complexion of the courts—although often they do—nor does it mean that they are always successful in their attempts to change the courts' outlook and philosophy.

As for Supreme Court nominees, presidents are circumscribed by chance, for although a vacancy on the Court has on average come up about every two years, some presidents have been denied the privilege of receiving their "quota" of two nominations. In his four years as

president, Jimmy Carter made no appointments, while in his first
three years in office, Richard Nixon made four, and in his first two
years, Bill Clinton made two. Interestingly, President Carter explicitly
stated an intention to remove political considerations from the appointment of all federal judges, although as far as the Supreme Court
was concerned, his pledge went untested.

On three occasions in recent history, presidents have been given
and taken the opportunity to try to change the political complexion of the Court. Roosevelt did so after 1937, Nixon after 1969,
and Reagan after 1981. In Roosevelt's case, the Court had repeatedly struck down New Deal legislation on the grounds that it was
an unconstitutional exercise of the Interstate Commerce Clause
and violated "substantive" due process under the Fourteenth
Amendment. In the face of the possible collapse of his economic recovery program, Roosevelt attempted to "pack" the Court by asking Congress to increase the number of justices by one for every existing justice over seventy years old, up to a maximum of fifteen.
His strategy was clear—to tip the ideological balance of the Court
away from the so-called Four Horsemen of Conservatism (Justices
Butler, McReynolds, Sutherland, and Van Devanter) toward a more
liberal stance. He failed in the Court-packing plan largely because
by the time it reached the critical stage in a not too enthusiastic
Congress, one of the conservatives, Van Devanter, had retired.
Roosevelt then proceeded to fill this and other vacancies, which
came thick and fast during the next few years, with "New Dealers"
or justices sympathetic to an enhanced federal role in economy and
society. He was remarkably successful. Almost all of his nine appointees toed the New Deal line, and the Court kept well out of
economic affairs during the 1937–1953 period.

The second dramatic instance of political use of the appointment
power occurred during the first two years of the Nixon administration. One of Richard Nixon's 1968 campaign pledges had been to
replace the liberals of the Warren Court with "strict construction-
ists" or conservatives less prone to the advancement of civil rights
and liberties characteristic of the Warren era. He was given a
golden opportunity to do just this, for four vacancies occurred during the 1969–1971 period. One of these was for chief justice, and
the president lost no time in nominating Warren Burger, chief judge
of the District of Columbia Court of Appeals, to the position.
Burger, a conservative Republican from Minnesota, remained chief
justice until 1986.[6]

Nixon's next two nominees encountered serious resistance in the Senate. Only rarely in the twentieth century have Supreme Court nominations been rejected, and it is a remarkable testimony to Nixon's political insensitivity that his second and third nominations, Clement Haynsworth and Harrold Carswell, were voted down in the Senate. Both were undistinguished as jurists, and Carswell, in particular, had acquired a dubious record on civil rights in the Southern courts from which he hailed. Their rejection illustrates well the simple fact that presidential discretion over appointments is limited. A president may nominate a conservative or a liberal but not an incompetent or a bigot. A Senate judiciary committee well versed by the American Bar Association, leading jurists, and interested groups will see to that. Richard Nixon did, however, succeed with his next three appointments, Harry Blackmun, Lewis Powell, and William Rehnquist. Rehnquist was a solid conservative (but a respected jurist), while the others were known as at least moderately conservative.

The Reagan experience was different again. Sandra Day O'Connor, nominated in 1981, was a respected judge who was chosen largely because she was a woman. A conservative but no ideologue, O'Connor replaced the moderate Potter Stewart, an Eisenhower appointee. In 1986, when Chief Justice Burger retired, Reagan elevated William Rehnquist to the chief justiceship and nominated Judge Antonio Scalia to fill the vacancy. Both moves were highly strategic. Rehnquist was known as a conservative on all major questions. His nomination inspired considerable opposition in the Senate, but he was eventually confirmed. Scalia was also known to favor the Reagan agenda, but his nomination met with little resistance.

These controversies pale into insignificance compared with the nomination of Robert Bork following the resignation of Justice Lewis Powell in June 1987. Powell had long held the pivotal vote against the New Right agenda favored by the administration involving such issues as affirmative action and abortion. Robert Bork's tenure on the Court of Appeals was marked by a "strict constructionism," or a consistently conservative interpretation of the Constitution. During the lengthy nomination proceedings, Bork worked hard to convince the Senate Judiciary Committee that he was in fact a centrist rather than an ideologue of the right. But this inconsistency helped produce his eventual defeat by the widest margin ever (58 to 42). Reagan's next nominee, Douglas Ginsburg, was also a conservative but was obliged to withdraw following revelations that he had once smoked marijuana while in law school. Eventually, the Senate confirmed the nomination of Anthony Kennedy, a moderate and pragmatic conservative from California.

At the appellate and district court level, Ronald Reagan pursued a more overtly political strategy than any previous president. As one commentator put it: "The striking feature about Reagan's lower-court judges is that they are predominantly young white upper-class males, with prior judicial or prosecuting experience and reputations for legal conservatism established on the bench in law schools, or in politics."[7] By appointing large numbers of conservatives to the lower courts, President Reagan almost certainly changed the nature of lower-court decisions and therefore the sort of cases appealed to the Supreme Court.

During his presidency, George Bush was able to make two appointments. In 1990, he nominated David H. Souter to replace William Brennan, almost the last of the Court's liberals and first appointed in 1956. Souter was quickly confirmed by the Senate. In 1991, Bush nominated Clarence Thomas to replace Lyndon Johnson nominee Thurgood Marshall. Thomas was also confirmed in spite of allegations that he had sexually harassed a former employee, Anita Hill. Marshall was the first black member of the Court, and Thomas the second. Both Souter and Thomas became identified with the dominant conservative representation on the Court.

On coming to office, Bill Clinton was determined to make his administrative and judicial appointees "look like America." In terms of gender and ethnicity, the president was true to his word. However, relatively few of his judicial appointments were so liberal as to transform the judiciary from the conservative stance acquired during the Reagan and Bush years. Indeed, his first two appointments to the Court, Stephen Breyer and Ruth Bader Ginsburg, were widely regarded as moderates. Both nominations were easily confirmed by the Senate. The justices they replaced (Byron White and Harry Blackmun) were, on the face of it, more liberal than the new appointees. Clinton's nominations to the lower courts included a large number of women and African and Hispanic Americans. However, because such nominees are often also liberals, the Republican-controlled Senate Judiciary Committee delayed confirmations for months and even years. As a result, many district and appeals court judgeships remained vacant some years into the Clinton presidency.

There can be no doubt that the Burger Court was very different from the openly liberal Warren Court and that the Rehnquist Court has in turn proved more conservative than the Burger Court. Personnel changes partly account for these shifts, but presidents can never be sure that, once appointed, a justice will fulfill expectations. Appointed for life to the most respected forum in the land, many justices change their political philosophies once on the Court. Such was the case with Earl Warren, one-time conservative Republican governor of California, who was expected by his patron President Eisenhower to continue the self-restraint of the Stone and Vinson Courts. In civil rights and liberties and reapportionment, he did just the opposite. And although the Nixon appointees generally moved the Court to the right, they did not do so in a coherent and consistent manner. Liberal civil rights and liberties decisions did not suddenly cease in 1971, even if they became infrequent and interspersed with more conservative judgments.

Public and Political Opinion

Thus, the appointment power must by definition be limited, because even when presidents have made appointments, they have no direct control over the justices once they are on the Court. Presidents can, of course, appeal to Congress (as with the Court-packing plan) or to public opinion, but if such action becomes necessary, the independent influence of the president is lost. As noted in earlier chapters, public opinion is hard to define and almost impossible to measure. Beneath the surface, what most commentators mean by "public opinion" is a particular configuration of political power, expressed either through representative institutions or through the media or organized groups. Under this definition, only very rarely in American history has the Court challenged a dominant climate of opinion. Between the Civil War and 1937, for example, the Court acquired a reputation for defending the burgeoning capitalist interests of the period by striking down both state and federal legislation designed to regulate industry or protect workers from exploitation. The regulation of interstate commerce did not, the Court argued, extend to such matters as federal laws regulating child labor. Or, more important, entitlement of "due process of law" under the Fourteenth Amendment did not extend to *state* attempts to regulate industrial and commercial life. It applied directly only to federal-citizen relationships. As a result, between 1900 and 1937, some 184 decisions invalidated state regulatory provisions.

To be fair, a number of state laws were also upheld during these years, but the general stance of the Court was antiregulation or antigovernment "interference" in economic affairs. Crucially, however, public opinion generally paralleled the Court's stance, at least until 1929. Most presidents, Congress, and many state legislatures accepted the Supreme Court's judgments with relative equanimity. Not until the coming of the Great Depression in the early 1930s did the climate of opinion change dramatically. And when the Court began regularly to strike down federal New Deal legislation, it became politically isolated. Within two years, and following intense pressure from unions, Congress, and the president, the Court made its "switch in time that saved nine" and thereafter followed rather than led the other branches in the general area of economic policy. Figure 12.2 shows this transition well. From the early 1940s, the Court overturned few laws in the economic policy area, although it has become more active in this area since the 1960s.

During the 1940s and up to about 1957, the Court was deferential to Congress and the president on questions of "subversion" and national security. In case after case, the Court accepted the restrictions placed on citizens by the 1940 Smith Act, by the 1950 McCarren Act, and in the case of Japanese Americans, by executive fiat.[8] Not until the late 1950s, when public fears about Communist subversion began to subside, did the Court begin to relax the restrictions on Communists and others perceived to be subversive.

Even in civil rights it would be difficult to argue that the Court was acting in isolation from broader political and public opinion. *Brown v. Board of Education,* the landmark 1954 decision holding that racially separate facilities in education and other facilities were inherently unequal, may have been highly unpopular in the South, but it was welcomed in the North by many members of Congress and was not unpopular with the president. The primary influence of *Brown* was that it helped push opinion toward desegregation of the South, although enforcement problems apart (of which more later), it was 1964 before Congress, goaded on by a determined and proselytizing president, passed the first major federal civil rights act.

The apportionment decisions of the early 1960s, extending the principle of representation according to mathematical equality, first to state legislatures and then to congressional districts, were probably more widely unpopular with politicians than were the civil rights decisions. But they were not unpopular with citizens, most of whom stood to gain from a removal of the bias in representation

FIGURE 12.2   Number of Economic and Civil Liberties Laws (federal, state, and local) Overturned by the Supreme Court, 1900s–1980s, by Decade

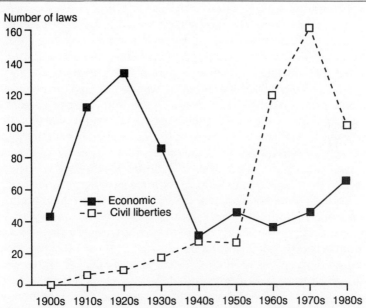

SOURCE: Various as compiled by Lawrence Baum, *The Supreme Court,* 5th ed. (Washington, DC: Congressional Quarterly Press, 1995), figure 5.2.

toward rural areas. Indeed, how could state and national politicians justify the gross inequities that had accumulated over time? The Court was a genuine innovator in this area, as it was in the realm of criminal defendants' rights.

Starting with *Mapp v. Ohio* in 1961 and continuing through to Earl Warren's resignation in 1969, the Court handed down a remarkable succession of decisions granting defendants the right to state-provided counsel and access to police files, extending the freedom from unlawful search and seizure, and generally providing much greater protection to arrested persons. Coming as they did during the disruptions of the 1960s, these changes were welcomed only by what eventually was a diminishing band of liberals. The dramatically increased activism of the Court in the civil rights and liberties area is shown by the number of acts declared unconstitutional from the late 1950s onward (Figure 12.2).

Undoubtedly, the Warren Court moved well ahead of public opinion in this area. Perhaps predictably, the Burger Court did not continue the same crusading spirit. In both civil rights and liberties, it was careful to qualify some of the more dramatic decisions of the 1960s. In one sense, the Burger Court was placed in a much more difficult position compared with the Warren Court, for it had to clarify highly complex and difficult questions raised but not settled during the Warren era. Hence, in school desegregation, the thorny problem of distinguishing between *de jure,* or legally sanctioned, and *de facto,* or naturally evolving, segregation emerged as the main civil rights issue. Generally, the Court argued that a past pattern of de jure segregation should be reversed via busing, but not (as generally prevailed in the North) if the segregation was de facto in nature.

Similarly, on the use of other affirmative action measures such as quotas, the Court had to grapple with the problem of choosing between *individual* rights under the Fourteenth Amendment and the *collective* rights of African Americans and other minorities who sought redress for a pattern of past discrimination. Individual rights generally prevailed. In criminal procedural rights, the Court limited the application of the "exclusionary rule," or the inadmissibility at trial of evidence culled during unlawful searches and seizures. And in a number of other areas, the Court reduced the protection afforded arrested persons.

Often the Court cannot predict the impact of its decisions on public opinion. The Burger Court, for example, handed down a decision on abortion in 1973 *(Roe v. Wade)* that seemed clear enough. The Court effectively established that a woman had an unrestricted right (following medical advice) to an abortion during the first three months of pregnancy. Hence, state laws banning or restricting abortion in this period were unconstitutional. States could restrict abortion the next three months only if there was a threat to a woman's health. In the final three months, states could ban abortion unless the woman's life was threatened. This compromise has, however, been seized by the pro-life, antiabortion interest groups and branded as a further example of the federal courts undermining public morals and the sanctity of family life. Little doubt exists that the decision precipitated debate and political controversy on an issue whose salience increased enormously during the last third of the century.

The Court's decisions on capital punishment, which provided moderately strict guidelines but left to the states the final decision on when (and how) a person should be executed, have also aroused great controversy. In both this instance and abortion rights, debate on the issues has passed onto the broader political stage. But they have not left the judicial policy agenda. Controversy on where individual rights begin and end must by necessity concern the courts, and given government's intimate involvement both in granting and denying rights to citizens (indeed in exercising a power over life and death in the two examples just cited), the Court's involvement must also continue.

With the appointment of Souter and Thomas, the Rehnquist Court moved clearly to the right. Indeed, the two most liberal members of the Court in 1993 were Nixon appointees, Harry Blackmun and John Paul Stevens. As earlier noted, the Clinton appointees, Stephen Breyer and Ruth Bader Ginsburg, did not shift the Court leftward in ideological terms because they replaced liberals rather than conservatives.

Predictably, therefore, the Rehnquist Court has advanced the conservative agenda, especially on moral and social issues and in the general area of federalism. As was discussed in Chapter 4, in a number of areas the Court has revived and enhanced the Tenth Amendment's reserve clause and the Eleventh Amendment's sovereign-immunity principle. By so doing, it has promoted administrative and policy diversity among the states. However, it has been reluctant to strike down as unconstitutional any of the landmark liberal decisions of the Warren and early Burger Courts in the moral conscience areas, such as *Roe v. Wade* or *Miranda v. Arizona* (on the rights of accused persons). Instead, it has argued cases on narrower grounds, often leaving to state and local officials the final decision on how the law should be interpreted. This approach frequently has narrowed the applicability of the landmark cases. In the 1992 case *Planned Parenthood of Southeastern Pennsylvania v. Casey*, for example, a divided Court upheld the right of states to restrict access to abortions, but it stopped short of invalidating *Roe v. Wade*.

By avoiding constitutional precedents, the Court has left open to Congress the opportunity to pass laws reversing its decisions. And Congress has seized the opportunity: In the 1991 Civil Rights Act, it overturned the 1989 *Patterson v. McLean Credit Union* decision that limited an employee's ability to sue for damages if subject to racial harassment on the job. The Court has also been reversed by statutory interpretation over laws involving abortion and affirmative action. The Court's reduced judicial activism in the civil rights and liberties areas is demonstrated by the data in Figure 12.2. It should be pointed out that on many of the social issues, the " moderate conservatism" of the Rehnquist Court has not been particularly out of tune with public opinion, and its cautious approach results partly from its reluctance to set headline-grabbing constitutional precedents.

Thus, only rarely has the Court consciously moved against prevailing public and political opinion, and when it has done so, it has not been for long. Two important qualifications must be applied to this generalization. First, the Court has been reluctant to challenge— or has never for long challenged—a program or policy supported by the other branches and one perceived to be crucial to the integrity of the union (the status of slavery in the North), to national security in wartime or "emergency" conditions ("subversion" in the two world wars and afterward), or to the running of the economy (the New Deal legislation). However, when there is no consensus on a policy— especially when Congress and the president are in serious disagreement—the Court plays a central role in arbitrating the conflict.

This role is illustrated by two dramatic examples in recent history. In 1952, President Truman seized the nation's steel mills on the grounds that industrial disputes were undermining production and the Korean War effort. The Court quickly condemned the seizure as an unconstitutional infringement on the legislative powers of Congress. In 1974, the Court declared that executive privilege did not protect President Nixon's taped conversations from being used in the courts and Congress to investigate the Watergate wrongdoings. On both occasions, Congress was unsympathetic to the president's position, and significantly, so was broader public opinion.

More recently, the Burger Court showed little reluctance to make deliberations affecting the separation of powers. In *Buckley v. Valeo* (1976), some key features of the 1974 Campaign Finance Act were struck down (see Chapter 9). Later, in *Immigration and Naturalization Service v. Chadha* (1983), the legislative veto was declared unconstitutional. Following this decision, the capacity of Congress to control the discretionary powers given to executive agencies was greatly curtailed. Finally, in 1998, the Rehnquist Court struck down the 1995 line-item-veto law (permitting the president to veto part rather than all of a law) as a violation of the separation of powers in the Constitution (*Clinton v. New York City*).

As noted, since 1988, the Court has generally strengthened the Tenth Amendment by favoring state objections to federal guidelines. Thus, federal power has been weakened in relation to the states through such cases as *New York v. United States* (1992), involving federal guidelines on the disposal of radioactive waste, and *Printz v. United States* (1997), involving federal rules on enforcement of the Brady Handgun Violation Prevention Act. Finally, in 1986, the Court declared the mandatory spending cuts required by the Gramm-Rudman-Hollings Deficit Reduction Act an unconstitutional violation of the separation of powers.

The second qualification to the Court's deference to prevailing public and political opinion is that when it does challenge them in areas involving the behavior of myriad individuals, rather than a few institutions or political leaders, it tends to experience serious problems in enforcing its decisions or in predicting their precise impact on public opinion.

Lack of Enforcement Powers

Without their own police force, army, or bureaucracy, the courts cannot enforce their decisions unless their authority is accepted by those who do exercise coercive powers. Moreover, the Supreme Court depends on lower courts (federal and state) to implement its decisions, and these courts may not always interpret or accept the Court's judgments in an unambiguous fashion. The most celebrated examples of judicial recalcitrance and obstruction involved the enforcement of civil rights in the South. Following *Brown v. Board of Education*'s 1954 directive that Southern schools should desegregate "with all deliberate speed," Southern federal district courts were assigned the job of enforcing the order. Appointed by presidents on the advice of local politicians and party faithfuls, district judges reflect local conditions and interests—and prejudices. Very few of the Southern district judges of the 1950s and 1960s were integrationists, and most resisted—mainly through delays of one sort or another—the order to desegregate.

In fact, not until its 1969 decision in *Alexander v. Holmes County Board of Education*—some fifteen years after *Brown*—did the Supreme Court finally make it mandatory to desegregate immediately By then, of course, the Court was supported by the not inconsiderable weight of the 1964 Civil Rights Act with its array of compliance and enforcement procedures. The figures on racial segregation demonstrate this point well. In 1963, nine years after *Brown,* only 45 percent of black students in the South attended schools where any whites were present. By 1971, this figure had increased to 85.6 percent.

More rarely, a state or local political actor may openly defy a Court order, as happened in Little Rock, Arkansas, in 1957 when Governor Orval Faubus used the local militia forcibly to prevent black children from entering a high school. Only the eventual use of federal troops on the instruction of President Eisenhower enabled the black children to enter the school. Much more common is evasion of the directives of the Supreme Court, not only by other courts or by outright defiance but through ignorance, deception, or the simple fact that complete enforcement is technically impossible to achieve. This has been the case with such criminal law decisions as *Miranda* and *Gideon,* which laid down strict procedures for the interrogation of suspects. As research has shown, arrested persons often do not know their rights, police officers are frequently ignorant of the correct procedures, and even when informed, can compromise them.

Similarly, the decisions of the early 1960s outlawing special prayers and Bible reading in public schools *(Engel v. Vitale, Abington School District v. Schempp)* as infringements of the First Amendment's freedom of religion clause have proved difficult to enforce. Indeed, although neither the Burger nor the Rehnquist Court had by 1998 seriously compromised the principles laid down in *Engel* and *Schempp,* both were under considerable pressure to do so.

The Court, the Public, and Politics

It is often argued that the greatest limitation on the political power of the Court is "judicial self-restraint," or a conscious decision by the justices to avoid the political thicket by deferring to the other branches (or to public opinion) rather than causing great controversy by departing from the dominant opinion. This is a strong premise, although self-restraint is more a matter of political common sense than, as some jurists have argued, something that can be justified solely on philosophical grounds. Judges may search for a "higher principle" inherent in the Constitution, or they may be convinced that government "interference" in the economy is always a bad thing. Sooner or later, however, they must take cognizance of the political and social environment in which decisions are made. As noted, the Supreme Court is seriously constrained by this environment; it is not an institution apart from politics but one that is an organic part of the polity and society.

If the Court rarely challenges the dominant political forces in society, what use then is the institution of judicial review? Three crucial functions can be identified from the preceding discussion: (1) The Court arbitrates between federal and state law. In terms of the stability and integrity of the union, this is undoubtedly its most important function. (2) Judicial review provides the Court with an apparently neutral point of reference (the Constitution) for arbitrating between the different branches of government—although historically this has tended to work only when one branch (the executive) is relatively isolated from congressional and public opinion. (3) Judicial review can help defend individual freedoms under the Bill of Rights and Fourteenth Amendment. Of course, there have been numerous occasions when the Court has clearly failed to defend such freedoms, as with the internment of Japanese Americans in 1942. But—and this is the strongest argument in favor of judicial review under the Bill of Rights—the legislative and executive branches would have denied these freedoms even in the absence of judicial review. Its presence is usually beneficial, therefore, in the sense that when the Court deviates from the other branches, it does so by favoring the individual. As the civil rights and especially the civil liberties cases of the 1950s and 1960s demonstrate, this thrust can involve radical, if sometimes temporary, departures from prevailing political and public opinion.

Finally, how has the Court responded to the much more fragmented polity and society characteristic of the 1990s? In a word, uncertainly. As suggested, the Burger and Rehnquist Courts had to confront questions involving moral absolutes where *any* compromise would have been unacceptable to some. Issue politics, combined with the increasingly technical nature of cases, can produce a situation in which the Court hands down highly contentious decisions. Issue politics produces odd, unpredictable political coalitions that find it almost impossible to please everybody. The Court's decisions on abortion and capital punishment, for example, involved issues where the subsequent lines of opposition and support were complex and unpredictable. In some other areas—campaign finance, for instance—the technicalities of the question are so formidable that the Court has produced decisions whose consequences have been unexpected and perhaps undesirable. As mentioned, the Rehnquist Court, whose conservatism was little changed by the Clinton nominations, has been reluctant to make precedent-setting constitutional decisions on such questions as affirmative action, the treatment of illegal immigrants, and abortion in the face of deeply divided public opinion.

The Court may, however, be forced into making decisions in these and other areas given that during the mid- and late 1990s, state legislatures and state initiatives passed highly controversial and possibly constitutionally unsound measures on such issues as the medical use of marijuana, term limits for legislators, the legal rights of homosexuals, the provision of state benefits for illegal immigrants, and the status of affirmative action programs. In these and other areas where public opinion is deeply divided, the Court is in a no-win situation. Unambiguous decisions on one side or the other would alienate sections of public opinion or the other branches. Avoiding clear judicial commitments has been the general thrust of recent Courts, but this approach does not help to resolve the unmet expectations of the public.

In sum, the caution and ambiguity in recent Supreme Court policy have done little to fulfill what is perhaps the Court's most vital task—the legitimization of the system in the eyes of the citizenry. In the words of Felix Frankfurter:

> A gentle and generous philosopher noted the other day a growing "intuition" on the part of the masses that all judges, in lively controversies, are "more or less prejudiced." But between the "more or less" lies the whole kingdom of the mind, the difference between the "more or less" are the triumphs of disinterestedness, they are the aspirations we call justice. . . . The basic considerations in the vitality of any system of law is confidence in this proximate purity of its process. Corruption from venality is hardly more damaging than a widespread belief of corrosion through partisanship. Our judicial system is absolutely dependent upon a popular belief that it is as untainted in its workings as the finite limitations of disciplined human minds and feelings make possible.[9]

Notes

1. "Supreme Court" and "the Court" are used interchangeably for the remainder of the chapter.

2. The most important class of cases here are those where *state* high court decisions declare a federal law unconstitutional, or where the constitutionality of state law is in doubt.

3. Loren P. Beth, *Politics, the Constitution, and the Supreme Court* (New York: Harper and Row, 1962), pp. 31–32.

4. *Schenck v. United States* (1919).

5. The Supreme Court decision that sanctioned such cases, *Chisholm v. Georgia* (1793), aroused great controversy at the time.

6. The position of chief justice became vacant quite fortuitously for Nixon. President Johnson had nominated Associate Justice Abe Fortas as Warren's successor, but during the Senate hearings into Fortas's suitability, it was revealed that, among other things, in 1966 he had received a $20,000 fee from a millionaire who at the time was being investigated (and later was convicted) for fraud. Fortas's nomination was withdrawn.

7. David M. O'Brien, "The Reagan Judges: His Most Enduring Legacy?" in Charles O. Jones (ed.), *The Reagan Legacy: Promise and Performance* (Chatham, NJ: Chatham House, 1988), p. 75.

8. The Smith Act made it unlawful to advocate the overthrow of the U.S. government, and the McCarren Act required "subversive organizations" to register with the Subversive Activities Control Board. In 1942, West Coast Americans of Japanese descent (many of them citizens) were arbitrarily interned in concentration camps by the governor of California (ironically, Earl Warren, later the champion of individual freedom on the Court) as a threat to internal security. The Court failed to hear the cases arising from this action until 1944 and then argued them on procedural rather than constitutional grounds.

9. Quoted in David F. Forte, *The Supreme Court in American Politics* (Lexington, MA: D. C. Heath, 1972), pp. 93–94.

Further Reading

A good introduction is Lawrence Baum, *The Supreme Court*, 5th ed. (Washington, DC: Congressional Quarterly Press, 1995). For a comparative analysis, see also Henry J. Abraham, *The Judicial Process: An Analysis of the Courts in the United States, England, and France*, 7th ed. (New York: Oxford University Press, 1998). For two journalists' vivid account of how the Court operates, see Bob Woodward and Scott Armstrong, *The Brethren: Inside the Supreme Court* (New York: Simon and Schuster, 1979). An analysis of the Burger Court is Herman Schwartz (ed.), *The Burger Years: Rights and Wrongs in the Supreme Court, 1969–1986* (Harmondsworth, Middlesex, and New York: Penguin, 1988). On the Rehnquist Court, see David G. Savage, *Turning Right: The Making of the Rehnquist Supreme Court* (New York: Wiley, 1992). For a compendium of Supreme Court information, see Kermit L. Hall, *The Oxford Companion to the Supreme Court* (New York: Oxford University Press, 1992). Also see Hall's *Oxford Guide to the United States Supreme Court Decisions* (New York: Oxford University Press, 1999). The classic work on the Court and civil rights and liberties is Henry J. Abraham and Barbara A. Perry, *Freedom and the Court*, 7th ed. (Oxford and New York: Oxford University Press, 1998).

13

Regulating Morality: Civil Rights and Liberties and Conscience Issues

I have a dream that one day this nation will rise up and live out the true meaning of its creed: "We hold these truths to be self-evident: that all men are created equal."

—*Martin Luther King Jr.*

It would be easy to infer from earlier chapters that decisionmaking in the American political system is so fragmented and dispersed that the resulting policies are not amenable to simple characterization; that the open and pluralistic nature of the system produces a politics of confusion and unpredictability. There is a great deal of truth to this, but it would be wrong to leave the analysis without inquiring further into the nature and consequences of policymaking in the United States. The purpose of the next four chapters is, therefore, to add perspective and balance to earlier conclusions by examining how policymaking has developed in four important areas—the regulation of morality and social, economic, and foreign policy. The discussion focuses on the following three questions:

1. How does policy develop over time? How do changes in administration and the domestic and international environment change the ways in which policy is formulated and implemented?
2. Related is the crucial question of the role that political institutions and processes play in the political system. Is it

now more difficult to produce effective public policy than in the past? Is the system capable of satisfying myriad public demands while at the same time preserving the ethos of limited government that is at the heart of the American public philosophy?

3. To what extent do policy systems differ in style and substance one from another?

Obviously, these questions have no definitive answers, and discussion of each area must, of necessity, be limited to the main issues involved. However, reference to more detailed analysis is provided when appropriate.

Overview of Morality Issues

American politics has always been infused with what Samuel Huntington has called a "creedal passion," or public demands that government should play a role in regulating the public and private behavior of citizens.[1] In spite of the Civil War and the passage of the Fourteenth and Fifteenth Amendments, between 1870 and the 1950s, most of the debate and controversy in this area rarely reached beyond state and local politics. Today, however, the federal government is intimately involved in regulating morality. From civil rights to abortion, prayers in public schools, and criminal procedural rights, federal rather than state and local standards and laws guide public morals. As with so many other areas of policy, the public is deeply ambivalent about (and often deeply divided over) this role. On the one hand, many Americans expect the federal government to be the final authority responsible for outlawing discrimination and protecting individual rights. On the other hand, many people become angry and disillusioned when this role fails to conform to their personal interpretation of what is moral and just.

This tension is, arguably, much greater in the United States than in most comparable countries. Americans are, in comparison with citizens in such countries as Germany and France, deeply distrustful of government and strongly devoted to the protection of individual freedoms. But quite deep divisions over the meaning of "individual freedom" exist that have few parallels in Western Europe. Nowhere in Europe, for example, are such issues as abortion, gun control, or prayers in public schools debated with the intensity and passion as they are in the United States.

This chapter addresses the role of the federal government in these and related areas. Special emphasis is paid to the ways in which the role of the federal government has changed in the latter half of the twentieth century.

Civil Liberties

Civil liberties are usually interpreted as those rights protected under the Bill of Rights (the first ten amendments to the Constitution) and the due process clause of the Fourteenth Amendment. Typically, therefore, they include freedom of speech, religion, and assembly; the right to a fair trial and due process; freedom from unlawful search and seizure; and the right to bear arms. In most countries, the terms "civil rights" and "civil liberties" are used interchangeably, but in the United States, civil rights have come to mean the right to be free from discrimination on grounds of race, ethnicity, religion, gender, disability, or sexual preference.

Until the twentieth century, protection under the Bill of Rights was, in fact, quite limited. By arguing that the Constitution applied to federal law and therefore the Bill of Rights was not applicable to state law, the Supreme Court effectively left the protection of liberties to the various state constitutions. In many parts of the United States, and especially in the South, numerous state laws were passed that today would be considered an affront to the rights of citizens. The most famous of these were the infamous "Jim Crow" laws excluding African Americans from full participation in society. But in many other areas, including the treatment of alleged political "subversives," religious minorities, women, and arrested persons, the protection afforded by many states was very limited. How has political action and discourse changed in these areas over the past century?

Freedom of Speech

Starting with *Gitlow v. New York* (1925), which established that First Amendment freedom of speech rights applied to state law, the Supreme Court gradually began to extend the Bill of Rights to state law. Not until after 1937 did the Court begin consistently to take this approach and in particular to argue that the states had an obligation to provide for due process under the Fourteenth Amendment and that as the Bill of Rights provided for due process, so these rights should be protected by the states. The technical term used was the *incorporation* of the Bill of Rights. After World War II and accelerating during the 1960s, all the Bill of Rights protections—from free speech to the right to counsel for arrested persons—were incorporated into state law.

This period of judicial activism coincided with the incumbency of the liberal Warren Court. In case after case, the Court extended the protection afforded to citizens under the Bill of Rights. Initially, the most important cases concerned First Amendment freedom of speech cases. Between 1919 and 1957, the Court consistently sided with restrictive federal and state laws against the rights of individuals in this area (notwithstanding, in the *Gitlow* case the Court upheld New York's right to proscribe speech while incorporating that law under the equal protection clause). Often these decisions translated into action against anarchists, Communists, and other "un-American" organizations. In many instances, the Court invoked the "clear and present danger" test, claiming that Communist activity was a clear threat to the union (see Chapter 12). In *Yates v. United States* (1957), the Court argued that membership in the Communist Party was not in itself a threat, and in *United States v. Robel* (1967), the Court effectively established that such membership was protected under the First Amendment.

Today, it is difficult to imagine Congress passing a law specifically proscribing the right to join a particular political organization or banning the publication of a particular political tract. Even the Ku Klux Klan and similar organizations enjoy First Amendment protection. Generally, federal authorities pursue *acts* of political violence or espionage. With the exception of proscribing individuals from urging others to perform acts of violence, the expression of *beliefs* is broadly protected under the law.

Freedom of speech extends beyond political freedoms, of course. It also applies to such areas as obscenity and libel. As for the latter, the American media have more freedom to publish unsubstantiated facts about groups and individuals than the media in many other countries, as tabloid stories about movie stars and other public figures show. Although this freedom has been challenged in the courts, it continues to be better protected than what is often called the individual's right to privacy. Most jurists argue that the publication of obscene materials is not protected by the First Amendment, but laws proscribing such material are often viewed as infringements of freedom of speech. This distinction arises mainly because, apart from child pornography, it is almost impossible to define what is and what is not obscene. In one important area, however, the Supreme Court has been active. In 1997, it struck down the 1996 Communications Decency Act, which sought to restrict Internet pornography that might be accessible to those under eighteen. The Court maintained that the law was too vague and that any attempt by the government to regulate the content of speech was a threat to the free exchange of ideas.

Criminal Procedural Rights

It would be fair to say that although freedom of speech rights are of fundamental importance to democracy, they have generally not aroused as much passion and debate as some other Bill of Rights issues, including criminal procedural rights. As with free speech, the constitutionality of most state laws in this area went untested until the 1960s. During that decade, however, the Warren Court greatly strengthened the rights of accused and arrested persons to invoke the Fourth, Fifth, and Sixth Amendments. *Gideon v. Wainwright* (1963) established the right to counsel irrespective of the ability to pay. *Escobedo v. Illinois* (1964) prevented the police from carrying out *any* interrogation until a lawyer was available. *Mapp v. Ohio* (1961) greatly extended the "exclusionary rule," or how much evidence could be used that the police uncovered during "search and seizure." Only if the police had proper authority to search and the evidence found was relevant to that search could it be used in court. In other words, if the police legally entered a property looking for weapons but found drugs, the drugs could not be used as evidence in a subsequent trial. *Miranda v. Arizona* (1966) established the precedent that arrested persons should be read their rights (essentially the right to remain silent).

These and other cases represented a transformation in the rights of the accused, but they were hardly without controversy, for they coincided with a rapid increase in crime, especially in the country's inner cities. Cause and effect are difficult to establish in this area, but there is little doubt that law enforcement officials believed that restrictions placed on the power to search and to interrogate were making it difficult to arrest and convict criminals—and especially those with the resources to make full use of the system. The public, too, grew increasingly disenchanted with courts that seemed too "soft" on crime. Eventually, both the subsequent Burger Court and the later Rehnquist Court gradually narrowed the meaning and application of almost all of these rulings.

As far as the exclusionary rule is concerned, police now have much greater freedom both to enter property and to use evidence found during search and seizure so long as it was found in "good faith." This effectively means they can use anything found during a search as evidence. The Court has also greatly expanded the power of the police to use warrantless searches and has chipped away at the effect of the *Miranda* warning. For example, in *Arizona v. Fulminante* (1991), the Court argued that evidence culled by undercover police (such as confessions) was permissible even though clearly suspects cannot be told of their right to silence in such cases. In effect, therefore, although none of the famous Burger decisions has been overturned, their application has been progressively narrowed.

A further area of controversy concerns the status of the death penalty—in particular, whether it constitutes "cruel and unusual punishment" under the Eighth Amendment. Doubts about the constitutionality of the death penalty led all states to postpone executions from the mid-1960s. In the 1971 case *Furman v. Georgia,* the Court held that as such laws were then administered, there was a random element in deliberations leading to the death penalty that was unacceptable. No executions occurred until after 1976 when the Court upheld the penalty in those cases where juries could consider the unique circumstances of every case. Since then, executions have proceeded at an accelerating rate, with Texas leading the way with 152 executions between 1976 and early 1998 (Table 13.1). Critics argue that the death penalty remains "cruel and unusual" both because most of those executed are poor and members of minority groups, and because convicted persons must withstand many years of appeals and stays of execution before they are finally put to death.

Although public opinion remains strongly pro–capital punishment, increasing publicity about hasty and poorly managed trials, mistakes, and the enormous variations in state policy in this area (Table 13.1) have led to a softening of opinion in recent years. Interestingly, many other countries, and especially those European states that abolished capital punishment many years ago, view American practices in this area with a mixture of horror and contempt.

334

TABLE 13.1   Executions in America as of April 1998

Death Row Inmates by Jurisdiction			
California	504	Arkansas	39
Texas	425	Kentucky	29
Florida	368	Oregon	23
Pennsylvania	216	Idaho	19
North Carolina	199	Washington state	19
Ohio	180	U.S. government	18
Alabama	163	Maryland	17
Illinois	156	Delaware	17
Oklahoma	127	New Jersey	15
Arizona	121	Utah	11
Georgia	119	Nebraska	11
Tennessee	96	U.S. military	8
Nevada	92	Montana	6
Missouri	87	Connecticut	5
South Carolina	73	Colorado	4
Louisiana	72	New Mexico	4
Mississippi	60	South Dakota	2
Virginia	46	Kansas	1
Indiana	45		

Executions by State Since 1976			
Texas	152	Nevada	6
Virginia	50	Utah	5
Florida	43	California	4
Missouri	32	Mississippi	4
Louisiana	24	Nebraska	3
Georgia	22	Maryland	2
Alabama	17	Pennsylvania	2
Arkansas	16	Washington	2
South Carolina	14	Oregon	2
Illinois	11	Montana	2
Arizona	11	Kentucky	1
Oklahoma	10	Wyoming	1
North Carolina	9	Idaho	1
Delaware	8	Colorado	1
Indiana	6		

SOURCE: Death Penalty Information Center, as reproduced in *Los Angeles Times,* May 31, 1998, p. A7.

A final area of controversy in the civil liberties area is the Second Amendment's right "to keep and bear arms." Supporters of this amendment, and in particular the National Rifle Association (NRA), argue that Congress and the state governments should keep gun-control laws to a minimum. Following the assassination attempt on President Reagan in 1981, Congress passed the Brady Bill requiring a waiting period for firearms purchases. Later the 1994 Crime Control Bill banned certain categories of assault rifles. Although most members of the public support stronger gun-control measures, opponents are better organized, well funded, and highly focused. Only after guns are used in such violent outrages as the high school massacre in Littleton, Colorado, in April 1999 are passions aroused, and then the antigun movement receives real impetus. Again, controversy in this area has uniquely American characteristics. Nowhere else do interest groups organize with such passion and conviction on the basis that the right of the citizenry to access and bear arms is an inviolable right.

The Establishment of Religion

Americans have always been ambivalent about the relationship between church and state—a sentiment that stems in part from the status of religion in the early republic. On the one hand, the First Amendment guarantees the "free exercise" of religion. On the other hand, it prohibits the government from "establishing" a religion. To the founding fathers, the "free exercise" of religion meant the freedom to set up religious groups and denominations free from government control. But initially, at least, these were always Christian groups. From the very beginning of the republic, state and local governments provided support for Christian organizations and especially schools.

In recent years, debate and controversy over the proper role of government in this area have never been far from the surface. For some, a "high wall of separation" between church and state should be maintained; for others, an intermediate or accommodationist position is preferred. As in other conscience issues, the Supreme Court has been active in this area, and especially so with regard to the complex problems of religious aid for schools and religious instruction in schools. In *Engel v. Vitale* (1962), the Court declared unconstitutional even the briefest of nondenominational prayers in schools. Later, and following a public outcry in many states and

communities, it progressively softened its position, until in *Lemon
v. Kurtzman* (1971), it laid down specific rules on what was permitted and what was not. Most important, the decision required
that any government aid to schools have a clear secular purpose
and that there be no "excessive governmental entanglement" with
religion.

What the *Lemon* directive means in practice has been up to the
courts to decide, and although the Rehnquist Court has not always
been consistent in this area, it has broadly favored the accommodationist position. Certainly, federal, state, and local governments
do provide direct and indirect aid for parochial schools ranging
from income tax deductions to the provision of remedial teachers
under the 1965 Elementary and Secondary Education Act. As with
capital punishment, the Court has followed rather than led public
opinion in this area.

Abortion

As noted in Chapter 12, few areas of public morality have aroused
as much passion as the issue of abortion. Along with capital punishment, abortion is usually discussed in terms of moral absolutes.
For the pro-life opponents of the practice, abortion is tantamount
to the murder of the unborn. For pro-choice advocates, the issue is
couched in terms of a woman's freedom to exercise control over
her own body. Often this argument is expressed in terms of the individual's right to privacy.

Since the landmark *Roe v. Wade* decision that effectively sanctioned abortion in the first three months of pregnancy throughout
the United States, pro-life supporters have used a wide variety of
tactics to get the decision reversed or at least to restrict its application. At the legislative level, both Congress and a number of state
legislatures have restricted access to abortion by reducing or elimi-
nating government aid, requiring that the parents of minors seeking to terminate be informed, limiting the location of abortion clinics, and requiring women to seek counseling before terminating.
State courts and ultimately the Supreme Court have generally upheld these laws, although at no point has the Rehnquist Court
struck down the principles inherent in *Roe v. Wade*. Because the
two Clinton appointees to the Court, Ruth Bader Ginsburg and
Stephen Breyer, support the right to choose, it is unlikely that *Roe
v. Wade* will be reversed in the near future.

Pro-life groups have sometimes gone beyond the legislative and judicial process and have taken various forms of direct action against abortion clinics and staff. These range from picketing and demonstrations to, in the most extreme cases, the murder of doctors and abortion proponents.

Although public opinion is broadly pro-choice, it is unlikely that the abortion issue will cease to divide citizens both politically and socially. Within the Republican Party, for example, abortion has become a particularly difficult issue, especially at the presidential level. Pro-life supporters look to Republican politicians to support their agenda. At the same time, Republican presidential candidates cannot afford to alienate the broad mass of voters who are pro-choice. As a result, several Republican candidates, including Bob Dole in 1996 and George W. Bush in 2000, have attempted to take a middle position, arguing that although they are personally against abortion, the decision should ultimately be for the individual to make. Such a position is naturally unacceptable to those who see the issue in terms of moral absolutes.

Equality and Civil Rights

"Civil rights" in the United States is usually used as a synonym for the provision of equal rights for racial and ethnic minorities. Discrimination does, of course, affect other social groups, including women and the disabled. This section addresses the evolution of public policy with regard to all of these groups.

Racial and Ethnic Minorities

In the mid-twentieth century, no area of public policy aroused as much passion and bitterness as the question of the desegregation of the South. Following the notorious 1883 Supreme Court decision in *Plessey v. Ferguson* that declared the 1875 Civil Rights Act unconstitutional, most of the Southern states enacted "Jim Crow" laws that institutionalized segregation and discrimination. As a result, the Southern states evolved into dual societies with African Americans segregated from whites in education, employment, transportation, and public accommodations. In addition, they were subject to a range of barriers to voting that effectively disenfranchised them.

The civil rights movement began after World War II, which had the dual effect of mobilizing many African American males and inducing a mass migration of blacks to the war factories in the North. Both events helped to reinforce the perception among blacks that conditions in the South were totally unacceptable.

The National Association for the Advancement of Colored People (NAACP) had long been active in fighting discrimination and by the 1940s was actively supporting lawsuits aimed at discriminatory practices. After some minor victories, the breakthrough came in 1954 with the landmark *Brown v. Topeka Board of Education* Supreme Court decision. The case involved an eight-year-old girl who was required to attend an all-black school five miles from her home rather than an all-white school a short distance away. Invoking the equal protection clause of the Fourteenth Amendment, the Court argued that separate facilities in education were "inherently unequal." In a related 1955 decision, the Court ordered Southern schools to desegregate "with all deliberate speed."

The Court's ruling in *Brown* provoked a storm of protest in the South, including clear efforts to obstruct the implementation of the law. Desegregation did eventually begin in earnest but not until further court action and the passage of the 1964 Civil Rights Act that added legislative teeth to the judicial decisions (see the chronology of civil rights action in Table 13.2).

The 1964 act, together with the 1965 Voting Rights Act, transformed the legal status of Southern blacks. Separate public facilities disappeared, and the number of African Americans registered to vote eventually approached white levels. Controversy hardly evaporated, however. Indeed, it increased as many of the issues raised by discrimination became national rather than specifically Southern in nature.

The first such issue was the distinction between *de facto* (naturally evolving) and *de jure* (legally imposed) segregation. Most of the segregation in the South was clearly de jure in nature, and the Supreme Court consistently argued that it was unconstitutional and should be reversed. Hence in *Swann v. Charlotte-Mecklenberg* (1971), the Court sanctioned busing within a district that had a long history of legally mandated segregation. This and subsequent cases raised the question of the status of de facto segregation in the North, where patterns of residential segregation led automatically to separation in schools. In general, the Court sanctioned busing to achieve racial balance within districts where there was a clear pat-

TABLE 13.2   Chronology of Civil Rights and Political Action,
1948–1971

1948	In *Shelley v. Kramer* the Supreme Court makes racially restrictive covenants in housing unenforceable. President Truman signs an executive orer desegregating the armed forces.
1954	In *Brown v. Board*, the Court establishes that separate educational facilities are inherently unequal.
1955	The Court orders Southern schools to desegregate "with all deliberate speed."
1956	Montgomery, Alabama, bus boycott (which followed Rosa Parks's refusal to sit in the "blacks only" back section of the bus) ends following Supreme Court decision outlawing segregation on buses.
1957	Creation of the Southern Christian Leadership Conference. Martin Luther King Jr. named as first president. Troops sent to Little Rock, Arkansas, to enforce desegregation of Central High School. Passage of 1957 Civil Rights Act establishes the U.S. Commission on Civil Rights.
1960–1965	Continuing civil rights demonstrations in the South, including "Freedom Rides" to force desegregation of transportation, and other nonviolent protests. Many demonstrators are arrested or assaulted by police. The most notable demonstration was the March on Washington for Jobs and Freedom in 1963 during which Martin Luther King delivered his "I have a dream" speech.
1964	The omnibus 1964 Civil Rights Act outlaws discrimination in education, employment, and public facilities. Passage of the Twenty-fourth Amendment prohibits poll taxes in federal elections. Martin Luther King Jr. awarded Nobel Peace prize.
1965	Civil Rights Act bans discrimination in voting and orders the dispatch of federal registrars to Southern voting districts.
1968	Martin Luther King Jr. assassinated. Widespread rioting follows, including demonstrations just blocks from the U.S. Capitol. Civil Rights Act bans discrimination in housing.
1971	Supreme Court decision in *Swann v. Charlotte-Mecklenburg* sanctions busing within a school district that has a long-standing pattern of segregation.

tern of *intent* to separate by race. However, it proved more reluctant to bus children across district lines and to remedy de facto discrimination where no intent to separate was evident. Nonetheless, the issue proved politically explosive in a number of jurisdictions, including Detroit and Boston, and increasingly during the 1970s and 1980s, the courts proved reluctant to impose busing plans on communities.

These cases also relate to the second area of controversy: What were the limits of *affirmative action,* or attempts to redress a past pattern of discrimination? Affirmative action is inherently problematical because it involves a clash between the liberal notion of what the *individual* is worth and the *collective* interests of a group or race. After the civil rights revolution of the 1960s, many federal, state, and local laws were enacted involving the use of affirmative action devices such as racial-preference quotas. However, in *Regents of the University of California v. Bakke* (1978), the Supreme Court found that a quota of 16 places reserved for minorities out of 100 available at the Davis Medical School was a violation of a qualified white applicant's rights under the Fourteenth Amendment. In other words, the individual rights of the white applicant were given higher priority than the collective rights of minorities who had suffered discrimination in the past and who were therefore disadvantaged. Since *Bakke,* the Supreme Court—and in particular the Rehnquist Court—has progressively weakened the meaning and application of affirmative action programs, including the use of quotas.

The decline of affirmative action was confirmed when the Supreme Court refused to review California's 1997 Proposition 209 banning "preferential treatment" for minorities in state programs. This voter initiative ended effective affirmative action in the University of California and elsewhere in the state. As a result, the number of blacks and Hispanics entering some of the more prestigious University of California campuses dropped significantly after 1997. In 1998, voters in Washington state also passed an initiative banning "preferential treatment for minorities."

Gender

The struggle for women's equality has in many ways paralleled the civil rights movement. Although women won the right to vote under the Nineteenth Amendment in 1920, they continued to be subject to extensive discrimination in a wide range of areas from employment to education to housing. The first major advance was the passage of the Equal Pay Act of 1963 banning wage discrimination in a range of job categories. One year later, all the prohibitions on discrimination in the 1964 Civil Rights Act also were applied to gender. Under this law, an Equal Employment Opportunities Commission (EEOC) was created to enforce equal employment conditions for women and minorities.

Underfunded and overburdened with cases, the EEOC made little headway into unequal pay, however, a fact that led many women's organizations to call for an Equal Rights Amendment (ERA) to the Constitution that would guarantee equality of treatment. In spite of a major campaign launched by the National Organization for Women (NOW), passage by Congress in 1972, and the support of Presidents Nixon and Carter, the ERA managed to muster only thirty-five of the thirty-eight state votes necessary for passage. The ERA effort was subject to a seven-year deadline with a three-year extension and therefore expired in 1982. Thus women continue not to be specifically mentioned in or protected by the U.S. Constitution.

Notwithstanding this setback, women's groups have been able to advance sexual equality in a number of areas by taking both the legislative and judicial routes. The Equal Credit Act of 1974 (amended 1976) grants equal access to financial credit. In 1993, Congress passed the Family and Medical Leave Act that provides women (and men) up to twelve weeks unpaid leave to tend to a newborn or sick family member. Although considered a significant advance, this law falls far short of the support provided in most other developed states, most of which allow for paid leave for the birth and care of the newborn.

On the judicial front, the Supreme Court has handed down a succession of decisions limiting sexual harassment, reinforcing equal pay, and ending discriminatory practices against pregnant women. One of the most celebrated of these cases affected the Virginia Military Academy's (VMI) ban on female cadets. Along with another all-male school, The Citadel in South Carolina, VMI was ordered to admit women cadets. By 1999, notwithstanding continuing harassment of females in such schools, women were being admitted in larger numbers. Some of the most far-reaching Court opinions have been written by Justices Sandra Day O'Connor and Ruth Bader Ginsburg, thus demonstrating that the incumbency of women in positions of power can make a significant difference in how women are treated in society.

Woman have, in fact, made major advances in politics, business, and other professions. As mentioned in Chapter 2, however, their journey is still continuing.

Disability

In total, some 20 million Americans suffer from some sort of disability (hearing, speech, sight, mental, or mobility impairment). Unlike for ethnicity and gender, however, legislative protection for the disabled has been relatively uncontroversial. As early as 1948, discrimination against the disabled in the federal civil service was outlawed. Later in 1964, the Architectural Barriers Act required all federal buildings to be accessible to the disabled, and the 1988 Civil Rights Restoration Act added disability to the list of categories in which federal funds could be withdrawn for discriminatory practices. The most important legislation was the 1990 Americans with Disabilities Act (ADA), which provided for comprehensive access for the disabled to all public buildings, transportation, and other public facilities.

As with other civil rights acts, how the ADA works out in practice will depend on administrative enforcement and judicial interpretation. It is easy to be complacent in this area, but it is interesting to note that the protection afforded disabled Americans is considerably greater than in many other countries, including many of the European welfare states. Perhaps this emphasis reflects the overarching importance of *equality of opportunity* as a value in American society. Most Americans would balk at the idea that simply because some people must use a wheelchair they should be denied access to the social and economic opportunities available to others.

Conclusion

This chapter has not addressed all those areas that could be included under the general heading of government regulation of public morality. Discrimination against older Americans and against gays and lesbians is also a matter for public debate and government action. Older Americans are represented by the American Association of Retired Persons (AARP), which with 30 million members lobbies hard both to protect Social Security and other benefits and to fight discrimination against the old in employment, housing, and medical care. Gays and lesbians continue to suffer extensive discrimination in housing and employment. They have achieved a degree of success in some communities, but many more have passed antigay ordinances—for example, prohibiting openly gay persons from teaching in public schools.

With these and all the other issues discussed earlier, citizens look to governments and increasingly to all three branches of the federal government for guidance and protection. This activity puts additional pressures on the political system. When, as with abortion and capital punishment, the issues involve moral absolutes, governments are, by definition, unable to please everybody. The nationalization of these issues in recent years thus helps raise public expectations of what government can do, but it also means that for many citizens, government action will result in disappointment—or even in anger and frustration.

One thing is certain—all of these civil rights and liberties and conscience issues will continue to crowd the policy agenda. More open and accessible political institutions, together with increasingly vocal demands for redress among minorities, women, and other groups, will ensure that these issues will not fade away.

A further and obvious conclusion to be drawn from the preceding analysis is that there is no single policy system that can accommodate the diverse and complex ways in which governments at all levels attempt to regulate public morality. Because this general area involves constitutional rights, the courts are, by definition, intimately involved. But as noted, the courts, and in particular the Supreme Court, have failed to provide consistent and coherent leadership on moral questions. The representative institutions of American government, including the presidency and Congress, are also involved, of course. But in contrast to how such areas as economic and foreign policy are managed, there is rarely a clear and predetermined policy agenda on civil rights and liberties and the other conscience issues awaiting presidents and members of Congress when they accede to power. Instead, these policymakers tend to react to outside events, such as civil rights demonstrations or a mass shooting incident, rather than take the lead. This reactive rather than proactive stance demonstrates well the perils of promising too much in policy areas where arguments are so often couched in terms of moral and political absolutes.

Notes

1. Samuel Huntington, *American Politics: The Promise of Disharmony* (Cambridge, MA: Harvard University Press, 1981).

Further Reading

The best account of the Supreme Court's role in the civil liberties area is by Henry J. Abraham and Barbara A. Perry, *Freedom and the Court: Civil Rights and Liberties in the United States*, 7th ed. (New York: Oxford University Press, 1998). Nicholas Lehmann's *The Promised Land: The Great Black Migration and How It Changed America* (New York: Knopf, 1991) provides a vivid account of black migration to the North. Taylor Branch has written two excellent volumes of a planned three-volume biography of Martin Luther King, *Parting the Waters: America in the King Years, 1954–1963* and *Pillar of Fire: America in the King Years, 1963–1965* (New York: Simon and Schuster, 1988 and 1998). Jane J. Mansbridge, *Why We Lost the ERA* (Chicago: University of Chicago Press, 1986), examines the reasons for the failure of the Equal Rights Amendment. A good discussion of the politics of abortion is provided by Barbara Craig and David O'Brien, *Abortion and American Politics* (Chatham, NJ: Chatham House, 1993). On disability, see Robert A. Katzman, *Institutional Disability: The Saga of Transportation Policy* (Washington, DC: Brookings Institution, 1986).

14

Social Policy in America:
Self-Reliance and
State Dependence

Sooner or later cuts in Social Security and Medicare which provide benefits for older Americans are unavoidable, because the alternatives—huge tax increases or peacetime budget deficits—are worse and probably politically unacceptable.

—*Robert J. Samuelson*

This is not the end of welfare reform; it is the beginning.

—*President Clinton, on signing welfare reform, August 22, 1996*

Governments have always been more reluctant to intervene in the general area of social policy in the United States than they have in Western Europe. Indeed, it was not until the 1930s that the federal government laid down a framework of law providing for welfare and Social Security benefits for the poor and the old. Even then, the extent and level of welfare coverage were limited. Contributory earnings-related pensions applied only to certain kinds of workers. Welfare was restricted to families with dependent children (in effect, mothers and children) and was distributed through the states on a matching federal-state basis. As a result, great disparities in the provision of welfare from state to state developed—disparities that remain to this day.

Housing and health, moreover, were not considered legitimate parts of federal social policy until the 1960s, and since then, housing subsidies have been subject to periodic cuts to the point that during the Reagan years, subsidies for the construction of new housing all but disappeared—if only temporarily. Only education has been universally accepted as a legitimate part of the social policy agenda. But until very recently, it was always local and state governments, rather than the federal government, that provided for elementary, secondary, and higher education.

The roots of the American antipathy to anything but limited and selective social benefits are not difficult to identify. They lie in the strongly held notions of self-reliance that have been discussed a number of times in earlier chapters. By the 1970s, however, some areas of social policy had become established as proper and legitimate roles for the federal government. Almost all of these involved earnings-related Social Security benefits for widows, widowers, the disabled, the blind, and, above all, the old. Most Americans now consider these benefits to be rights, not handouts by the government. There is, in fact, a sizable "handout" element in the Social Security program, because benefits are not strictly related to what has been paid in. In addition, Medicare, the program providing medical aid for the old, is also now considered a right, even though the redistributive element in the program is considerable (benefits rarely relate precisely to what recipients have paid in). Finally, many Americans, even those on the political right, look more benignly on the welfare programs for the old and disabled, such as Supplementary Security Income, than they do on other welfare programs. Clearly, the elderly are given a special status as a group who cannot be expected to help themselves.

The same sympathy is not, paradoxically, extended to children in poor families who, though provided with a range of welfare benefits, do not fare as well as do the old. One reason for this disparity is the problem of ensuring that benefits received by parents do in fact reach needy children. Because of this and the belief among many politicians that many of those on welfare can and should be capable of supporting a family through work, what used to be the two main welfare programs—food stamps and AFDC (Aid to Families with Dependent Children)—were always politically vulnerable. Similarly, medical care for the poor (Medicaid) is less well protected than Medicare.

TABLE 14.1   Major Federal Social Policy Legislation, 1935–1996

1935   Social Security Act—established the basic old-age, survivors, and disabled insurance program, as well as unemployment insurance and the main welfare program, Aid to Families with Dependent Children (AFDC).

1937   Public Housing Act—provided limited grants for the construction of municipal housing.

1964   Food stamps—the provision of stamps that the poor can exchange for food.

1965   Creation of Medicare (medical care for the old) and Medicaid (medical care for the poor).

Elementary and Secondary Education Act—federal aid for local school authorities in disadvantaged areas.

1968   Housing Act—the provision of housing subsidies for the owners and renters of low- and moderate-income housing.

1971   Supplementary Security Income (SSI)—the provision of welfare benefits for older citizens.

1988   Family Support Act—requires states to provide work or training programs for welfare recipients.

1996   Personal Responsibility and Work Opportunity Reconciliation Act (PRWORA)—limits recipients to five years of benefits (with some exceptions). Consolidates federal programs as block grants for the states. Limits welfare benefits for young mothers.

As can be seen from Table 14.1, most of the major social policy bills were enacted during the New Deal and the Great Society period of the 1960s. Since then, there have been numerous amendments to the original legislation but, until 1996, no wholesale reform. In fact, reform attempts have come from left and right, with the most recent assault on the system from the right being led by the Republican 104th Congress. In 1996, Congress did pass a welfare reform bill that President Clinton eventually signed. The grandly titled Personal Responsibility and Work Opportunity Reconciliation Act abolished AFDC and instead provided the states with block grants to fund their own programs.

What accounts for the particular shape of social policy programs
in the United States? This question has both institutional and ideological answers.

Federalism

Federalism has always had an important influence on welfare provision in the United States. AFDC was originally organized on a
matching basis with the states with the result that benefits varied
greatly from state to state. In 1996, for example, the maximum
monthly benefit payable to a one-parent family of three in Alaska
was $923 compared with just $120 in Mississippi. Cost-of-living
differences among states account for part but by no means all of
this difference. Food-stamp benefits also vary from state to state
but were partly designed to make up for the AFDC inequities.

Federalist sentiment was also an important influence on the 1996
welfare reforms. Since the passage of the law, it is up to the states
to create welfare plans designed to reduce the number of recipients
to a minimum. How, precisely, the states will replace welfare with
"workfare" over the longer term remains to be seen, however.
Some states such as Wisconsin and Minnesota implemented plans
quickly and reduced their welfare rolls accordingly, whereas others
such as California had much less success. Two things seem certain:
Over the next several years, the pressure will be on the states to reduce the number of people on welfare, and for the first time since
before the New Deal, the states will become the main providers of
income support for families. As can be seen from Figure 14.1, although the welfare participation rate has fallen dramatically since
1994, the real test of the new system will come if and when unemployment rises to the high levels characteristic of the 1970s and
1980s.

Social Security, Medicare,
and the Electoral Connection

As suggested earlier, Social Security has a special status as a protected set of measures in the United States. In 1982, President Reagan attempted to cut benefits but failed because of fierce opposition from Congress and public opinion generally. More recently,
Newt Gingrich and the Republican 104th Congress made a serious

FIGURE 14.1   Welfare Participation and Unemployment

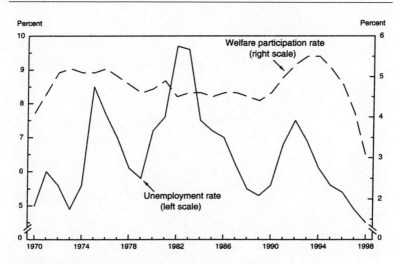

SOURCE: *Economic Report of the President 1999,* Washington, DC, 1999, chart 3.11.

attempt to cut back on the *projected increase* in the cost of Medicare over the next several years. This threat provoked a storm of anger from older Americans and their organizations. Most Americans, regardless of their economic position, expect to receive Medicare benefits at some time during their lives. By attacking the burgeoning cost of the program (see Figure 14.2), Gingrich was taking a considerable political risk. Even though he was not planning to cut Social Security, there was a widespread impression that this would be next on the list. Meanwhile, during the 1996 election campaign, President Clinton could project himself as the guardian of these programs and accuse Gingrich and the Republicans of being mean-spirited and insensitive to the needs of the old. It seems likely that these events helped Clinton to victory in the 1996 presidential elections.

Social insurance (mainly old-age pensions) is easily the largest item in the nondefense federal budget (Figure 14.2), and as an entitlement program, it is effectively uncontrollable. Increasingly, however, benefits for the old, which have little or no contributory

FIGURE 14.2   Composition of Federal Spending, 1970–1995

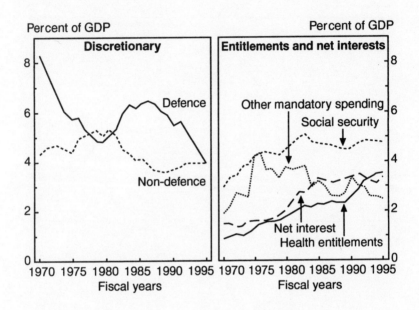

SOURCE: *Economic Report of the President, 1996,* Washington, DC, 1996, chart 2.11.

element (SSI, Medicare, and Supplementary Medicare), are also electorally protected. As Figure 14.2 shows, health benefits are also increasing rapidly in cost, and it was this very rapid growth that inspired Gingrich to propose what were in effect modest cuts.

Although the Republicans may have been politically foolish to propose such measures, there is no doubt that, in the longer run, they are needed. The fundamental problem with Social Security and with Medicare is that the number of *contributors* to the programs through payroll taxes will gradually *decrease* sometime early in the twenty-first century while the number of *beneficiaries* will *increase*. To put it another way, when the "baby-boom" generation (those born between about 1945 and 1965) retires, there will be fewer workers in the labor force to replace them.

FIGURE 14.3 Social Security Receipts, Spending, and Reserve
Estimates, 1992–2035

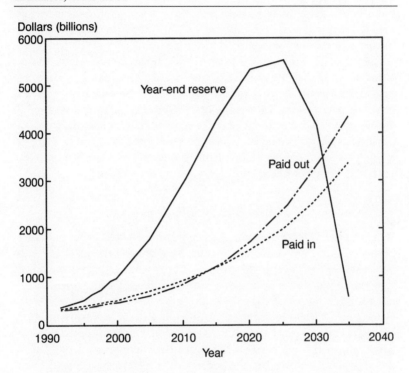

SOURCE: Harold W. Stanley and Richard G. Niemi, *Vital Statistics on
American Politics* (Washington, DC: Congressional Quarterly Press,
1994), figure 12.2.

This is an actuarial problem facing all welfare states at century's
end, but in fact it is not as serious in the United States as in some
countries, especially Italy and France, given that the American
birthrate is one of the highest among richer countries. Nonetheless,
something will have to be done about the problem over the next
decade. This is amply demonstrated by Figure 14.3, which shows
what will happen to the Social Security Trust Fund by 2035 if no
reforms are instituted. Congress originally created a trust fund to

ensure that the program was self-financing and immune to "raids" by the federal government. A large surplus will build up as the baby-boom generation pays in increasing sums as their incomes increase. After about 2025, however, the program will slide inexorably toward insolvency.

Aware of this pending shortfall, President Clinton made the reform of Medicare and of the Social Security system a priority for his second term. As a lame-duck president, he faced no political costs in attempting such reforms. Whether Congress would go along with what would have to be sizable cuts or tax increases, or both, was another matter, however. One thing is certain: The spiraling cost of these entitlement programs will remain firmly at the center of the political agenda for some years to come.

Philosophy of Self-Reliance

Whereas the elderly and the disabled are protected, younger, able-bodied citizens are under increasing pressure to take jobs and support themselves. The 1988 Family Support Act required the states to provide work or training programs for all welfare recipients, but not until the passage of the 1996 Personal Responsibility and Work Opportunity Reconciliation Act did the federal government fully embrace a philosophy of self-reliance. Under the act, welfare recipients cannot receive benefits for more than five years. In addition, the eligibility criteria for the receipt of Supplemental Social Security, food stamps, and other benefits were narrowed to include only the very needy. Indeed, Democrats and Republicans are now committed to "workfare," or the linking of benefits to training and jobs. It remains to be seen how the new law will work out in practice, but for families, workfare is not a realistic option unless accompanied by comprehensive child care. The 1996 legislation did include some provision for child care spending, but it was widely perceived to be inadequate. In addition, some critics have noted that reducing the welfare rolls during a period of rapid economic growth—and in some areas, a labor shortage—is one thing, but maintaining this situation when the economy slows and unemployment rises may prove more difficult.

An interesting aspect of the widespread public concern about the growth in welfare expenditure and the related belief that most welfare recipients are scroungers rather than the deserving poor is

FIGURE 14.4   Federal Outlays by Function, Fiscal 1996

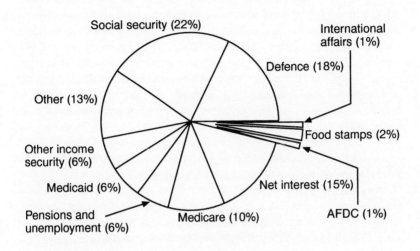

NOTE: AFDC is aid to families with dependent children.
SOURCE: *Economic Report of the President, 1996,* Washington, DC, 1996, chart 2.12.

that, in relation to the size of other federal programs, public assistance spending is quite low. As can be seen from Figure 14.4, the major welfare programs in 1996 (food stamps and AFDC) accounted for just 3 percent of federal spending. The category "other income security" also contains a number of programs for the poor, but the major item here is Supplementary Security Income (SSI), which provides welfare mainly for older Americans and the disabled. This program has not been subject to major public criticism. Whatever the objective situation, Democrats and Republicans have shown a determination to cut the welfare rolls, and as noted (Figure 14.1), their efforts have been remarkably successful since the mid-1990s.

Health Care Reforms

When he took office, Bill Clinton was determined to reform America's health care system. His motives were twofold. First, as a reforming Democrat, he wanted to extend medical coverage to the 15 percent of Americans who were totally without medical insurance. Second, he wanted to stem the spiraling cost of medical care. He delegated the job of producing a health care plan to his wife Hillary and to Ira Magaziner, an old confidant and author of books on U.S. industrial policy. After fifteen months, they produced an outline Health Care Security Act that, among other things, required employers to provide health care coverage, extended coverage to the whole population, created an internal market device called alliances to purchase coverage and services, and placed price controls on insurance policies.

The plan was submitted to Congress in October 1993. Twelve months later, it was still in Congress, never to emerge as legislation. What went wrong? Most commentators agree that some of the blame must be attributed to the plan itself. It did propose the creation of a new bureaucracy; it was unpopular with business and especially with smaller companies; and it was not at all obvious that it would cut costs. As a result, it was heavily criticized in Congress, where it was referred to a number of committees, each with different priorities. Alternative plans were eventually drawn up by congressional Democrats and Republicans, but these proved unacceptable to the White House. Indeed, the president and his team proved less than adept at guiding the legislation through Congress—although to be fair, any major reform of the health care system, however well steered through Congress, would have encountered difficulties.

The major problem with this policy area is that Americans' health care has developed into a three-tier system—those individuals with private insurance coverage, those in health maintenance organizations (HMOs), and the uninsured. The emergence of HMOs, which use market criteria to cost (and limit) health care provided by doctors and hospitals, already constitutes a major change in the system. Around 140 million Americans are in HMOs, and there is widespread disquiet at the way they operate. Providing health care for the approximately 40 million who have no health care would, unless taxes were to be increased, imply a further squeeze on what has become the most important part of the health care system. In sum, an effective low-cost reform to provide for the uninsured could only be achieved at the expense of the majority. Such a situation is not amenable to easy solutions—and especially not when the major priority of government is to maintain a balanced budget without increasing taxation. It now seems, indeed, that a major overhaul of health delivery systems is unlikely to occur for some years.

Conclusion

Perhaps the most remarkable development in American social policy since the 1980s is the virtual abandonment by Democratic leaders of the sort of redistributive measures associated with the New Deal and the Great Society. Although Social Security and Medicare remain politically sacrosanct, welfare and a number of other income support programs are now viewed with hostility. For Republicans and those on the right, it was always thus. Today, they have been joined by many Democrats.

In this sense, the status of a major aspect of American social policy has returned to its pre–New Deal position. Income support should be provided for the truly needy who are unable to work. Any adult who is able to work must do so or forfeit the support of the state. There is, however, a major difference between the New Deal era and today. Put simply, as far as Social Security and health care are concerned, most Americans expect the federal government to play an important role. Indeed, their expectations in both areas have, if anything, been increasing over recent years. At the same time, the political system has been unable to institute major reforms because reform must entail either increased taxation or reduced benefits. In this sense, Social Security and health care capture nicely the theme of this book: high public expectations married to deep distrust of an enhanced federal role. Only in the welfare area have public demands been met. But as indicated, welfare provision has always been viewed with suspicion in the United States, and reform has been achieved largely because the traditional supporters of welfare—the Democrats—see welfare cuts as both possible and politically expedient.

Further Reading

On the origins of social policy, see Theda Skocpol, *Protecting Soldiers and Mothers: The Political Origins of Social Policy in the United States* (Cambridge, MA: Cambridge University Press, 1995). On recent changes in welfare policy, see Charles Noble, *Welfare as We Knew It* (New York: Oxford University Press, 1997), and Anne Marie Cammisa, *From Rhetoric to Reform: Welfare Policy in American Politics* (Boulder, CO: Westview Press, 1998). On health care, see Thomas E. Mann and Norman J. Ornstein (eds.), *Intensive Care* (Washington, DC: American Enterprise Institute, 1995).

15

Managing Economic Change

Sometimes magic works, sometimes it doesn't. For a generation after World War II, America had (as Tom Wolfe put it) a "magic economy.". . . In less than thirty years everything doubled. That is the real earnings of the typical worker, the real income of the typical family, consumption per capita. "In 1973 the magic went away."

—*Paul Krugman*

As recently as 1965, a section on economic policy in a textbook on American politics would not have been considered necessary. Today it is essential. Not since the 1930s have economic issues dominated the policy agenda as they do now. Abroad, America's standing has changed in a new and often hostile international economic order. At home, maintaining steady growth with low inflation and balanced budgets has become the number one domestic policy priority. It hardly needs stressing that the state of the economy is vitally important, not only for the economic role of governments in society and the ways in which they tax citizens and allocate expenditure, but also for the health of the polity. It is small wonder, then, that economic policy came to dominate the agenda of the 1980s and 1990s. Governments, moreover, are now irrevocably involved in economic affairs. Some 35 percent of gross domestic product is accounted for by government expenditure at all levels; federal regulation of industrial and commercial affairs, from environmental protection to antimonopoly law, is widespread; and by manipulating aggregate levels of expenditure and taxation and altering the supply of money in the economy, all federal governments now accept the need to "manage" the economy. Regulation has been discussed elsewhere (Chapter 10), and this section's aim is to study economic management policies and in particular to identify those forces that shape the economic policy making agenda. As with social policy, particular attention is paid to the relationship between public expectations and the objective performance of the government in the economic policy area.

State and Economy in the United States

As Chapter 2 emphasized, the traditional view of the United States is of a country where the state plays a relatively minor role. In contrast to the burgeoning welfare states and mixed economies of Europe, convention has it that Americans prefer market to public mechanisms to distribute goods and services in society. By most simple quantitative measures, this view has some validity. The United States is low on scales measuring the percentage of GDP accounted for by public expenditure and of taxation's share of GDP.

The data in Table 15.1, however, show that America is closer to such countries as Australia and Spain than it is to Japan, so it might be more accurate to label Japan rather than the United States as the "exception" (Table 15.1). Although the trend in U.S. expenditures has been upward, there has been no dramatic change since the late 1950s, the increase being from about 27 to 35 percent of GDP. Of course, if measured over a longer time span, then the growth of public expenditure has been dramatic. In 1930, the percentage of GDP accounted for by public expenditure was less than 10 percent. Much of the increase since then has been a result of massively enhanced defense spending and, since the early 1960s, of the partial replacement of defense expenditure with spending on a range of domestic programs. The key feature of federal government expenditures alone is the rapid growth in spending precipitated by the two world wars and by the New Deal. Apart from a brief period during World War I, until the early 1930s less than 5 percent of GDP was accounted for by federal spending. Since 1945 it has been rising slowly and erratically until falling in very recent years, and today it is around 20 percent of GDP (Figure 15.1).

Whatever the relative position of the United States, the sheer size of all government budgets should not be underestimated. In 1998, the federal government alone spent nearly $1.7 trillion, and total expenditure of all governments comes to over $2.4 trillion. As Figure 15.2 shows, the gap between this expenditure and income—the fed-

TABLE 15.1   Public Expenditure as Percentage of GDP and in Dollars Per Capita, Late 1980s

	%GDP	%OECD Mean	Per Capita Expenditure PPP $a	%OECD Mean
United States	35.3	81	6,473	121
Canada	42.8	99	7,368	138
Norway	48.1	111	7,410	139
Switzerland	30.1	69	4,767	89
Sweden	60.0	138	8,262	155
Denmark	55.7	128	7,375	138
Germany	43.2	99	5,755	108
Japan	27.2	63	3,585	66
France	48.4	112	6,197	116
Finland	38.2	88	4,904	92
Australia	35.0	81	4,414	83
United Kingdom	42.9	99	5,293	99
Netherlands	54.0	124	6,616	124
Italy	45.2	104	5,538	104
Belgium	50.6	117	5,972	112
Austria	47.3	109	5,517	104
New Zealand	41.9	97	4,475	84
Spain	36.1	83	3,134	59
Ireland	50.4	116	3,801	71
Greece	43.0	99	2,736	51
Portugal	37.6	87	2,368	44
Average	43.4		5,331	

aPPP is purchasing-power parity

SOURCE: Organization for Economic Cooperation and Development (OECD), reproduced in Richard Rose, "Is American Public Policy Exceptional?" in Byron Shafer (ed.), *Is America Different?* (New York: Oxford University Press, 1991), table 7.2.

eral debt—increased rapidly until 1992, so that by the mid-1980s, the size of the deficit had become the number one economic issue.

As in every other developed economy, American governments—and particularly the federal government—have enormous potential power over economic activity. By increasing spending and lowering taxation, government can stimulate the economy. Conversely, lower spending and higher taxes can lower the level of economic activity. Used in this way, fiscal policy is a major tool of macroeconomic pol-

FIGURE 15.1   Federal Outlays as a Percentage of GNP/GDP, 1869–2002

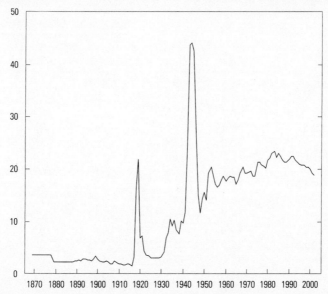

NOTE: Averaged by decade for 1869–1888. Percentage of GNP is shown through 1929, percentage of GDP thereafter. Figures for 1997–2002 are estimates.

SOURCE: Harold W. Stanley and Richard G. Niemi, *Vital Statistics on American Politics, 1997–98* (Washington, DC: Congressional Quarterly Press, 1998), figure 11.1.

icy. Other tools include control over credit and the money supply, both of which are currently in fashion as means of fighting inflation.

American government affects the economy in a number of other ways, most of which can be contained under the general description of microeconomic policy. Microeconomic policy is concerned not with pulling fiscal and monetary levers to affect the general direction in which the economy moves, but rather with a range of policy instruments that affect the specific behavior of individuals, firms, sectors, and regions. Hence, industrial policy, labor relations, education, training, and regional and urban policy are typical microeconomic tools.

Regulatory policy can also be a microeconomic device, although, as noted in Chapter 10, it is often motivated by noneconomic considerations such as the promotion of equality or the protection of the environment.

FIGURE 15.2   Federal Budget Deficit as a Percent of GDP

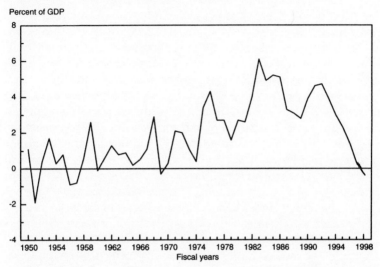

SOURCE: *Economic Report of the President 1998,* Washington, DC, 1997, p. 27.

It hardly needs mentioning that this range of macro- and micro-policies is not perceived by policymakers as a coherent set of inter-related instruments. Neither do the policies always complement one another according to some coherent economic rationale. If anything, the very opposite applies. Politicians and bureaucrats are not in agreement as to which policy should be applied at any par-ticular time; and the policies themselves often compete with, rather than complement, one another; or as the economists would put it, *trade-offs* exist between (say) education and training policy and taxation, or between inflation and unemployment.

Any attempt to identify the scope and limitations of economic policy in any society requires an analysis of institutional and ideo-logical factors. How do these constrain economic policy making in the United States?

Ideology and Economic Policy

As the discussion in earlier chapters showed, ideology plays an im-portant part in shaping the policy agenda or in influencing which issues or alternative policies are available for debate and discussion at any one time. In most Western countries, economic policy has been influenced by three distinct philosophies, each of which has its defenders among economists as well as its political champions. On the right, economic liberals look to the market for salvation. In the center, Keynesians believe that when the market fails to provide full employment and steady growth, governments should step in and, via increased spending and borrowing, stimulate demand. On the left, socialists place the market in a subordinate position in relation to a public sector that would plan the allocation of resources in society. Socialist solutions are effectively excluded from the policy agenda in the United States and by century's end were discredited almost everywhere else. They carry connotations of collectivism unacceptable in a society so infused with economic individualism.

Until the 1980s, most debate involved clashes between liberals and Keynesians. Much of the politics of economic policy, then, centered on levels of taxation and spending and on the extent to which credit and the money supply should be controlled. Prior to 1933, liberal economics dominated; not until the New Deal and World War II did federal governments begin to "borrow and spend their way out of trouble," either to stimulate a depressed economy or to produce war materiel on a massive scale.

To the economic liberal, high levels of government expenditures are bad enough, even if they are covered by taxation. But deficit spending and loose money-supply policies are even worse, for these lead directly to inflation and, so the argument runs, eventually to disaster. Economic liberals' antipathy even to higher levels of government expenditure adequately financed by taxation derives from their conviction that the market is the only efficient and acceptable allocator of resources. When governments allocate, they do so wastefully and inefficiently. Of course, the free marketeers accept that governments have to play some role, especially in defense. But the essence of their philosophy is to reduce what has become a very intrusive role in society and always to ensure that what expenditure remains is recovered by taxation.

During the late 1930s and 1940s, Keynesian thinking dominated, and successive federal governments ran up large deficits, the peak being reached in the admittedly unusual conditions of wartime in 1943 when, in one year, a $54.8 billion deficit amounted to some 35 percent of GDP. Interestingly, though most of the postwar period is usually labeled "Keynesian," total federal debt as a percentage of

GDP declined steadily until 1970, although it rose sharply thereafter until leveling off in the early 1990s only to fall sharply thereafter. As debt increased, spending rose, and in recent years there has been a tendency toward increased domestic, rather than defense, spending. To the economic liberal (a supporter of the free market), the latter may be justifiable, but the former rarely is.

The liberal position was given further stimulus by the events of the early and mid-1970s. During the 1971–1973 period, loose money-supply policies were accompanied by steep rises in commodity prices, culminating in the 1973–1974 fourfold increase in oil prices. These fueled inflation and wrought serious damage on the supply side of the economy. Producers, in other words, found their costs increasing rapidly. Their incentive to produce and invest was greatly undermined, resulting in a drop in output and rising unemployment. The ensuing recession convinced many in the Ford and Carter administrations that the way back to economic health lay in re-creating the right production and investment environment—low taxes, inflation, and interest rates. This cure, they argued, could be achieved only if governments avoided overstimulating demand through expenditure and borrowing. But neither president was very successful in keeping government spending down, and when elected in 1980, President Reagan made a much stronger pledge to cut expenditure, borrowing, and taxes and therefore provide an amenable investment environment. How Ronald Reagan's new economic program fared is discussed later.

Notwithstanding a near consensus by the late 1990s on the need for liberal, free-market economics, conflicts over the consequences of liberal policies remained. Many in the Democratic Party and in the labor unions continued to advocate Keynesian solutions, and most commentators remained wary of the political feasibility of exclusively free-market solutions, whatever their economic merits. In addition, many political leaders voiced concern about the social consequences of expenditure cuts. As established in earlier chapters, federal, state, and local governments are now irrevocably involved in the business of providing a wide range of economic and social services whether they like it or not. The public *expects* a wide range of services from the federal government, and the tension between this plain fact and the prevailing liberal economic philosophy is considerable and unlikely to disappear in the immediate future.

The liberal-Keynesian conflict in economic policy is essentially about macroeconomic management. What then of the relationship between ideology and microeconomic policy? In some respects, adopting interventionist microstrategies to solve economic problems is more of a challenge to liberal ideology than is Keynesian demand management: Industrial or regional policy assumes that governments can and should interfere with individual economic actors or sectors by providing incentives, subsidies, loans, or guidance.

Perhaps for this reason, the United States has less consciously planned and developed industrial, regional, and labor market policies than any comparable country. Indeed, there *is* no federal industrial or regional strategy worth the name, and training and labor force policies are more ameliorative ad hoc measures than true labor market strategies. Japan and France, by way of contrast, have had highly developed industrial policies involving centrally coordinated resource and investment planning. In Japan's case, industrial planning by sector has involved close linkages among government, corporations, and unions. Such corporatist arrangements were, until recently, quite alien to the American way of doing things.

Nonetheless, during the 1970s, a number of commentators, noting the relatively poor economic performance of the United States, called for a federal industrial policy. These calls went unheeded and all but faded away amid the free-wheeling economic boom of the middle and later Reagan years. By the early 1990s, however, industrial policy had returned to the center of the economic stage. Slow or even negative economic growth continued for several years, and increasingly invidious comparisons were made between the performance of American as opposed to Japanese and German industry.

By 1993, the incoming Clinton administration was committed to an economic strategy that could be interpreted as industrial policy, including an economic stimulus package: infrastructure investment, a federal training program, and special help to facilitate innovation in high-growth industries such as microchips and genetics. Very early in the first Clinton term, however, the advocates of industrial policy, and especially Labor Secretary Robert Reich, were eclipsed by economic and political events. The economy recovered rapidly from 1993, thus partly removing the need for an economic stimulus package. This recovery was, moreover, steady and noninflationary. Further government expenditure may have resulted in "overheating" and renewed inflation.

As important for the fate of the package were dissenting voices from within the administration. The deputy director of the Office of Management and Budget, Alice Rivlin, had written a book, *Re-*

viving the American Dream, in which she argued that the economy needed less, not more, federal government expenditure and regulation. Although her perspective was at first unpopular, by the middle of 1993, her views, rather than Reich's, were on the ascendant within the White House. Finally, there was deep disquiet among Republicans in Congress that the stimulus package represented a giant pork-barrel giveaway. This combination of factors killed the stimulus package in Congress. Indeed, by the end of 1993, the entire industrial-policy question had slipped from the policy agenda.

Of course, the United States has had a range of industrial policies for many years, from loans provided by the Small Business Administration to aid for urban transportation and interstate highway schemes, to employment-creation programs for poor cities and rural areas, to investment incentives for commercial and industrial development. At the state and local levels, similar programs and schemes exist. Crucially, however, these have in the main been ad hoc and uncoordinated and have emerged as a result of the lobbying and bargaining processes outlined in earlier chapters. They cannot, therefore, be considered as part of an economic or industrial *strategy.*

Institutions and Economic Policy

The relationship between ideology and political and social institutions has inspired debate within social science for many years. In American politics, for example, the issue has never been resolved of whether federalism is a cause of a limited federal planning and coordinating role in society or whether it has been maintained as a result of the power of liberal ideology. Whatever the causal directions, there can be no doubting that institutional arrangements continue to have a profound effect on economic policy making. Indeed, some would argue that the institutional constraints are such that no administration can effectively manage the American economy. What are the constraints?

Federalism and Localism

Chapter 5 referred to competitive interdependence in U.S. intergovernmental relations and showed how the federal government is now locked in a symbiotic relationship with lower-level governments. Thus, although the federal government continues to hand out large sums of money to states and localities, it is no easy thing to withdraw this largesse in line with economic imperatives. State and local governments have multiple channels of access to officials in Washington, and, notwithstanding recent cutbacks in federal aid, formidable political resources can be harnessed to defend federally funded programs. Of course, to a greater or lesser extent, this strategy is used everywhere, but the institution of federalism gives to individual states added legal weight in their efforts to maintain federal funding.

Federalism also encourages "highest common denominator" options when funds are being allocated. In other words, the federal government finds it very difficult to discriminate among states according to some rational economic principle. When Washington is providing regional economic or research and development aid, for example, who gets what depends more on lobbying, criteria of equity, or mere chance than on the needs of economy. The failure to develop a coherent microeconomic strategy must in part be related to this phenomenon.

State and local governments also have independent revenue sources, which can weaken the scope and substance of federal fiscal policy. Federal revenues account for only about 60 percent of all government income in the United States; the remainder is derived from state and local sales, property, and income taxes. Constitutionally, and in marked contrast to the situation in a country like Britain, the federal government cannot *directly* affect these revenues. It is easy to make too much of this point, however. Runaway spending by subnational governments is uncommon. Many state constitutions prohibit deficit spending, and the bulk of government debt in the United States has been incurred at the federal level. But, in a rather indirect sense, the fiscal activities of state and local governments do affect the federal budget, for their fiscal problems, together with opposition by their respective publics to increased state and local taxes, can lead to calls for federal revenues to fill the gaps left by tax-limitation measures. Some commentators have, indeed, pointed to the paradoxical possibility that antipathy toward impersonal government and high taxes will lead to greater centralization at the state and federal levels.

Separation of Powers

When studying economic policy making in the United States, foreign observers usually look first to the budgetary process and in particular to the conflicts between Congress and the president that the spending power produces. Given the American concern with macropolicy and with controlling spending, this tension is perhaps not surprising. Indeed, as Chapters 8–11 showed, battles over spending are the very essence of presidential-congressional politics. Much of the conflict derives from a simple constitutional fact: Congress, and in particular the House of Representatives, was given the power to raise taxes and appropriate money for the executive branch to spend. As the role of the government has expanded, so the need for institutional mechanisms to coordinate and control spending has also increased. Thus, the president and Congress have improved and streamlined their budgetary bureaucracies, each intent on providing the other branch with a coherent spending and taxing policy.

On the executive side, the first important item of legislation was the 1921 Budget and Accounting Act that created the Bureau of the Budget, a bureaucracy designed to provide improved budget advice and review for the president. At first, the Bureau of the Budget was intended to help control spending—an objective in line with the prevailing laissez-faire or liberal philosophy that spending was essentially a bad thing. All changed with the coming of the New Deal, when, under the leadership of Franklin Roosevelt, the bureau became a partisan for increased spending in opposition to a sometimes hostile Congress. The bureau was also formally incorporated into the Executive Office of the President during this period, and its staff increased from 40 to more than 600.

The next significant law was the 1946 Full Employment Act, a piece of legislation that effectively endorsed Keynesian demand management by pledging the federal government to full-employment policies. Among other measures, the legislation created the Council of Economic Advisers, a further White House innovation but this time one designed to encourage presidents to pursue "rational economic policies to foster and promote free competition, to avoid economic fluctuations or to diminish the effects thereof, and to maintain employment, production, and purchasing power." The 1946 act also mandated the president to produce an annual economic report to document economic performance over the previous year and to provide Congress with a program for the coming year.

Since 1946, successive presidents have experimented further with the budget machinery, usually to inject rationality into burgeoning federal budgets. Lyndon Johnson ordered the adoption of planning-programming-budgeting systems (PPBS), effectively a technique to link spending with preconceived planning priorities. Jimmy Carter, in turn, adopted zero-base budgeting, or budget plans organized from the bottom up according to spending limits rather than according to specific program objectives. The latter adapts spending to (say) the construction of so many miles of interstate highway or to a particular objective in the space program and thus tends toward expenditure rising incrementally. The point about these and other innovations is that they reflect presidents' growing concern with the sheer size of the budget and the need to present Congress with a coherent spending plan.

Congress has responded with its own innovations. The 1946 legislation, for example, created a joint Economic Committee consisting of seven senators and seven House members to provide Congress with a total view of the economy and aid the legislature's response to presidential initiatives. More recently, the 1974 Budget Reform Act created a Congressional Budget Office, together with Budget Committees, to provide House and Senate with a coherent view of budget making and instill a sense of spending priority rather than to proceed incrementally as had been the case in the past. In the first few years of this innovation, congressional control appeared to improve, but fundamental problems of budget making soon reappeared. These resulted simply because Congress's role is negative rather than positive—or, as noted in Chapter 9, "the president proposes and Congress disposes."

Economic management is first and foremost an executive responsibility. Until the reforms, the role of Congress was confined to trimming, tinkering with, or otherwise modifying the president's budget on an ad hoc basis. After the reforms, the congressional budget committees played a more prominent role that almost certainly made the budget process more cumbersome. The budget timetable has remained essentially the same: In the spring of Year One, the departments and agencies submit their expenditure estimates to OMB. OMB then spends several months reviewing—and often cutting—these estimates until the president formally submits the budget to Congress in late January of Year Two. During the ensuing nine months, the budget committees work with the legislative and appropriations committees to reconcile competing interests and objectives until a final budget resolution or reconciliation is passed in September before the beginning of the financial year on October 1.

During the first years of the Carter presidency, the system seemed to work moderately well, but the economy then was growing rapidly and deficits ultimately came quite close to the president's projections. Between 1980 and 1995, the situation was transformed, first by deepening recession and later by deficits far exceeding expectations. This period also brought the most radical and frenzied activity in the politics and procedures of congressional budget making ever experienced.

The turmoil started in the first few weeks of the Reagan administration, when the president submitted major changes for spending in 1982, 1983, and 1984. Large increases in defense spending and cuts in domestic programs were proposed. Parallel, quite radical cuts in taxation were also introduced into Congress. On the budget side, a new resolution, known as Gramm-Latta I (after Delbert L. Latta, the ranking Republican on the House Budget Committee, and Phil Gramm, a leading Democratic conservative on the committee), instructed fifteen House committees and fourteen Senate committees on how their budgets would be slashed over the next three years. The amounts involved—$36, $47, and $56 billion in each of these years—were huge. Finally, the resolution was framed in such a way that any subsequent supplementary appropriations would be very difficult to achieve. In reaction to these draconian measures, congressional committees submitted a mass of new legislation designed to reassert traditional congressional power. The administration, fearing a sudden increase in spending, accepted a modified resolution (Gramm-Latta II), which was finally passed, very speedily, in August.

Although the final bill imposed less extensive cuts than those originally planned, this particular budget experience was almost the antithesis of the slow, incremental, deliberative process for which Congress is famous. In retrospect, it is clear that President Reagan was fortunate to have the support of three key groups in Congress—the conservative Republicans, conservative Southern Democrats (the "Boll Weevils"), and, crucially, moderate Republicans (the "Gypsy Moths"). This coalition also helped the administration achieve quite startling tax cuts in the same session. Always a fragile arrangement, the coalition showed signs of collapse even by late 1981, and after 1982 the administration was much less successful in handling Congress.

Within Congress, the traditional centers of budgetary power, the appropriations committees and subcommittees, reasserted their influence. During his last few years in office, Reagan found it easier to deal directly with these committees rather than work through the budget committees, which were prone to tinker endlessly with the details of the budget. The events of 1981 were, in other words, exceptional. The experience showed, however, that Congress was at least capable of rapid response to presidential economic initiative. It also demonstrated the growing influence of the Office of Management and Budget, which, under the leadership of David Stockman, assumed a central position as designer and as manager of government-spending priorities.

The problem of dealing with the deficit was sufficiently serious to inspire Congress, under pressure from the administration, to pass the Gramm-Rudman-Hollings Deficit Reduction Act in 1985. By imposing on Congress a timetable for mandatory spending cuts, the law would indeed have solved the budget deficit, with major cuts falling on defense and the discretionary programs. In 1986, however, the Supreme Court declared the mandatory provisions of the law unconstitutional violations of the separation of powers. As a result, the legislation became merely advisory and produced much smaller cuts than originally anticipated.

George Bush faced a Democratic Congress intent on defending a range of entitlement and other domestic programs. In each of Bush's four years in office, Congress and the president were at loggerheads on the budget. That lack of progress, together with a weakening economy, resulted in the ballooning of the deficit during the 1989–1992 period (Figure 15.2).

Budget drama continued with the first Clinton administration. During his first two years in office, things went relatively smoothly. Congress was still in the hands of the Democrats, the economy was growing steadily, and the president's budget included expenditure cuts that helped reduce the budget deficit during 1993 (Figure 15.2). All changed with the election of a Republican Congress in 1994, however. Under the leadership of House Speaker Newt Gingrich, the Republicans were intent on extensive cuts in federal social spending for fiscal year 1996. The president and Congress failed to agree on a budget by the October 1995 deadline, and this stalemate resulted in a much publicized partial shutdown of the federal government. "Nonessential" workers were laid off, national parks closed, and the crisis was not resolved until early 1996.

These events were not repeated in 1996, mainly because of the political costs to all parties of being seen as uncooperative during an election year. During 1997 and 1998, a buoyant economy helped reduce the annual deficit to zero, and budget crises took second place to other aspects of presidential-congressional relations—not least the president's serious personal and political problems. Nonetheless, future economic downturns will surely return conflicts over the budget to the center of the political stage. This is especially true in an era of divided government.

The economic problems of the 1980s and 1990s highlighted another important institutional relationship that is peculiarly American: the unique political position of the American central bank, the Federal Reserve System. Created in 1913, the Federal Reserve is a "decentralized" central bank consisting of twelve Federal Reserve Districts governed by a board in Washington. Congress deliberately gave the board some autonomy from the president, and in recent years, the chairmen of the board have asserted their independence to some effect. This is important because the Federal Reserve has special responsibility for implementing monetary policy and in particular for setting interest-rate levels. With budget deficits increasing, one recent chairman, Paul Volcker, insisted on controlling the money supply through a policy of high interest rates. Although at first the Reagan administration accepted the Federal Reserve's policy in this area, by late 1982, serious disagreement had emerged between Volcker and Donald Regan, the Treasury secretary. Volcker continued to insist on a tight money policy, whereas some members of the administration wanted some relaxation to help lift the economy out of recession. Later, Volcker became a vocal critic of the rapidly appreciating dollar, but the administration generally viewed this as a problem for other countries. In these countries, central banks, if not the creatures of executives, are often significantly less autonomous than the Federal Reserve System.

George Bush had an easier time with a Federal Reserve under the chairmanship of Alan Greenspan—although the president did call for a more rapid reduction in interest rates during the 1991–1992 recession than the Federal Reserve eventually sanctioned. Greenspan continued as chairman during the Clinton administration. Bill Clinton was fortunate, however, that during the whole of his first term, the economy grew steadily without threatening inflation. As a result, interest rates were kept relatively low, and the Federal Reserve's fine-tuning of the economy remained essentially noncontroversial. During Clinton's second term, however, deepening crisis in the world economy again raised the political salience of the Federal Reserve and eventually culminated in 1998 in calls for coordinated interest-rate cuts among all the richer countries, led by the United States, to alleviate the problem.

Economic Policy and Public Expectations

In many respects, the economic policy making system resembles the social policy system. In both, the chief executive has the major responsibility for policy formulation and implementation, and in both he or she faces competition from other centers of power—notably Congress, executive departments and agencies, state and local governments, and organized interests. There are, however, some important qualitative differences between the two policy areas. Economic policy is obviously more important in the sense that most other domestic and foreign policies depend on it. All parties and politicians have interests in economic performance, and all believe that the federal government must play a key role in economic management. They may disagree—sometimes radically—on what that role should be, but no one disputes the need for economic policy.

Social policy, in contrast, is considered by many on the right not to be a legitimate concern of the federal government. The great paradox of social policy is the incontrovertible fact that dozens of federal programs exist in the absence of central coordination and control. Control problems apply to economic policy, too, of course, but not in quite the same way. Measures of economic performance—inflation, growth, interest-rate levels, the deficit, unemployment—exist to provide a focus of activity for policymakers, as does the budgetary process itself. Nonetheless, macroeconomic management is shared among at least three major institutions—presidency, Congress, and Federal Reserve—which is highly unusual in comparative context. And microeconomic policy making is as confused and incoherent as social policy. What the two policy systems do share in common is that both are attempting to solve apparently intractable problems. Most other countries are experiencing similar difficulties of economic and social management, but in few are institutional arrangements organized in such an apparently inconvenient manner.

In conclusion, some reference to the growing consensus on economic management during the late 1990s should be mentioned. Much of this consensus revolves around two themes. The first is the almost universal perception that the budget must be kept in surplus without increasing taxation. Holding this consensus together may prove relatively easy while the economy is growing. Should it falter, however (as it always has in the past), the institutional conflicts inherent in the American system will receive fresh impetus. The second and related dimension to the consensus is the wide acceptance that free markets at home and abroad are the only mechanisms that can produce lasting prosperity. This means less government interference at home and the achievement of open markets in international trade.

Although every recent administration has been committed to both premises, it is clear that preaching the merits of limited government cannot easily be reconciled with the fact that the demands on government programs remain high. A felicitous combination of circumstances in the late 1990s may have temporarily solved the budget deficit problem, but the underlying dynamics of the separation of powers and complex and conflicting public expectations of government have not changed. Americans continue to expect good health care, pensions, and education as well as secure and well-paying jobs. Moreover, they hold the federal government accountable for economic errors that undermine these objectives. The distributional conflicts that are the heart of economic policy remain and will surely continue to test American political institutions and processes for many years to come.

Further Reading

A general review of economic policy is provided by Paul Peretz (ed.), *The Politics of American Economic Policy Making* (New York: M. E. Sharpe, 1996). On the budget and deficits, see Robert Reischauer (ed.), *Setting National Priorities: Budget Choices for the Next Century* (Washington, DC: Brookings Institution, 1997). On economic ideas, see Peter Hall, *The Political Power of Economic Ideas* (Princeton: Princeton University Press, 1998). The annual *Economic Report of the President* (Washington, DC: U.S. Government Printing Office, yearly) provides a clear account of recent and predicted U.S. economic performance.

16

The American World Role

Oliver Cromwell once said that a man-of-war is the best ambassador. That's not really quite true. As the negotiations with North Korea proved, the best approach is a good ambassador backed up by a man-of-war.

—Defense Secretary William Perry, 1994

Today, as an old order passes, the new world is more free but less stable. Communism's collapse has called forth old animosities and new dangers. Clearly America must continue to lead the world we did so much to make.

—President Clinton, Inaugural Address, 1992

Since the 1940s, the United States has been transformed from one of six or seven world powers with a standing army of under 200,000 and few foreign alliances or military bases into a country with a military machine of 1.5 million men and women under arms (over 250,000 of whom are stationed overseas), alliances with nearly fifty countries, and unrivaled military and diplomatic status and capacity. From being isolationist and contemptuous of the "corruption" and imperialism of the old European powers, the United States is itself, in spite of recent reverses, now in a position to exploit and dominate other countries and, unlike the prewar powers, literally to determine the fate of all humankind.

The country's political processes and institutions have not always handled these new responsibilities well. Indeed, one school of thought argues that a country infused with a past characterized by a combination of isolationism and idealism is ill suited to playing the role of world police officer. Certainly, there have been many foreign and military policy mistakes in the postwar era, including the Vietnam War, which caused serious domestic conflict and terrible suffering and instability throughout Indochina. This chapter does not, however, concentrate on normative questions of fortune and folly in American foreign policy. Instead, the discussion focuses on the policymaking process and on the constraints imposed on foreign policy by institutional arrangements and public opinion.

The Institutional Context

As with social and economic affairs, it is somewhat misleading to refer to an American foreign *policy,* for there are at least three distinct types of foreign and defense policies. There is, first, strategic foreign policy, or the general stance of the United States in relation to other countries over time. Scholars have been quick to identify two competing themes in the postwar period—realist and idealist. Realism is, simply, the pursuit of "national self-interest" and is associated with international power politics and the implementation of policies that have clear military, diplomatic, or economic benefits.[1] Idealism, in contrast, injects a moral or normative element into policy, as implied by such presidential rhetoric as "making the world safe for democracy" or achieving "peace with honor" in Vietnam. These two characterizations of strategic policy are discussed later. Although strategic policy is influenced by the broader society and polity, its main institutional context comprises the presidency, the National Security Council (NSC), and the State Department.

Second, crisis management is a crucial part of foreign policy. Since World War II, a number of conflicts—the Berlin airlift, Suez, the Cuban missile crisis, numerous military actions in Indochina, American reactions to military activity in the Middle East including the Gulf War, and intervention in Bosnian and Kosovo—have involved the United States in quick crisis-management decisions. Generally, the presidency and National Security Council are the institutional foci of these decisions, although the longer a crisis drags on, the more likely are Congress and the public to become involved. Just this happened with the yearlong 1979–1980 Iranian hostage crisis.

Third, logistical or structural defense policy involves the deployment of billions of dollars worth of materiel and over a quarter million personnel around the globe. As was established in earlier chapters, this process entails voters, organized interests (defense contractors), state and local governments, congressional commit-tees, and the more obvious institutions of the Department of De-fense and the presidency. This policy system is much more open and accessible than strategic and crisis-management policy, but it is almost certainly less fragmented and pluralistic than the processes associated with social or economic policy. Oligopolistic defense in-dustries are protected by government contracts,[2] and the defense budget has a powerful base of support in Congress.

These three contrasting institutional settings for foreign and de-fense policy do impinge on one another. Logistics and weapons sys-tems can influence strategic thinking (the cruise missile) and crisis management (the Iranian hostage crisis, the bombing of Libya, the Gulf War), and strategic considerations are obviously important determinants of logistical policy. Similarly, crisis management is profoundly affected by the strategic context. During the Cuban missile crisis, for example, President Kennedy referred constantly to the infringement of an American sphere of influence (the West-ern Hemisphere) that was a long-established part of American for-eign policy.

How has decisionmaking in each of these policy areas changed over time? Perhaps obviously, crisis management has always pri-marily been the prerogative of the president and his closest aides in the NSC. Quick response requires tightly knit decisionmaking structures, and as commander-in-chief, the president has the con-stitutional as well as political position to assume the leadership of such structures. This does not mean that the president and the aides are completely insulated from the outside world during a cri-sis and make their choices according to strictly rational criteria. As Graham Allison has shown in his brilliant study of the Cuban mis-sile crisis, at least three competing models of decisionmaking can be used to explain the events of the crisis, two of which put great premium on outside information and political and bureaucratic procedures and pressures.[3] But compared with other policymaking processes in American government, crisis management is relatively free from political and societal pressures.

The main development in strategic foreign policy making in the postwar period has been the gradual centralization of power in the president and NSC at the cost of State Department influence. This shift appeared most graphically in the eclipse of some recent secretaries of state in the shadow of national security advisers—most notably Henry Kissinger under Nixon (although he eventually became secretary of state) and Zbigniew Brzezinski under Carter. Presidents have increasingly eschewed the State Department and its secretaries, because they can represent independent sources of authority and control over particular issues and areas. Certain countries or policy options are championed within the department, and it is simply not convenient for presidents to have to join battle with the professional bureaucrats when foreign policy is formulated. White House–departmental antagonism occurs in other areas, of course, but within foreign policy, presidents do have the option of, if not ignoring the State Department, at least of bypassing it. The State Department effectively has no domestic constituency, and its officials are unusually neutral and apolitical, versed as they are in the arts of diplomacy and moderation. Thus, whereas presidents may find it almost impossible to disregard the Departments of Defense, Agriculture, or Commerce, they can almost do this in the case of State.

Foreign policy is also more insulated from the other "traditional" centers of power in American government. House and, particularly, Senate Foreign Relations Committees are important forums for discussion and criticism, but their function is qualitatively different from (say) those of the Armed Services and Agriculture Committees with their entrenched relationships with big spending bureaus and powerful corporate clients.

In other words, foreign policy decisionmaking is different. Within the White House, the NSC is uniquely important, and, in theory at least, consistency and coherence are almost certainly more achievable in foreign affairs than in many domestic areas. It may be, of course, that clarity and coherence can lead to greater errors of judgment and strategy, and that more pluralistic arrangements would lead to greater moderation. But it should be noted that in *cross-national* context, American presidents are not particularly free from institutional and political constraints in foreign policy making.

Public and congressional opinion has been exerted on presidents with increasing intensity since the events of Vietnam and Watergate. Earlier chapters have catalogued some of these constraints, including the 1973 War Powers Act. President Reagan's 1983 remark, when he heard of British Prime Minister Thatcher's carefully disguised visit to the Falklands, that he "couldn't even go to church in secret" reveals a great deal. Presidents and their policymakers are constantly exposed to public scrutiny. They may be able to secrete themselves away in the NSC and plan general strategy, and they may also be relatively free from direct and immediate congressional or bureaucratic pressure. But they still must operate in the context of the American political system, with all that this implies in terms of openness and accessibility. For example, individual ethnic groups, such as Americans of Cuban or Jewish origin, constantly monitor the administration's policy toward Cuba or Israel. Right-wing caucuses, such as Jesse Helms's National Congressional Club, campaign strongly in favor of a hard line toward Cuba. Since the Vietnam War, the involvement of American troops in counterinsurgency wars abroad has become especially difficult because of the ever present potential for serious domestic political opposition. This was graphically illustrated in the case of the U.S.-led NATO bombing of Kosovo in 1999. Using air power alone to solve the problem was directly a result of the domestic political costs of the alternative—American casualties resulting from the use of ground troops.

In addition, the openness of the American system can lead to the conflation of domestic and foreign policy in ways that are unusual in some other countries. Presidents have been accused of using foreign interventions to divert attention from their domestic troubles. Such allegations were leveled at President Reagan following the U.S. invasion of Grenada in 1983 and at Bill Clinton following his decision to attack terrorist installations in Sudan and Afghanistan in 1998.

The openness of the official system has led to the evolution of an "unofficial" foreign policy system on at least two occasions. Such was the case during the period 1969–1973 when illegal acts were committed in Southeast Asia. More dramatic were the events of the Iran-Contra affair, which involved the creation of an alternative foreign policy machinery in the White House under the guidance of NSC adviser John Poindexter, CIA chief William Casey, and Colonel Oliver North. By agreeing to secure the release of American hostages in Lebanon by selling arms to the Iranians, the proceeds from which would go to help the Contras fighting for the overthrow of the Sandinista regime in Nicaragua, these officials were acting contrary to the spirit and to the letter of the law. President Reagan and Secretary of State George Shultz either did not know of these events or were only vaguely aware of them, a situation that reflected the extent to which the president had lost control of this particular policy system during his second term. But the culprits in the Iran-Contra affair were discovered, thus perhaps demonstrating the greater degree to which public and press opinion can expose the errors of foreign policy compared with the situation in Britain and France.

American Foreign Policy in the Post–Cold War World

Until recently, the most striking feature of American foreign policy was the overwhelming influence of the realist, as opposed to idealist, school. In the context of the Cold War, American policy was couched in terms of self-interest—indeed, in terms of national survival. The ideological struggle between East and West centered on territory (in Europe and in the Third World) and on economic interest (was capitalism or communism to be the model for world development?). During the early and mid-1980s, the Reagan administration elevated this competitive struggle to the top of the policy agenda. Increased defense spending and military action in the Middle East, Grenada, Libya, and Central America were all justified in terms of the national interest. By the late 1980s, signs that this particular perspective on international relations was becoming obsolete were clearly evident, and by 1992, conditions had changed to the point that presidents were making reference to what was called "the new world order."

The crucial change was, of course, the demise of the Soviet Union and more generally of communism as a viable alternative to capitalism. Even in China, the last major redoubt of political communism, a rejection of the centralized resource allocation of economic communism had occurred. Communism's collapse did not transform the realist focus of American foreign policy. The Gulf War, for example, was fought at least in part to protect the West's oil supplies. But it did greatly complicate the business of identifying where, exactly, America's national interest lay. When there was an identifiable enemy whose economic and political system was so obviously alien to Americans, justifying high defense spending and the deployment of U.S. troops abroad was relatively easy. Today, such justification is harder. Instead of appealing to self-interest, the new world order appeals to humanitarian motives. In Somalia, Bosnia, and most dramatically in Kosovo, no American interests

FIGURE 16.1   Perceptions of the Soviet Union and Attitudes on Defense
Spending

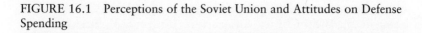

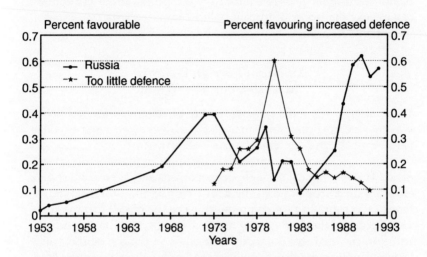

SOURCE: William R. Thompson, "Foreign Policy, the End of the Cold War, and the 1992 Election," in Bryan C. Jones, *The New American Politics: Reflections on Political Change and the Clinton Administration* (Boulder, CO: Westview, 1995), figure 11.4.

were directly threatened, yet American troops, aircraft, and ships
were deployed under the auspices of a UN-sponsored humanitarian
mission. It remains to be seen whether the United States can continue to play this role—especially in terms of winning the support
of the American people.

Public attitudes toward defense spending and how these relate to
the Cold War are amply demonstrated by Figure 16.1. Note the
dramatic change in attitudes toward the Soviet Union in the late
1970s and the early 1980s and the associated rise in the need for
increased defense expenditure. When the late 1980s and the early
1990s brought the collapse of communism in Eastern Europe, a
steep rise in public regard for the Soviet Union (or Russia) and a
sharp decline in the perceived need for defense spending occurred.
Defense spending did indeed decrease following these events. Ex-

pressed as a percentage of GDP, defense spending fell from well over 6 percent in the mid-1980s to an estimated 3 percent in 1998 (Table 16.1). Defense spending is now no longer the largest item in the federal budget. As recently as 1960, it accounted for more than 50 percent of all federal spending. By 1998, it had shrunk to under 17 percent (Table 16.1).

Even so, the United States remains easily the world's most powerful military force. In terms of rapid deployment, the United States has no peer. Only U.S. forces can be moved rapidly around the world to meet a crisis or emergency. No other country has this capacity. This fact alone puts pressure on American politicians to embrace global policing and to take on a humanitarian, rather than realist, role. Post–Gulf War U.S. involvement in Somalia, Bosnia, and Kosovo is best understood in these terms. In the future, action may additionally be taken against international terrorist groups and individuals, such as occurred with the 1998 American attacks on terrorist facilities in Sudan and Afghanistan. Finally, the American role in brokering peace, whether it be in Israel, Northern Ireland, or Bosnia, is facilitated by a background of U.S. military and economic power. Such missions will no doubt continue. The danger comes when the costs of intervention, whether measured in terms of expenditure or in terms of American lives, become too great for public opinion to tolerate. Should this happen, there is always the possibility that America will revert to the isolationist stance typical of the pre-1941 period. So far, however, internationalism has prevailed. Supporters of isolationism in both the Democratic Party (usually on foreign economic policy issues) and in the Republican Party certainly exist, but no president of any party has espoused the cause. Even the post-1994 Republican leadership in Congress, including House Speakers Newt Gingrich and Dennis Hastert and Senate majority leader Trent Lott, broadly supported President Clinton's foreign policy positions.

Conclusion

It is important to stress that realist thinking has not been *replaced* with idealist values. It is more that both are now important in explaining the motives behind American actions abroad. As emphasized earlier, militarily, the United States is now more privileged than ever before. In the late 1980s, who would have remotely

TABLE 16.1 Defense Spending as a Percentage of Federal Outlays and GDP, 1960–1998

	Defense Spending (percentage of)	
	Federal Outlays	Gross Domestic Product
1960	52.2	9.5
1965	42.8	7.5
1966	43.2	7.9
1967	45.4	9.0
1968	46.0	9.7
1969	44.9	8.9
1970	41.8	8.3
1971	37.5	7.5
1972	34.3	6.9
1973	31.2	6.0
1974	29.5	5.7
1975	26.0	5.7
1976	24.1	5.3
1977	23.8	5.1
1978	22.8	4.8
1979	23.1	4.8
1980	22.7	5.1
1981	23.2	5.3
1982	24.9	5.9
1983	26.0	6.3
1984	26.7	6.2
1985	26.7	6.4
1986	27.6	6.5
1987	28.1	6.3
1988	27.3	6.0
1989	26.6	5.9
1990	23.9	5.5
1991	20.6	4.8
1992	21.6	5.0
1993	20.7	4.6
1994	19.3	4.1
1995	17.9	3.8
1996	17.0	3.6
1997	16.9	3.4
1998 (est.)	16.8	3.2

SOURCE: *Statistical Abstract of the United States, 1998* (Washington, DC, 1998), table 542.

guessed that the United States would, by 1997, be negotiating with Russia over the eastward expansion of NATO? The United States is more circumscribed in terms of defining its new mission and in building domestic support for an active role abroad. This applies to "traditional" foreign policy and to foreign *economic* policy. As indicated earlier, the United States now operates in a much more interdependent world. Important questions of foreign policy are raised in many international economic activities involving the United States—its relations with the European Union, negotiations over the General Agreement on Tariffs and Trade (GATT) and the North American Free Trade Area (NAFTA), and contributions to the International Monetary Fund and the World Bank. Clearly these issues have a much greater input from domestic politics than do most traditional foreign policy areas.

This interdependence often makes it difficult to distinguish clearly between different policy systems, and there is no doubt that it makes the business of government more burdensome. Given the external constraints imposed by interdependence and the internal pressures resulting from a fragmented and open political system, it is not surprising that presidents have sought to centralize decision-making in the White House. Such efforts are likely to continue, because external constraints are growing rather than diminishing. Divided government aggravates the tendency for Congress to provide an "alternative" foreign policy. And since Vietnam, the public expects low-cost (in terms of American lives and public expenditure) but effective foreign policy. Apart from the Gulf War, however, the foreign policy system has not been subject to a severe test for some years. It remains to be seen how a much more open and constrained policy environment will perform should decisionmaking be subject to such a test either in foreign or foreign economic policy in the years to come.

Notes

1. The classic account of the realist position is by Hans J. Morgenthau, *In Defense of the National Interest* (New York: Knopf, 1951).

2. The top eight arms contractors in 1996 were Lockheed Martin, Boeing/McDonnell Douglas, Tenneco, General Motors, Northrop Grumman, Raytheon, General Electric, and Loral.

3. Graham T. Allison, *Essence of Decision: Explaining the Cuban Missile Crisis* (Boston: Little, Brown, 1971).

Further Reading

A textbook treatment of foreign policy is provided by Thomas L. Brewer and Lorne Teitelbaum, *American Foreign Policy: A Contemporary Introduction* (New York: Prentice-Hall, 1997). For an analysis of the problems facing American foreign policy in the post–Cold War era, see Robert J. Lieber, *Eagle Adrift* (New York: Addison-Wesley; Longman, 1977). Also see Peter Trubowitz, *Defining the National Interest: Conflict and Change in American Foreign Policy* (Chicago: University of Chicago Press, 1998). Eric Nordlinger, in *Isolationism Reconfigured* (Princeton: Princeton University Press, 1995), provides a defense of the neoisolationist position.

17

The American Political System at Century's End

With people whom we distrust, it is as difficult to do business as to search for scientific truth, arrive at religious harmony, or attain justice. When one must first question words and intentions, and start from the premise that everything said and written is meant to offer us an illusion in place of truth, life becomes strangely complicated.

—Charles Wagner

Assessing the American Polity

No political system is perfect. Most regimes are fragile in the extreme, lasting no more than a few years or decades. Others may be longer-lived but fail the tests of equality, justice, and democracy. Some simply fail to provide citizens with basic protection against violence and disorder, or with the minimum of food and shelter necessary for human survival. By these very elemental measures, the American system has been highly successful. The basic constitutional structure has remained unchanged for more than 200 years. Few regimes are as stable, and none has been more successful at generating wealth. Violence has always been a feature of American society, but only very rarely has it translated into politically motivated civil disorder. Inequalities of wealth and income are considerable—and certainly greater than in comparable developed countries. This problem should not be underestimated, but wealth and income inequalities have never threatened the stability of the system.

Measuring justice and democracy is notoriously difficult, of course, but the United States almost certainly scores high on both counts compared with other countries. No one questions the availability of institutional mechanisms for democracy in America or the opportunity for participation in politics. In the sense that public discourse is essentially free from government controls and basic rights are protected by the courts, the United States also does more to promote justice and equity under law than most countries.

Until quite recently, a major criticism directed at the system was the apparent inability of the federal government successfully to manage economic affairs, including the capacity to compete with other countries and to balance the budget. By the late 1990s, however, the budget was balanced, and U.S. economic performance stood out as a beacon of light in a turbulent and unpredictable international economy.

Why, given this record of success, do Americans continue to expect so much from government while simultaneously distrusting their government and public officials? And what are the likely consequences of this new public philosophy of disenchantment? Earlier chapters pointed to the answers to these questions, most of which concern the relationship between the institutional structure of American government on the one hand and the unique American political culture on the other. This relationship is now examined in more detail.

Institutional Fragmentation

The founding fathers deliberately created an institutionally fragmented political system in order to limit the possibility of power being usurped either by a single person or by a particular group or faction. Although they were brilliantly successful in achieving this objective, the resulting fragmentation has made the business of governing problematical in the United States. Earlier chapters showed how federalism and the separation of powers have combined to make it inordinately difficult to create clear and unambiguous public policies. Comparison with those countries that lack these institutional checks makes the point.

In New Zealand and the United Kingdom, for example, governments intent on transforming the public sector by privatization and the application of market principles to government programs have achieved almost all their objectives. The progress of similar reforms in the United States, even with the support of first Republican and then Democratic presidents, has been much slower. Congress and presidents have found it difficult to agree on how, exactly, the reforms should be implemented. Progress at the state and local level has depended on the policies of individual states and localities and has thus varied from area to area.

More serious have been failures associated with substantive areas of public policy such as health care and campaign finance reform. With both, the separate constituencies of president and Congress have worked against each other to such an extent that little has been achieved—even though a broad consensus exists that reform is urgently needed in both areas. Recent changes in the party system and in Congress have, if anything, served to aggravate rather than soothe the effects of jurisdictional fragmentation by making compromise and bargaining between president and Congress more fractious and conflictual than it used to be.

Conflict between the two branches reached an embarrassing climax with the impeachment of President Clinton in 1998. In spite of the weak constitutional case against the president and low levels of public support for congressional action, a partisan House of Representatives persisted and eventually voted for articles of impeachment in late 1998. Trial in the Senate, although conducted with some dignity, produced the outcome that all observers expected—acquittal. Many foreign commentators were puzzled by this series of events. How could a great nation such as the United States embroil itself in such a damaging confrontation between the two major branches of government, for what looked like such irrelevant offenses? Part of the answer must lie in the high expectations many Americans continue to hold for those in high office, despite a long history of wrongdoing in government. But impeachment was also facilitated by the fundamental antagonism between president and Congress that constitutional arrangements permit.

As was shown in Chapter 12, the Supreme Court has been unable to resolve these differences by brokering conflict between the two branches. This is mainly because the Court only has negative powers. It is meant to resolve differences between the branches when a matter of great constitutional interest is raised, such as the insistence by the Nixon White House not to release the Watergate tapes to Congress. When the differences are *political,* the Court can do little. In addition, in those areas such as federalism and the conscience issues where Court decisions may have made public policy less ambiguous, the Rehnquist Court has, for the most part, kept out of the "political thicket" by arguing cases on narrow rather than broad constitutional grounds. This approach may reflect the fact that the public is itself deeply divided on such issues as abortion and affirmative action.

Open Government and Pluralistic Politics

There is no doubt that many of the problems associated with jurisdictional fragmentation have been aggravated by what has become a much more accessible and pluralistic political system. As earlier chapters showed, Americans can voice their interests and grievances more effectively than ever before. This openness applies both to public opinion broadly defined and to the activities of organized interests. Public opinion makes itself felt in a number of ways, whether it be through the ballot box, members of Congress reading their mail or watching the polls, or presidents following their approval ratings. The openness of the system had reached such a state by 1998 that it almost came to resemble caricature, as the broadcast of the taped deposition by President Clinton to the Starr inquiry showed.

In addition, organized interests are active at every level of politics. Corporations, labor unions, and promotional groups all work hard to protect and promote their interests. Through the use of "soft money" advertising, some groups add to such issues as abortion and affirmative action an adversarial tone that may project opinions more extreme than those held by the public at large.

Furthermore, an extensive and highly commercial public media are constantly hungry for news and political happenings. Their influence permeates almost all public discourse, and they now play a key role in election campaigns at every level. No one disputes the value of the freedom to disseminate information, but the particular way the media operate in the United States (and indeed are used by well-financed political campaigns) can have the effect of distorting and misleading, rather than educating, the public.[1] Although openness is increasingly a characteristic of public affairs in comparable political systems, nowhere has it developed to the degree prevalent in the United States. A good illustration of this is the attention paid to U.S. service personnel involved in foreign wars. When personnel are injured, captured, or lost, television crews rush to the affected families for national coverage. In France and the UK, similarly affected families are rarely the subject of intense media attention.

Governments often intervene to reduce publicity. Unlike in the United States, secrecy can usually be assured if necessary.

Limited Government and Public Expectations

Open government and a pluralistic politics (some commentators even call it hyperpluralism) thrive when it is possible to access a range of political institutions operating at several levels. In other words, this combination seems almost designed to raise the expectations of mass publics and organized interests alike. The great paradox is, of course, that institutional fragmentation was deliberately instituted by the founding fathers to *limit* government, not to increase public expectations of what it can do. Yet the philosophy of limited government continues to this day. Surveys repeatedly show that Americans distrust the state and are more imbued with notions of self-reliance than are the citizens of comparable countries. This attitude shows itself in Americans' distrust of big government and in a general aversion to taxing and spending.

When it comes to the federal government's provision of *specific* benefits, however, Americans expect a great deal. Indeed, a wide range of services and programs provided by the federal government have now achieved the status of citizen's *rights,* rather than benefits that may be withdrawn should conditions warrant it. This notion of entitlement certainly applies to Social Security, Medicare, and many other social programs. In addition, few seriously expect that the federal government's role in protecting the environment, the consumer, and the employee in the workplace will suddenly end in the near future.

Disputes over the exact extent of this role and how it should be shared with the states will continue, but most Americans expect some leadership role from the federal government in these areas. Similar disputes surround the conscience issues, such as abortion, penal standards, and affirmative action. Many also look to the federal government to address the growing income and wealth inequality that has become a prominent feature of American society. Few would argue that such inequality is in the public interest, but correcting it through government action, such as by legislating significant increases in the minimum wage or taxing the wealthy, is clearly incompatible with a limited-government philosophy.

The same contradictions surround America's world role. Most Americans expect the United States to play a key role both in protecting democracy and freedom and in maintaining a stable and healthy international trading environment. At the same time, many are deeply ambivalent about the costs of such actions, including the potential price paid in American lives and the economic costs of supporting such international bodies as the United Nations and the International Monetary Fund.

Reform and Renewal

As the quotation at the beginning of this chapter indicates, distrust can be damaging. Disillusionment with political processes and institutions can undermine the legitimacy of the political system. In many countries, it is just such sentiments that lead to a breakdown of the regime. Although regime change in the United States seems a very distant prospect, declining faith in the polity is viewed by most observers as a serious development. It greatly hinders efforts to institute and legitimize much needed reforms. In the worst-case scenario, disillusionment may help the political fortunes of extremists and demagogues. No sensible commentator believes that "solutions" to this problem exist in the sense that public expectations will suddenly be lowered or that Americans' attitudes toward government will miraculously be transformed. There is, however, no shortage of suggested reforms, most of which offer at least partial solutions.

One thing is certain—there is no constituency of support for fundamental constitutional change. Calls for the abolition of the separation of powers and the introduction of a parliamentary system have always fallen on deaf ears and will almost certainly continue to do so in the future.[2] Instead most commentators today call for changes in the way in which Americans think about politics. Quick-fix and gimmicky solutions should be replaced by longer-term thinking solutions. Hence, public officials and public discourse should be educating the public on the nature of policy commitments (such as the funding of Social Security) and on the need for individuals to take on more personal responsibility for their future (such as saving for retirement or educating their children).[3] In effect, these pleas ask for a rethinking of what citizens expect from government. In most instances, proponents think the public should be educated to expect less but to do more in the context of families and local communities to help each other.

The difficulty, of course, is that many of the problems that affect modern America are not amenable to family- or community-based solutions. Such objectives as affordable health care, a balanced budget, full employment, and an effective foreign policy can only be achieved through government. And when the economy falters or American interests are threatened by foreign powers, the electorate is quick to call for firm and decisive action from the federal government. The fundamental dilemma of attempting to reconcile raised public expectations with a deep suspicion of what government can and should do is, therefore, likely to remain the identifying feature of the American system for many years to come.

Notes

1. See the discussion in C. Eugene Steuerle, Edward M. Gramlich, Hugh Heclo, and Demetra Smith Nightingale, *The Government We Deserve: Responsive Democracy and Changing Expectations* (Washington, DC: Urban Institute, 1998), chap. 5.

2. See, in particular, Charles M. Hardin, *Presidential Power and Accountability: Towards a New Constitution* (Chicago: University of Chicago Press, 1974); James L. Sundquist, *Constitutional Reform and Effective Government* (Washington, DC: Brookings Institution, 1987).

3. See Steuerle et al., *The Government We Deserve*, chap. 6.

The Constitution of
the United States of America

We the people of the United States, in order to form a more perfect union, establish justice, insure domestic tranquility, provide for the common defense, promote the general welfare, and secure the blessings of liberty to ourselves and our posterity, do ordain and establish this Constitution for the United States of America.

Article I

Section 1.
All legislative powers herein granted shall be vested in a Congress of the United States, which shall consist of a Senate and House of Representatives.

Section 2.
The House of Representatives shall be composed of members chosen every second year by the people of the several states, and the electors in each state shall have the qualifications requisite for electors of the most numerous branch of the state legislature.

No person shall be a Representative who shall not have attained to the age of twenty five years, and been seven years a citizen of the United States, and who shall not, when elected, be an inhabitant of that state in which he shall be chosen.

Representatives and direct taxes shall be apportioned among the several states which may be included within this union, according to their respective numbers, which shall be determined by adding to the whole number of free persons, including those bound to service for a term of years, and excluding Indians not taxed, three fifths of all other Persons. The actual Enumeration shall be made within three years after the first meeting of the Congress of the United States, and within every subsequent term of ten years, in such manner as they shall by law direct. The number of Representatives shall not exceed one for every thirty thousand, but each state shall have at least one Representative; and until such enumeration shall be made, the state of New

Hampshire shall be entitled to chuse three, Massachusetts eight, Rhode Island and Providence Plantations one, Connecticut five, New York six, New Jersey four, Pennsylvania eight, Delaware one, Maryland six, Virginia ten, North Carolina five, South Carolina five, and Georgia three.

When vacancies happen in the Representation from any state, the executive authority thereof shall issue writs of election to fill such vacancies.

The House of Representatives shall choose their speaker and other officers; and shall have the sole power of impeachment.

Section 3.

The Senate of the United States shall be composed of two Senators from each state, chosen by the legislature thereof, for six years; and each Senator shall have one vote.

Immediately after they shall be assembled in consequence of the first election, they shall be divided as equally as may be into three classes. The seats of the Senators of the first class shall be vacated at the expiration of the second year, of the second class at the expiration of the fourth year, and the third class at the expiration of the sixth year, so that one third may be chosen every second year; and if vacancies happen by resignation, or otherwise, during the recess of the legislature of any state, the executive thereof may make temporary appointments until the next meeting of the legislature, which shall then fill such vacancies.

No person shall be a Senator who shall not have attained to the age of thirty years, and been nine years a citizen of the United States and who shall not, when elected, be an inhabitant of that state for which he shall be chosen.

The Vice President of the United States shall be President of the Senate, but shall have no vote, unless they be equally divided.

The Senate shall choose their other officers, and also a President pro tempore, in the absence of the Vice President, or when he shall exercise the office of President of the United States.

The Senate shall have the sole power to try all impeachments. When sitting for that purpose, they shall be on oath or affirmation. When the President of the United States is tried, the Chief Justice shall preside: And no person shall be convicted without the concurrence of two thirds of the members present.

Judgment in cases of impeachment shall not extend further than to removal from office, and disqualification to hold and enjoy any office of honor, trust or profit under the United States: but the party convicted shall nevertheless be liable and subject to indictment, trial, judgment and punishment, according to law.

Section 4.

The times, places and manner of holding elections for Senators and Representatives, shall be prescribed in each state by the legislature thereof; but the Congress may at any time by law make or alter such regulations, except as to the places of choosing Senators.

The Congress shall assemble at least once in every year, and such meeting shall be on the first Monday in December, unless they shall by law appoint a different day.

Section 5.

Each House shall be the judge of the elections, returns and qualifications of its own members, and a majority of each shall constitute a quorum to do business; but a smaller number may adjourn from day to day, and may be authorized to compel the attendance of absent members, in such manner, and under such penalties as each House may provide.

Each House may determine the rules of its proceedings, punish its members for disorderly behavior, and, with the concurrence of two thirds, expel a member.

Each House shall keep a journal of its proceedings, and from time to time publish the same, excepting such parts as may in their judgment require secrecy; and the yeas and nays of the members of either House on any question shall, at the desire of one fifth of those present, be entered on the journal.

Neither House, during the session of Congress, shall, without the consent of the other, adjourn for more than three days, nor to any other place than that in which the two Houses shall be sitting.

Section 6.

The Senators and Representatives shall receive a compensation for their services, to be ascertained by law, and paid out of the treasury of the United States. They shall in all cases, except treason, felony and breach of the peace, be privileged from arrest during their attendance at the session of their respective Houses, and in going to and returning from the same; and for any speech or debate in either House, they shall not be questioned in any other place.

No Senator or Representative shall, during the time for which he was elected, be appointed to any civil office under the authority of the United States, which shall have been created, or the emoluments whereof shall have been increased during such time: and no person holding any office under the United States, shall be a member of either House during his continuance in office.

Section 7.

All bills for raising revenue shall originate in the House of Representatives; but the Senate may propose or concur with amendments as on other Bills.

Every bill which shall have passed the House of Representatives and the Senate, shall, before it become a law, be presented to the President of the United States; if he approve he shall sign it, but if not he shall return it, with his objections to that House in which it shall have originated, who shall enter the objections at large on their journal, and proceed to reconsider it. If after such reconsideration two thirds of that House shall agree to pass the bill, it shall be sent, together with the objections, to the other House, by which it shall likewise be reconsidered, and if approved by two thirds of that House, it shall become a law. But in all such cases the votes of both Houses shall be determined by yeas and nays, and the names of the persons voting for and against the bill shall be entered on the journal of each House respectively. If any bill shall not be returned by the President within ten days (Sundays excepted) after it shall have been presented to him, the same shall be a law, in like manner as if he had signed it, unless the Congress by their adjournment prevent its return, in which case it shall not be a law.

Every order, resolution, or vote to which the concurrence of the Senate and House of Representatives may be necessary (except on a question of adjournment) shall be presented to the President of the United States; and before the same shall take effect, shall be approved by him, or being disapproved by him, shall be repassed by two thirds of the Senate and House of Representatives, according to the rules and limitations prescribed in the case of a bill.

Section 8.
The Congress shall have power to lay and collect taxes, duties, imposts and excises, to pay the debts and provide for the common defense and general welfare of the United States; but all duties, imposts and excises shall be uniform throughout the United States;

To borrow money on the credit of the United States;

To regulate commerce with foreign nations, and among the several states, and with the Indian tribes;

To establish a uniform rule of naturalization, and uniform laws on the subject of bankruptcies throughout the United States;

To coin money, regulate the value thereof, and of foreign coin, and fix the standard of weights and measures;

To provide for the punishment of counterfeiting the securities and current coin of the United States;

To establish post offices and post roads;

To promote the progress of science and useful arts, by securing for limited times to authors and inventors the exclusive right to their respective writings and discoveries;

To constitute tribunals inferior to the Supreme Court;

To define and punish piracies and felonies committed on the high seas, and offenses against the law of nations;

To declare war, grant letters of marque and reprisal, and make rules concerning captures on land and water;

To raise and support armies, but no appropriation of money to that use shall be for a longer term than two years;

To provide and maintain a navy;

To make rules for the government and regulation of the land and naval forces;

To provide for calling forth the militia to execute the laws of the union, suppress insurrections and repel invasions;

To provide for organizing, arming, and disciplining, the militia, and for governing such part of them as may be employed in the service of the United States, reserving to the states respectively, the appointment of the officers, and the authority of training the militia according to the discipline prescribed by Congress;

To exercise exclusive legislation in all cases whatsoever, over such District (not exceeding ten miles square) as may, by cession of particular states, and the acceptance of Congress, become the seat of the government of the United States, and to exercise like authority over all places purchased by the consent of the legislature of the state in which the same shall be, for the erection of forts, magazines, arsenals, dockyards, and other needful buildings;—And

To make all laws which shall be necessary and proper for carrying into execution the foregoing powers, and all other powers vested by this Constitution in the government of the United States, or in any department or officer thereof.

Section 9.

The migration or importation of such persons as any of the states now existing shall think proper to admit, shall not be prohibited by the Congress prior to the year one thousand eight hundred and eight, but a tax or duty may be imposed on such importation, not exceeding ten dollars for each person.

The privilege of the writ of habeas corpus shall not be suspended, unless when in cases of rebellion or invasion the public safety may require it.

No bill of attainder or ex post facto Law shall be passed.

No capitation, or other direct, tax shall be laid, unless in proportion to the census or enumeration herein before directed to be taken.

No tax or duty shall be laid on articles exported from any state.

No preference shall be given by any regulation of commerce or revenue to the ports of one state over those of another: nor shall vessels bound to, or from, one state, be obliged to enter, clear or pay duties in another.

No money shall be drawn from the treasury, but in consequence of appropriations made by law; and a regular statement and account of receipts and expenditures of all public money shall be published from time to time.

No title of nobility shall be granted by the United States: and no person holding any office of profit or trust under them, shall, without the consent of the Congress, accept of any present, emolument, office, or title, of any kind whatever, from any king, prince, or foreign state.

Section 10.
No state shall enter into any treaty, alliance, or confederation; grant letters of marque and reprisal; coin money; emit bills of credit; make anything but gold and silver coin a tender in payment of debts; pass any bill of attainder, ex post facto law, or law impairing the obligation of contracts, or grant any title of nobility.

No state shall, without the consent of the Congress, lay any imposts or duties on imports or exports, except what may be absolutely necessary for executing its inspection laws: and the net produce of all duties and imposts, laid by any state on imports or exports, shall be for the use of the treasury of the United States; and all such laws shall be subject to the revision and control of the Congress.

No state shall, without the consent of Congress, lay any duty of tonnage, keep troops, or ships of war in time of peace, enter into any agreement or compact with another state, or with a foreign power, or engage in war, unless actually invaded, or in such imminent danger as will not admit of delay.

Article II

Section 1.
The executive power shall be vested in a President of the United States of America. He shall hold his office during the term of four years, and, together with the Vice President, chosen for the same term, be elected, as follows:

Each state shall appoint, in such manner as the Legislature thereof may direct, a number of electors, equal to the whole number of Senators and Representatives to which the State may be entitled in the Congress: but no Senator or Representative, or person holding an office of trust or profit under the United States, shall be appointed an elector.

The electors shall meet in their respective states, and vote by ballot for two persons, of whom one at least shall not be an inhabitant of the same state with themselves. And they shall make a list of all the persons voted for, and of the number of votes for each; which list they shall sign and certify, and transmit sealed to the seat of the government of the United States, directed to the President of the Senate. The President of the Senate shall, in the presence of the Senate and House of Representatives, open all the certificates, and the votes shall then be counted. The person having the greatest number of votes shall be the President, if such number be a majority of the whole number of electors appointed; and if there be more than one who have such majority, and have an equal number of votes, then the House of Representatives shall immediately choose by ballot one of them for President; and if no person have a majority, then from the five highest on the list the said House shall in like manner choose the President. But in choosing the President, the votes shall be taken by States, the representation from each state having one vote; A quorum for this purpose shall consist of a member or members from two thirds of the states, and a majority of all the states shall be necessary to a choice. In every case, after the choice of the President, the person having the greatest number of votes of the electors shall be the Vice President. But if there should remain two or more who have equal votes, the Senate shall choose from them by ballot the Vice President.

The Congress may determine the time of choosing the electors, and the day on which they shall give their votes; which day shall be the same throughout the United States.

No person except a natural born citizen, or a citizen of the United States, at the time of the adoption of this Constitution, shall be eligible to the office of President; neither shall any person be eligible to that office who shall not have attained to the age of thirty five years, and been fourteen Years a resident within the United States.

In case of the removal of the President from office, or of his death, resignation, or inability to discharge the powers and duties of the said office, the same shall devolve on the Vice President, and the Congress may by law provide for the case of removal, death, resignation or inability, both of the President and Vice President, declaring what officer shall then act as President, and such officer shall act accordingly, until the disability be removed, or a President shall be elected.

The President shall, at stated times, receive for his services, a compensation, which shall neither be increased nor diminished during the period for which he shall have been elected, and he shall not receive within that period any other emolument from the United States, or any of them.

Before he enter on the execution of his office, he shall take the following oath or affirmation:—"I do solemnly swear (or affirm) that I will faithfully execute the office of President of the United States, and will to the best of my ability, preserve, protect and defend the Constitution of the United States."

Section 2.
The President shall be commander in chief of the Army and Navy of the United States, and of the militia of the several states, when called into the actual service of the United States; he may require the opinion, in writing, of the principal officer in each of the executive departments, upon any subject relating to the duties of their respective offices, and he shall have power to grant reprieves and pardons for offenses against the United States, except in cases of impeachment.

He shall have power, by and with the advice and consent of the Senate, to make treaties, provided two thirds of the Senators present concur; and he shall nominate, and by and with the advice and consent of the Senate, shall appoint ambassadors, other public ministers and consuls, judges of the Supreme Court, and all other officers of the United States, whose appointments are not herein otherwise provided for, and which shall be established by law: but the Congress may by law vest the appointment of such inferior officers, as they think proper, in the President alone, in the courts of law, or in the heads of departments.

The President shall have power to fill up all vacancies that may happen during the recess of the Senate, by granting commissions which shall expire at the end of their next session.

Section 3.
He shall from time to time give to the Congress information of the state of the union, and recommend to their consideration such measures as he shall judge necessary and expedient; he may, on extraordinary occasions, convene both Houses, or either of them, and in case of disagreement between them, with respect to the time of adjournment, he may adjourn them to such time as he shall think proper; he shall receive ambassadors and other public ministers; he shall take care that the laws be faithfully executed, and shall commission all the officers of the United States.

Section 4.
The President, Vice President and all civil officers of the United States, shall be removed from office on impeachment for, and conviction of, treason, bribery, or other high crimes and misdemeanors.

Article III

Section 1.
The judicial power of the United States, shall be vested in one Supreme Court, and in such inferior courts as the Congress may from time to time ordain and establish. The judges, both of the supreme and inferior courts, shall hold their offices during good behaviour, and shall, at stated times, receive for their services, a compensation, which shall not be diminished during their continuance in office.

Section 2.
The judicial power shall extend to all cases, in law and equity, arising under this Constitution, the laws of the United States, and treaties made, or which shall be made, under their authority;—to all cases affecting ambassadors, other public ministers and consuls;—to all cases of admiralty and maritime jurisdiction;—to controversies to which the United States shall be a party;—to controversies between two or more states;—between a state and citizens of another state;— between citizens of different states;—between citizens of the same state claiming lands under grants of different states, and between a state, or the citizens thereof, and foreign states, citizens or subjects.

In all cases affecting ambassadors, other public ministers and consuls, and those in which a state shall be party, the Supreme Court shall have original jurisdiction. In all the other cases before mentioned, the Supreme Court shall have appellate jurisdiction, both as to law and fact, with such exceptions, and under such regulations as the Congress shall make.

The trial of all crimes, except in cases of impeachment, shall be by jury; and such trial shall be held in the state where the said crimes shall have been committed; but when not committed within any state, the trial shall be at such place or places as the Congress may by law have directed.

Section 3.

Treason against the United States, shall consist only in levying war against them, or in adhering to their enemies, giving them aid and comfort. No person shall be convicted of treason unless on the testimony of two witnesses to the same overt act, or on confession in open court.

The Congress shall have power to declare the punishment of treason, but no attainder of treason shall work corruption of blood, or forfeiture except during the life of the person attainted.

Article IV

Section 1.

Full faith and credit shall be given in each state to the public acts, records, and judicial proceedings of every other state. And the Congress may by general laws prescribe the manner in which such acts, records, and proceedings shall be proved, and the effect thereof.

Section 2.

The citizens of each state shall be entitled to all privileges and immunities of citizens in the several states.

A person charged in any state with treason, felony, or other crime, who shall flee from justice, and be found in another state, shall on demand of the executive authority of the state from which he fled, be delivered up, to be removed to the state having jurisdiction of the crime.

No person held to service or labor in one state, under the laws thereof, escaping into another, shall, in consequence of any law or regulation therein, be discharged from such service or labor, but shall be delivered up on claim of the party to whom such service or labor may be due.

Section 3.

New states may be admitted by the Congress into this union; but no new states shall be formed or erected within the jurisdiction of any other state; nor any state be formed by the junction of two or more states, or parts of states, without the consent of the legislatures of the states concerned as well as of the Congress.

The Congress shall have power to dispose of and make all needful rules and regulations respecting the territory or other property belonging to the

United States; and nothing in this Constitution shall be so construed as to prejudice any claims of the United States, or of any particular state.

Section 4.
The United States shall guarantee to every state in this union a republican form of government, and shall protect each of them against invasion; and on application of the legislature, or of the executive (when the legislature cannot be convened) against domestic violence.

Article V

The Congress, whenever two thirds of both houses shall deem it necessary, shall propose amendments to this Constitution, or, on the application of the legislatures of two thirds of the several states, shall call a convention for proposing amendments, which, in either case, shall be valid to all intents and purposes, as part of this Constitution, when ratified by the legislatures of three fourths of the several states, or by conventions in three fourths thereof, as the one or the other mode of ratification may be proposed by the Congress; provided that no amendment which may be made prior to the year one thousand eight hundred and eight shall in any manner affect the first and fourth clauses in the ninth section of the first article; and that no state, without its consent, shall be deprived of its equal suffrage in the Senate.

Article VI

All debts contracted and engagements entered into, before the adoption of this Constitution, shall be as valid against the United States under this Constitution, as under the Confederation.

This Constitution, and the laws of the United States which shall be made in pursuance thereof; and all treaties made, or which shall be made, under the authority of the United States, shall be the supreme law of the land; and the judges in every state shall be bound thereby, anything in the Constitution or laws of any State to the contrary notwithstanding.

The Senators and Representatives before mentioned, and the members of the several state legislatures, and all executive and judicial officers, both of the United States and of the several states, shall be bound by oath or affirmation, to support this Constitution; but no religious test shall ever be required as a qualification to any office or public trust under the United States.

Article VII

The ratification of the conventions of nine states, shall be sufficient for the establishment of this Constitution between the states so ratifying the same.

Done in convention by the unanimous consent of the states present the seventeenth day of September in the year of our Lord one thousand seven hundred and eighty seven and of the independence of the United States of America the twelfth. In witness whereof We have hereunto subscribed our Names,
[Names omitted]

Amendments to the Constitution of the United States

[The first 10 Amendments were ratified December 15, 1791, and form what is known as the Bills of Rights.]

Amendment I (1791)
Congress shall make no law respecting an establishment of religion, or prohibiting the free exercise thereof; or abridging the freedom of speech, or of the press; or the right of the people peaceably to assemble, and to petition the government for a redress of grievances.

Amendment II (1791)
A well regulated militia, being necessary to the security of a free state, the right of the people to keep and bear arms, shall not be infringed.

Amendment III (1791)
No soldier shall, in time of peace be quartered in any house, without the consent of the owner, nor in time of war, but in a manner to be prescribed by law.

Amendment IV (1791)
The right of the people to be secure in their persons, houses, papers, and effects, against unreasonable searches and seizures, shall not be violated, and no warrants shall issue, but upon probable cause, supported by oath or affirmation, and particularly describing the place to be searched, and the persons or things to be seized.

Amendment V (1791)
No person shall be held to answer for a capital, or otherwise infamous crime, unless on a presentment or indictment of a grand jury, except in cases arising in the land or naval forces, or in the militia, when in actual service in time of war or public danger; nor shall any person be subject for the same offense to be twice put in jeopardy of life or limb; nor shall be compelled in any criminal case to be a witness against himself, nor be deprived of life, liberty, or property, without due process of law; nor shall private property be taken for public use, without just compensation.

404   The Constitution of the United States of America

Amendment VI (1791)

In all criminal prosecutions, the accused shall enjoy the right to a speedy and public trial, by an impartial jury of the state and district wherein the crime shall have been committed, which district shall have been previously ascertained by law, and to be informed of the nature and cause of the accusation; to be confronted with the witnesses against him; to have compulsory process for obtaining witnesses in his favor, and to have the assistance of counsel for his defense.

Amendment VII (1791)

In suits at common law, where the value in controversy shall exceed twenty dollars, the right of trial by jury shall be preserved, and no fact tried by a jury, shall be otherwise reexamined in any court of the United States, than according to the rules of the common law.

Amendment VIII (1791)

Excessive bail shall not be required, nor excessive fines imposed, nor cruel and unusual punishments inflicted.

Amendment IX (1791)

The enumeration in the Constitution, of certain rights, shall not be construed to deny or disparage others retained by the people.

Amendment X (1791)

The powers not delegated to the United States by the Constitution, nor prohibited by it to the states, are reserved to the states respectively, or to the people.

Amendment XI (1798)

The judicial power of the United States shall not be construed to extend to any suit in law or equity, commenced or prosecuted against one of the United States by citizens of another state, or by citizens or subjects of any foreign state.

Amendment XII (1804)

The electors shall meet in their respective states and vote by ballot for President and Vice-President, one of whom, at least, shall not be an inhabitant of the same state with themselves; they shall name in their ballots the person voted for as President, and in distinct ballots the person voted for as Vice-President, and they shall make distinct lists of all persons voted for as President, and of all persons voted for as Vice-President, and of the number of votes for each, which lists they shall sign and certify, and transmit sealed to the seat of the government of the United States, directed to the President of the Senate;—The President of the Senate shall, in the presence of the Senate and House of Representatives, open all the certificates and the votes shall then be counted;—the person having the greatest number of votes for President, shall be the President, if such number be a majority of the whole number of electors appointed; and if no person have such majority, then from the persons having the highest numbers not exceeding three on the list of those voted for as President, the House of Representatives shall choose immediately, by ballot, the President. But in choosing the President, the votes shall be taken by states, the representation from each state having one vote; a quorum for this purpose shall consist of a member or members from two-thirds of the states, and a majority of all the states shall be necessary to a choice. And if the House of Representatives shall not choose a President whenever the right of choice shall devolve upon them, before the fourth day of March next following, then the Vice-President shall act as President, as in the case of the death or other constitutional disability of the President. The person having the greatest number of votes as Vice-President, shall be the Vice-President, if such number be a majority of the whole number of electors appointed, and if no person have a majority, then from the two highest numbers on the list, the Senate shall choose the Vice-President; a quorum for the purpose shall consist of two-thirds of the whole number of Senators, and a majority of the whole number shall be necessary to a choice. But no person constitutionally ineligible to the office of President shall be eligible to that of Vice-President of the United States.

Amendment XIII (1865)
Section 1.
Neither slavery nor involuntary servitude, except as a punishment for crime whereof the party shall have been duly convicted, shall exist within the United States, or any place subject to their jurisdiction.

Section 2.
Congress shall have power to enforce this article by appropriate legislation.

Amendment XIV (1868)
Section 1.
All persons born or naturalized in the United States, and subject to the jurisdiction thereof, are citizens of the United States and of the state wherein they reside. No state shall make or enforce any law which shall abridge the privileges or immunities of citizens of the United States; nor shall any state deprive any person of life, liberty, or property, without due process of law; nor deny to any person within its jurisdiction the equal protection of the laws.

Section 2.
Representatives shall be apportioned among the several states according to their respective numbers, counting the whole number of persons in each state, excluding Indians not taxed. But when the right to vote at any election for the choice of electors for President and Vice President of the United

States, Representatives in Congress, the executive and judicial officers of a state, or the members of the legislature thereof, is denied to any of the male inhabitants of such state, being twenty-one years of age, and citizens of the United States, or in any way abridged, except for participation in rebellion, or other crime, the basis of representation therein shall be reduced in the proportion which the number of such male citizens shall bear to the whole number of male citizens twenty-one years of age in such state.

Section 3.
No person shall be a Senator or Representative in Congress, or elector of President and Vice President, or hold any office, civil or military, under the United States, or under any state, who, having previously taken an oath, as a member of Congress, or as an officer of the United States, or as a member of any state legislature, or as an executive or judicial officer of any state, to support the Constitution of the United States, shall have engaged in insurrection or rebellion against the same, or given aid or comfort to the enemies thereof. But Congress may by a vote of two-thirds of each House, remove such disability.

Section 4.
The validity of the public debt of the United States, authorized by law, including debts incurred for payment of pensions and bounties for services in suppressing insurrection or rebellion, shall not be questioned. But neither the United States nor any state shall assume or pay any debt or obligation incurred in aid of insurrection or rebellion against the United States, or any claim for the loss or emancipation of any slave; but all such debts, obligations and claims shall be held illegal and void.

Section 5.
The Congress shall have power to enforce, by appropriate legislation, the provisions of this article.

Amendment XV (1870)
Section 1.
The right of citizens of the United States to vote shall not be denied or abridged by the United States or by any state on account of race, color, or previous condition of servitude.

Section 2.
The Congress shall have power to enforce this article by appropriate legislation.

Amendment XVI (1913)
The Congress shall have power to lay and collect taxes on incomes, from whatever source derived, without apportionment among the several states, and without regard to any census of enumeration.

Amendment XVII (1913)

The Senate of the United States shall be composed of two Senators from each state, elected by the people thereof, for six years; and each Senator shall have one vote. The electors in each state shall have the qualifications requisite for electors of the most numerous branch of the state legislatures.

When vacancies happen in the representation of any state in the Senate, the executive authority of such state shall issue writs of election to fill such vacancies: Provided, that the legislature of any state may empower the executive thereof to make temporary appointments until the people fill the vacancies by election as the legislature may direct.

This amendment shall not be so construed as to affect the election or term of any Senator chosen before it becomes valid as part of the Constitution.

Amendment XVIII (1919)

Section 1.

After one year from the ratification of this article the manufacture, sale, or transportation of intoxicating liquors within, the importation thereof into, or the exportation thereof from the United States and all territory subject to the jurisdiction thereof for beverage purposes is hereby prohibited.

Section 2.

The Congress and the several states shall have concurrent power to enforce this article by appropriate legislation.

Section 3.

This article shall be inoperative unless it shall have been ratified as an amendment to the Constitution by the legislatures of the several states, as provided in the Constitution, within seven years from the date of the submission hereof to the states by the Congress.

Amendment XIX (1920)

The right of citizens of the United States to vote shall not be denied or abridged by the United States or by any state on account of sex.

Congress shall have power to enforce this article by appropriate legislation.

Amendment XX (1933)

Section 1.

The terms of the President and Vice President shall end at noon on the 20th day of January, and the terms of Senators and Representatives at noon on the 3d day of January, of the years in which such terms would have ended if this article had not been ratified; and the terms of their successors shall then begin.

Section 2.
The Congress shall assemble at least once in every year, and such meeting shall begin at noon on the 3d day of January, unless they shall by law appoint a different day.

Section 3.
If, at the time fixed for the beginning of the term of the President, the President elect shall have died, the Vice President elect shall become President. If a President shall not have been chosen before the time fixed for the beginning of his term, or if the President elect shall have failed to qualify, then the Vice President elect shall act as President until a President shall have qualified; and the Congress may by law provide for the case wherein neither a President elect nor a Vice President elect shall have qualified, declaring who shall then act as President, or the manner in which one who is to act shall be selected, and such person shall act accordingly until a President or Vice President shall have qualified.

Section 4.
The Congress may by law provide for the case of the death of any of the persons from whom the House of Representatives may choose a President whenever the right of choice shall have devolved upon them, and for the case of the death of any of the persons from whom the Senate may choose a Vice President whenever the right of choice shall have devolved upon them.

Section 5.
Sections 1 and 2 shall take effect on the 15th day of October following the ratification of this article.

Section 6.
This article shall be inoperative unless it shall have been ratified as an amendment to the Constitution by the legislatures of three-fourths of the several states within seven years from the date of its submission.

Amendment XXI (1933)
Section 1.
The eighteenth article of amendment to the Constitution of the United States is hereby repealed.

Section 2.
The transportation or importation into any state, territory, or possession of the United States for delivery or use therein of intoxicating liquors, in violation of the laws thereof, is hereby prohibited.

Section 3.
This article shall be inoperative unless it shall have been ratified as an amendment to the Constitution by conventions in the several states, as provided in the Constitution, within seven years from the date of the submission hereof to the states by the Congress.

Amendment XXII (1951)
Section 1.
No person shall be elected to the office of the President more than twice, and no person who has held the office of President, or acted as President, for more than two years of a term to which some other person was elected President shall be elected to the office of the President more than once. But this article shall not apply to any person holding the office of President when this article was proposed by the Congress, and shall not prevent any person who may be holding the office of President, or acting as President, during the term within which this article becomes operative from holding the office of President or acting as President during the remainder of such term.

Section 2.
This article shall be inoperative unless it shall have been ratified as an amendment to the Constitution by the legislatures of three-fourths of the several states within seven years from the date of its submission to the states by the Congress.

Amendment XXIII (1961)
Section 1.
The District constituting the seat of government of the United States shall appoint in such manner as the Congress may direct:
A number of electors of President and Vice President equal to the whole number of Senators and Representatives in Congress to which the District would be entitled if it were a state, but in no event more than the least populous state; they shall be in addition to those appointed by the states, but they shall be considered, for the purposes of the election of President and Vice President, to be electors appointed by a state; and they shall meet in the District and perform such duties as provided by the twelfth article of amendment.

Section 2.
The Congress shall have power to enforce this article by appropriate legislation.

Amendment XXIV (1964)
Section 1.
The right of citizens of the United States to vote in any primary or other election for President or Vice President, for electors for President or Vice

President, or for Senator or Representative in Congress, shall not be denied or abridged by the United States or any state by reason of failure to pay any poll tax or other tax.

Section 2.
The Congress shall have power to enforce this article by appropriate legislation.

Amendment XXV (1967)
Section 1.
In case of the removal of the President from office or of his death or resignation, the Vice President shall become President.

Section 2.
Whenever there is a vacancy in the office of the Vice President, the President shall nominate a Vice President who shall take office upon confirmation by a majority vote of both Houses of Congress.

Section 3.
Whenever the President transmits to the President pro tempore of the Senate and the Speaker of the House of Representatives his written declaration that he is unable to discharge the powers and duties of his office, and until he transmits to them a written declaration to the contrary, such powers and duties shall be discharged by the Vice President as Acting President.

Section 4.
Whenever the Vice President and a majority of either the principal officers of the executive departments or of such other body as Congress may by law provide, transmit to the President pro tempore of the Senate and the Speaker of the House of Representatives their written declaration that the President is unable to discharge the powers and duties of his office, the Vice President shall immediately assume the powers and duties of the office as Acting President.

Thereafter, when the President transmits to the President pro tempore of the Senate and the Speaker of the House of Representatives his written declaration that no inability exists, he shall resume the powers and duties of his office unless the Vice President and a majority of either the principal officers of the executive department or of such other body as Congress may by law provide, transmit within four days to the President pro tempore of the Senate and the Speaker of the House of Representatives their written declaration that the President is unable to discharge the powers and duties of his office. Thereupon Congress shall decide the issue, assembling within forty-eight hours for that purpose if not in session. If the Congress, within twenty-one days after receipt of the latter written declaration, or, if Congress is not in session, within twenty-one days after Congress is required to assemble, determines by two-thirds vote of both Houses that the President is unable to discharge the powers and duties of his office, the Vice President shall continue to discharge the same as Acting President; otherwise, the President shall resume the powers and duties of his office.

Amendment XXVI (1971)
Section 1.
The right of citizens of the United States, who are 18 years of age or older, to vote, shall not be denied or abridged by the United States or any state on account of age.

Section 2.
The Congress shall have the power to enforce this article by appropriate legislation.

Amendment XXVII (1992)
No law varying the compensation for the services of the Senators and Representatives shall take effect until an election of Representatives shall have intervened.

Index